# FROMMER'S

## COMPREHENSIVE TRAVEL GUIDE

# ORLANDO '91
### INCLUDING ALL DISNEY ATTRACTIONS

## by Marylyn Springer

PRENTICE
HALL
PRESS

NEW YORK • LONDON • TORONTO • SYDNEY • TOKYO • SINGAPORE

**FROMMER BOOKS**
Published by Prentice Hall Press
A division of Simon & Schuster Inc.
15 Columbus Circle
New York, NY 10023

PRENTICE HALL PRESS and colophons are registered trademarks of
Simon & Schuster Inc.

ISBN 0-13-326950-7
ISSN 0899-2940

Manufactured in the United States of America

# CONTENTS

I. INTRODUCING ORLANDO AND CENTRAL FLORIDA    1

II. GETTING TO AND AROUND ORLANDO AND DISNEY WORLD    15

III. DOZING IN DISNEY WORLD AND ORLANDO    25

IV. DINING IN DISNEY WORLD AND ORLANDO    64

V. AFTER DARK IN DISNEY WORLD AND ORLANDO    86

VI. SPORTS IN DISNEY WORLD AND ORLANDO    100

VII. SHOPPING IN CENTRAL FLORIDA    111

VIII. EXPLORING THE MAGIC KINGDOM    117

IX. EPCOT: A VISIT TO TODAY'S WORLD—AND TOMORROW'S    157

X. DISNEY-MGM STUDIOS: A STAR-SPANGLED MOUSE    189

XI. DISNEY AND THE BEANSTALK: GROWS, GROWS, AND GROWS    197

XII. A STAR IS BORN: ORLANDO'S UNIVERSAL APPEAL    201

**XIII.** MORE THINGS TO SEE AND DO IN
CENTRAL FLORIDA                    207

INDEX   230
    General Information   230
    Sights and Attractions   235
    Accommodations   238
    Restaurants   240

# MAPS

**Orlando and Vicinity   21**
**Orlando   57**
**Walt Disney World and EPCOT Center   124**
**The Magic Kingdom   126–7**
**EPCOT Center   161**
**Disney-MGM Studios   193**
**Universal Studios   205**
**Florida Orientation   211**

*For DAS,*

*a dreamer of dreamers and*

*the architect of a magic kingdom*

## Inflation Alert

It is hardly a secret that inflation continues to batter the United States as it does everywhere else. The author of this book has spent laborious hours attempting to ensure the accuracy of prices appearing in this guide. As we go to press, we believe we have obtained the most reliable data possible. Nonetheless, in the lifetime of this edition the wise traveler will add 15% to 20% to the prices quoted throughout these pages.

# INTRODUCING ORLANDO AND CENTRAL FLORIDA

**A** silvery tower, glowing diamond bright, soars up into a million stars. A rainbow of flags flutters in the breeze. A swan floats idly by, its feathers as ethereally white as clouds. Beneath the shimmering battlements, a golden princess in wisps of blue chiffon trips daintily across the drawbridge. Around her in this mystical land, flowers grow in pristine perfection, lights twinkle in magical patterns, marshmallow waves crest on a sea of sapphires.

Here life is carefree, ceaseless childhood. Here you go on the greatest adventure of all, a glorious journey right out of reality into the world of your imagination, a world that smells of cookies baking, tastes of cotton candy, and tinkles with the sound of music.

Here bitter is sweet, monsters are playmates and black clouds are just silver linings turned inside out. Here everything is perfect, and anything goes.

This crazy-crumpet, topsy-turvy teacup, Mad Hatter heaven, peopled by ducks who quack jokes, flat-footed houndogs, nice mice, and elephants that fly, is indeed a magic kingdom, perhaps the only place on earth that asks you please *not* to be serious.

Here you live in a treehouse, dance with ghosts, sip cognac under the Eiffel Tower and schnapps in the Black Forest. You sniff sulfurous fumes pouring from prehistoric earth, discuss politics with a robot, ride a spaceship, pet a whale, and reinvent the wheel.

Dancing with you down the yellow brick road are tipsy toads and beautiful princesses, roaring jaguars and whimsical fountains, wicked pirates, and waltzing bears.

Like no other place on earth, Central Florida is where you send reality on vacation and get down to your imagination. It is where you sow the seeds of fantasy—and reap a whirlwind of wonder.

## BEGINNING WHERE IT BEGAN

Who would ever have figured that here in the land of the brave and the free a meek little creature beloved by few, loathed by many, would one day become a national hero?

But that's just what happened when the creative mind of cartoonist Walt Disney dreamed up a better mousetrap that was eventually to capture the child in all of us—Walt Disney World.

Dredge back into your memory and up will pop that M-i-ccccc, k-e-yyyyyy, M-o-u-s-e refrain that many of us sang when little curly-haired Annette Funicello and her all-American cohorts in Mouse ears enlisted us in the Mickey Mouse Club.

Children all over America, then all over the world, joined that bunch of mouse-lovers, got a set of plastic ears, and sat down in front of the television to laugh and sing with Annette as Disney's crazy characters cavorted across the stage.

Little Annette and her playmates grew up, but many a Mouseketeer remained a child at heart. Memories of those mouse-, duck-, and rabbit-filled Saturday mornings are still strong in many hearts—and still capable of creating a little mistiness in even the most jaded eye.

Those magical moments of childhood live on in even the most sophisticated of us, making Mickey an ageless creature. His dragging tail and big ears can turn us in seconds from reality-facing adults to squealing children, eyes aglow with excitement, hearts full of the wonder that only imagination can create.

But no one—not you, not even your toddler—loves Mickey more than Orlando's entrepreneurs. For them the Mouse roared his way through Central Florida turning boondock into boomtown. For them Mickey is a phenomenon whose image has acquired icon status here in Central Florida. You see those big ears, that red suit, and those yellow gloves everywhere: smack in the middle of a high-powered executive's desk lamp; holding a telephone in a banker's office; or peeking beneath the monogrammed cuff of a Harvard grad's Ivy League, button-down Oxford cloth.

It was Mickey who turned this collection of cow pastures into a city and turned many of the meek into millionaires. These good ol' boys and girls aren't forgetting it either: "I have a little shrine in my bedroom," swears one now-prosperous hotelier. "Every morning I get up, pull the tiny drapes in the shrine open . . . and kiss Mickey's feet."

Yes, indeed, a little mouse changed the face of this land forever and cynical realist that you are, he will worm his way into your heart mere minutes after you arrive here. Fight it as you will, sooner or later that smug smirk will disappear, your eyes will begin to glow, and you will clap and cheer as gleefully as all the other "youngsters" around you, your overlay of sophistication swept away by the wide-eyed eternal child that lives within each of us.

Then Disney "imagineers" did it again, sinking millions of dollars into a new creative effort called Experimental Prototype Community of Tomorrow (EPCOT). Planning on this multimillion project began when the cartoonist decided he wanted Walt Disney World (WDW) to keep growing and changing. Since it was no secret that the mass of the population was growing from baby boom to young adulthood, clever Disney World planners set out to create something that would appeal to the adult in all us children.

To do that they combined the magic of life-size animated figures with the latest technology available from some of the nation's largest corporations. What they came up with is a look into the future as inspiring and scientific as it is entertaining.

Here in this Disney "world," laser beams and liquid neon create volcanic eruptions and steamy swamps. Solar energy moves you around, and oddball agricultural advances make your garden grow in places where plants have never before sprouted.

At EPCOT you peek far beneath the earth into a tumultuous subterranean world where oil bubbles and burns. You trace humankind's history from scratchings on cave walls to millisecond satellite communications, from the invention of the wheel to the creation of moon-bound rockets.

Your imagination soars, stimulated by the weird and wonderful images only Disney's huge staff of imaginations could create. You get a look at the ways in which past can become future, and future can become a spectacle we never imagined in our wildest dreams.

At yet another new "world," Disney creators introduce you to the world around you *now*. You see the Eiffel Tower and the Doges' Palace, hear the atonal harmonies of Japan and China, taste the teas of the United Kingdom, and yodel with an Alpine maid. Here in World Showcase you visit the Great Wall of China on a screen that wraps around you in a massive circle created by nine cameras that were transported to parts of China never before filmed for a Western audience. You go on a shopping spree in Mexico, plummet over Niagara Falls, ride in the Calgary Stampede, and streak over the Brittany coast.

In 1989, the park introduced its third massive attraction, **Disney-MGM Studios,** where you go behind the scenes to see what makes celluloid dreams happen. Sprawling across no less than 100 acres of Disney's 25,000-acre property in Central Florida, this new diversion includes a visit to a motion-picture and television studio, a theme entertainment park with shows and several ride-through attractions.

Here you stroll Hollywood Boulevard populated by hopeful starlets, art deco–designed restaurants and shops harking back to Hollywood's halcyon days in the 1920s and 1930s. A replica of Grauman's Chinese Theater looms up along the boulevard and in it you meet Disney's usual array of AudioAnimatronics characters who come out to play with live actors.

Shops are everywhere, of course, as they are throughout the Magic Kingdom and EPCOT. Here they offer collectibles from famous motion pictures, everything from movie scripts to costumes, movie magazines, trade papers, movie soundtracks, videotapes, posters, and a studio newspaper weekly. Shades of *Variety*.

On a walking tour you can visit soundstages, special-effects demonstrations, dubbing and editing studios, and a Sneak Preview Theater, which features upcoming releases.

Back here, too, you'll see Disney artists at work creating the storyboards and characters and putting them all together to make those zany Disney cartoon characters come alive.

Now there is even more afoot at this massive park which has been breaking attendance records year after year and packs them in at the rate of 50,000 to 60,000 a day in busy seasons.

In 1989 the park added **Pleasure Island,** a 16-acre cluster of nightclubs, including one at which you can dance—or roller skate!

Add to that **Typhoon Lagoon,** a new 56-acre water wonderland, four times the size of Disney's River Country and featuring five-foot waves crashing in a lagoon big enough for surfboards.

Take a ride—literally—around the body at the new Metropolitan Life EPCOT exhibit called the **Wonders of Life.**

Cavort at the **Caribbean Beach Hotel,** a 2,112-room rainbow-hued hotel, or at two other new hotels, the **Dolphin** or the **Swan,** a splashy 2,200-room complex overlooking a lagoon.

Add all that together and you've got the biggest amusement park in the world, an attraction that is well on its way to becoming the world's single most popular attraction.

It's all there waiting for you, the magic of a child's small world and the wonders of an adult's rapidly expanding horizons. Strange new worlds and old familiar ones touched by that star-struck Disney magic that turns mundane into mysterious, humdrum into heady.

But Disney World is not all there is to this sandy central strip of Florida.

As adorable as the Mouse is, he has plenty of competition. So much, in fact, that Orlando tourist officials who once suggested you could see it all in three days, now say you'll need a week, better yet two—or three—to make the most of the magic.

Legion is the competition for your attention and, let's face it, for your tourist dollar. Sweet Shamu, the world's heftiest ballet star, pirouettes his four tons gracefully on an enormous tail and plants gentle, if somewhat damp, kisses on willing cheeks at Sea World. Champion water-skiers fly through the sky and form human skiing pyramids in the shimmering waters of Cypress Gardens.

But all is not tourist here. Before Disney's arrival, Orlando was, after all, just a sleepy little village where life moved slowly most days and hardly at all on others. Amid the plastic and the neon that accompanied Disney World here, you can still find sun-dappled streets with huge trees dripping Spanish moss, and the sparkling azure waters of Orlando's dozens of lakes.

Take time to do some exploring, via the convention and visitors bureau's self-guided auto tour, for instance, and you'll turn up gem after gem: a rambling Tudor-style manse beside a sand-trimmed lake; verdant rolling hills lined with verandahed Old Florida homes, kept primped and painted; serene small parks and impressive large ones filled with strange and beautiful tropical exotica.

Roam the byways around Orlando. Discover glamorous small towns like Winter Park, which calls itself, justifiably, Little Europe, or a New England–village look-alike called Mount Dora, dotted with lakes, rocky bluffs, and citrus trees.

It's all here, as it has been since Orlando got its name from hero-soldier Orlando Reeves, killed by a Native American arrow after he saved the tiny village with his warnings of an impending raid. It's all here, just as it has been since an enclave of 85 pioneers settled here in 1875, but these days you have to spend a little time searching for the real Orlando.

When you find it, in all its pristine antique elegance, you'll discover an intriguing side of this city of many faces, a region of Florida lovingly endowed by nature, built by people, and made famous by a mouse—a magic kingdom indeed.

# THE REASON WHY

You come to Orlando not for the sun, sand, and salt spray that attracts 42 million visitors a year to the rest of the Sunshine State, but because you want to see what all the Central Florida hoopla is about—and you won't be disappointed.

Here the smiles are genuine and the welcome warm. A section of the state untouched by the sophistication of neighboring cities farther south on this peninsula, Central Florida is just a little more innocent, a little more trusting, a little less cynical.

Soft Southern drawls are common here, but they mix easily with the clipped consonants of Northern arrivals and the distinctive accents of West and Midwest.

Things move a little more slowly in Central Florida, so you're expected to demonstrate the patience and good manners exhibited by those who have learned to live with the procrastination that often prevails here.

Roll with the tide a little. Throw off some of the I-want-it-now aggressiveness that gets things done in big cities. Lean into this quiet village-turned-metropolis, and it will repay your patience with the warmest of welcomes, the most loyal of friendships, and a gentle goodwill that's often missing in more cosmopolitan climes.

# CLIMATE

You may not have come here for sand and sea, but you can rest assured the temperatures will be in the usual balmy Florida ranges. It will always be warmer here than in any more northern city from which you may hail. Because Orlando is smack in the center of the state, however, it benefits less from cooling—and warming— breezes generated over the ocean. So this city is often a few degrees colder in winter and warmer in summer than other places in the state. A sweater or shawl should cover most of the winter weather, however, with perhaps a jacket for some extra-cold days in January and February.

You can expect cool (cold is considered a four-letter word in Florida) temperatures from mid-December through March, with temperatures rarely dropping below the 50s, Fahrenheit. From March on, ever-warmer temperatures prevail, up to record-breaking 90s to 95s in the hottest days of summer. Things begin to cool down again about early October, when an Indian summer, just a little warmer than you find in New England, brings cooling relief.

In summer, the fewer clothes the better, with this exception: Keep in mind that your winter-white body is not prepared for the burning Florida sun. Don't head off for a day at Disney World or one of the other attractions dressed in the bare minimum. You will, in a word, fry. Instead, layer a few things on and take them off if you're too warm, but keep them handy to slip back on when the sun starts to burn.

## SUNTANS AND SUNBURNS

If it's sun you want, that's what Central Florida will give you—it has plenty to spare. What Central Florida cannot yet provide is a cure for sunburn. Hoteliers and doctors, if need be, will hold your hand, commiserate, bring you an aspirin, and smear some aloe plant jelly on your back, but all of that is cold comfort when you're on fire.

No matter how innocent those rays of sunshine may look zipping through the window, no matter how many clouds seem to be between you and the sun, Ole Sol is attacking your epidermis. Skin that has spent months, perhaps years, swaddled in clothes and far from the warming rays is no match for that golden glow. Suntan oils can help, but recall what happens when you apply heat to a frying pan full of oil, and you'll get some idea of how your unsuspecting cells are being sautéed.

Sun-screening lotions are effective products. Combined with a sensible sunning schedule and a few protective pieces of clothing—like broad-brimmed hats, sunglasses, and cover-ups—they will earn you a nice tan, without that tattletale trail of peeled skin. A tanning schedule that works for many goes something like this: Stay out of the sun between 11am and 2pm, at least for the first few days. During other hours, get only 10 minutes of sun the first day, 15 the second, then 25, 35, 50, 75, and on the seventh day 105 minutes.

## HURRICANES, RAIN, AND TROPICAL STORMS

Storms make dramatic headlines, so you have probably heard about Florida's headliner clashes with the forces of nature. No doubt about it, hurricanes are frightening, even to those who have sat out many a roaring wind, but—and this is the important part for visitors—they are *never* a surprise.

Thanks to a hardworking weather service and some pilots with strong stomachs and iron nerve, Floridians now know far in advance when a storm is brewing. Pilots fly into the eye of the storm and keep tabs on its progress, reporting to Floridians, who plot it on weather charts with the aplomb other Americans apply to crossword puzzles. Everyone begins to batten down long before a storm nears land.

What's more, because it's an inland city, Orlando gets the brunt of far fewer storms. If one does reach this far into the state, it has usually wound down to a bad-tempered rainstorm by the time it arrives.

Most important to you, as a visitor to the state, is that you will have plenty of time to leave the area, or the state, if a big wind is about to blow. But even if you stay, rest assured that strict building codes have forced builders to create structures as impervious as possible to wind and rain damage. Besides, emergency crews with lots of practice are always on hand to help you weather the storm. Officially, the season for these storms is June to November, but summer storms are rare — most occur between August and November.

In Florida, rain is not much like rain anywhere else in the nation. This state is part of the tropics, so rainstorms here are likely to be awesome sights for newcomers. It rarely rains in boring gentle drizzles or all-day downpours here. Instead, the sun suddenly disappears behind huge black clouds, the sky rumbles and roars, lightning begins to flash, and from the sky pours a violent lashing rainstorm, the intensity of which will awe and perhaps terrify you. Down it comes with ear-splitting, eye-blinding intensity, then, poof, it's gone as quickly as it came. Sun returns, blazing down on the waters, shattering droplets into a cataclysm of rainbows, spreading nature's art gallery across the sky.

You needn't fear one of these downpours, just get out of it into someplace dry and protected — and don't forget all that advice you've heard on staying safe in a thunderstorm. You also needn't leave wherever you are just because it's started to rain. In most cases those drops will disappear very soon, or slacken to a fine mist that may dampen your shirt but won't stop your spirits. Floridians are used to this kind of rain, so all attractions are well prepared with plenty of raincoats for sale and lots of interesting places where you can seek shelter until the sun returns.

Just so you'll know: June, July, August, September, and October get the most rain — about six or seven inches a month usually — November through May about half that.

Finally, Orlando is one of the few places in the state that experiences early-morning fogs. Most longtime Florida dwellers have forgotten what a fog looks like and how to cope with it, so traffic tends to jam when the gray rolls into town. Once again, however, that indomitable sunshine generally sweeps away the soup by mid-morning, so don't bother to change your plans if you can't see the building next door at 6am some morning. All will be well. Soon.

# VISITOR INFORMATION

Central Florida has 12 very busy years of experience in answering the questions and the needs of travelers, so you'll find plenty of places in the state and in this region ready, able, and more than willing to answer your questions.

## GENERAL FLORIDA TOURIST INFORMATION

Start at the top, the **Florida Division of Tourism,** Visitor Inquiry Section, Department of Commerce, Fletcher Building, Room 422, 101 E. Gaines St., Tallahassee, FL 32399 (tel. 904/487-1462), where Floridians with all the answers—and all the brochures—can tell you everything you ever wanted to know, and perhaps far more, about the Sunshine State and this popular Central Florida region. Mention any specific interest you might have, and they'll respond with lots of information on how and where to do what you want to do. Florida also has a fine publication, *Florida Vacation Guide,* which is free and crammed with information on all regions of the state.

If you're an outdoor type, the **Florida Department of Natural Resources,** Office of Communications, Marjory Stoneman Douglas Building, Room 613, 3900 Commonwealth Blvd., Tallahassee, FL 32399 (tel. 904/488-7326), has files and files of information on state parks and what each has to offer.

Fishing and hunting fans love Central Florida, which abounds with game and with great freshwater fishing holes. You can get all the details on where to find the whoppers from the **Florida Game and Freshwater Fish Commission,** 620 Meridian St., Tallahassee, FL 32399 (tel. 904/488-4676), which will tell you all you need to know, stopping just short of guaranteeing you a fish or venison dinner.

One Central Florida county has so many lakes it's called Lake County. At the **Leesburg Chamber of Commerce,** Box 269, Leesburg, FL 32749 (tel. 904/787-2131), you can get a rundown on fish camps and guides.

If hunting is your game, call this toll-free number to find out what season is when: 800/282-8002. They also have fishing information here.

If you're interested in camping, the **Florida Campground Association,** 1638 N. Plaza Dr., Tallahassee, FL 32308 (tel. 904/656-8878) has a long list of campgrounds in Florida and descriptions of camp facilities. Another camping and parks information resource is the **National Parks Service,** U.S. Department of the Interior, Washington, DC 20025, which has general information on national parks in Florida.

Hikers can find out what trails make interesting hikes from the **Florida Trail Association,** 3008 NW 13th St. (mailing address: P.O. Box 13708), Gainesville, FL 32604 (tel. 904/378-8823).

Travel agents are very well informed people who have a wealth of information at their fingertips and computers. They'll be happy to help you plan a trip to the state.

If you're a frequent flier, the travel agent's bible, **Official Airline Guides,** 2000 Clearwater Dr., Oak Brook, IL 60521 (tel. toll free 800/323-3537), publishes a *Pocket Flight Guide* that's crammed with information on airlines flying to the area and around the state.

## CENTRAL FLORIDA TOURIST INFORMATION

Take your questions—and your troubles if need be—to the **Orlando/Orange County Convention and Visitors Bureau,** 8445 International Dr., Orlando, FL 32187 (tel. 407/345-8882), where smiling and well-informed Orlandoites are on hand to help weekdays from 8am to 5pm.

Orlando publishes a handy guide called *The Visitor's Guide,* which includes information on attractions, hotels, and restaurants in the region. It's free and can be obtained from the convention and visitors bureau.

In the tiny cow capital, Kissimmee, you find the **Kissimmee Chamber of Commerce** at 320 E. Monument Ave., Kissimmee, FL 32741 (tel. 407/847-3174), and the **Kissimmee/St. Cloud Convention and Visitors Bureau** at 1925 E. Irlo Bronson Memorial Hwy., P.O. Box 2007, Kissimmee, FL 32742 (tel. 407/847-5000, or toll free 800/327-9159, in Florida 800/432-9199), both as fiercely loyal to their small town as they are down-home friendly in their welcome.

In **Winter Park** write or call the chamber at 150 N. New York Ave., Winter Park, FL 32790 (407/644-8281) and in Mount Dora the chamber is at Alexander St. and Third Ave., P.O. Box 196, Mount Dora, FL 32757 (tel. 904/383-2165).

## WALT DISNEY WORLD AND EPCOT INFORMATION

A huge staff is on hand at **Walt Disney World** to answer your questions. Call them at 407/824-4321 or 824-2222.

To make reservations at hotels on Disney World property, call 407/824-8000 or 407/W-DISNEY (best time to call is after 5pm, when things slow down a bit), or write to **Walt Disney World Reservations,** P.O. Box 10100, Lake Buena Vista, FL 32830. Ask for a copy of the *Walt Disney World Vacation Guide,* which explains all the hotels and facilities in the World. Walt Disney World Travel Co., P.O. Box 22094, Lake Buena Vista, FL 32830 (tel. 407/828-3232), also has a number of money-saving package tours that include admission to Disney World, hotel, and often transportation. They'll be happy to send you a brochure outlining them.

## USEFUL INFORMATION

For police or medical emergency anywhere in the area, dial 911 ... For **minor medical problems,** Family Treatment Center, 6001 Vineland Rd., one block west of Kirkman Rd. (tel. 351-6682), is open 8am to 8pm daily and accepts MasterCard and VISA for payment ... For medical help 8am to 11pm, call the Central Florida Medical Service (tel. 648-9234). Some doctors listed by the service will even make "house" calls at your hotel or motel ... To find out what **weather** to expect, call 851-7510 in Orlando ... Get a **baby-sitter** by contacting your hotel's guest services desk ... **Pet emergencies** can be handled at the Veterinary Emergency Clinic, 882 Jackson Ave., Winter Park, FL (tel. 644-4449) ... For an anytime snack or meal, **Denny's,** 5800 International Dr. (tel. 351-1581), is near Disney World on International Drive and is open 24 hours . . . **Western Union** is at 800/325-6000 . . . Your **film** can be developed overnight at Champagne Color Camera, 1917 N. Orange Ave. (tel. 894-3362), and at many hotel guest services desks . . . Get **out-of-town newspapers** at Orange Avenue News, 59 N. Orange Ave. (tel. 422-0954) . . . If you don't mind admitting your age, you "senior citizens" can save a bundle of money during Orlando's Senior Season, from September to mid-December, when dozens of attractions and hotels offer discounts up to 50% to anyone 55 and up. The convention and visitors bureau can give you exact details on Senior Season . . . **Gooding's,** which can be found at several locations in the Orlando area, is a grocery store open 24 hours. Closest one to the Disney area is at Crossroads Shopping Center, 1252 Fla. 5356 (tel. 827-1200) near the entrance to Lake Buena Vista and the Disney Hotel Village just off I-4.

# TIPS ON FOOD AND LODGING

Traveling happy as opposed to hectic is often just a matter of a little planning, so here are a few tips for making your Central Florida sojourn as trouble-free as possible.

## HOTELS AND MOTELS

Every part of Florida has a high season. So Orlando has its prime time too, when hotels and motels are packed and everything else keeps pace.

In Central Florida that time is Christmas, when the thundering hordes come pouring into Disney World, Sea World, and the rest, to see what imagination can create for Christmas. Sure, you can take your chances, but driving from hotel to motel to guesthouse looking for a room is a pretty silly way to spend your vacation. You can avoid that fate with the simplest of remedies: Reserve ahead. That goes for other holiday periods, too—Easter, Thanksgiving, Washington's Birthday, and the busiest summer months of June, July, and August, when youngsters are out of school and lots of other people are planning the same summer sojourn you are.

There are dozens of moderately priced hotels and motels in Central Florida and many representatives of major national chains like Howard Johnson, Holiday Inn, and Days Inn. Here are the toll-free numbers for the major chain operations in the moderate price bracket so you can call and check them out. **Days Inn** (tel. 800/325-2525); **Best Western** (tel. 800/528-1234); **Econo Lodge** (tel. 800/446-6900; in Virginia 800/582-5882); **Holiday Inn** (tel. 800/465-4329); **Howard Johnson** (tel. 800/654-2000); **Quality Inns** (tel. 800/221-2222); **Ramada Inns** (tel. 800/272-6232); **Red Carpet Inns** (tel. 800/521-1962); **Rodeway Inns** (tel. 800/228-2000); **Scottish Inns** (tel. 800/251-1962); **TraveLodge** (tel. 800/255-3050).

A few words on saving money on Florida hotel rooms. Small motels on U.S. 192, Orange Blossom Trail, and Colonial Drive are cheaper (sometimes 50% or more) than hotels at or in Disney World. There's no doubt about it: Hotels on Disney World property are expensive, but their cost needs to be balanced against transportation expenses elsewhere, particularly if you're flying in and renting a car. Since all transportation is free inside Disney World property, you might find that you spend less by renting a room there, after you add in the cost of a car rental, gasoline, and the like. You may also *not* come out cheaper, but think about it.

A boon for budget-watching families is the area's no-charge-for-children policy. Only the smallest motels charge for children (usually kids under 18, but check age cutoffs to be sure), and then it's often only a nominal charge, nothing likely to break the bank account. That no-charge edict assumes that you and the youngsters are sharing a room, however, which requires a considerable amount of camaraderie. Families who'd like to stretch out a bit without kicking someone's shoes under the bed might consider villa accommodations—I've named some in Disney World and some outside—which offer many amenities and plenty of parental privacy.

As everywhere, motels and hotels closest to the action, such as those by Disney World, tend to be the most expensive, with prices dropping as you go farther afield. Major resorts are an exception to that, however. Naturally those with fewer amenities, such as on-premises restaurants and game rooms, are less expensive.

Prices I've quoted are for a room for two, and almost always include in the price two children up to the age of 18. Those prices, at least at most motels and hotels, do change seasonally, with highest rates charged at the most popular visiting times—holidays and summer—dropping in January, after Easter until mid-June, and from about the first week in September to Thanksgiving.

## RESTAURANTS

Nothing changes faster in Florida than restaurants, which seem to go into and out of business faster than you can whip cream. I've tried to recommend restaurants here that have been around long enough to be considered winners in the war of the whisks, but I'm offering no guarantees on prices or continued existence.

One happy note, however. Restaurants in Orlando tend to be less expensive than their counterparts elsewhere in the state. Even posh, elegant restaurants considered expensive by Orlando standards are unlikely to top $25 to $30 a person for dinner. Many, many more—hundreds in fact—offer fine fare at moderate prices with entrées in the $10 to $20 bracket and often at budget rates under $10.

What's more, Florida is the home of the early-bird special, so if you're one of those people who like getting out to dinner before 6pm, you can often find complete dinners in the $10 range, particularly in less busy seasons.

I've tried to indicate here what I think you'll pay per person for dinner entrées, which in Florida usually include salad, vegetable, meat, bread, butter, and often coffee. If you like a bottle of wine or a martini or two before, and something sweet after, your bill will naturally rise accordingly.

Central Florida restaurants are much more casual than their counterparts in almost any other section of the state. Here, a tie is reserved for only the most spectacular dining spots, and you'll see many men without them even there. For men, a sports jacket in hand, not necessarily on shoulders, is good insurance and will do just fine, even in peak seasons.

At most moderately priced restaurants in the area, you'll feel overdressed in anything more than a golf shirt. However, need I say that T-shirts, cutoff blue jeans, sandals, and scruffy-looking things are outré most anywhere these days?

For women, dresses or good-looking pants outfits go anywhere, designer jeans almost anywhere. A warm blazer or shawl is worth its weight in summer, when some restaurants turn air conditioners down to Arctic temperatures, as well as in winter, when nature adds a little of its own air conditioning.

## Local Foods

Florida has some interesting culinary treats you may not have encountered before, and you'll find most of them right here in Central Florida.

So much seafood comes from the waters on either coast that it's hard to know where to start, but you might try pompano, a delicate, flaky white fish much loved by gourmets and often baked inside special paper. Stone crabs are a renowned Florida treat, and it's nice to know no one has to kill anything to get them. Stone crab fishermen on the state's west coast capture the crabs, break off one large claw, and throw the crabs back into the deep, where they grow another claw to replace the missing pincer. Stone crabs are best during their harvest season from mid-October to mid-May. After that they'll come from the freezer. Eat them cold or steamed with melted butter.

Florida lobsters, which seemingly appear on every single menu in the state, are nothing like their Maine counterparts. Instead, they're much smaller and much cheaper, although their flavor is comparable. (I expect plenty of argument on that statement.)

Apalachicola oysters are a Florida specialty, grown up in the curve of the Panhandle. They're as different from their Bon Secour, Alabama, brothers as they are from any other oysters, so try them and become an oyster connoisseur. Rock shrimp, sometimes called "langostinos," are something like shrimp-size lobsters. Clams and scallops are abundant—there are two kinds of scallops, bay and deep-sea, the former much tinier and sweeter.

Fresh hearts of palm occasionally show up on Orlando menus. A delicacy far superior to the canned variety, they're cut from the heart of the cabbage palm using a technique learned from the Seminoles. Once you try them, you'll be spoiled for the canned variety forever.

From the many nationalities that have merged on this land (Bahamians, Cubans, Indians, Spanish, English, French), Floridians have acquired a taste for crusty Cuban bread; steaming conch chowder (made from the creature that lives inside those shells you "listen" to); paella, a rice, seafood, and vegetable combination; piccadillo, a mix of ground meat, olives, and raisins in a spicy sauce; pilau, a spicy stew found in the St. Augustine area; and creole foods.

You'll find these and many, many other foreign flavors in Orlando, plus some of the best home-cooking of any section of the state—fried chicken, corn, fresh vegetables right off the farms of neighboring Zellwood, and strawberry shortcake piled with massive berries from the fields of nearby Plant City.

## Citrus

There's something breathtakingly beautiful about the citrus groves that blanket the rolling hills of this central section of the state. Orange and gold fruit add a pointillist's touch to mile after mile of emerald green—stretching from horizon to horizon.

In cold snaps, those old tires you see piled up in the fields are odoriferously burned to heat the air and keep frost from the delicate fruit. Huge sprinklers serve much the same function by keeping the ground wet and warm to ward off frost.

At groves throughout Florida, you can get out in the field and pick your own oranges, grapefruit, lemons, and limes right off the tree, then recover from your labors with a free glass of fresh-off-the-tree orange juice! Send some home to friends here or abroad. If you're taking fruit home by plane, be sure to put your name or some identifying ribbon on it, since everyone else on the plane is likely to have some too. You can't take the fruit into Canada or abroad personally, but you can ship it there.

You'll find citrus of some kind in the area every month of the year. Here's a catalog of some of the different kinds you can try:

**Navel oranges**—best from November to January, recognizable by their tiny "navels" and smooth skin, usually almost seedless and easily peeled.

**Valencia oranges**—March to July, juicy and aromatic.

**Temple oranges**—January to March, a favorite eating orange with a lightly pitted skin.

**Murcott oranges**—February to April, almost red inside.

**Hamlin oranges**—October to December, a juice orange, seedless, thick-skinned.

**Pineapple oranges**—December to February, very juicy and very sweet.

**Tangelos**—December to March, a cross between a tangerine and an orange, with an easy-peel skin.

**Tangerines**—December to February, the zipper-skin fruit.

**Duncan grapefruit**—October to May, very juicy and seedy, with a thick, pale-yellow skin.

**Seedless grapefruit**—November to June, smooth yellow skin, few seeds.

**Pink seedless grapefruit**—October to May, rose-colored interior.

Other interesting fruits are the tiny pucker-inducing kumquats, often used in jellies; Persian limes (the big green ones); Key limes (the little yellow ones imported here from Key West); and Ponderosa lemons, often nearly as big as a large orange.

You can even try citrus wine! It's made at Florida Vineyard and Fruit Gardens at Orange Lake, between Gainesville and Ocala, and sold in most liquor and some grocery stores in Orlando, as well as at roadside Stuckey's stores along the Florida Turnpike.

Citrus candies and jellies, goat's milk fudge, and coconut patties are favorites in Florida, too. You can buy coconuts (which, if they're ripe, are brown and slosh when you shake them), already hulled, in grocery stores.

Food festivals are favorite entertainment in Florida and range from the corn festival in nearby Zellwood each May to the Strawberry Festival in Plant City in February.

# II

# GETTING TO AND AROUND ORLANDO AND DISNEY WORLD

**O**nce upon a time, getting to and around Orlando was only a little less difficult than a cross-country trek by mule train. Roads had all the "too's" of a driver's worst nightmares: too few, too narrow, too crowded, too bad.

But no more. Now there are few, if any, areas in the state as accessible as Central Florida, which has a road system much envied by more populous areas of the Sunshine State.

That same once-upon-a-time nightmare also applies to Orlando's airport, once little more than a cleared cow pasture, but today a full-fledged jetport. In 1982 and 1990, in fact, Orlando International Airport proudly opened sleek new terminal buildings with nearly 100 gates and runways long enough to welcome no less an aircraft than that airborne record-breaker, British Airways' supersonic Concorde (the Concorde doesn't land here yet but may in the near future).

Rest assured that beloved Mouse does not miss an opportunity even here: At Orlando airport, arrivals can stroll right off the plane and over to a Disney information desk where tickets, information, maps, and even a set of Mouse ears are available!

Those arriving by train can step off on the platform at Kissimmee, the official Walt Disney World Amtrak stop, and from there it's only minutes to the Kingdom by car, bus, taxi, or hotel jitney.

Finally, for those arriving by car—and that's far and away the way most people get here—four- or six-lane highways streak into and through the area from every direction.

In fact, getting here can be fun. Billboards along roadways entice you to area attractions so colorfully, amusingly, and informatively, you'll begin to be caught up in the excitement of this giggly slice of the Sunshine State long before you step onto the macadam of Main Street, U.S.A.

# GETTING THERE FROM ANYWHERE

## BY AIR

Airlines include American, Bahamasair, Continental, Delta, Eastern, Midway, Northwest, Pan Am, TWA, United, and USAir. Some international airlines, including Air Canada, Air France, Mexicana, VASP, Virgin Atlantic, Icelandair, KLM, and Ward Air bring throngs of foreign visitors here. All of those airlines touch down at Orlando International Jetport, a sleek, modern facility still small enough to be simple to negotiate.

British Airways, which flies to more destinations than any other airline in the world, has added Orlando to its impressive list of destinations. Those who want to arrive in real style can do so aboard British Airways' supersonic Concorde, which doesn't land here yet, but does land in Miami, a five-hour drive away.

Orlando's $300-million airport sports attractive boutiques, even a unisex barber/beauty shop. An intriguing collection of restaurants features everything from a raw bar, at which oysters, clams, lobsters, stone crabs, and shrimp are bedded down on huge ice-filled scallop shells, to a cappuccino-and-croissant bakery, a tropical drink bar and a food court with everything from egg rolls to pizza.

Elevated trains whiz you from plane to the central terminal for baggage pickup, then rental cars, taxis, buses—even a Cadillac limousine—will meet you at the door; everything seems to work with fast-paced efficiency. It's quite a step into the future for this once-sleepy little conglomerate of villages called Central Florida.

## BY TRAIN

Every day Amtrak's shining Silver Meteor and Silver Star streak southward from New York's Penn Station. The **Silver Star** departs at about 9am, arriving in Kissimmee the next morning. For afternoon travelers the **Silver Meteor** leaves at about 4:30pm, arriving in Kissimmee at midday the following day. Official address of the **Kissimmee station** is 416 Pleasant St.

If you're headed for downtown Orlando, you can leave the train at the **Orlando station** located about a mile from the downtown area at 1400 Sligh Blvd. Both trains arrive at that station about 20 minutes earlier than they get to Kissimmee, which is farther south. That is one of the reasons it's a good idea to get an Orlando map from the visitors bureau before you leave home. You'll save yourself driving time and money when you arrive.

Major stops on the New York to Orlando run include Newark, Trenton, Philadelphia, Wilmington, Baltimore, Washington, Richmond, Raleigh, Columbia, Savannah, and Jacksonville.

At Jacksonville the Silver Star splits, so part of the train can travel to the St. Petersburg/Tampa area, part to Miami. The Silver

Meteor splits just south of Kissimmee for the same two destinations, so it's wise to note which car you're on and where it's going.

From those splits you can deduce that trains also can take you *from* Miami, St. Petersburg/Tampa, and various smaller cities in between to Orlando and Kissimmee.

If you're headed north from Miami, the Silver Meteor leaves at 8:51am EST daily and arrives in Orlando at 2:18pm. You can also catch that train at Hollywood, Fort Lauderdale, Deerfield Beach, Delray Beach, West Palm Beach, Sebring, and Winter Haven stops. Fares in 1990 were $46 one way, $53 to $92 round trip depending on the day and seating.

To reach Orlando/Kissimmee from Tampa/St. Petersburg, you can take the Silver Meteor, which leaves Tampa at 11:32am and arrives in Kissimmee at 1:14pm, in Orlando at 1:50pm. The Silver Star leaves Tampa at 7:30pm and arrives in Kissimmee at 8:44pm, in Orlando at 9:15pm.

Fares on the major north-south run between New York and Orlando in 1990 were $145 one way, $174 to $290 round-trip. Discounts of all kinds and for all reasons (families, senior citizens, students, military—it goes on and on) are as prevalent on Amtrak as they are on airlines, so be sure to tell travel agents or Amtrak reservations personnel as much as you can about yourself and your travel plans, so they can help you find the best bargain.

Amtrak "All Aboard America" fares divide the nation up into four regions, with fares based on the number of regions in which you'll be traveling. A money-saver, this fare offers a $189 price for all travel in one region, between New York or Washington and Florida, for instance.

Since the New York to Orlando journey takes 24 hours or more, you might consider a "slumber coach," which is the railroad's economy sleeper. It is a private compartment with dual or single upper and lower berths that are stowed efficiently away during the day so you can enjoy the passing scenery from a seat. There are also foldaway sinks and unenclosed toilet facilities in these compartments which only have storage for small pieces of luggage (check your others with the bell captain). You must add the cost of these sleeping accommodations—$90 to $145 single, $155 to $174 double, one way, depending on season—to the fares to come up with the total cost of the journey by sleeper. Unlike other sleeping accommodations, this sleeper category does not include meals.

Another accommodation level on Amtrak is called a "roomette." That is a room for single travelers only, and includes a Murphy bed–like, pull-down sleeper plus unenclosed lavatory facilities. Additional cost for the roomette is $163 to $203 one way, including meals.

Finally, a couple or an adult with one or two small children can reserve a bedroom furnished with a couch-like seat or two lounge chairs facing each other, plus upper and lower berths and enclosed toilet facilities. Supplement for these quarters is $300 to $435 each way, depending on the season in which you're traveling. Some of these sleeping quarters have adjacent compartments which can be joined to create a suite for a family or group traveling together.

Meals are also included in this sleeping category. Other Silver Service amenities include a hospitality basket with wine and goodies.

If you're coming to Florida from Europe, you can buy a national **USA Railpass** available only to overseas visitors. Prices are $299 for 45 days of unlimited train travel, not only in Florida but throughout the U.S. Children two through 11 pay $150. Top European travel companies like Thomas Cook, American Express, and Kuoni are among the many European travel agents who can arrange passes for you. Some airlines and rail travel offices can, too.

Other Amtrak values include a 45-day **Eastern Region Pass** for $179, allowing unlimited travel and stopovers east of the Mississippi River in a region extending from Montréal and Chicago in the north to Miami and New Orleans in the south. Three other regional passes are available in other parts of the nation.

Those headed for St. Petersburg, Sarasota, and other cities on Florida's west coast will discover that although the train now travels only to Tampa, Amtrak has begun a service called **Amtrak Thruway Service** which meets you at the station in Tampa and takes you by bus to other cities along the western coastline of the state.

Amtrak also can help you save money. **Tour packages** available from the company offer savings on car rentals, hotels, and attraction admissions. For information on those packages and for Amtrak timetables, Rail Planner, and route guides, write to Amtrak, Box 7717, Itasca, IL 60143, or call the railroad, toll free, in any of the continental states at 800/USA-RAIL.

Good news! **Auto-Train** (tel. 407/323-4800) is back on track again, offering you the convenience of a car in Florida without any of the inconvenience of driving it there. Operated by Amtrak, Auto-Train begins at Lorton, Va., and ends at Sanford, Fla., about 23 miles from Orlando. You drive your car aboard the train in Lorton, which is about a four-hour drive from New York, about two from Philadelphia, and practically no distance at all from Washington, D.C. Both here and in Sanford, Fla., the Auto-Train station is not the same as the station you would use if you were catching a regular Amtrak train. In both cases they are in different locations which will be carefully explained to you when you book a ticket.

Next, you settle into a coach seat or bedroom and the next morning at 9:30am you roll into the station at Sanford. Round-trip cost of this simple way to avoid up to 2,000 miles of driving is $169 to $280 for each adult, depending on the season in which you're traveling, and $298 to $490 per car. Singles pay $140 in peak season, $99 in off-peak season. Off-peak, by the way, is October through May, peak is June through September.

If you want to rent a bedroom compartment aboard the train, you pay an additional $179 to $358 for a sleeper accommodating two travelers. Amtrak's off-peak excursion fare saves you money if you are able to go to Florida and return within 45 days. Those intent on a longer stay pay the fares quoted. Amtrak often has other kinds of discounts, so it's wise to ask lots of questions.

Auto-Train leaves either Lorton or Sanford daily at 4:30pm, arriving at its destination the following morning.

## BY BUS

Buses are often, although not always, the budget way to travel. If you like the idea of leaving the driving to them, you might consider traveling to Orlando on the nation's major bus line, **Greyhound/ Trailways** (tel. 407/843-7720).

Express buses have cut the time you'll spend getting here, but you still should plan on at least 36 hours from Chicago to Miami, about 28 from New York, 24 from Washington, and about three days from Los Angeles.

Once you're in Florida, buses can take you from even the smallest village to Orlando.

What's more, Greyhound/Trailways offers package-tour programs (two- or three-day or longer) that can save you money on hotels, attractions, and transportation costs.

There's a one-day trip from Fort Lauderdale that leaves the station about 6am, whizzes you to Disney World, and gets you back again about midnight, for $78 adults, $58 children, including park admissions, transportation, and breakfast.

Also check the tours run by **Gray Line** (tel. 407/422-0744).

## BY CAR

To ask several Florida travelers for the best route to Central Florida from your hometown is to discover why horse races are popular: a difference of opinion. Every driver who's ever hit the highroad to the Sunshine State has a special way to get here and is convinced that's the *only* way to go. If you can't decide who's right, you might consider joining the American Automobile Association (AAA), which offers members a free route-mapping service. There are a number of other motor clubs, too, offering various services from insurance to maps, breakdown help, even bail bonds if you run afoul of the speed laws. Included among those clubs are Allstate, Amoco, Ford, Gulf, Montgomery Ward, Exxon, Mobil, and Texaco Motor Clubs.

Whichever route you select to get you to the state line, once there you'll find friendly Floridians on hand to greet you at **Welcome Stations** set up at key state border crossings. Those stations are located at Yulee (Hwy. I-95), Hillyard (U.S. 1 and U.S. 301), Campbellton (U.S. 231), Jennings (Hwy. I-75), Pensacola (Hwy. I-10), and in Tallahassee in the new Capitol Building. Here smiling greeters are armed with masses of helpful pamphlets, friendly smiles, and even a welcoming glass of orange juice!

Costs of automobile travel have not changed radically in recent years. The American Automobile Association (AAA), which keeps records of such costs, figures estimated daily driving costs at about $173 daily for a family of four—two adults and two children—for lodging and meals, and $8.40 in car expenses for each 100 miles traveled (based on an average of 23 miles a gallon). AAA (tel. 407/ 444-7000 in Orlando) says be prepared to adjust these estimates up or down depending on the popularity of the region in which you are driving.

## BY SHIP

Well, that's fudging a bit—you can't really get here by ship but you can now visit the Mouse for a few days and rest up from the experience with a few days at sea.

You can do that aboard shiny red cruise ships operated by Premier Cruise Lines, which happens also to be the "official" cruise line of WDW. Aboard the lines *Star/Ship Majestic, Star/Ship Oceanic,* or *Star/Ship Atlantic,* you can sail off to the Bahamas on three- or four-day voyages that depart from Port Canaveral, about 45 miles east of Orlando. Packages team the cruise with a visit to Walt Disney World and toss in airfare, hotel accommodations, a rental car, tickets to the theme park, and a tour of Spaceport, USA at the Kennedy Space Center. You can take the cruise before or after you visit the park. A travel agent can make all the arrangements for you and will have brochures outlining the details of the cruise line's packages.

# GETTING AROUND

Every major rental-car agency in the nation has an office in Orlando, and dozens of smaller independent operators do business here as well, making this one of the most competitive markets in the nation. That means you can find rental-car rates in Central Florida that are as low—and often lower—than any in the nation.

National Car Rental is the official Walt Disney World rental-car agency and has, or is included in, a number of package-tour programs that offer price reductions on attraction admissions and car and hotel prices. Hertz, Avis, Budget, Dollar, and other major national chain operations also have package tours that include Disney World.

A bargain leader in Central Florida and elsewhere in the state is Alamo, which allows you (as do some but not all other car rental companies), to pick up a car from most of its many locations in Florida, such as Miami, Fort Lauderdale, or West Palm Beach, and drop the car in Orlando at no extra charge and vice versa. Rates begin at about $80 a week, sometimes less, for air-conditioned, subcompact cars (a two-door Chevette, for instance), including unlimited mileage. An optional collision damage waiver is available for about $13 to $15 a day additional but is sometimes included in the price.

If you're considering a car rental in Orlando, there are two things you should do. First, ask a travel agent to help you check prices, or make some telephone calls yourself to the toll-free numbers of rental-car agencies to ask about rental rates for the time you'll be in Florida. If you're flying to Florida, you might also ask if the company has special price offers in conjunction with any airline. It is getting almost as complicated to work your way through the maze of rental-car rates as it is to discover all the bargain-flight fares available to Florida, but it is always worth the trouble.

**ORLANDO AND VICINITY**

Second, check with your insurance agent to see what insurance coverage you already have, and how much of it covers you in a rental car. If you are covered for collision, for example, and are willing to risk a few hundred dollars in deductible fees if the car is damaged, you can often waive collision insurance and save yourself a pile of money. Florida residents who have insurance covering them in a rental car can waive other insurance charges too, but sometimes must leave a refundable cash or credit-card deposit. You can often waive other insurance add-ons, and you should do so, if you are already insured elsewhere. Read your policy and the small print on the rental contract.

In Florida, by the way, most rental-car companies set the minimum rental age at 21 for men, 18 for women when reserving through an airline or travel agent, 25 years old when booking directly. A few have even set a maximum age. You must also have a credit card or be willing to leave a deposit in cash at the rental agency while you have the car. Deposits are, of course, returned when you return the car undamaged.

Here are the toll-free numbers of some of the largest and best-known rental-car companies: **Alamo,** 800/327-9633; **Avis,** 800/331-1212; **Budget,** 800/527-0700; **Dollar,** 800/421-6868; **Value Rent A Car,** 800/327-2501; **Hertz,** 800/654-3131; and **National,** 800/328-4567. Avis, Budget, Dollar, Hertz, and National have rental desks in the terminal at Orlando airport, but all the others can easily be reached by phone and will pick you up and take you to their rental desks, returning you to the airport at the completion of your rental contract.

**Mears Transportation Airport Limousine** 320 W. Gore St., Orlando (tel. 423-5566), operates airport limousine service to area hotels. You'll find the limousines, which really are 11-person vans, outside the terminal building on the second floor. Prices range from $12 to $18 for a one-way ride to hotels in the Orange Blossom Trail area and to International Drive, and rise for the ride to Lake Buena Vista, Kissimmee area, Walt Disney World hotels, downtown Orlando hostelries, and farther afield. Children's fares (for ages 4 to 14) are $3 lower and you can save several dollars on both child and adult fares by buying a round-trip ticket.

Some hotels offer free shuttle service from the airport. You can even call many of them free from the airport, using telephones at consoles in the baggage claim area.

For a taxi, try **Yellow Cab** (tel. 699-9999), which charges $2.25 a mile for the first mile, $1.30 for every mile thereafter. You'll pay $20 to $25 to Lake Buena Vista/Disney World, and hotels on U.S. 192 in Kissimmee.

If you'd like to arrive in style, **Carey Limousine** (tel. 855-0442) has a booking booth at the luggage pick-up area too, and will bring a Cadillac limousine or a presidential stretch limo around for you. Rates are about $4 higher than taxi fares and run from about $60 to $90 for most destinations. If there are enough of you traveling together, you might even save money.

Do keep in mind that distances are great in Central Florida's flatlands, so don't expect just to drop into Sea World and walk over to Disney World—it's four miles just from Disney's first entrance sign to its parking lot! If you're planning to sample some of the area's great dining spots and lively nightlife, you'd be wise to rent a car, since taxi fares over the distances here can be enormous, and public transportation, great during the day, isn't much after attraction closing hours.

If Disney World and its fellow sights are your major interest and you're not planning to do much other exploring, you'll find Orlando has plenty of transportation from hotels to the major fun spots. Some hotels operate their own shuttle buses to the major attractions and those that don't, ask shuttle bus operators in the area to stop at their doorstep to pick up their guests.

**Gray Line** (tel. 422-0744) operates much of what moves on wheels in Orlando. It operates regular bus service from the airport to Disney World hotels and to International Drive area hotels. Buses leave from both sides of the second floor of the terminal baggage claim areas 24 hours a day.

The line's big bruisers also ply between attractions and International Drive area hotels. You can ride to Sea World or Walt Disney World for $7 one-way for adults or children. Gray Line also operates trips to other attractions throughout central Florida (Kennedy Space Center, Busch Gardens), for prices ranging from $20 to $30.

In Lake Buena Vista, **shuttle buses** that operate on an every-15-minutes schedule stop at all hotels and finally at the entrances to the Magic Kingdom and EPCOT. They're free to hotel guests who simply display a pass issued by the hotel. Flags painted on the sides of the buses identify where they're going. Buses operate from 8am to 2am, so you can take in the nightlife at Disney World.

You can even rent a motor home and buzz about in style here. **Holiday RV Rental,** 5001 Sand Lake Rd., Orlando, FL 32819 (tel. 407/351-3096; or toll free 800/351-8888; in Fla. 800/351-6666) has all sizes of recreational vehicles for rent for prices ranging from $550 to $800 a week.

# GETTING YOUR BEARINGS

If there's one place in Florida that really deserves the description "sprawling," it's Orlando. First, there are a dozen or so suburbs large enough to be cities in their own right but too small to be easily differentiated from Orlando's urban sprawl. Second, the city itself sprawls over mile after flat mile of highway-beribboned countryside.

Finding your way around isn't as difficult as it might be, however, thanks to a carefully constructed network of roadways that can speed you from one suburb to the next—and even across the state, east toward Cape Canaveral and Daytona or west to Tampa.

Here are a few clues to finding your way around this brash and booming territory.

Main east-west artery is **Highway I-4,** which runs from Tampa on the state's west coast to Daytona on the east and conveniently zips right through Orlando. If you see the sun dipping off to the west, indicating you're driving north or south, don't panic. At times the road does indeed take a north-south twist. Just keep in mind the Tampa-to-Daytona orientation, take a careful look at an area map, and you'll be all right. Exits from this major expressway take you to Disney World, Sea World, Church Street Station, downtown Orlando, International Drive, Lake Buena Vista, Altamonte Springs, and Winter Park, to name just a few. Highway I-4 is likely to be the expressway you'll get to know best, since most attractions and hotels are located on or near it.

The main east-west route past the entrance to Disney World is **U.S. 192** which stretches from Kissimmee, past many inexpensive motels and restaurants, to U.S. 27.

A quick east-west route is a road called the **Beeline.** It intersects with Highway I-4, crosses other major arteries like Route 436, Orange Blossom Trail, and the Florida Turnpike, then zips eastward to Cape Canaveral. It's a quick way to the World from the airports, too.

Another east-west byway is the **East-West Expressway,** which is north of the Beeline and streaks scenically across Orlando. It can be reached from Highway I-4.

**Route 436** is a major roadway that forms a beltline around Orlando's east side from the Beeline, past the East-West Expressway and Colonial Drive, then bends west to cross U.S. 17/92 and some outlying suburbs.

That street with the picturesque name, **Orange Blossom Trail** (also called Route 441), is a north-south road with plenty of motels and restaurants and no dearth of traffic either.

Another "orange" street, **Orange Avenue,** parallels Orange Blossom Trail but is located farther east and goes past downtown landmarks, as does **Colonial Drive** (Route 50).

Once you've found your way around the city and to Walt Disney World, you'll need to know that the 28,000 acres—a total of 43 square miles—owned by Disney here are divided into several sections.

There are three theme parks here and a fourth is promised by Disney officials. For the moment those **three theme parks** are WDW's Magic Kingdom, spread across 100 acres; EPCOT Center sprawling across 260 acres; and Disney-MGM Studios occupying about 110 acres of Central Florida.

Beyond that, the Mouse's Kingdom stretches across the landscape to include: **Discovery Island,** an outdoor, no-bars bird and animal nature preserve; **River Country,** a playground with pools, slides and inner-tube diversions; **Typhoon Lagoon,** a wonderland with scary waterslides, a tranquil tubing lagoon, a fish-filled—and even shark-inhabited (these don't bite)—play pool, beaches, picnic tables and all the South Seas island accoutrements.

Here, too, on Disney's awesome hunk of Central Florida landscape are 2,500 acres worth of golf courses, sports facilities, hotels, and a shopping plaza with another even larger mercantile center soon to come.

# III

# DOZING IN DISNEY WORLD AND ORLANDO

You probably never considered it possible to live happily with a mouse, but when there's magic around, *anything* can happen! What better place to let yourself roll with that magic than in Mickey's Magic Kingdom?

When you stay right here where Mickey, Pluto, and Dumbo are tucked in each night, the magic keeps going from your first morning orange juice until the last glittering fireworks fade from the sky.

That's the way Walt Disney and his workers planned it when they crowned their Magic Kingdom with two fabulous, fantasy hotels: one a quick trip to your very own Fantasy Island, the other an adventure in tomorrow, with a capital "T."

Fabulous usually carries a rather high price tag, however. That's the case at Disney World, where you will pay quite a few pretty pennies for the privilege of proximity. There are mitigating factors, however, the major one of which is the availability of free transportation. When you stay in one of the hotels owned and operated by Disney, or in seven others privately owned but located on Disney World property, you can abandon the trusty auto and leave the driving entirely to their shuttle system.

Visitors who fly to Orlando intent on spending most of their time at Disney World, with perhaps a tour or two to other area attractions, can find some very comfortable and luxurious places to bunk and forgo the expense and hassle of a car.

If, however, you think you'd like to look around this very lovely part of Florida and want to have the convenience of a car at your doorstep, you can find plenty of moderately priced accommodations just a short drive from Disney World and from many of the other attractions in the area.

It is crucial to remember that distances are great here in Central Florida. You cannot spend the morning at Disney World and stroll over to Sea World or Universal Studios for lunch. You cannot, in fact, stroll over to Universal or Sea World at all unless you're a marathon walker. It is miles just from the first Disney entrance sign to the parking lot, and farther yet between attractions.

What I want to emphasize here is that you have several basic decisions to make before you land in Disney land.

If you plan to fly here, you must decide if you want to rent a car and save some money on hotel accommodations, or forgo the car and splurge on hotels at Disney World, where you do not need a car. You can, of course, see some of the other area attractions on package tours, but without a car you'll probably have to forgo a look at other attractions, Orlando's charming suburbs, and some of the intriguing restaurants and nightlife here.

If you're driving here and owe yourself a splurge, there's no better place to take it than at some of the very attractive and interesting hotels on Disney property.

If you want to keep your costs down, you can do that by taking advantage of moderately priced hotels and motels that are just a short drive from the park.

# ACCOMMODATIONS IN DISNEY WORLD

## DISNEY WORLD HOTELS

So what are these fabulous places I've been raving about? Let's take a look at hotels owned and operated by Disney World. (Book all these in–Disney World hotels by calling 407/824-2000 or 407/ W-DISNEY or by writing Walt Disney World Reservations, Box 10100, Lake Buena Vista, FL 32830.)

If you listen very hard at Disney's **Polynesian Village,** you may hear the plaintive strains of that little character, Tatu, crying "Zee Plaaaane, boss, zee plaaane." So quickly do you become part of the South Seas atmosphere here that right at the reception desk you begin wondering why you didn't pack a sarong. Thatched roofs, waterfalls, "longhouses" set amid jungle, lily ponds, tonga torches, grass-skirted maidens, fire dances—one fantastic place indeed to lei your head.

Enter the lobby and stroll into the center of a jungle where perhaps the only thing missing is a volcano! Water trickles over rocks, palms soar to the three-story-high ceiling, anthuriums peek flaming red ears out from behind more than 75 species of tropical flora. Look closely and you'll spot an orchid or two nestled among the greenery. This intriguing spot is called the Great Ceremonial House, and it's where you'll find most of the hotel's sybaritic restaurants, lounges, and shops.

Nine two- and three-story longhouses streak down the sides of this complex, which is bounded by a sparkling white beach. Named for Pacific Islands, the longhouses are home to 853 rooms. The largest ones are in Oahu, and suites are in Bali Hai, to name a couple. South Seas luxury in your room translates to one king-size or two queen-size beds, plus carpets, big closets, and dressing rooms. Rooms can accommodate five, even six if the sixth is a toddler. Suites are available for four to eight fantasy-seekers.

Sleeping is the least interesting thing you can do here. There are all kinds of boats to rent, from pedal boats to pontoons to outrigger canoes. There are two super swimming pools, including a Swimming Pool Lagoon, set amid rocks that form a waterslide you reach by splashing and spluttering your way through a waterfall.

You'll find a children's playground, a game room called Moana Mickey's Fun Hut, outdoor bars, and a shop in the Great Ceremonial House where you can buy a grass skirt after you really begin to get into the spirit of this place.

You get to this touch of Fantasy Island Orlando-style via the monorail that takes you right to the door. It's just one stop from the Magic Kingdom, so you can see what I meant when I said you don't need a car.

What you'll pay for all this depends primarily on which view you select: in ascending order, pool-view rooms, garden-view rooms, marina- or lagoon-view rooms, all ranging in price from $190 to $245. There is no charge for guests under 18. Each additional adult in a room is $15. Rates are a little lower in spring and fall.

Onward to Disney's second fanciful creation, the **Contemporary Resort Hotel,** where Tomorrowland comes to life. For openers, the monorail runs right through the *middle* of this hotel! There are few experiences more awesome than arriving aboard a whooshing monorail and stepping right out into the lobby. For that matter, there are few experiences more awesome than just riding that monorail through the lobby whether or not you're staying at the hotel.

A towering A-frame, the Contemporary would have fit right into *Star Wars.* It's sleek, it's practically supersonic, and it most certainly is contemporary.

Largest of the Walt Disney World hostelries, the Contemporary has 1,052 rooms in an imposing central tower and two garden wings. Just as the Polynesian tends to slow and soothe you, the Contemporary sends your pulses racing, your imagination soaring. That's why some people like it not at all, and others never cease to be awed by its exciting aura of future shock.

Disney World doesn't stint on luxury at either of these two hotels. At the Contemporary, you'll find large, luxurious, and spotlessly maintained rooms with two queen-size or one king-size bed. As in the Polynesian, rooms can accommodate five and even six, if the sixth is under three. You can choose rooms in the tower ($210 to $230, depending on the date), where some complain that slow elevators are an inconvenience, but where everyone agrees you have a fabulous view of the lake and its intriguing Electrical Water Pageant. From rooms on the other side of the tower, Cinderella Castle provides an ever-changing, ever-enchanting view complete with fireworks at special times of the year.

Garden Wings flank the main tower. Rooms in these three-story buildings are just as attractive but seem more sedate and re-laxed. Prices here are $180 to $205 a day double, and children under 18 are free.

Suites are also available at higher prices, and in the Garden Wing they come in several configurations, including studios for two with a parlor and sleeping area with a king-size bed; one-bedroom suites, which sleep up to six in a bedroom and parlor with two double sleep sofas; and suites, which can accommodate seven in bedroom and parlor. Perfect for really big families or several couples.

There's no dearth of activities here. You can send the children off to the game room (or sneak there yourself), where they will dis-appear for hours, perhaps days, lost in the wonderland of games ranging from skee ball to air hockey, from Space Invaders to whatev-er other electronic game is new and exciting.

While they're gone, weary parents can try their feet at waterskiing, their arms at swimming in two very large pools (there's even a special pool for teenagers), or they can exercise it all on sail-boats, or pedal boats, pontoons, or shuffleboard courts, playing volleyball, or jogging at nearby Fort Wilderness. If you're not up to any of that, settle into a good movie—three Disney films are shown daily.

Shopping? Of course, and in some very posh shops located on what the hotel calls its Grand Canyon Concourse.

In 1988, Walt Disney World opened the first new hotel in many years to be built right on Disney property—joining the Con-temporary and the Polynesian. Called the **Grand Floridian Beach Resort,** Box 10,100, Lake Buena Vista, FL 32830 (tel. 407/824-8000), this 900-room structure harks back to days of yore in Flori-da. Sprawling across 40 acres alongside the Seven Seas Lagoon between the Magic Kingdom and the Polynesian Village Resort, the Grand Floridian was designed to recall the grand old days when John D. Rockefeller, Thomas Edison, and Pres. Theodore Roose-velt hied on down to the Florida sun each winter.

While Florida developers Henry Flagler and Henry Plant would be quite awestruck to discover that their railroads had in these contemporary times produced a monorail, there it is, stopping right at the Grand Lobby entrance to the hotel.

Here you will find soaring ceilings, wicker rockers beneath pad-dling ceiling fans, and a veritable forest of intricate Victorian woodwork—indeed, there are 60 miles of wooden scrollwork here!

Capped by a red shingle roof, the towers of this fanciful cre-ation combine to create an impressive yet delicate facade.

Only the look of the place is antique. Inside, every modern comfort can be yours, from fancy suites complete with bars to cozy hideaway seating areas where complimentary Continental break-fasts and evening cocktails are served by the concierge.

Here in the Grand Lobby you whiz about the levels in an open-cage elevator, are entertained in the serenity of an aviary, and are at all times surrounded by a forest of palms, the Victorian tree of choice. Five stories above you is a Victorian ceiling inset with three stained-glass domes, glittering chandeliers, and ornate metal scrolls.

All that is just in the main building. Then there are five four- and five-story lodge buildings, all decked out in soft spring pastels with printed wall coverings, armoires, light wood furniture, marble-top sinks with antique fittings, and, of course, more Victorian woodwork. Most rooms have two queen-size beds and a day bed, while suites offer a parlor and one to three bedrooms.

Even the hotel's shops stay in theme: You can buy in Summerlace, a ladies' shop; Commander Porter's, a men's shop; and M. Mouse Merchantile . . . need we tell you?

When you hunger and thirst, head for the Gasparilla Grill and Games, where you top your own burger with the accoutrements of your choosing, or slip into Victoria & Albert's, where a royal elegance reigns. For a taste of Floridiana, try Flagler's, where the menu features some of Florida's favorites, ranging from citrus-topped chicken to the ubiquitous Key lime pie. Outside along the shoreline, the octagonal Narcoossee Nick's offers oysters, clams, shrimp, and other seafood treats in a suitably seaside atmosphere complete with open beams and a typical Disney "legend" about Narcoossee Nick.

Evenings, the attention focuses on the hotel's white beach, where the Grand Floridian's Seaside Clambake takes place. At that event you dine on gator tail, roast pig, Florida lobster, clams, mussels, and corn on the cob, prepared over open pits and in copper kettles.

Recreational opportunities include a wide variety of water sports, from rental boats to a swimming pool and windsurfing boards.

Rates at this sparkling new addition to Walt Disney's World are $215 to $355, depending on room location.

In 1989, the **Caribbean Beach Resort,** Box 10,100, Lake Buena Vista, FL 32830 (tel. 407/824-8000), a massive 2,112-room property made its debut, and that is good news for budget watchers: It is billed as the first moderately priced hostelry ever built by Disney World. Moderate here at WDW is defined as in the $74 to $105 double range.

This new creation is composed of village clusters of two-story buildings spotlighting the styles of Trinidad, Martinique, Barbados, Aruba, and Jamaica—lots of pastels, metal roofs, and the laid-back, lazy feeling that is an integral part of Caribbean life.

Roadways winding through the resorts connect the villages which are linked to the Walt Disney World transportation system, although not by monorail. Six counter-service restaurants offer bakery treats, barbecued food, and native Caribbean fare, as well as the usual beef and seafood selections.

With a name like that, there is, of course, a beach, a swimming pool, a waterfall, and slides. Sailboats, canoes, and paddleboats fill the lagoons and a 1.4-mile tropical promenade is perfect for joggers and bicyclists.

These hotels are very, very popular, and reservations are *absolutely necessary* as far ahead as possible. If you aren't successful at first, try, try again, since cancellations do happen here as everywhere. Try, try again at **Central Reservations** (tel. 407/824-8000 or W-DISNEY; if you speak Spanish, French, Italian or German, call 407/824-7900) and don't hang up—the phone often rings five minutes or more before it's answered to keep you from paying while you're on hold. A deposit of one night's rate is required 21 days after the reservation is accepted and will be refunded if you cancel within five days before your scheduled arrival. Reservations are automatically canceled if a deposit is not received.

If you should arrive before check-in time (3pm) or want to leave after check-out time (11am), you can leave your luggage and go about your play. These hotels operate luggage-storage areas and will take care of your belongings until you return.

While those four hotels are Disney's top showplaces, there are two more Disney-owned properties here, both of them quieter spots, off the beaten monorail path, and both quite interesting in their own right.

First of these is the **Disney Inn,** formerly Golf Resort Hotel, a 288-room spot originally built to serve as a golf clubhouse. Rooms here are a little larger, have a mini-suite look, are decorated in pretty country prints and located in a two-story building behind the lobby. From a quiet corner of your private balcony or patio, you can gaze out over the golf course or a peaceful green woodland. Here too, rooms can accommodate up to five, plus a sixth small one, in two queen-size beds, topped with quilts, and a sofa sleeper. Two suites here can tuck in seven sleepy visitors.

You don't golf, you say? No matter, no one will come knocking at your door demanding a starting time, although if that's what you want, it's certainly available on two par-72 courses: the Magnolia, which plays from 5,903 to 7,253 yards, and the Palm, which plays from 5,785 to 6,951 yards. Disney doesn't overlook the small ones even on the golf course—there's a Wee Links six-hole, 1,150-yard course for the youngsters.

Naturally the resort also has a swimming pool, and for tennis buffs there are two lighted tennis courts open from 8am to 10pm daily.

Finally there's a small game room to keep the children occupied and a Garden Gallery Restaurant.

Rates at the Disney Inn are $175 to $185 a day with a view of the woods, the pool or the golf course. Suites are $275 and higher. As at all the Disney hotels, children under 18 are free.

The last of the Disney resorts is far from the last resort. It's one of my favorites, and if you like a feeling of seclusion and absolute privacy, this may prove to be your choice, too. Called **Walt Disney World Village Villas,** the resort is several clusters of villas, dubbed Vacation Villas, Fairway Villas, Club Lake Villas, and, most intriguing of all, Treehouse Villas.

All are apartment villas, which means they have kitchen facilities, so families, particularly large ones, can save money by doing some of their own cooking. What's more, the apartments are all big, roomy places where everyone can spread out, so you're not tripping over books and shoes on your way to the closet, as often happens in hotel rooms.

Let's start with the **Vacation Villas.** Here you'll find cathedral ceilings in the living room, plush and comfortable furnishings, and plenty of space to roam around. You can choose a one-bedroom villa for four with a queen-size bed in the bedroom and a queen-size sleeper sofa in the living room, or a two-bedroom villa for six with queen-size or twin beds in each bedroom and that big sofa sleeper in the living room. One additional small person can be accommodated in each of the units (small means under four years old in the one-bedroom, under 12 in the two-bedroom).

A super-elegant part of the Vacation Villas is a section called Grand Vista Suites, which are two- and three-bedroom *homes* where you're treated to bed-turndown service, daily newspapers delivered to your door, refrigerators stocked with staples when you arrive, and lovely furnishings. Whew!

Rates at the one- and two-bedroom Vacation Villas are $225 to $305; rates at the Grand Vista Suites are $775 to $850, depending on size of the home, and including use of an electric cart and bicycles.

**Club Lake Villas,** now also called **Club Suites,** were designed for use by conference attendees participating in meetings at the resort's nearby conference center. They're not as large as other villas but are very sophisticated and sleek with a wet bar in a sitting area and a bedroom with two double beds set off slightly from the sitting area. Rates are $150 to $175.

A one-bedroom deluxe club suite ($230 to $255) also is available and accommodates five with Jacuzzi, two queen-size beds upstairs and a convertible sofa downstairs. All this, by the way, is hard by the tranquil waters of a sparkling blue lake. Other facilities at these villas include a swimming pool and three tennis courts as well as a golf course.

**Fairway Villas** are all handsome two-bedroom units located near the 10th, 11th, 17th, and 18th fairways of the Lake Buena Vista Club Golf Course. Here you'll find imposing cathedral ceilings in woodsy two-bedroom units with cedar siding on the exterior and rough-hewn wood trim on the inside. Contemporary furniture pulls it all together and huge expanses of glass bring the outside world inside. They're very impressive places to while away the non-park hours and can sleep six plus a child under 12. Rates for the two-bedroom villas for six are $250 to $305 a day.

Finally, my favorites, the **Treehouse Villas,** are fascinating quarters plunked down deep in a shady pine forest. So cleverly do these octagonal creations on stilts blend into their serene surroundings, you may have difficulty finding the forest for the trees . . . er, treehouses. Each has three bedrooms with queen-size bed and comfortable furnishings, a small kitchen, a living room with a convertible sofa, and two baths. All that is on the second floor of the treehouse, encircled by tall glass windows and a wraparound deck where you can meditate on the beauties of the forest around you. On the ground-level floor of the treehouses, you'll find a den and utility room with a washer and dryer.

So lovely is it here, it may never occur to you to look for anything else to do, but if you must, there could hardly be a more entrancing spot for jogging, and the canals that wind about here are a haven for fishing fanatics. Swimmers can head over to the pool at the Lake Buena Vista Club.

Rates for the three-bedroom treehouses for six are $270 to $295 a day. There is no charge for additional occupants of the quarters.

Naturally, facilities of this size take up quite a bit of space, so it is helpful to have a car to get around the villas and to get from them to the Magic Kingdom. Although Disney has, of course, provided transportation, you can also rent electric carts for $30 a day to zip around in the serene style befitting these attractive resorts.

None of the villas has a restaurant, but if you want to dine out, you can zip over to the Lake Buena Vista Club or to Walt Disney World Shopping Village.

Once again, Disney people have thought of everything, so you'll find a Gourmet Pantry chock full of goodies right down to pastries. You can pick up groceries or order them delivered to your villa free—if you're not there, they'll even arrange to put them right in your refrigerator for you! Call them at 828-3886 from outside or by dialing a number on your room phone. That, folks, is service with a capital "S."

Other facilities include swimming at three different pools, a game room, and one more golf course, the Lake Buena Vista course, in addition to the two at the Golf Villas, plus tennis courts, and boating on the lake.

At the center of the villa complex is the Pool Pavilion, where you can rent those electric carts and bicycles, and use laundry and vending machines, electronic games, and pinball gizmos.

Check-in spot for Vacation Villas, Club Lake Villas, Treehouse Villas, and Fairway Villas is the Reception Center 1901 Lake Buena Vista Dr., in the Walt Disney World Village Hotel Plaza (more about that shortly) between the Viscount Hotel and Grosvenor Resort in Lake Buena Vista.

It is important to note here that while the Villas and the Disney Inn are on Disney property, they are not as close to the Magic Kingdom as the Polynesian, Grand Floridian, and Contemporary hotels and cannot be reached by monorail. You get from the villas to the Walt Disney Shopping Village, the Ticket and Transportation Center at the entrance to the Magic Kingdom, and to the Polynesian, Grand Floridian, and Contemporary hotels by bus, each conveniently identified with colored flag so you can easily tell which goes where. For a complete look at Disney World's transportation system, see Chapter VIII.

## FANCY CAMPING IN DISNEY WORLD

Finally, here are accommodations for those who do not only like the great outdoors but like to be right out there in it as much as possible. Number one locale for that at Disney World is a cozy enclave known as **Fort Wilderness**. For some reason this spot is one of Disney's lesser-known attractions and one that's often confused with the Magic Kingdom's other western-oriented area, Frontierland. Fort Wilderness, however, is not an attraction, in the strict-est sense, although it is an attractive spot designed for campers and those who like the ambience of camping but can do without the drudgery.

Here's how Fort Wilderness works: For campers there are 892 campsites, 90 of them set up for tents and the rest rented to trailer campers. Each site is 25 by 65 feet and located in one of 21 clusters through which roads loop and twist. Each site has 110/220-volt electrical outlets, water, a barbecue grill, picnic table, and disposal hookup. In each cluster you'll find rest rooms, showers, an ice ma-chine, telephones, and a laundry room. Up to 10 campers can settle into a site for $35 to $46 a day, depending on season and location. There's a maximum stay of 14 nights.

Which are the best sites? Well, it depends what you are looking for in a Disney World campsite. Sites numbered from 100 to 500 are near the lakeside beach, the Trading Post, and Pioneer Hall. Farthest away from all that are numbers 1500 to 1900, which are located amid the loveliest and densest concentration of greenery.

If you can't quite face the idea of a trailer or tent, Disney has thought up a way to provide for you. Throughout the campground you'll find 363 air-conditioned Fleetwood Travel Trailers, 35 feet long and equipped to sleep and feed six. Everything's there, from a can opener to a dishwasher and microwave, from a bedroom with a sink, color television, and double bed or bunks, to a living room with a convertible sofa, television, and sink. There's also a bathroom in each trailer and daily maid service. Quite a "camping" experi-ence, eh? There's just one no-no: You can't have camping equipment on the site, and everyone sleeping there must do so inside the trailer. Rates for the four- or six-person trailers are $155 to $165 a night.

Rest assured you will not starve at Fort Wilderness, even if you choose not to avail yourself of groceries at the Meadow or Settle-ment Trading Posts, open from 8am to 10pm in winter, to 11pm in summer. You can get hot dogs, hamburgers, and the like at the Beach Shack by the lake or the Campfire Snack Bar in Pioneer Hall. For more substantial fare, there'a the Trail's End Café, a cozy log cafeteria with beamed ceiling and simple homey cooking, in Pio-neer Hall. Later, from 9pm to 12:30am, pizza rolls out of the oven here; and beer, sangría, and soft drinks flow from the taps as happy munchers chuckle over the silent movie or participate in a sing-along.

Which brings us to what there is to do here: plenty. Most fun is the Hoop-Dee-Doo Musical Revue, which takes center stage three times a night at 5, 7:30, and 10pm. So popular is this show that res-ervations are required. Make them as far ahead as possible by calling Central Reservations 824-8000. If the first show's completely booked, you can get on a waiting list by turning up at the Pioneer Hall Ticket Window prior to the next show and explaining your plight.

While you're watching the antics that occur after the velvet cur-tain opens, you'll chow on some down-home cookin' in the form of barbecued ribs, corn on the cob, fried chicken, and strawberry shortcake. There is plenty to eat as well as plenty to watch at one of these rip-roaring evenings. Tickets are $30 for adults, $24 for young people 12 to 20, and $16 for children 3 to 12.

City kids who don't get much opportunity to sit around a campfire will love another of Fort Wilderness's activities, a campfire sing-along that occurs near the Meadow Trading Post. Also on the bill there are free Disney movies and cartoons, a marshmallow roast and canoe excursion, called the Marshmallow Marsh Excursion, which paddles off to a special spot where excursionists can watch the Electrical Water Pageant at 9:45pm nightly while less adventuresome campers take up a seat on the beach.

More? You can swim in the lake, pedal around on bicycles, or paddle around in boats, play basketball, baseball, tetherball, softball, or volleyball, jog on a 2.3-mile course, fish, go horseback riding on guided trail rides, try waterskiing, drop in on the village blacksmith, the Petting Farm, or the horse barn, stroll a Wilderness Swamp Trail, and last, perhaps least, play in a games arcade.

Pets, by the way, must be housed in a special kennel here ($6 for overnight stay).

Buses and watercraft connect Fort Wilderness to the rest of the Disney World Kingdom with schedules available at Guest Services. More on the various modes of transport in Chapter VIII's section on transportation in and around the Magic Kingdom.

## HOTELS IN WALT DISNEY WORLD VILLAGE HOTEL PLAZA

Walt Disney World Village Hotel Plaza is quite a mouthful, but it adequately describes seven major Orlando hotels located on Disney property. While they occupy prime land among the thousands of acres owned by Disney World in Central Florida, these hotels are not owned by Disney World but by separate corporations which lease their land from Disney.

All of which means little to visitors except in one particular: These hotels are all very, very close to the Magic Kingdom and have free, frquent, and reliable transportation to the Kingdom, River Country, EPCOT, and, in fact, to all points in Walt Disney World day and night. You can also get reduced rates at Disney attractions, like River Country and Discovery Island, at these hotels, and because they have had a rather special status, you can get a seat at dinner shows ahead of the general public.

Just as meaningful, of course, is the quality of these accommodations. In a word, they are tops. All offer modern, luxurious surroundings, all the amenities, and a friendly welcome.

There are several ways to get to the hotels, but the easiest for new arrivals is the Lake Buena Vista exit from Highway I-4 (this exit also bears the route number SR 535). Signs direct you to the entrance, where you'll know immediately you have happened upon something special. You're transported from flatlands, sand, and scrub palms to a world of emerald-green lawns, median strips filled with greenery and colorful plantings, and best of all, chic, sleek resorts that do not use neon and Day-Glo colors to attract your attention. Instead they get that attention in the best way of all, with tastefully decorated, well-maintained buildings and beautiful grounds.

Hotel signs are subtle announcements, all the same size and color, alerting you to your arrival at these very attractive hostelries. Their luxury costs about $100 to $150 a night.

Guests' pets can stay at WDW Kennels, too, for $6 a night.

The first hotel you'll encounter as you enter here is the **Viscount Hotel,** Box 22205, Lake Buena Vista, FL 32830 (tel. 305/828-2424 or toll free 800/348-3765; in Florida 800/423-1022). Once the kids are safely tucked in here, parents can zip up to the 18th-floor Top of the Tower Nightclub, where they'll have one of the best seats in town for fireworks at the Magic Kingdom.

Viscount, part of the huge Trusthouse Forte chain, provides two queen-size beds in every room and attractive decor. You'll find plenty of smiling service, a game room and swimming pool to play in, and a coffee shop and lounge to retreat to after a long day in the park. Room rates are $109 to $159, year round, for up to four people in a room. In slower months the hotel often features some great bargain package prices. Ask.

Next in line is the **Grosvenor Resort,** 1850 Hotel Plaza Blvd., Lake Buena Vista, FL 32830 (tel. 407/828-4444 or toll free 800/624-4109). Formerly the Americana Dutch Resort Hotel, this high-rising hostelry got a new name and a new face when it became the Grosvenor. Now you'll find the hotel's huge lobby decked out in rattan and soft teal and rosy hues, reminiscent of Victorian-era shades. Ceiling fans whirr and a lobby bar called Crickets offers a respite from Disney-ing. Those who want no respite from the Mouse can find him in many guises in the hotel's Disney-packed shop, which also stocks resort clothes and all the little things you forgot.

Sumptuous hospitality has always been a byword of this hotel and that remains true. Rooms here offer twin double beds, some have king-size sleepers, and all are handsomely decorated in shades of teal, rust, and buff. Another unusual feature here: videocassette players and a 200-film library from which to select the perfect movie to begin or end a day. You'll find a small stocked bar and refrigerator; bathrooms are big and amply supplied with fluffy towels.

A particularly interesting feature of this hotel is its dining room, Baskerville's, which sports—are you ready?—a Sherlock Holmes Museum. Right in the middle of this dining spot is a glass-enclosed re-creation of Sherlock's parlor with everything in it—right down to his tobacco and his correspondence stabbed with a knife. Furnishings, details, even the newspaper, are straight from tales of 221B Baker St., quite a showstopper in an area dominated by Mouse-mania.

If that's not enough for you, nip into Moriarty's Pub where a portrait of that fiendish criminal who plagued Holmes lords it regally over darts players and imbibers.

Rates at this lakeside resort, which also sports two outdoor pools, a hot tub, horseshoe playground, shuffleboard, and lighted tennis, handball, and racquetball courts, are $99 to $150 a day—higher for suites, naturally.

On the other side of the primped and planted roadway that twists through this complex of hotels is the soaring **Hotel Royal Plaza,** 1905 Hotel Plaza Blvd., Lake Buena Vista, FL 32830 (tel. 407/828-2828 or toll free 800/248-7890), which not long ago spent jillions on a massive renovation designed to modernize every nook of this attractive property.

A 17-story tower houses part of the resort's rooms and is flanked by two two-story wings. In the center of it all is one very large swimming pool. Every room has a private balcony, and all are tastefully decorated in contemporary colors. You can massage away your aches and pains in a sauna or Jacuzzi, but if you have more energy left after a day at Disney, you can have a go at the game room, shuffleboard courts, or four tennis courts.

For dining, El Cid restaurant offers steaks and seafood ($15 to $25 for entrées). There's a coffee shop called the Knight's Table, plus two bars, La Cantina, and a disco called Giraffe, which happens to be the only disco on Disney World property, so it's quite popular. Amenities include four restaurants, a beauty salon, heated swimming pool, sauna, whirlpool, putting green, shuffleboard, and four lighted tennis courts you can play on for free.

Listen, if it's good enough for Bob Hope and Michael Jackson, then surely you . . . Both those fellows were guests here in recent years, so the resort once named two suites after them. Rates range from $130 to $170 for double rooms year round. If you want to sleep where Michael or Bob slept, you'll pay $375 to $555.

That mainstay of the tired American traveler, **Howard Johnson,** 1805 Hotel Plaza Blvd., Box 22204, Lake Buena Vista, FL 32830 (tel. 407/828-8888, toll free 800/223-9930), makes an appearance here, too. So popular did Ho Jo's prove to be at Disney World that the company not long ago added a six-story annex wing. Mainstay of the property, however, is a 14-story tower, which features two glass elevators and a plant-bedecked atrium. Children always seem partial to Howard Johnson and that is the case here, where the young ones are lured by a whizzing, whirring game room; two swimming pools; and a kiddie pool.

Rooms are spacious, attractively decorated, and equipped with everything you'd expect to find in a major hotel. This chain has had many years' practice in welcoming weary travelers, and you'll find smiling, responsive service and plenty of it. What's more, you can get something to eat at any hour of the day or night in the hotel's restaurant, which offers all the usual Howard Johnson specialties, including all those flavors of ice cream, of course.

Rates range from $125 to $175 year round; there is no charge for children under 18.

Among latest hotel chains to seek a piece of Mouseland is the **Hilton at Disney World Village,** which opened a new hotel in this little enclave at 1751 Hotel Plaza Blvd., Lake Buena Vista, FL 32830 (tel. 407/827-4000, or toll free 800/445-8667). So how did Hilton decide to face the competition of the masses of hoteliers here? Simple, electronically. Get in the elevator here, press the button for the third floor, and shortly a disembodied voice says, "Third floor, going up."

This sort of state-of-the-art digital-push-button-computerized-electronic wizardry turns up everywhere in the hotel from a digital telephone system that uses the touch of a single button to adjust heating or air conditioning, control television, and call hotel service personnel to lights that turn on and off by themselves when people enter or leave the room. Elevators are controlled by microcomputers that talk to you and rooms open with tamperproof magnetic cards.

Spacious hotel rooms in this 10-story building are done up in pretty contemporary pastels with attractive furnishings and big windows.

If you're traveling with the youngsters and would like to do without them for a few hours, a special Youth Hotel here offers accommodations for children 3 to 12 years old complete with video room, snack bar, and play area with meals and scheduled recreation provided.

Complimentary transportation to both Disney World parks is provided by the hotel, which also has two restaurants. One, the American Vineyards Restaurant, is all dolled up in brass and features American regional cuisine like hickory-smoked Vermont turkey and Florida stone crabs; the other's a lively informal family spot called County Fair, which offers breakfast, lunch, and dinner buffets and an old-fashioned family-style dinner. Hot dogs, hamburgers, and fresh fruit are available at poolside too. There are also two tennis courts, two lounges—Rum Largo featuring tropical drinks in a greenhouse and John T's Plantation in the lobby—with entertainment, a swimming pool and spray pool for the youngsters, and a health club with whirlpool, steamroom, and sauna.

An 814-room hotel, Hilton at Disney World Village charges $135 to $180 for rooms, depending on their size and location in this three-wing building.

Another hotel on this posh block is the **Buena Vista Palace,** 1900 Buena Vista Dr., Lake Buena Vista, FL 32830 (tel. 407/827-2727; or toll-free 800/327-2990; in Florida 800/432-2920). An $85-million creation towering 27 stories over the lake and sporting no fewer than 841 rooms, this hotel was completed in 1983 and remodeled in 1987, so if you like modernity, you can be sure you'll find the latest innovations here.

That renovation created marble floors inlaid with handwoven tufted carpets, crystal chandeliers, and a nifty lobby bar topped by a gazebo. Another innovation here: the first-ever complete children's program at a Disney World hotel. It comes complete with professional recreational director supervising daylong children's activities and a summer camp.

Buena Vista Palace has four towers, with many rooms that exit right onto a balcony rather than a hallway and 22 suites with international themes. Decorated in the latest styles and colors, the hotel features a bridge across a lagoon to a recreation area where you will find two swimming pools set in lush tropical plantings. This attractive hotel has come up with an interesting architectural innovation:

You enter on an upper level of the hotel where a serene, unhurried atmosphere prevails because all the guest services—reservations, car rentals, swimming pool exits, and the like—are located on the first floor. You'll find an interesting Australia-related Outback Restaurant here that's reached by a private elevator; another restaurant, Arthur's, is a gourmet haven high atop the tallest tower overlooking EPCOT—a sensational view and an 800-bottle "wine cellar in the sky." Rates are $145 to $240 year round.

Newest of the hotels in this handsome collection of Lake Buena Vista hostelries is **Pickett Suites Resort,** 2305 Hotel Plaza Blvd., Lake Buena Vista, FL 32830 (tel. 407/934-1000 or toll free 800/PICKETT). Pickett Suites differs from all its Disney-property competitors in a way that is sure to interest families and is likely to intrigue other travelers as well: This hotel has no rooms, only suites.

A showy cluster of 229 two- or three-room suites, Pickett Suites boasts custom-designed furniture, remote-control televisions in living room and bedroom, in-suite movies, and a stocked, built-in refrigerator.

They've thought of everything here, closets with skirt hangers, two vanities, full-length mirrors, built-in hair dryers, even a third television set in the bathroom. Coffee/tea makers and microwave ovens are also available. Most suites have two double beds plus a sofa bed that folds out into an additional sleeper; if there are more than four of you traveling together, two-room suites are available.

Tropical bird aviaries are all the rage in hotels these days, and Pickett Suites provides a two-story aviary surrounded by a Parrot Patch Restaurant and Lounge. Outside, there's a poolside bar, ice-cream parlor and game room.

Sports fans can swim in the resort's heated pool or whirlpool while the youngsters splash in the wading pool. There are tennis courts and golf at Walt Disney World Golf Courses. Since it also is on Disney property, the hotel is part of the Walt Disney World bus transportation system, which whizzes you from hotel front to park front in minutes at no cost.

Rates at the resort are $165 to $375 for one-bedroom suites, higher for two-bedroom accommodations.

## NEW HOTELS AT EPCOT CENTER

Even as you read, hotels are rising at Walt Disney World which, according to its chief honcho, will by 1995 add 11,000 hotel rooms to the thousands that are already on WDW's 25,000 acres of Central Florida land.

Among the newest are two interesting resorts that snuggle into their own little corner of the World just a niggle away from the entrance to EPCOT Center. Trams transport you quickly between the parks and these two interesting hotels.

You won't have any trouble finding them—just look for two huge swans and two huge dolphins towering over the landscape.

First of the two to be completed was the 758-room **Swan,** operated by Westin Hotels, at 1200 EPCOT Resort Dr., Lake Buena Vista, FL 32830 (tel. 407/934-3000, the Disney reservations office at 407/934-7639, or toll free 800/228-3000). Atop this 12-story building painted in an odd but riveting turquoise and coral pattern are two massive swans, each 45 feet tall and weighing in at 28,000 pounds.

Handsomely decorated rooms here sport a pineapple theme in salute to that fruit's long association with hospitality. Colors are bright, tropical pastels and rooms feature in-room safes, clock radios, multichannel cable television, voice mail telemessaging, minibars, separate dressing areas, hair dryers, bathrobes, daily newspaper delivery, and 24-hour room service.

On the 11th and 12th floors, suites and a special concierge level offers extra amenities.

Swimming at the Swan occurs in the hotel's big pool while tan fans head for a strip of beach alongside the lagoon that winds around this hotel.

You'll also find a health club, game room, beauty salon, shops, lighted tennis courts, and an activities program for children 4 to 12.

Palio, an Italian restaurant, is a pleasant spot with fresh pasta and other offerings on display at the entrance and the Garden Grove Café, snuggled away in a two-story circular greenhouse, also has lunch and dinner. All three meals are offered in the Splash Grill at poolside and Kimonos and the Lobby Court Lounge purvey potables.

Rates at the Swan are $185 to $325 double year round, higher for suites.

One rarely finds dolphins and swans in the same spot but here at Disney, as you certainly will discover, almost anything can happen.

Perhaps that's why the **Walt Disney World Dolphin** is joined to the Swan by a scenic covered walkway that bears considerable resemblance to a circus tent in color and fanciful form.

Wayyyy up top of the 27 floors of this triangular-tower hotel operated by the Sheraton Corp., you'll spot two huge dolphins, of like size and weight to their swan counterparts. A bit more dramatic than the Swan in exterior architecture, the Dolphin features a wildly tropical ambience with a massive waterfall cascading down the face of the triangle and splashing from one giant seashell to the next until it reaches a dolphin-trimmed, shell-shaped pool at the bottom of its trip.

Nearly twice as large as the Swan, the Dolphin has 1,509 rooms with seven concierge floors (12 through 18), two pools and a themed swimming grotto, a beach, a health club, eight tennis courts, a children's program, shops, game room, beauty salon, airline and car rental desks, and a vast array of meeting rooms.

There are no fewer than seven restaurants here including an Italian trattoria, a steak and seafood restaurant, an ice-cream shop, Asian restaurant, 1950s-style cafeteria, a café with an international menu. Add to that: two lounges and a nightclub.

**Walt Disney World Dolphin** is at 1500 EPCOT Resort Blvd., Lake Buena Vista, FL 32830 (tel. 407/934-4000 or the Disney reservations service at 407/934-7639, or toll free 800/227-1500 or 800/325-3535). Rates at the resort are $171 to $285 double year round, higher for suites and concierge-level accommodations.

Soon to come nearby are the smaller Yacht Club and Beach Club hotels, scheduled to open in 1991.

# ACCOMMODATIONS IN AND AROUND ORLANDO

It did not take long for Orlando's canny entrepreneurs to see that the Mouse and EPCOT might make them rich. Consequently, in what seemed mere minutes, dozens of new hotels and motels sprung up on the flat sands and cow pastures of Central Florida. There are now so many that the first-time visitor may be overwhelmed by the constant assault of a barrage of signs and buildings that stretch out in every direction from Disney World.

Welcome, however, to a buyer's market! Not for a decade have prices in Orlando been so advantageous for the traveler—or so bargainable! But Central Florida continues to boom with higher and higher numbers of visitors streaming into the region. All those new and repeat visitors had by 1990 set new attendance records at nearly every Central Florida attraction, and there seems to be no end to the increases in sight.

That means, however, that although price competition is still keeping prices down, they may not stay down. Once increasing at flashpaper speed, hotel construction here has slowed—although Walt Disney World has nearly 3,000 rooms under construction or just completed and has plans for another 8,000 in the next few years.

What all that means to you is that if Disney is in your dreams, now is the time to do it. Prices rose little in 1989 and 1990, but the beginnings of change are in sight. Major hotels have confidently returned to $150- to $200-range daily rates and are reporting occupancy rates much envied by other parts of the state.

Still, the stunning proliferation of hotel quarters has undeniably led to a price war, the likes of which you are not likely to find anywhere else in Florida—or perhaps the world! In slow spring and fall months, signs advertising rooms for $9.95 per person can be seen and it's even gotten to the point that small hotel operators are bargaining down their own prices on the telephone when you call them for reservations. Some are advertising: "Make us an offer."

"If you're going to stay two or three days, come down on the second day and talk to us and we'll see if we can't do something about lowering the price," an anxious motel owner told me. And he was prepared to make a deal on a room that was only $27 a night!

To describe every one of the raft of newcomer hotels would take a book of its own, so suffice to say that if you drive into the area and begin looking for a spot to settle, begin looking on U.S. 192. Small motels, and some not so small, have sprung up along this wide highway that is sometimes called the Highway to the Worlds. Those "worlds" refer primarily to Walt Disney World, the entrance to which is reached from this highway, but also to Sea World, just a splash away, and Circus World, about 15 to 20 minutes away.

Those newcomer motels, which seem to have sprung up like the proverbial mushrooms in less than two years, are all pretty stock material, both in ambience and in price. You'll find basic cement-block structures with clean but unprepossessing quarters: two chairs, a table, usually two double beds covered with floral bedspreads, a dresser, often a small dressing area, and a bathroom. Owners and operators of these often family-run motels are as exotic as their motels are not: Some are Chinese, many are Indian, some are Latin Americans, and, of course, many are Americans.

Price? About $35 to $50 year round, sometimes a few dollars less.

While they're not head-turning beauties, these motels do offer a decent, if non-chic, place to put your head each evening when you weave in exhausted from a long day at one or more of Orlando's many attractions. They have the added benefit of proximity to Disney World, which is not likely to be more than a 10- or 15-minute drive away.

What's more, roads are so many, so good, and move you so quickly from place to place in the Orlando area, you need not feel obliged to settle in right next to Mouseland. If you have a car, there is an enormous range of hotel choices. If you don't, public transportation can whisk you from all but the most remote spots right to Disney World and other attractions. Several tour companies operate in the area, picking up passengers at most hotels, delivering them to the doors of Disney World, Sea World, Circus World, and the rest, then bringing them safely home again.

To make matters even easier, hotels and motels in the area are clustered in several general locations: along U.S. 192 to Kissimmee, on International Drive in an area called Florida Center, downtown, and near the airport. I've divided them up geographically for you, beginning with those closest to the Kingdom and fanning out to the airport.

## JUST OUTSIDE DISNEY PROPERTY

Plunked down all by itself in the countryside just outside Disney World's acreage but still technically in Lake Buena Vista is **Vistana Resort,** on Route 535, at 13800 Vistana Dr., Lake Buena Vista, FL 32830, at the Lake Buena Vista exit from I-4 (tel. 407/239-3100 or toll free 800/327-9152, in Florida 800/432-9197). There probably is no quieter retreat outside the Disney Villas than Vistana's own villas, which are two-bedroom town-house–style dwellings, complete with balconies or patios.

Designed as condominium homes, these pastoral palaces feature the most contemporary furnishings in living and dining rooms, attractive woven wall hangings, and an ambience even the most critical traveler is sure to love. Some accommodations have high, beamed ceilings; most sport videocassette players, microwave ovens, and hydro-massage tubs.

You can settle in here and do some of your own cooking in a fully equipped kitchen, or just luxuriate in doing nothing at all in tranquil surroundings that include maid service, washers and dryers in each villa, three pools, a casual eatery, jogging trail, and scheduled activities.

Tennis is the major focus of this 50-acre complex so you'll find enough courts for Wimbledon, free play, and frequent discounts on tennis instruction and clinics as well as on Disney tickets. Transportation to Disney World and Sea World is $5 round trip.

Rates at Vistana, which has an even more impressive addition called The Palms, where water architecture achieves new heights, are $195 to $275 depending on the season.

A money-saver just outside Lake Buena Vista's Hotel Plaza entrance (but just a few hundred yards away) is **Days Inn Lake Buena Vista**, S. State Rd. 535, Lake Buena Vista, FL 32830 (tel. 407/239-4646 or toll free 800/325-2525). Two pools here should please youngsters as well as adults, and there's a nice quiet air about the place that's soothing after a long hot day. You'll find 245 rooms here, including five efficiency units with full kitchens, six rooms with king-size beds, and rooms with refrigerators. Tucked away under rustling pines, Days Inn features a coin laundry, game room, and movies, as well as bright tropical decor and lots of glass to let in the sunlight you came here to see. There's also an attractive casual restaurant for family dining and a cocktail lounge with entertainment, plus free transportation to the Magic Kingdom, EPCOT, and to Lake Buena Vista Village Shopping Center. Rates range from $75 to $95 year round, depending on season; efficiencies and suites higher.

Hyatt Hotels hit Orlando with a bang—make that a splash—when the hotel chain opened its dramatically showy new hotel in Lake Buena Vista just west of the Disney World Village Hotel Plaza area.

You'll see Hyatt's stepped-pyramid building rising out of the woodlands as you drive by on Highway I-4. To get to the **Hyatt Regency Grand Cypress Hotel**, 1 Grand Cypress Blvd., Orlando, FL 32819 (tel. 407/239-1234, or toll free 800/228-9000), take the SR 535 (Lake Buena Vista) exit from I-4 and head west to the second traffic light. There you turn left (a sign directs you). Just a short distance down that road is the entrance to this hotel, which is just the first project in a massive development underway here.

First, of course, came the hotel, which is now one of the chic-est showplaces in Orlando. Chief among its showy attributes is a quite incredible swimming pool featuring a dozen waterfalls crashing into it and a suspension bridge swaying over it. You can swim around and into rock grottoes, slide down a slippery waterslide set in rock, and imbibe at a grotto bar.

In the hotel itself, an 18-story atrium soars skyward and a fortune's worth of Asian artworks are scattered casually about hotel and grounds. Streams trickle through the lobby and ivy cascades down from high overhead.

The rooms are lovely, no question about it. In a special 11th-floor Regency Club, where rates are $350 a day, rooms are outfitted with a loveseat and chair tucked into a sitting area fronted by glass doors through which the pool's dozen waterfalls are visible. King-size beds are trimmed in light woods and headboards have insert fabric designed to match bedspreads.

Other rooms in the hotel are a bit smaller but by no means small. They range in price from $200 to $230 double and are also decorated in the most contemporary of furnishings in pale pastels, mauves, salmon, pink, light woods, and with handsome paintings.

When you've explored all the nooks and crannies of that spectacular swimming pool, you can sail, windsurf, canoe, or paddle boat about a 21-acre lake or sun on 1,000 feet of white-sand beach. Boat rentals, sailing lessons, and bicycle rentals are moderately priced.

A tennis and recreational complex offers tennis courts, a racquetball court, shuffleboard and volleyball playgrounds. Tennis fees are $3 an hour and a tennis clinic is complimentary.

A children's playground keeps the youngsters busy, and nature trails lure walkers and joggers.

Jack Nicklaus has added his signature to an 18-hole golf course, which is restricted to registered guests of the hotel and their friends. Greens fees are $65 to $95, including bag storage, club cleaning, unlimited range use, and carts.

A nine-hole pitch-and-putt course is a challenge and a health club offers a weight and exercise room fitted out with shiny new equipment, a sauna, Jacuzzi, massage studio, and jogging clinics—and a grotto bar nearby in which to recuperate.

A game room features video playthings for the youngsters and there's an outdoor playground as well.

Three restaurants offer an intriguing variety of places to dine. In the Cascade restaurant, Hyatt's two-level version of a coffee shop, a dramatic bronze mermaid keeps cool beneath a 35-foot waterfall. A pianist entertains here—at breakfast!

Atop the rocks and waterfalls a woodsy restaurant called Hemingway's pays tribute to Key West's favorite son. Prices for steaks and seafood are in the $18 to $26 range for entrées.

La Coquina, Hyatt's most elegant and most expensive restaurant, is a two-story triumph overlooking the lake. Here a harpist plays as you dine on French and continental entrées in the $19 to $29 range. Figure about $90 a couple for an elegant dinner.

At the White Horse Saloon, dress is casual, servers are cowboy-clothed, and the fare is prime rib, prime rib, and prime rib for prices in the $25 to $45 range, depending on the size of the cut you order.

Cocktail lounge enthusiasts can visit Trellises, the lovely lobby bar tucked among streams and ferns, or the Hurricane Bar in Hemingway's, where a strolling musician provides evening entertainment and bartenders create a combustible daiquiri called the Papa Doble.

## ON U.S. 192

This is the highway that leads straight to the Disney World entrance, and here you'll find a surprising number of moderately priced motels and a few major resorts as well. I'll start with the Orlando Hyatt Hotel, which tops the price list, and work down to some of the smaller, less elaborate spots for budget-watching vacationers.

The **Hyatt Orlando Hotel,** 6375 W. Irlo Bronson Memorial Hwy., Kissimmee, FL 32741 (tel. 407/396-1234 or toll free 800/228-9000), can be so much fun on its own you may be tempted some days to skip the Magic Kingdom and participate in a little of the magic this hotel goes all out to create. For openers, every building here is painted a different color, delicate pastels all, designed to make it easier to find your way around this massive complex which includes 946 rooms, four (!) swimming pools and four kiddie pools, tennis courts, a shopping mall complete with package store, a game room with electronic toys, and a tot lot for the toddlers. There's even a helicopter on the front lawn if you'd like a bird's-eye view of the *other* Magic Kingdom.

Rooms here are spacious, with big dressing areas fitted out with all the little touches Hyatt so thoughtfully includes, from shower cap to French-milled soap and shampoo. The earthy tones in the rooms are soothing, while the attractively landscaped grounds offer shady and sunny spots to while away a few restful hours.

For dining there are several restaurants, including the Summerhouse, open 6:30am to 11pm for breakfast and dinner buffets, and the Market Place, a big deli featuring pizza, all kinds of short-order treats, take-out service, and what they like to call "gourmet groceries," open the same hours. Palm Terrace Restaurant offers Orthodox Union Kosher meals. Finally, at Limey Jim's, an intimate dining spot that features continental cuisine, you can work your way through five or six courses, ending in a finale of a specialty—liqueur-laced coffees. Expect to pay about $30 to $50 here for dinner.

Single or double rates are $119 to $129, with suites ranging up from $140.

There are two attractive resorts on the west side of Highway I-4, Sheraton Lakeside Inn and Orlando Vacation Resort. Both are reasonably close to the Magic Kingdom, and both offer top-quality accommodations.

**Sheraton Lakeside Inn,** 7711 Vine St., U.S. 192 West, Kissimmee, FL 32741 (tel. 407/828-8250 or toll free 800/325-3535) has 652 rooms, a seafood saloon, lounge, deli, two heated pools and two pools for the toddlers, a boat dock, paddleboats, mini-golf, tennis courts, and poolside gazebos. Rates here year round are $83 to $115; children under 17 stay free at any time of year.

The nearby **Comfort Inn,** 7571 W. Irlo Bronson Memorial Hwy., U.S. 192 West, Kissimmee, FL 32741 (tel. 407/396-7500 or toll free 800/218-0064, in Florida 800/218-0087), is a pretty place on a strip of highway packed with fast-food restaurants, shops, and chain hotels. Located just one mile from Walt Disney World, the hotel has 282 spacious rooms, each with two double beds decorated in cheerful prints. There's a shuttle service to Disney World, color television, free local phone service, a pool, game room, boutique, laundry facilities, and a cozy restaurant open for breakfast and dinner (prices in the $4 range for big breakfasts, under $10 for steak, seafood, and Italian dinner favorites). Rates are $36 to $94 all year.

Floridians were born with superlatives in their mouths, so you can expect to find the world's largest, biggest, strangest, and all the other "ests" well represented in this competitive locale. Which brings us to a stopping spot the Days Inn chain calls the world's largest **Days Suites**. It's at 5820 W. Irlo Bronson Memorial Hwy., Kissimmee, FL 32741 on U.S. 192 just east of Highway I-4 (tel. 407/396-7900 or toll free 800/327-9126, in Florida 800/432-9103.) This local representative of the Days Inn chain offers about what you've come to expect in these low-cost but high-quality-for-the-money operations. Days Suites, by the way, differ from Inns in that rooms are larger and come with cooking facilities. Here in Kissimmee's Days Suites, rooms also boast 700 square feet of living space, patios or balconies, and amenities that include three swimming pools, playground, and barbecue. Located less than three miles from the Kingdom, the resort charges $75 to $125 ($10 more for poolside rooms) and children are free.

If you're looking for spacious accommodations in the region, take a look at **Orange Lake Country Club,** 8505 W. Irlo Bronson Memorial Hwy., Kissimmee, FL 32741 (tel. 407/846-0000 or in Orlando 407/239-0000 or toll free 800/327-4444, in Florida 800/432-8888). Accommodations here include villas that sleep eight on king-size beds in the master bedroom, queen-size beds in a second bedroom and a convertible sofa in the living room. There are two bathrooms, color television, microwave ovens, washer and dryer, and kitchens with all you need to cook for eight.

Orange Lake Country Club also has studio efficiencies that sleep four and also have equipped kitchenettes with microwave oven.

Created by Kemmon Wilson, founder of the Holiday Inn chain, this resort has just about every diversion you can dream up: a 27-hole golf course, 16 tennis courts including 10 lighted courts, four racquetball courts, waterskiing, sailing, fishing and jet-skiing on an 80-acre lake, an Olympic-sized swimming pool and a smaller heated pool, plus two whirlpools. You can play on a mini-golf course, have a go at some video games, or work out in a fitness center. When you're starving after all that activity, head for the resort's tropically furnished restaurant, perhaps with a stop at the cocktail lounge or pool bar.

Rates at this big new resort are $99 to $125, depending on the size of the accommodations.

**Radisson Inn Maingate,** 7501 W. Irlo Bronson Memorial Hwy. (U.S. 192), Kissimmee, FL 32741 (tel. 407/396-1400 or toll free 800/333-3333), is an attractive choice for those who want to be close to Walt Disney World. Located just a few minutes drive from the main gate, Radisson Inn is sleekly modern from its colorful woven wall hangings to its plant-bedecked restaurant and bar, with entertainment and dancing. That modernity continues in rooms, which are decorated in warm tropical colors and come complete with lots of little extra amenities. Tucked into the middle of the several wings of this hotel is a swimming pool and outside are a jogging trail, two lighted tennis courts, and a playground for the youngsters. A deli-style café caters to those youngsters too and even offers take-out service. Rates are $65 to $98 double, with children under 17 free.

Back on the east side of U.S. 192, **Larson's Lodge,** 2009 W. Vine St., Kissimmee, FL 32741 (tel. 407/846-2713 or toll free 800/327-9074), is owned and operated by the friendly Larson family, who try hard to give this resort a home-away-from-home atmosphere. You'll first see an imposing wood-and-brick structure at the entrance, backed by a tiled lobby, where you'll be greeted with a smile. Resort facilities include a game room, boutique, two heated pools, a whirlpool, tennis courts, sundeck, restaurant, and lounge —everything right down to a little picket fence around the children's play area. In the resort's four-story wings are 200 attractively decorated rooms, each with two double beds, a sitting area, and picture windows. To make dinner time simple, right next door is a Black Angus Steakhouse, where you can chow down on some simple barbecue fixins for under $15. Rates for a room for two at Larson's Lodge is $39 to $70 year round, an efficiency $10 more, and at any time children under 18 are free.

**Rodeway Inn Eastgate,** 5245 Irlo Bronson Memorial Hwy., Kissimmee, FL 32741 (tel. 407/396-7700 or toll free 800/432-3864; in Florida 800/992-2302), is a two-story building with spacious rooms overlooking pool or patio. Children can amuse themselves on the inn's playground and there's a coin laundry to make quick work of playground results. A game room and miniature golf course provide amusements for both adults and children and there's the requisite pool for splashers. A restaurant here offers reasonably priced continental cuisine (entrées in the $10 to $15 range) and a poolside bar dispenses potables. Rates at the Rodeway Inn Eastgate are $35 to $65 including children year round.

A few rungs down the luxury ladder, you'll find **Colonial Motor Lodge,** 1815 W. Vine St., Kissimmee, FL 32741 (tel. 407/847-6121). Furnishings are basic, and rooms are neat and clean and big enough for a budget-watching family. There are 40 apartments and motel units with two double beds. You'll also find two swimming pools and a game room. For these simple but adequate accommodations, you'll pay $54 to $60 for two-bedroom apartments, $36 to $50 for motel units in peak seasons, less in spring and fall, with no charge for children under 12, $4 each for others.

One of my favorite budget spots is **King's Motel,** 4836 W. Irlo Bronson Memorial Hwy., Kissimmee, FL 32741 (tel. 407/396-4762), a small quiet spot that shares a little lake with an adjoining motel called **Lakeview** (another adequate budget motel). Shady pines drop fat pinecones, and there's a tranquil view of the lake. You can use the resort's boat for a little watery expedition. A swimming pool and barbecue pavilion overlook the lake, too. Motel units here have cable television, two double beds, and bright colors, and rent for $50 to $60 year round. Two-bedroom apartments are just $75, and there's no charge for children under 16. Others are $3 each.

**Econo Lodge Maingate East,** 4311 W. Irlo Bronson Memorial Hwy., Kissimmee, FL 32741 (tel. 407/396-4213 or toll free 800/365-6935), is still another appealing resort on this highway which, despite its different names, is one big road. Nestled in a grove of massive oaks, this Econo Lodge is a rustic resort with rooms that are thoroughly modern and colorful. Wide picture windows offer a view of those huge, old oak trees towering over a shady swimming pool. Rates year round are $46 to $72 per person including meals.

If you've got a hamburger fan in your group, you can't go wrong at the **Sunrise Motel,** 801 Vine St., Kissimmee, FL 32741 (tel. 407/846-3224)—it's next door to a McDonald's, and there's a Burger King across the street! In quality, the Sunrise Motel fits right into those levels—nothing fancy, just small, simply furnished rooms lined with paneling and decorated in bright colors. Sunrise is about a 15-minute drive from Disney, and room charges are $25 to $45 for two ("or whatever I can get," meaning it may not hurt to bargain here). Children under 16 are free.

Here's a brief look at some of the more attractive possibilities spotted on a recent expedition:

**Embassy Motel,** 4880 W. Irlo Bronson Memorial Hwy., Kissimmee, FL 32741 (tel. 407/396-1144 or toll free 800/325-4827, in Fla. 800/432-0153), is a pleasant spot that recently added 100 rooms, 22 of them overlooking pretty Lake Cecile. Complimentary coffee bubbles in the lobby and there's a game room, plus laundry facilities and a swimming pool. A two-story motel with big windows across the front of every room, the Embassy is located four miles east of Walt Disney World. Medium-sized rooms have two double beds outfitted in attractive earth tones, color television, and dressing area. Prices here are $25 to $70 year round.

On the same lake you'll find **Park Inn International,** 4960 W. Hwy. 192, Kissimmee, FL 32741 (tel. 407/396-1376 or toll free 800/327-0072, in Fla. 800/432-0276), a pretty spot. Arches add a Mediterranean touch to the two-story buildings here, and sparkling Lake Cecile in the back is a good place to send the kids exploring while you grab a few minutes' peace. There's a small swimming pool in the middle of the resort, also a Jacuzzi, game room, beach, playground, and water sports. Some rooms here are equipped with compact stove/sink units, so you can ship up the occasional lunch for yourself. Nearby a small shopping area features plenty of souvenirs and a family-style restaurant. Rates are $39 to $59 double.

**Budget Host Inn Main Gate East,** 6051 W. Hwy. 192, Kissimmee, FL 32741 (tel. 407/396-1748 or toll free 800/288-4678), offers the basic but comfortable quarters this chain has been providing for quite a number of years at a building with the faintest touch of Swiss chalet. They're running quite a large operation here, with game room, laundry room, gift shop, playground, swimming pool, and shuttle service to Disney World and to the airport. Rates are $37 to $65 year round, suites $46 to $70.

**Holiday Inn-Kissimmee,** 2145 E. Hwy. 192, Kissimmee, FL 32743 (tel. 407/846-4646 or toll free 800/465-4329), and **TraveLodge Kissimmee Flags,** 2407 W. Hwy. 192, Kissimmee, FL 32741 (tel. 407/933-2400 or toll free 800/352-4725, in Florida 800/432-4554), are both represented along this highway. Each offers clean, comfortable quarters just like those you'd find in those chains' representatives anywhere in the nation. Rates are $49 to $75 year round at either property.

**Buena Vista Motel**, 5200 W. Hwy. 192, Kissimmee, FL 32741 (tel. 407/396-2100), has an alluring, spanking-clean look about its blue and white buildings. That same simple but attractive atmosphere continues in the rooms, which are basic but well-kept and serviceable. There's a pretty swimming pool here, too. Rates are $30 to $50 year round.

**Central Motel**, 4698 W. Hwy. 192, Kissimmee, FL 32741 (tel. 407/396-2333), has Chinese-red doors and a swimming pool at the rear of the building. Brick-trimmed doors welcome you to standard motel rooms with orange and brown floral-print decor. Rates here are $25 to $50 year round.

If you like Mediterranean architecture, you'll find hints of it at **Casa Rosa Inn**, 4600 W. Hwy. 192 (tel. 407/396-2020), painted in a delicate pink hue. Surroundings are especially attractive here: The motel's set in a small wooded area. Free coffee, free VHS movies, too. Rates are $32 to $52, higher for suites.

**Sun Motel**, 5020 W. Hwy. 192, Kissimmee, FL 32741 (tel. 407/396-2673), is another of the multitude of tiny family-owned motels that have risen here in the last few years. This one is currently owned by a Chinese family who employ a bustling Chinese maid in a peaked straw hat and typical Chinese blues. Rates are $30 to $58.

Still more motels along U.S. 192 that are neat, clean and fall in the $30 to $60 price range year round are:

**The Palm**, 4519 W. Irlo Bronson Memorial Hwy., Kissimmee, FL 34741 (tel. 407/396-0744), a pleasant spot with stone siding, a heated pool, and attractive rooms.

**Enterprise Motel**, 4121 W. Vine St., Kissimmee, FL 34741 (tel. 407/933-1383), a bright, cheerful brand new spot with queen-size beds, HBO television service, and a swimming pool at the rear of the building so your poolside reveries are not disturbed by traffic noise.

**Spacecoast Motel**, 4125 W. Irlo Bronson Memorial Hwy., Kissimmee, FL 34741 (tel. 407/933-5732), which has some rooms with whirlpool, plus remote-control color television and free HBO service, plus king- and queen-size beds, efficiencies, and suites. It's 3½ miles from Walt Disney World and EPCOT Center.

**Hawaiian Village Inn**, 4559 W. Irlo Bronson Memorial Hwy., Kissimmee, FL 34741 (tel. 407/396-1212 or toll free 800/821-9503, in Florida 800/342-0137), with 114 newly redecorated rooms, each with two extra-long double beds, kitchenette in some. There's a swimming pool off on one side of the building, a small and simple restaurant, and a lounge with big-screen television. Package rates here can save you money, too. Rates are $30 to $45 year round.

To give you some more $30 to $75 options in the busiest months, here are the names of a few of the many small places offering basic accommodations, usually a swimming pool, and, best of all, proximity to Disney World and the other playgrounds here:

**Chalet Motel,** 4741 W. Hwy. 192, Kissimmee, FL 34741 (tel. 407/396-1677); **Chateau Motel,** 4657 W. Hwy. 192, Kissimmee, FL 34741 (tel. 407/847-3477); **Maple Leaf Motel,** 4647 W. Hwy. 192, Kissimmee, FL 34741 (tel. 407/396-0300); **Key Motel,** 4810 W. Hwy. 192, Kissimmee, FL 34741 (tel. 407/396-6200).

## INTERNATIONAL DRIVE/FLORIDA CENTER

Florida Center is a name applied to an area that roughly surrounds International Drive, a major thoroughfare near Disney World. With all the attractions, hotels, motels, fast-food restaurants, and shops that are located here, Florida Center and International Drive practically qualify as a mini-Disney World. I guarantee you won't have any trouble keeping the kids busy around here on non-Disney days. Just send them to the Places of Learning, Wet 'N Wild, Mystery Fun House—see what I mean? To get here, leave Highway I-4 at the International Drive–Sand Lake Road exit and head east on Sand Lake Road (also known as Route 528A).

It was only to be expected that Sea World would not sit idly by and let Disney World have all those hotels on its property. That's why you will now find a brand, spanking new hotel, **Stouffer Orlando,** 6677 Sea Harbor Dr., Orlando, FL 32821 (tel. 407/351-5555, toll free 800/327-6677), right across the street from Sea World.

On the outside this towering new hotel presents a rather bland white façade sparked only by a bright blue tile roof. But on the inside, whoooeee! Built in quadrangle style, the hotel's four wings surround a lobby bigger than a couple of football fields. Birds chatter in an atrium, fish swim in the waters surrounding a multilevel cocktail lounge, and visitors stroll past buildings designed to look like a small village.

Describing this skylight-topped hotel is not an easy task. For openers, the "lobby," which is really an inner courtyard delineated by the four wings of the hotel, looks like no lobby you've ever seen before. Cupola-topped buildings in soft greens and blues open to reveal an aviary, an ice cream parlor, a gazebo-like dining center and a cocktail lounge. A couple of leaping plaster dolphins beside the entrance to the lounge keep Sea World firmly in mind.

Three other restaurants reside here, one a subtly decorated, black-lacquered Hai-Feng Oriental restaurant; another a handsome and high-priced Atlantis gourmet dining room (figure $35 to $50 a person for dinner); another a rather grandiose 24-hour coffee shop that becomes a steak and seafood dining room at night.

The best rooms, to my mind, are those on the north and south sides of the buildings. They have pretty French doors leading to flowerbox-trimmed balconies overlooking the magnificence of the lobby below, while the others, although just as handsomely decorated, overlook Sea World on one side, the outskirts of Orlando on the other. They have not missed anything in these rooms; remote control television, comfortable armchairs, lovely pastel decor, marble-clad double-sink bathroom sporting a huge white clamshell full of everything from shampoo to a little sachet of potpourri. Quite a place indeed. Rates at Stouffer Orlando are $169 to $229 year round.

International Drive is booming. Lined with hotels of every size and architectural description, this busy drive just minutes from Sea World, Disney World, and many other Central Florida attractions is now also home to a hotel with a very special feature that only one other hotel in the world can boast: a quacking duck parade.

Unlike the ducks at Walt Disney World, these quackers are the real thing and they march more or less in formation every day at the sparkling new **Peabody Hotel,** 9801 International Dr., Orlando, FL 32819 (tel. 407/351-4000 or toll free 800/COCONUT). On the stroke of 11am every day, out strut the Peabody's legendary ducks. After a ride down on the elevator from their home up-top somewhere, they march in puffed-breast splendor across to the lobby fountain, quacking everyone up as they go. A tradition that began at this hotel's sister property in Memphis many years ago, the ducks are a small but significant part of this handsome and elegant hotel.

Rooms are spacious and beautifully decorated in tranquil contemporary shades. There's a pool, athletic club, and four lighted tennis courts, and it's close to the attraction action. But after the ducks, everything else is just icing anyway. Rates at this standout on International Drive are $145 to $225, with higher prices buying you more space and concierge amenities. Suites are, of course, higher, ranging up to $1,200.

It won't take you long to spot the **Orlando Marriott,** 8001 International Dr., Orlando, FL 32819 (tel. 407/351-2420 or toll free 800/228-9290). It may, in fact, take you longer to find your way around this sprawling resort. A recent major renovation added 437 rooms to the 640 with which it began, making it one of the largest hotels in the area. Strolling around this huge 45-acre complex, with its rooms clustered into villas named after flowers, is like strolling through a large, showy garden ornamented with little lagoons, ponds, and fountains. Inside the villas you'll find big picture windows, contemporary earthy colors, deep carpets, oversize beds; in some rooms a big, comfy couch and chair and, in some, a kitchenette, too. There are many amenities: lighted tennis courts, two kiddie pools, three pools with sundecks and wooden platforms for scenic sunning, two game rooms and a play area, and a gift and sundry shop. In the handsome dining room, called The Grove, you can dine on seafood and sizzling steaks in the $15 to $20 price range and enjoy nightly entertainment. Marriott charges $110 to $120 double year round. Children under 18 are free.

Those who love to swim ought to adore **Radisson Inn & Justus Aquatic Center,** 8444 International Dr., Orlando, FL 32819 (tel. 407/345-0505 or toll free 800/752-0003). Designed to lure swim competitions, this new hotel has an Olympic-size swimming pool topped by a hydraulic roof that opens or closes for the weather, plus high diving boards, marked lanes, electronic timing equipment, even underwater observation rooms. For those who are content just to watch some of the nation's top swimmers and divers, there are

3,000 seats available in this "natatorium." Opened in early 1985, the Radisson cost $25 million and already its pool is being touted as the pool to upstage Fort Lauderdale's nationally known Swimming Hall of Fame.

For those who want to keep fit but aren't water babies, Radisson has installed a state-of-the-art fitness center with a mind-boggling array of exercise equipment. Justus Human Performance Laboratory offers 17 different diagnostic tests ranging from assessment of body composition to maximal exercise tolerance to help you figure out which muscle machine to attack.

Confirmed slugabeds will be relieved to know that they can just pull up a chair beside the hotel's quiet pool or try a round or two of racquetball, tennis, or handball on the hotel's courts.

Even swimmers must sleep, however, and here they can do that in large, lovely rooms outfitted in muted contemporary colors, often peach and gray tones. Each has two queen-size beds or a king-size sleeper. Another unusual touch: in-room safes. Radisson's lobby is quite lovely, too, all outfitted in deep forest green sparked by quite unusual, starkly contemporary, fresh floral arrangements. Here you dine cafeteria-style in an airy coffee shop. Evenings there's entertainment in the hotel's Sweetwater Lounge. Rates at the 300-room hotel are $79 to $99 year round.

Before Walt Disney World's Magic Kingdom made its appearance here, one of Orlando's best-known attractions was its many deep-blue, spring-fed lakes. These days, travelers speeding through on major highways or racing from one man-made attraction to another rarely see those sparkling lakes, which are often hidden away on backroads. There is, however, one hotel that has forsaken the world of glitzy lobbies and fake rocks to focus on the natural beauty of one of the region's largest lakes. Called the **Sonesta Village Hotel on Sand Lake,** 1000 Turkey Lake Rd., Orlando, FL 32819 (tel. 407/352-8051, or toll free 800/343-7170), this resort is different in another way: It has no hotel rooms! Instead, Sonesta Village offers 370 two-story villas strung out in a long, winding cluster of town-house–like structures, each with its own living room, small kitchen, dining room, and bath downstairs, and large bedrooms and a second bathroom upstairs. Tall glass doors frame green lawns rolling down to the lake. Light wood and wicker furnishings are outfitted in soothing contemporary colors. All villas have two double beds in each bedroom and a convertible sofa in the living room, as well as a television in each room.

Circling around the edge of one of the area's largest lakes, this 97-acre resort gives visitors a closeup look at a natural spring lake that has maintained much of its wilderness character. As you sit on a private terrace overlooking green lawns that slope gently to the shore, a snowy egret stalks by in search of lunch. While it seems as far as Mars from the hustle of Orlando's other hotel enclaves, Sonesta Village only feels remote. Actually, it's right in the middle of things, about 10 minutes from the airport and from the region's major attractions, including WDW. Sea World is just across I-4, about a mile away.

At this $100 million resort you'll find a formal restaurant, a casual café, a lounge with entertainment, and an ice-cream shop. For amusement there are sailboats and paddleboats, waterskiing and parasailing, fishing, a health club, pool and whirlpool spas, tennis courts, a children's activities program and a playground, even a tranquil wooden boardwalk that stretches out into the lake. Rates year round are $125 to $180 for a one-bedroom villa, $180 to $270 for a two-bedroom villa. Friendly folks at Guest Services here can arrange transportation to Walt Disney World for you for $7 per person roundtrip.

**Hilton Inn Florida Center,** 7400 International Dr., Orlando, FL 32819 (tel. 407/351-4600 or toll-free 800/327-1363, in Florida 800/332-4600) occupies the entrance to the north end of International Drive, convenient to Disney World, and has a monster of a pool, covered by a roof. If you want sun, there's a second pool outside. A 400-room hostelry that includes 20 suites, the resort also features a tropical garden. Hilton Inn has spent quite a lot of money refurbishing this hotel in recent years and now it has a bright contemporary look and a delightfully tropical feeling. There's patio dining outside under that slick roof and a woodsy inside dining room with prices in the $10 range. Lots of families find their way here, since children stay free at the resort. There's also complimentary airport transportation. Rates are $54 to $104 year round.

Another huge resort in this vicinity is the **Court of Flags,** 5715 Major Blvd., Orlando, FL 32819 (tel. 407/351-3340 or toll free 800/268-1133). Located west of Highway I-4, the Court of Flags spreads out over 25 acres of grounds. It's easy to get lost here, but even that can be entertaining, since in your wanderings you'll stumble across three swimming pools, three hot tubs in a landscaped grotto, a wading pool for children, a video game room, a shopping arcade, lighted tennis courts, lounges, a tour desk, and two saunas. A buffet restaurant called the Center Court Café features continental cuisine in the $15 to $20 range and the resort's Worst Bar is a legend. Contemporary colors accent the 824 spacious rooms and there are private balconies for quiet moments. Two people pay $125 to $150 year round and children under 18 are free; those under six *eat* free, too.

Another comparatively new hotel in the area is **Sheraton World,** 10100 International Dr., Orlando, FL 32819 (tel. 407/352-1100 or toll free 800/325-2525, in Florida 800/341-4292). It's right next door to Sea World and at last count had 800 rooms. Built in 1980, this very contemporary spot is rigged out in arched wicker headboards and framed prints. A skylight sends rays of sunshine down on the brickfloored lobby, and bright banners add lively touches of color. Families gravitate to the Brasserie Restaurant, while parents often sneak off to the adjoining lounge. You'll find three heated swimming pools here, five tennis courts, a Jacuzzi, fitness room, mini-golf course, ice-cream parlor, deli, game rooms, and poolside gazebos that make a pleasant retreat from the sun. Sheraton charges $108 to $128 double all year and children under 18 stay free in the newly renovated rooms.

A little farther along International Drive, you'll find **Las Palmas Inn,** 6233 International Dr., Orlando, FL 32819 (tel. 407/351-3900 or toll free 800/432-1175, in Florida 800/432-1175), right across the street from Wet 'N Wild, a watery wonderland for children and adults. Spain has influenced Las Palmas, which sports lots of dark wood and a red-tiled roof. Spacious rooms are newly redecorated. There's a pool bar for cooling off on hot afternoons, a playground and game room for the youngsters, and an inexpensive restaurant and lounge, Las Brisas. Rates are $62 to $82 year round.

**Star Quality Resort,** 5905 International Dr., Orlando, FL 32819 (tel. 407/351-2100 or toll free 800/327-1366, in Florida 800/247-3737), has a cylindrical tower that soars over Florida Center, and a huge "Q" on top makes it an unmistakable landmark. You can see all over Orlando from the top of this 21-story hotel, which features 298 attractively decorated rooms. Rooms have double beds, in-room safes and movies, plus dressing areas. To entertain you there are two pools, a game room, saunas, boutiques, a lounge with entertainment, and a restaurant. There are even a barber shop and beauty salon. Rates here are $42 to $80 depending on season.

Working down to the lower end of the price range, you'll find **Davis Brothers Motor Lodge,** 6603 International Dr., Orlando, FL 32809 (tel. 407/351-2900 or toll free 800/722-2900), a chain operation with cafeterias whose prices are a budget-watcher's dream. A nice combination of inexpensive rooms and meals here in the heart of Disney territory. Even your canine friends are welcomed at Davis Brothers Motor Lodge, where bright, spacious rooms are $37 to $90 year round. Buffet-style meals in the cafeteria are in the $5 range!

Sweden House, home of those bounteous all-you-can-eat buffets, is already a resident of **Gateway Inn,** 7050 Kirkman Rd., Orlando, FL 32819 (tel. 407/351-2000 or toll free 800/327-3808, in Florida 800/432-1179), so if you're traveling with a passel of chow hounds, you are likely to find this a perfect plunk-down spot. An attractive family resort, Gateway Inn wraps itself around three sparkling pools and features bright and spacious rooms. A playground with swings should keep the youngsters busy, and if that's not enough, there are video games, miniature golf, a sundry shop, and, for escapist parents, the Lion's Den cocktail lounge. Gateway Inn, which offers free transportation to area attractions, recently added 104 new wicker-furnished havens and a $500,000 lobby. Rates are $44 to $72 year round; under 16 are free.

There's plenty of patriotism at the **1776 Resort Inn,** 5858 International Dr., Orlando, FL 32819 (tel. 407/351-4410 or toll free 800/327-2115). In the heart of Florida Center, the 1776 sprawls around courtyards and a heated pool. Paths wind through the grounds and past rooms that feature wide windows overlooking trees and shrubbery. Bright tropical decor is a feature of the spacious rooms here and outside there's a whirling ride for the kids, a shady poolside lounge for parents. Prices are the same year round: $38 to $58 for poolside rooms, rooms with two double beds, or king-size beds, and no charge for children under 18 sharing a room.

Are you ready for a resort with 100 electronic game machines and an 18-hole miniature golf course? It's the perfect way to occupy dear little Dudley while you get in some serious sunning and swimming, and it can be yours at the **Days Inn Universal Studios East,** 5827 Caravan Ct., Orlando, FL 32819 (from I-4 take the exit to Route 435 N.; tel. 407/351-3800 or toll free 800/327-2111), which bills itself as a family resort and has all the family-entertainment paraphernalia to prove it. You can browse in Barber's gift shop, dine on country cooking, or toss back something cool in Coconuts. There are big and little pools at the resort, and large rooms decorated in contemporary hues. Double rooms year round range from $50 to $100. Children under 17 are free.

## A BED AND BREAKFAST INN

In 1987, Britisher Janet Barnet bought a big old house with a slightly tarnished reputation and set out to turn it into one of the area's first bed and breakfast inns, the **Unicorn Bed and Breakfast,** 8 S. Orlando Ave., Kissimmee, FL 32741 (tel. 407/846-1200). Perched at the intersection of Emmett Street and Orlando Avenue in the often-sleepy village of Kissimmee, this B&B occupies quite an imposing Old Florida house built in 1901—and for Florida that is old indeed.

Upstairs you'll find a one-bedroom suite with living room and separate bedroom with a trundle daybed any kid would love. Everywhere in the nine rooms now in operation, you'll find new wallcoverings, new closets, brand new bathrooms, some antiques, and lots of nice comfortable furniture. A glassed-in veranda on the second floor of the inn offers a lofty view of the passing world.

Janet has nine rooms in operation now, a new kitchen, and a cozy dining room of which she's very proud. The inn is nine miles from Walt Disney World—not far on this region's wide highways, but just far enough to give you a look at Kissimmee, an attractive, historic Florida city few travelers ever see. Rates at this spot are $65 year round and include breakfast.

## AT UNIVERSAL STUDIOS FLORIDA

One could hardly get closer to this impressive new attraction than the **Twin Towers Hotel,** 5780 Major Blvd., Orlando, FL 32819 (tel. 407/351-1000 or toll free 800/327-2110) which does, indeed, tower over the landscape hereabouts. Once known as the Sheraton Twin Towers, this hotel in 1990 underwent a massive top-to-toe renovation to the tune of $29 million. Now you'll find soft pastels in the handsomely decorated rooms and a wide variety of amenities from tennis and paddleball courts to a health club, a big outdoor pool, whirlpool spa, poolside bar, restaurants, and lounges. Golf and fishing are nearby. Twin Towers is just a few minutes walk from the entrance gate to Universal so if you're headed to this new attraction, this is the perfect stopping spot—and it's just steps away from Hard Rock Café as well. Rates are $125 to $195 double year round.

## DOWNTOWN ORLANDO

Not too many cities anywhere, and certainly few in Florida, can boast, as can Orlando, a sparkling blue lake right in the middle of downtown. Benches set around the lake offer a tempting spot to while away some contemplative minutes as ducks paddle by and fountains shoot skyward. Despite its inviting location, however, the world grew away from downtown Orlando as it has from many cities, leaving behind aging hotels and some imposing Old Florida neighborhoods. In recent years, however, entrepreneurs and hoteliers have begun to cast an eagle eye on downtown Orlando. Some changes are in store, and some have already taken place.

To take a look at this metamorphosis in the making, take Highway I-4 to the 17/92 exit and head north to Washington Street.

Here you'll find the star of downtown Orlando's slow but sure renewal: the **Harley Hotel,** 151 E. Washington St., Orlando, FL 32801 (tel. 407/841-3220 or toll free 800/321-2323). When I saw what the Harley renovation had done, I could hardly believe my eyes: from the quiet colors, modern prints, and comfortable chairs in the hotel rooms to the entrancing Café on the Park. Plunk yourself down here, gaze out over a smashing view of Lake Eola, and revel in this glamorous atmosphere of brass, leaded glass, deep burgundy velvet, and dark wood. Rates are $70 to $109 double all year, $55 on weekends.

There's a Howard Johnson in the area, too, and by now you probably know what to expect at this chain. I only mention the **Howard Johnson Midtown** at 2014 W. Colonial Dr. and Tampa Ave., Orlando, FL 32804 (tel. 407/841-8600 or toll free 800/654-2000), because it's managed by Mac Finnane, a very nice man who runs a *very* nice Howard Johnson's in the midtown area of Orlando. How nice is *very* nice? Well, this one once won the highest rating in Florida in the Howard Johnson quality assurance program, and that's nice by any standards. You will see that the honor is deserved when you find rooms steadily refurbished and get a look at an attractive new landscaping project just completed. This Ho-Jo's is near lots of restaurants and shops and only about a 20-minute drive from Disney World. A new restaurant here features American favorites with a few Greek selections thrown in for adventuresome palates. Rates at the hotel are $48 to $52 year round.

If you like small places, the **Davis Park,** 221 E. Colonial Dr., Orlando, FL 32801 (tel. 407/425-9065, toll free 800/468-3550), may be just what you have in mind. In Orlando just 75 units makes it a small place, so owners Carroll and Toni Chapin like to say they're operating "a village atmosphere in the heart of Orlando." There's a coziness about the place, too, from paneled rooms with big dressing areas to a small brick-and-wood restaurant where you'll find inexpensive prices. A few rooms have cooking facilities, and top rates are $39.50 to $49.50 double, about $3 cheaper for singles. Davis Park is about a 20-minute drive from Disney World.

**Best Western Orlando Inn,** 3330 W. Colonial Dr., Orlando, FL 32801 (tel. 407/299-6710 or toll free 800/528-1234, in Florida 800/432-8609), prides itself on being newer than Walt Disney World and now it's newer still! Recently remodeled, the resort features attractive and spacious rooms surrounding a winding swimming pool and a lovely landscaped garden area. Rooms have two double beds and some have couches so you can really settle in for a relaxed holiday. King-size bed fanciers will find some rooms with those big recliners and there are even rooms for nonsmokers. Denny's Restaurant, a 24-hour spot, offers meals in the $10 range or less and the Rod and Gun Pub has a large-screen television where weary parents can sneak off for a couple of relaxing hours away from their darlings. Two people pay $42 to $80, year round.

**Orlando Motor Lodge** is a little removed from the usual byways. This lakeside charmer is on U.S. 17/92 at 1825 N. Mills Ave., Orlando, FL 32803 (tel. 407/896-4111, toll free 800/222-4273). Take the Princeton exit from Highway I-4. You'll find trim lake view rooms, a pool, a romantic lake, a coffee shop for breakfast, and bargain rates: $28 to $38 double in peak season, $3 additional for rooms with kitchen. Children under 12 are $2; others an additional $3 a day.

## AIRPORT AREA

Orlando's impressive jetport is not far from the Magic Kingdom and other Orlando attractions, and it's a good spot to begin looking for a room when other motels closer to attractions are filled. There are some very attractive hostelries here, and thanks to plenty of multilane highways, they're easy to reach.

Tops among hotels convenient to the airport is the **Gold Key Inn,** 7100 S. Orange Blossom Trail, Orlando, FL 32809 (tel. 407/855-0050 or toll free 800/327-0304; in Florida 800/432-0947), a very special and cozy place. In the lobby there's a brick fireplace flanked by plump couches arranged on a perky flowered carpet. Massive beams dominate the room and there are usually fresh flowers. In your room you'll find comfortable armchairs, reproductions of old English prints, tile bath, and the small touches that make this more an inn than a hotel. For the more active, there are a putting green, tennis, and a swimming pool, and a restaurant surrounded by tropical gardens. Shuttle buses stop here to take you to attractions.

Gold Key's Piccadilly Restaurant is an award-winning spot famous locally for its homemade soups, gently seared steaks, delicately roasted prime rib, and excellent seafood, all presented in an atmosphere that glows in the light of candles, with stained-glass windows, floral prints, and heavy wood beams.

Rates at Gold Key, which is as close as you're likely to come to a country inn in Orlando, are $66 to $86 year round.

Across the street is **TraveLodge Gardens,** 7101 S. Orange Blossom Trail, Orlando, FL 32809 (tel. 407/851-4300, toll free 800/255-3050), with attractive, large rooms in tropical colors and rates of $50 to $65 double year round. The resort sports two heated pools, one for children, nonsmoking rooms, free transportation to and from the airport, and Gray Line bus service to attractions.

## WINTER PARK

Winter Park is not right down the street from Disney, but it's such a beautiful hideaway that for my money it's well worth the 20- or 30-minute drive to area attractions. So lovely is this small city that it is an attraction in itself, a tiny diamond glittering proudly among quite a few rhinestones.

Located just north of Orlando and about 15 miles from Disney World, Winter Park is comparatively easy to find and worth the trouble. Just exit from Highway I-4 at Colonial Drive East, turn north at Mills Drive, and east again on Orange Avenue. You can also exit Highway I-4 at Fairbanks Avenue and follow that street east to Park Avenue, where you'll turn left.

You'll land right in the middle of a town that likes to call itself "Little Europe" and with good reason. Many of its fabulously beautiful mansions are European in style, its streets are small and packed with shops as elegant and intriguing as any you find in posh European shopping areas, and its ambience is pure Europe, from splashing fountains to tiny courtyards tucked between buildings.

As you roll or stroll down Winter Park's main street, Park Avenue, look up and you'll see an ornate balcony, decked with pots of scarlet geraniums and sparkling white wicker furniture. That's the **Park Plaza Hotel,** 307 Park Ave., Winter Park, FL 32789 (tel. 407/647-1072), a glamorous little hotel recently redecorated but still redolent with Old World, Old Florida touches, such as leaded-glass windows and a marble desk in the lobby. They've managed to blend antique elegance with modern convenience, using Cuban tile, brick trim, and whirring paddle fans. My favorite is a big room with brass beds, a sitting area, deep plush carpets, pretty pastel colors, and wing chairs. French doors open onto a balcony where you can gaze down on those lesser beings not up there enjoying this luxury, for which you will pay $100 to $125 for suite *avec* balcony, $65 to $75 for a room overlooking an enchanting courtyard, or the park across the street. Worth every hard-earned dime.

A family-owned hostelry, the **Langford Hotel** at 300 E. New England Ave., Winter Park, FL 32789 (tel. 407/644-3400), has been around since 1955 but keeps up to date with frequent modernization. Shaded by pines and a deep jungle of plants, the Langford provides a quiet retreat spiritually, if not geographically, in a tiny tropical garden with a little waterfall that glitters at night in the glow of lamplights. Some rooms are downright spectacular, with antique French chairs, crystal chandeliers, a striped silk chaise, patterned carpet, beveled mirrors, and Austrian drapes covering a glass entrance to a private balcony. Another hideaway is covered wall to wall in straw matting and filled with things African, from zebra-striped furniture to massive mahogany carvings. Latest addition: the Shangri La Health Club.

• In the hotel's Empire Room supper club, a long menu sports some tempting beef and seafood specialties ($15 to $20 range), and in the lounge the area's liveliest entertainment goes on stage in the form of floor shows and dance bands.

Year-round rates at the Langford are $65 to $85 double.

## IN SURROUNDING TOWNS

Let me say once more that because it's reasonably fast and easy to get from one place to another in Orlando, there's no reason why you shouldn't stay in one of the attractive small towns that dot the lake-strewn countryside. When you want to spend a day amusing yourself at the attractions, just hop in the car and zip on over there. Just don't forget you'll need a car!

Altamonte Springs is quite a few exits north of Disney World on Highway I-4, but it's a pretty town with several very good restaurants. If you don't mind about a 25-minute drive to Disney World, Sea World, and the like, stay here at the **Ramada Altamonte Springs,** 151 N. Douglas Ave., Altamonte Springs, FL 32701, off Hwy. I-4 at Rte. 436 (tel. 407/869-9000). It has the advantage of being a lulling distance from the crowds, and in a town near to several top restaurants and a huge shopping mall. If you think you'd like to stay up this way, this resort is the place to settle. Recent renovations have made the attractive spacious rooms even prettier and for play time there are tennis courts and a heated pool.

The inn's restaurant, Bloomer's, and its lounge, Wildflowers, are favorite imbibing and dinner spots for residents who retreat here for some top culinary treats and some flashily prepared flambé desserts. For more casual dining, the hotel's Sprig's Restaurant fills the bill. Prices at the former are in the $12 to $15 range, lower in the latter restaurant. Rates at the inn are $54 to $76 year round.

For those who like plenty of space in their accommodations, a hotel that opened in Altamonte Springs in 1985 offers not only rooms with plenty of space—all rooms are suites—but rooms with another touch unusual in Florida: wood-burning fireplaces. Called **Residence Inn by Marriott,** the hostelry is part of a nationwide all-suites hotel chain that has risen to popularity in recent years as this concept has swept the industry.

The suites here are decorated in contemporary style and each has a fully equipped kitchen with all the necessary appliances right down to a popcorn popper, plus a cozy dining area. You can choose a one- or two-bedroom or penthouse suite with king- and queen-size beds, one or two full baths and separate living room, the focal point of which is a fireplace.

In recent years, the hotel added 36 new studio suites and 12 penthouse suites, the latter sporting two bedrooms, king-size bed and queen-size beds, three television sets, and a full kitchen with even a microwave stocked with microwave popcorn.

The room rates buy you use of the resort's health club, as well as entitling you to a free grocery shopping service. Sports facilities include two heated whirlpools, a sport court for a variety of games, and an outdoor swimming pool. All guests are treated to complimentary Continental breakfast, served in the hotel's Gatehouse and a free copy of the local newspaper or the *Wall Street Journal*. Each evening, complimentary cocktails are served from 5 to 7pm.

You'll find the hotel at 270 Douglas Ave., Altamonte Springs, FL 32714 (tel. 407/788-7991 or toll free 800/331-3131), and year-round rates are $89 to $99 for a one-bedroom and $114 to $129 for two-bedroom penthouse accommodations which include a sleeping loft and Murphy bed.

**Ramada Inn West Gate** is in the little town of Clermont, smack in the middle of citrus country. You'll find it on U.S. 192 W at U.S. 27, Route 5, Box 62, Clermont, FL 32711 (tel. 813/424-2621 or toll free 800/228-2828). There are 194 spacious, comfortable rooms here on extensive grounds that also harbor an Olympic-size swimming pool, game room, playground, lounge, and dining room with moderately priced offerings. It's just six miles from Disney World, and rates for two are $40 to $80 year round.

Tennis is the focal point of the **Orlando Vacation Resort,** South U.S. 27, Clermont, FL 32711 (tel. 407/656-8181 or toll free 800/874-9064), where you'll find umpteen lighted tennis courts and much, much more. For instance, 233 attractive rooms with plenty of space and bright decor plus a homey little restaurant done up in an antique theme. Excellent food emerges from the kitchen, too, including fresh bread daily. Prices are in the $10 to $15 range. A $10-round-trip shuttle ride to Disney comes with the package, for which you'll pay $58 to $68 year round; children under 17 free.

Haines City is a tiny town near Cypress Gardens, only about a 30-minute drive to Disney World through some pretty country. Here you'll find a posh golf resort called **Grenelefe Resort and Conference Center,** 3200 Rte. 546, Grenelefe, FL 33844 (tel. 813/422-7511 or toll free 800/237-9459, in Florida 800/282-7875). One of the state's top golf and condominium resorts, Grenelefe has 950 acres of green grounds dotted with shady pines and huge spreading live oaks.

Condominium resorts always offer you plenty of living space in your quarters, and Grenelefe is no exception. All apartments are large, individually decorated by owners who must, nevertheless, meet rigid equipment standards. You'll find contemporary touches like lots of glass, wide dressing areas, big walk-in closets, kitchens equipped with everything from food processors to church keys, high sloping ceilings, and private balconies where you can enjoy some sweeping vistas of woodland paths.

Thirty-six of the resort's 54 holes of golf are rated among the top in the state. If you're not a golfer, there are four swimming pools, a spa and sauna, 20 tennis courts, and several restaurants and lounges. Double accommodations are $75 to $325 year round, higher for two-bedroom suites; children under 18 are free. If you'd like to have the resort staff meet you at the airport, that can be arranged for an additional fee.

A new restaurant here on the shores of Lake Mario is called the **Grene Heron** and is hardly the culinary outpost you'd expect way out here in this citrus-lined countryside. Decked out in rattan furnishings, Audubon prints and mirrored copper, the restaurant features flavored butters, creamy lobster bisque, oysters Rockefeller, and traditional favorites like rack of lamb modernized with touches of fruit, nuts, and wild rice. Swordfish with hazelnut butter is a specialty in this restaurant where prices are in the $15 to $28 range for dinner. Open 6 to 10pm Tuesday through Saturday, closed Sunday and Monday.

Last, and in some respects least, is a place for those *really* dedicated to a tan. Called **Cypress Cove,** it's the state's largest nudist resort, a couples-only spot located about 11 miles south of Kissimmee on Pleasant Hill Road, Route 2 (tel. 407/933-5870). No, I have not seen all there is to see here, but there is a lake, tennis courts, canoes, paddleboats, a campground, and rental units. Admission is $22 a couple, and you can rent a two-bedroom trailer for $80.50.

## A VERY SPECIAL PLACE

Mount Dora is a lovely old Florida village that has changed so little over the years you feel as if you're dropping back in time when you visit. Perched atop a high rise overlooking a lake, the town looks like a Vermont village that lost its way and turned tropical. It's lined with adorably designed antique shops, geranium-filled window boxes, pretty little boutiques, and houses sweet as a lace-trimmed hanky.

Raising its gabled head over four green acres that roll down to the diamond-tipped waters of the lake, **Lakeside Inn,** 110 S. Alexander St. (P.O. Box 1390), Mount Dora, FL 32757 (tel. 904/383-4101 or toll-free 800/556-5016), is a veritable oasis.

At the turn of the century, adventurous Yankees came here bent on getting a close look at the weird tropical wilderness about which they'd heard some tall tales. To house those visitors, some canny developer built a 10-room inn called Alexander House. Before long, boating became a national mania and the Alexander became the Lakeside Inn, a base for Mount Dora's annual regatta. During its long and venerable history, the Lakeside Inn welcomed many of the rich and famous, including former Pres. Calvin Coolidge, who spent the winter here in 1930.

Today you can settle into a rocking chair on the porch and leave all your cares behind as you gaze out over green lawns flanked by two wing buildings. Inside the main lodge, wood floors have been polished to a sienna glow, and small groupings of camelback couches and wing chairs welcome you to quiet talks by the fireplace. Tall windows, many of them cozy bays or gables, offer a dramatic view over the central swimming pool and the rippling lake beyond.

Rooms are togged out in delicate Laura Ashley prints and sport walk-in closets that hark back to the days when winter tourists came here for the *whole* winter instead of a week. In the two other buildings on the grounds, rooms are decorated in similarly handsome style, many of them with reproduction antique furnishings.

Evenings, visitors gather in a forest-green lounge where the chef produces a tray of delectable canapés on request. Later, the action moves to the dining room, where a huge circlet of bay windows creates a dramatic setting for candlelight dinners. Outside, a giant camphor tree rustles in the breeze.

Ellison Ketchum, manager and one of the three partners in this ambitious but very successful restoration, is happy to relate details of its renovation to antique buffs, restoration fans, and anyone else who will listen. Thanks to him and his helpers, the crack of croquet mallets once again echoes across the lake, and tea will be served promptly at 4pm, madame.

Lakeside Inn is a don't-miss about a 30-minute drive from Central Florida attractions and charges $75 to $125 year round.

## ANOTHER SPECIAL PLACE

Every time I visit Orlando I find a new treasure for my "memorable places" file. Howey-in-the-Hills is one of those, a little village hidden in the rolling citrus land. Here, too, is a special place called **Mission Inn,** Box 441, Howey-in-the-Hills, FL 32737 (30 miles northwest of Orlando off Exit 85 of Florida's turnpike on U.S. 19; tel. 904/324-3101 or toll free 800/874-9053; in Florida 800/342-4495).

Rising like a California mirage, the resort has a Spanish theme that permeates its 141 spacious rooms, 19 suites and villas, which feature panoramic views of the countryside or of an 18-hole golf course on hotel grounds. As one writer put it: "One expects to turn around any moment to find hood-shrouded monks tolling mission bells, or armored *conquistadores* strolling the plazas, swords slapping at their sides."

With 141 rooms and villas in three wings with evocative names like La Posada de San Miguel, and La Posada de San Angel, this resort is a small and well-kept secret among those who have learned of its charms.

Small as it is, it has all the extras you'd expect to find in a big resort. Mission Inn's golf course, first laid out in 1926, ranked in the top 20 of Florida's 841 courses. Recently, the hotel opened La Hacienda, a sleek, sky-lit restaurant offering Sunday brunch and daily breakfast and lunch service beside a columned fireplace. Other amenities include tennis courts, a jogging and fitness trail, volleyball, shuffleboard, sports instruction, heated pool, spa, exercise room, and a fleet of boats in a nearby lake.

Not too long ago, the resort discovered a magnificent old, double-decker yacht lying dead in the water at Daytona Beach, had it moved inland to a nearby lake, restored its beautiful woods, renamed it *La Reina,* and now operates it, much to the delight of guests.

Money-saving golf packages are available, and many of them include attendance at the Howie Barron Golf School. Spacious rooms and suites range from $75 to $335, higher for larger suite accommodations and villas. Limousine service can be arranged from Orlando's airport with 48 hours' notice and Mission Inn can also see to it that you get to Disney World.

## CAMPING

You can't miss **Yogi Bear's Jellystone Park Campground—** the bear's face is on billboards all over town. There are three of these parks in the area, but the closest to Disney World is a pretty wooded 600-site campground just four miles west of the park on U.S. 192 (8555 W. Irlo Bronson Memorial Hwy., Kissimmee, FL 32741; tel. 305/239-4148 or toll free 800/327-7115). You'll find a lake here, a mini-golf course, boating and fishing, a grocery store, restaurant, and gift shop, not to mention all kinds of special events. A rate of

$22 includes water, electric, and sewage hookup. Tent sites also are available for $17.

Second of Yogi's hangouts is a 500-site campground 10 miles east of Disney World (9200 Turkey Lake Rd., just off Hwy. I-4, Orlando, FL 32801; tel. 305/351-4394 or toll free 800/327-7115). The third is about 30 miles away in Apopka (U.S. 1, Box 2000, Apopka; tel. 305/889-3048 or toll free 800/327-7115). Rates and facilities are similar at all the campgrounds.

**Port O Call Campground,** 5175 U.S. 192, Kissimmee, FL 32741 (tel. 407/396-0110 or toll free 800/327-9120, in Florida 800/432-0766), is a massive lakeside place with a long list of facilities ranging from fishing and shuffleboard to game room, movies, bike and paddle boat rentals, weekend entertainment, and a fancy tropical rock-bedecked swimming pool. It's about five miles east of the gates to Disney World and charges $24 for two adults, no charge for children under 12, and additional adults pay $2. Fees include water, electric, and the rest of those camping necessities. Tenters pay $13.

If the Old West is a lure for you, **Fort Summit Camping Resort,** 2525 Frontage Rd., Davenport, FL 33837 (mailing address: P.O. Box 22182, Lake Buena Vista, FL 32830; tel. 813/422-5766 or toll free 800/424-4999; in Fla. toll free 800/424-1880), may be the place to settle. You roll into the stockade here and park it, podner. Lots of Western flotsam and jetsam make this an unusual camping resort, and it has all the necessary amenities, from a store to a snack bar, laundry, bathhouse, rec room with video games, swimming pool, and a barbecue powwow center. Rates are $13.50 for tenting, $19.95 double a night. Take I-4 west to Exit 23, make a right turn and you'll find it at the intersection of U.S. 27 and I-4.

# DINING IN DISNEY WORLD AND ORLANDO

Not long ago I heard a stress expert admonish an audience to spend less time worrying, since there's no end to what you can find to worry about and no "cure" for a worry anyway. He didn't say what to do if you're worried about worrying!

Which brings me to good news for those who may be harboring some niggling worries about the quality, quantity, availability, variety, or price of food in Orlando and Disney World. If you're even a little concerned, here's a little advice: Don't be. Finding a restaurant in the price, quality, and atmospheric bracket you're seeking is definitely not a problem in Central Florida; it's finding a square block *without* a tempting restaurant on it that's a real challenge.

If you doubt me, let it be known that in Disney World alone, there were no fewer than 75 restaurants before they added a couple dozen or so more at EPCOT and Disney-MGM—and that's not counting the umpteen popcorn stands, ice-cream wagons, chocolate-covered-frozen-banana purveyors, and other vendors in the Magic Kingdom . . . *and* it's not counting hotel restaurants in Lake Buena Vista's Walt Disney World Hotel Plaza.

Don't think, either, that all the restaurants in Orlando are inside Disney World. Entrepreneurs clever enough to lure a Disney World to a clutch of cow pastures in the middle of nowhere were certainly not zany enough to overlook the possibility that thousands of visitors streaming through the gates of Mouseland would sooner or later want to exchange silver for golden fried. A large number of those visitors being children, theirs were the first gastronomic desires to be satisfied. Thus, in the early days of its boom, Orlando and its environs were hog heaven for fast-food freaks.

It wasn't long, however, before burger-and-chicken creators discovered they could turn their culinary knowledge into even bigger dollars by creating restaurants for the palates of more discerning diners. Thus were born architecturally impressive and gastronomically top-notch eateries that soon were showing up on respected lists of the nation's best dining spots.

If you want to get your own look at the range from sublime to . . . well, less sublime in dining spots hereabouts, ride over to the suburb of Winter Park, Central Florida's gastronomic capital, and take a look at some enchanting dining spots behind Tiffany-style glass windows and in tiny courtyards.

Then to satisfy that craving for a double burger, hold the mayo, two orders of fries, and a shake, head for International Drive, where you'll find representatives of what seem to be every fast-food chain in the world—there's Pizza Hut, Arby's, Wendy's, McDonald's, Burger King, Denny's, International House of Pancakes, Perkins Cake and Steak, Steak and Ale, Cork and Cleaver, Bennigan's, Baskin-Robbins . . . and more, all on one short street!

Because Disney World is such a big place, to simplify your task of selecting an eating place I've listed restaurants located within Walt Disney World's Magic Kingdom and EPCOT in Chapters VII and VIII. That way, if hungers strikes as you tour the Magic Kingdom, EPCOT, or MGM Studios you can look right at the walking maps to discover which of the many restaurants is nearest you.

In this chapter, I've listed under restaurants *in* Disney World, those top spots throughout Disney World (including hotels in Walt Disney World Hotel Plaza) that I think you'll enjoy visiting for a leisurely meal, which usually means dinner, but can also be lunch and, at some spots, a sumptuous breakfast/brunch. Reservations are a must at some Disney World restaurants (and may be made up to 45 days in advance!). At the end of this section on "Restaurants in Disney World," I've put together a list of restaurants that take reservations and their phone numbers. The area code for all is 407.

Listed under restaurants in Orlando are some of the best choices in that city and in all the smaller outlying cities in this region—Winter Park, Fern Park, Altamonte Springs, Kissimmee, Maitland, and more.

# RESTAURANTS IN DISNEY WORLD

Let's start right at the top. To my mind that's the glorious, glamorous **Empress Lilly** (tel. 828-3900), a gleaming craft that looms up out of Lake Buena Vista like a ghostly dream. Named after Walt Disney's wife, this glittering triple-decker riverboat is Disney at its best: a fairyland of tiny white lights, the burnished glow of polished brass and mahogany, the sweeping elegance of velvet, damask, gingerbread trim, Victorian furniture, wide staircases, and etched glass. Even if you don't get a chance to try one of the three plush dining rooms here, don't miss stopping by for a visit. Try to go at night, when the twinkling lights that ring the *Empress*'s polished decks turn this permanently moored and entirely fanciful creation into a fantasyland par excellence.

As you stroll the Promenade Deck you'll find one of Disney World's most elegant—and most expensive—restaurants: **The Empress Room.** Lining the room are ornate moldings covered with $8,000-worth of gold leaf, and overhead is a massive brass chandelier dripping with shimmering crystals. Damask wallpaper, etched glass, handsome paneling, and a hushed atmosphere broken only by the delicate notes of harp melodies make this room a spot the French kings of Versailles would have found quite adequate, *merci.*

There's a handsome forest-green lounge for predinner imbibing and, as you might expect, prices match the upper-crust ambience. Entrée prices, for example, can go as high as $34 for dishes like oyster-stuffed veal chops or saddle of wild boar, but most entrées fall in the $20 to $30 category—figure $50 to $65 per person for dinner. Other tempters on the menu here include pâtés, chilled avocado soup, smoked duck with creamed horseradish, chicken in a sauce of cream and cider, and fresh mushroom salad; everything's à la carte. The Empress Room is open 5:30 to 10pm daily, and both reservations and jackets are required.

If you're not prepared to shell out shekels in those quantities, there are two other dining rooms on the *Empress Lilly* that are almost as tempting: the Steerman's Quarters and the Fisherman's Deck.

In the **Steerman's Quarters** you'll find yourself surrounded by heavy mahogany furnishings set off by a deep shade of red, wainscoting, and flower-sprigged wall coverings. Beef is king here, with several kinds of steaks and prime rib topping the list, and a delicious cheesecake bringing up the menu's aft end. Prices for entrées are in the $17 to $25 range, and the Steerman's Quarters is open noon to 3pm and 5:30 to 10pm daily.

Seafood is the center of attention in the **Fisherman's Deck** restaurant. Located on the forward promenade deck, its curving windows overlook the glittering lake outside. The decor is blue velvet and the atmosphere is sophisticated and glittering in the bi-level room where entrée prices run in the $17 to $49 range. Hours are the same as those in the Steerman's Quarters.

Dress aboard the *Empress Lilly* is dressy, with jackets suggested for men after 5pm. There's valet parking near the boat. No reservations are accepted at the Steerman's Quarters or the Fisherman's Deck, you just give your name to the host or hostess and wait in the Victorian elegance of the lounges aboard. In the Empress Room, however, reservations are required and can be made up to 30 days in advance at 828-3900.

Finally, if you just want to have some fun without food, stop by the **Baton Rouge Lounge,** where banjos twang, guitars strum, and there's a laugh-it-up good time going until 1am daily. More on that subject in Chapter V's nightlife rundown.

Running neck-and-neck for top honors in Disney dining is the **Polynesian Village's Polynesian Revue,** often called the Luau. You dine on typical luau cuisine, including a taste of poi, chicken, pork, and spareribs, while graceful hula hands tell tales of the South Pacific. This is one of the best Polynesian shows in the state, since many of the dancers have trained at Hawaii's famed Polynesian Cultural Center. There are three shows nightly at 4:30, 6:45, and 9:30pm. Show and dinner prices are $29 for adults, $23 and $25 for children. Reserve a seat for these popular productions: Call 824-8000.

That's the major production nightly, but children can also feast and be entertained at the hotel's **Children's Dinner Theater,** where prices are $5 an hour for some very entertaining baby-sitting.

Breakfast is a specialty at **Papeete Bay Verandah,** where you'll find a massive brunch on Sunday. Set aside a little resting and digesting time after one of these gargantuan repasts, which include fresh fruit, crêpes, smoked fish, and all the breakfast goodies you can imagine.

Dinner features some interesting tropical touches like coconut milk marinades, entrées steamed in leaves, pork served with peanuts and bananas, and honey-dipped chicken, all served beside the Seven Seas Lagoon, with the turrets of Cinderella Castle glittering in the distance. You can't match that, even in Polynesia!

Sunday brunch is $18.95 for adults, $8.50 for children. Dinner is $15 to $24.95 at Papeete Bay Verandah, and reservations can be made at 824-1391 a week or more in advance.

Similar breakfasts and dinners are available at the **Tangaroa Terrace** dining room near the Oahu longhouse and the hotel's coffee shop, **Coral Isle Café,** which also serves lunch. Duck with macadamia nuts is an unusual dinner specialty at Tangaroa Terrace, and french toast made with sourdough bread and bananas is a breakfast feature at both spots. Prices are similar to those in the Papeete Bay Verandah. Reservations can be made at 824-1360.

Coconut hot dogs? You betcha. At the hotel's **Barefoot Snack Bar** and **Tangaroa Snack Isle,** both open for snacks from lunch through dinnertime.

For sophisticated top-name entertainment and dining combined, the **Contemporary Resort** is the spot. Here in a 15th-floor aerie you feast on American and continental favorites like steaks, prime rib, and seafood while the lights of the Magic Kingdom glitter in the distance and, at special times of year, fireworks explode overhead.

The **Top of the World** is a popular spot for breakfast, lunch, and dinner. Prices for breakfast and lunch are in the $7 to $12 range, dinner is $45 for adults and $19.59 for children 3 to 12.

Buffet meals attended by Disney characters are popular at Disney World, and you'll find one each morning and evening—an all-you-can-eat extravaganza—in the Contemporary's **Contemporary Café.** No reservations are taken for dinner, when the buffet price is $15.50 for adults, $9.95 for children. At breakfast, Disney characters entertain from 8 to 11am. Prices are $9.95 for adults, $5.95 for children.

Those in search of cholesterol-free diet goodies can find sustenance at the **Grill Room,** a quiet spot on the fourth-floor Grand Concourse behind Coconino Cove. Breakfast, lunch, and dinner are served and feature all the usual choices plus seafood, veal, prime ribs, and some fancy poultry dishes for evening dining. There's a special menu for the small fry, too. Prices are in the under-$20 range, and it's open for all meals. Call 824-1000 for reservations.

More dining spots in the Contemporary? Of course. The **Outer Rim,** a raw bar and lounge where you can snack overlooking Bay

Lake; the **Fiesta Fun Center** for more snacking; and the **Dock Inn** at the marina for subs and great frozen bananas.

A little farther afield (but not far) from the Magic Kingdom is the Disney Inn which sports the **Garden Gallery Restaurant.** Sneak off here where things are busy at the other restaurants in Walt Disney World, and odds are you'll slip right into an empty spot and be glad you did. Because the Inn is a little off the beaten track (see Chapter III's discussion of hotels in Disney World), fewer people know about it, so it's less likely to be packed with day visitors. It's every bit as good and as attractive as any of the other restaurants in the World, too, and features more of those gigantic all-you-can-gorge breakfast buffets, lunch, plus impressive dinner cuisine that can range from fresh oysters, crab, and shrimp, or a platter of vegetable appetizers, to entrées of seafood, poultry in creamy sauces, or pink prime rib, topped off by a house specialty, french-fried ice cream. What's that? Would I spoil the surprise? The Garden Gallery is open for three meals, daily, and dinner's in the $13 to $35 range. You can make reservations at 824-2200.

For snacks at this resort it's the **Sand Trap,** a poolside eatery serving lunch and dinner as well as basic survival sustenance.

Finally, at Fort Wilderness, the **Trail's End Café** offers a down-home atmosphere of logs and heavy beams with country fixin's to match. Those of you who feel the day's gotten off to a bad start if you haven't launched into biscuits and gravy can satisfy those cravings here for less than $10. At other hours of the day, you'll find the likes of chicken pot pie, hot dogs and beans, spareribs, steaks, prime ribs, saucy ham, and roast turkey—simple foods, simply prepared and presented buffet-style, perfect for those days when you're fed up to here with snacks or haute cuisine. There are specially priced items for children and a make-your-own pizza every night from 4:30 to 9pm.

Snacking spot at the campgrounds is the **Campfire Snack Bar,** where reside all the hot dogs, chili dogs, hamburgers, and such you can consume. Open Friday only, 5 to 9pm.

## DINING WITH MICKEY, MINNIE, PLUTO AND THE GANG

There's no question about it: A mouse is royalty here in Walt Disney's fantasyland. So here comes your chance to dine at a royal table that some enthusiasts figure is better than Buckingham Palace.

Yes, you can rub the sleep from your eyes and breakfast with Pluto, break a Disney day sharing a table for two with Minnie, and, later, stare across the dinner table into the very large eyes of Chip 'n' Dale.

Here's a look at who's hosting what character party:

One or another of the Disney characters comes aboard the fancifully pretty *Empress Lilly* riverboat at 8:30 and 10am daily to host **Breakfast à la Disney.** Prices are $9.75 adults, $6.50 children 3 through 11. Reservations are required; call 828-3900 or 824-8000.

A variety of characters turn up at the Polynesian Hotel's Papeete Bay Verandah Sundays from 11:45am to 2pm for **Brunch with the Disney Bunch.** Prices are $18.95 adults, $8.50 children 6 through 11, free for children under 6. Reservations are wise; call 824-1391.

Melvin the Moose joins Chip 'n' Dale at **Chip 'n' Dale's Country Morning Jamboree,** an event that takes place daily at 8am and 9:45 pm in Pioneer Hall at Fort Wilderness. It's an all-you-can-eat, family-style breakfast, for which the tab is $12 adults, $9 children 3 through 11. Call 824-8000 for reservations.

At last, the ladies are getting into the act. None other than Minnie appears to welcome you to the **Minnie Menehune Character Breakfast** in the Polynesian Hotel's Papeete Bay Verandah. A daily event, the breakfast takes place between 7:30 and 10:30am. Adults pay $9.95, children 3 through 11 are charged $5.95. Make reservation at 824-2000.

Guess who drops by for **Mickey's Tropical Revue,** a luau-style character show at the Polynesian Hotel's Luau Cove each afternoon at 4:30pm. Adults pay $25 for this event, guests 12 to 20 pay $20 and children 3 through 11 pay $11. Reservations are required and can be made at 824-8000.

Those ubiquitous Disney characters turn up again each day at the Contemporary Hotel for the **Contemporary Café Character Breakfast,** served from 8 to 11am. Prices are $9.95 adults, $5.95 children 3 through 11. No reservations are required.

Busy little fellows, these cruising characters. They turn up yet one more time daily at the Contemporary Resort Hotel's **Contemporary Café Character Dinner Buffet.** A western, all-you-can-eat buffet, this dinner with Dumbo's pals takes place each evening at 5pm, winding up at 10pm. Adults pay $15.95, children 3 to 11 are charged $9.95. No reservations are required.

Moving right along now to Walt Disney World Village—when you're at the Disney Inn, you're almost there. When you do indeed arrive at this tastefully designed shopping mall, you'll find a bevy of restaurants as well.

If you like to see water rippling by as you dine, you'll love **Chef Mickey's Village Restaurant,** another gardener's delight, filled with plants and sporting a lovely view of Buena Vista Lagoon. Lunch on a light seafood salad or an omelet stuffed with artichoke hearts, or try a dinner of beef or seafood specialties. After dinner settle into a plump couch in the Village Lounge, lean back and listen to the sound in the area's number-one jazz club. Dinner prices are in the $18 to $25 range, lunch in the $6 to $8 bracket. The Village is open for brunch, lunch, and dinner daily (tel. 828-3723).

A popular place in the village is **Cap'n Jack's Oyster Bar** (tel. 828-3870) which, as you might guess, carries a fair supply of those bivalves, plus just about every other kind of seafood treat you can dream up—ceviche (marinated raw fish that's much better than it sounds), clams, shrimp, crab claws, and smoked kingfish. The atmosphere's informal, tropical, and fun. Try one of the special frozen daiquiris or margaritas in monstrous glasses to get things off to a ripping start. Lunch and dinner are served daily, and the price range is about $11 to $17.

**All American Sandwich Shop** is basic New York deli, perhaps minus a few of the umpteen selections you find in Big Apple delis. You can choose among several varieties of breads and dozens of cheeses and meats, then chow down on the extras, which include everything from baked beans to applesauce and imported or home-grown beers. For the ultimate Florida experience, dine outside on the terrace under a shower of blossoms from the trees that shade this cozy spot. Inside ceilings are high, and there are lots of tropical touches. In either locale prices are in the $5 to $10 range. Open for lunch and dinner daily (tel. 828-3883).

If you like country clubs, you'll love the **Pompano Grille** at **Lake Buena Vista Club,** where you'll often find room even when things are jammed at other hotels and Magic Kingdom restaurants. Here they go all out to provide enormous breakfasts which, on Sundays (10:30am to 3pm) are brunch feasts (adults, $16.95; children from 3 to 11, $8.95): eggs in all styles including Florentine (with spinach and hollandaise sauce), fruit-filled crêpes laced with vanilla sauce, and salads brimming with crisp vegetables or tropical fruit. Lunches and dinners are pleasant, too, in this serene spot overlooking a golf course, and a particular specialty at those meals is a meal-in-a-bowl onion soup covered with cheeses. Dinner and lunch prices run from $6.95 to $20 for entrées. For dinner and brunch, make reservations at 828-3735. Jackets are not required for dinner.

Fast food? Of course, at **Lite Bite,** which has burgers, dogs— like that. Prices: under $5.

Whether or not you're staying in Walt Disney World Village Hotel Plaza (which includes Grosvenor Resort, Hotel Royal Plaza, Viscount, Buena Vista Palace, Pickett Suites, and Howard Johnson hotels, see Chapter III), you can pop into these conveniently located hotel restaurants. Since they're all on Disney grounds, they're not far from Magic Kingdom and EPCOT Center and make a pleasant respite from the activities and crowds there.

At **Grosvenor Resort** you'll find **Baskerville's** (tel. 828-4444), where you'll dine in a Sherlock Holmes-ian atmosphere at breakfast, lunch, and dinner. Dinner entrées are in the $10 to $15 range.

If you're up at 7am and still going strong at midnight, you can find something to eat at **Hotel Royal Plaza's Knight's Table** (tel. 828-2828) coffee shop (prices $7 to $15), which also serves pizza out of the ovens in the evening. For atmosphere and leisurely dining, the hotel's **El Cid** restaurant (tel. 828-2828) is the place. Heavy on Spanish atmosphere—carved dark wood, red trimmings, pewter platters, and the like—El Cid counts among its specialties such beef and seafood specialties as chateaubriand and Maine lobster. Prices are in the $13 to $28 range for dinner, and hours are until 11p.m.

**Howard Johnson's** (tel. 841-8600) needs, as they say, no introduction. You already know that their fried clams are unbeatable, their ice cream a national passion, and their other offerings simple and predictable. Ho Jo's is open 6am to 10pm and has prices in the $10-and-under range.

**Chez Donut** is the favorite of youngsters and not-so-youngsters alike at the Viscount (tel. 828-2424). Breakfast and lunch buffets in the $5 to $7 range, and basic beef and seafood dishes ($13 to $16) are served in the **Palm Grill.**

Finally, a few tips on dining at Disney World. Try to avoid the most popular dining hours—8 to 10am, 11am to 1pm, and 7 to 9pm. During those hours, the popular breakfast and lunch buffets at Walt Disney World hotels and at restaurants within the Magic Kingdom and EPCOT are busy. If you must dine then, resign yourself to waiting in line. It will be worth it, though, since the Disney folks do go out of their way to please you.

If you're one of those people who goes berserk in lines, consider leaving the Kingdom or EPCOT at lunchtime and trying some of the restaurants at hotels in the World or in the WDW Shopping Village (although Village restaurants are busy on weekends, when local residents come here to shop).

Best bet is to get in on the early or late end of popular dining times, or avoid them altogether by snacking.

Guests at the seven Lake Buena Vista Resorts (Howard Johnson, Hilton, Viscount, Grosvenor Resort, Pickett Suites, Buena Vista Palace, and Hotel Royal Plaza) and at hotels owned by Disney World (the Contemporary, Polynesian, Disney Inn, Disney Villas, and Grand Floridian) can make reservations at EPCOT's restaurants in advance, but they are the only lucky travelers to be able to do so. If you're not staying at one of those resorts, you must hie on over to EPCOT and make your reservation as we have described.

At dinner, particularly during the busiest days at the park (see Chapter VIII), make reservations—and at the most popular restaurants (for instance, Polynesian Village's luau show, Top of the World at the Contemporary, Fort Wilderness's show, King Stefan's in Cinderella's Castle, and Liberty Tree Tavern in Liberty Square) make them as far in advance as possible—some shows can be sold out up to a year in advance.

Here's a quick at-a-glance rundown of **Disney World reservation numbers** for those spots which take reservations:

**Contemporary Resort:** Gulf Coast Room, 824-1000; Top of the World, 824-8000.

**Polynesian Village:** Papeete Bay Verandah and Tangaroa Terrace, 824-2000; Polynesian Revue (luau), 824-8000.

**Disney Inn:** Trophy Room, 824-2200.

**Magic Kingdom:** At King Stefan's in Cinderella's Castle and Liberty Tree Tavern in Liberty Square, reservations must be made in person on the day you're dining, so make that your first stop on arrival at the Magic Kingdom.

**Walt Disney World Village:** Empress Room on the *Empress Lilly,* 828-3900, and Lake Buena Vista Club, 828-3735.

**Fort Wilderness:** Hoop-Dee-Doo Musical Revue at Pioneer Hall, 824-8000.

In general, you can make reservations up to 45 days in advance if you're staying in a Disney World hotel and up to 30 days if you're bunking down elsewhere. Two exceptions: Reservations for the Top of the World's show can be made no sooner than 30 days before that show, and reservations in the Empress Room may be made 30 days in advance, no matter where you're staying.

# RESTAURANTS IN ORLANDO AND SURROUNDING CITIES

Dinner in an elegant garden? Or surrounded by the bejeweled glitter of Tiffany-style glass windows? In an old Florida inn or under the glow of chandeliers in a fountain-trimmed mansion?

You can try all that and more right here in Central Florida, where some of the most glamorous restaurants in the state are waiting to welcome you.

Supplementing those are dozens of small, family-run dining rooms, jeans-and-cotton-shirt spots where the atmosphere is cozy, intimate, and informal, the cuisine homey and all-American.

Because the decision on where to go for dinner is usually made by considering what kind of food you want, I've listed some of the area's most popular options by culinary specialty. You'll have fun trying them and even more fun finding your own candidates for "best restaurant" here in the land the Mouse built.

Remember that, unless otherwise specified, the prices I've cited are for entrées, which usually, but not always, include salad, one or two vegetables, and perhaps coffee as well.

## AMERICAN/CONTINENTAL

Golden light streams through a glass roof and glimmers on formal silver place-settings, etched-and-smoked-glass mirrors, lovely linens, and the green leaves of dozens of plants at **Park Plaza Gardens,** 319 Park Ave. S., Winter Park (tel. 645-2475). This small jewel of a restaurant overwhelms you with good things like seafood bisque, exotic shrimp in curry sauce, flounder meunière, veal with chanterelles, and baked Alaska. Open from 11:30am to 3pm and 6 to 10pm weekdays, to 11pm weekends, Park Plaza Gardens is a serene spot. You'll pay about $20 to $25 for dinner at this hideaway next door to the quaint Park Plaza Hotel. Sundays, a $14.95 champagne brunch is served from 11am to 3pm.

New American cuisine is one of the latest culinary styles to capture the American imagination, not to mention the palate. In Orlando, the place to seek out what this new preparation style is all about is **Pebbles,** 2110 W. Fla. 434, Longwood (tel. 774-7111). This pebble tossed into the stream of Central Florida cookery has made quite a ripple with such treats as linguine with duck sauce, creative salads topped with paper-thin Chinese noodles, and other unusual combinations of herbs and fresh ingredients. Just off I-4 in a small shopping center at Longwood, this very handsome restaurant is open 11am to midnight; prices are in the $10 to $18 range.

I've already raved about the Gold Key Inn, 7100 S. Orange

Blossom Trail (tel. 855-0050), so I'll continue the raves with a review of the inn's cozy **Piccadilly Restaurant.** Long an award-winner for its cuisine and attractive decor, this pretty pub-like spot surrounds you with the gleam of polished wood. The Piccadilly is bright with candles and fresh flowers, and provides a charming atmosphere in which to dine on roast beef with Yorkshire pudding, rack of lamb, or poached red snapper. Prices are in the $10 to $17 range. The restaurant is open for dinner from 6 to 10:30pm and for other meals from 7am.

Among the newest restaurant-nightspots in town is **Park Avenue Grille,** 358 Park Ave. N., Winter Park (tel. 647-4556). An upstairs-downstairs retreat right in the middle of this beautiful boulevard, Park Avenue Grille is all decked out in bay windows, a burgundy and white decor, tiled bars, brass rails, and enough plants to start a nursery. There's even a garden dining room. You'll find mesquite-grilled seafood, plus prime rib and steaks in both upstairs and downstairs dining rooms and attractive cocktail lounges in both locales as well. A piano trio plays nightly except Sunday and Monday for quiet listening and dancing. Prices are in the $12 to $17 range for dinner entrées and the restaurant is open from 11am to 11pm weekdays, later on weekends.

Not far from Disney World in the Hyatt Orlando Hotel is a spot called **Limey Jim's Restaurant,** 6375 Irlo Bronson Memorial Hwy. at Hwy. I-4 and U.S. 192 (tel. 239-4100 or 422-3106 from Orlando). Just where they got that name is anybody's guess. Here you can try all manner of delicacies ranging from steak au poivre to a palate-cleansing sherbet to liqueur-laced après-dinner café. You'll pay about $20 to $30 for dinner in a quiet, elegant atmosphere blessed with top-notch service and the soft melodies of a pianist. Limey Jim's is open from 6 to 10pm daily.

When Harley Hotels transformed a doddering old downtown hotel into the number-one downtown glamour spot, they didn't stop at the restaurant door. Here at **Café on the Park,** 151 E. Washington St., Orlando (tel. 841-3220), you'll find a place with decor as inviting as the food that's prepared in the kitchen. What's more, the view out over glittering Lake Eola, with its spouting fountain, is terrific, too. A bevy of mirrors here reflect delicate shades of peach, fresh flowers, shining tableware, and many a smiling face chowing down on the likes of prime rib, scampi, shellfish, and filet mignon. On Sunday, the brunch stretches for a mile or so, beginning with champagne and working through enough food to keep you going for a week or so. It's $16 for adults, $8.50 for children. Because it's part of a hotel, the dining room is open all day long, but the highlights are the Sunday brunch from 11am to 3pm; the luncheon buffet 11am to 2pm ($7.50), weekdays only; and dinner from 6 to 10:30pm daily for entrées from $13 to $19.

It's wonderful to see some of Florida's lovely old architecture saved. The salvation of the 4,000-square-foot Eldridge-McBride House was accomplished by the Townsend family, which has cut quite a wide swath through Orlando with its dining spots. A sprawling mansion that occupies a lovely spot beside a little lake called Martin's Pond in the village of Apopka, **Historic Townsend's Plan-**

**tation,** 604 E. Main St., Apopka (tel. 880-1313), is a Victorian delight all painted and primped and with its wide front veranda securely in place. Surrounded by a pristine white fence and rolling lawns, the house is once again a home, now welcoming the hungry in search of some top home-cooking. On the menu are such rib-sticking goodies as southern fried chicken with honey pecan sauce, pan-fried green tomatoes, deep-fried pickles, bourbon-marinated steak, beef pot pie, coconut-fried shrimp, and Cajun alligator tail. Those are accompanied by salad, hot breads, an array of fresh vegetables and potatoes.

High tea—with scones, double cream, strawberry preserves, berry tarts, cookies, tea sandwiches—and, oh yes, tea—is served from 3 to 5pm Monday through Saturday. For other meals, including a groaning lunch buffet table, the restaurant is open daily from 11:30am to 2pm and 5 to 10pm, closing an hour later on weekends, and at 9pm Sunday after brunch and dinner.

Townsend family members also operate **Townsend's Fish House and Tavern,** 35 W. Michigan St., Orlando (tel. 422-5560), where a woodsy-plantsy atmosphere draws a lively crowd of diners and imbibers. Trimmed in brass and copper with marble bars, Townsend's Fish House has a wine bar with 20 wines available by the glass, lots of burgers and grazing food for prices in the $13 range or less. Hours are 11am to 2:30pm weekdays and 5:30 to 10:30pm daily, much later in the tavern.

**Jordan's Grove,** 1300 S. Orlando (17-92), Maitland (tel. 628-0020), is a handsomely restored historic home on three shady acres in the village of Maitland. Jordan's has a changing menu focus on five food groups: seafood, pasta, veal, red meats, and fowl. Sunday, the restaurant features a sumptuous brunch from 11:30am to 2:30pm. Every day except Monday, hours are 6 to 10pm for dinner, and the restaurant is open 11:30am to 2:30pm weekdays for lunch. No dinners Monday night. Entrées are in the $15 to $30 range.

Step right up and hear all about the fun and frolic at the Rosie O'Grady Church Street Station emporium in Chapter V, but listen here to a word about Rosie's top restaurant, **Lili Marlene's Aviator's Pub and Restaurant,** 129 W. Church St. in Church Street Station (tel. 422-2434). Lili Marlene's is a comparatively quiet spot in this never-a-dull-moment entertainment complex. It's pretty, too: full of antiques, including a walnut fireplace once owned by the Rothschilds, massive furniture trimmed in velvet, lots of oak paneling, and stained glass. Take refuge here for a quiet dinner before you venture into the zany atmosphere that prevails in the rest of Rosie's. Steaks, seafood, and occasional French culinary touches are the fare at Lili Marlene's, where you'll pay about $15 to $20 for dinner, served from 5:30pm to midnight daily. Lunch is served from 11am to 4pm.

Whoo, whoo, the train's leaving for **The Bubble Room,** 1351 S. Orlando Ave., Maitland, FL 32571 (tel. 628-3331). The Bubble Room is like Christmas every day, with toy trains running all around this diverting restaurant filled with collections of items from the '40s. You'll never see everything there is to see here no matter how hard you try, so concentrate on the aged prime beef, fresh seafood, pork, poultry, and desserts that go wayyyy beyond mere sin.

Warble a little tune and you're all set for **Caruso's,** latest entry in the fanciful world of Orlando Entertains which brings you King Henry's Feast, Fort Wilderness, Mardi Gras, and the like.

A massive hunk of showy restaurant complete with towering Roman columns, Caruso's is a $5-million creation at 8986 International Dr. (tel. 363-7110 or toll free 800/347-8181). Shining white and standing tall this creation features a handpainted dome alive with cherubs happily cavorting around an Italian sky, acres of faux marble, gold leaf, tapestries and murals, singing waiters, and strolling entertainers.

There's a children's menu and plenty of interesting adult options. Great pastas, some good veal and poultry dishes are served here for prices in the $16 to $32 range. Caruso's warbles from 5 to 11pm daily with a Sunday brunch from 11am to 3pm. There's a lounge here, too.

## JAPANESE

**Ran-Getsu of Tokyo,** 8400 International Dr. (tel. 345-0044) rolls out the sushi bar and raps out the sashimi, tempura, and teriyaki in a handsome $3-million Japanese garden, complete with Japanese goldfish pond. Both showy and serene, this flashy new addition to International Drive eateries claims to have the largest sushi bar in Florida. There's also a kushiyaki bar, starring grilled tidbits of beef, fish, chicken, and vegetables so you can graze your way to nirvana. Authenticity is provided by chefs from Tokyo, and prices are in the $12 to $32 bracket, lower if you stick with sushi and kushiyaki. Hours at Ran-Getsu are 5 to 11pm daily.

**Benihana of Tokyo** is practically a household word by now but in case it's news to you, this chain of upscale Japanese restaurants is a top spot to introduce yourself to some good, reliable and not-too-exotic Japanese cookery. Here you sit at tables for eight. Front and center is a skilled Japanese chef with hand-is-quicker-than-eye talents that will make your head spin. These talented fellows chop, whack, flip, slice, sauté, and amaze. Dinner begins with a traditional little bowl of broth, moves on through shrimp appetizers and on to a beef or seafood selections, each prepared right in front of you and served by a kimono-clad lass. It all makes for gustatorial and prestidigitorial evenings that have made this dining spot both famous and successful. In Orlando you'll find Benihana's in the Hilton Hotel, 1751 Hotel Plaza Blvd., Lake Buena Vista (tel. 827-4865), and hours are 5 to 11pm daily.

## CHINESE

Seven stars around the moon, please. What on earth is that? Well, it's lobster, pork, chicken, snow-pea pods, mushrooms, baby corn, water chestnuts, bamboo shoots, and bok choy plus seven butterfly shrimp, that's what. And it's all here at **Jin Ho,** 400 S. Orlando Ave., Winter Park (tel. 628-2660), a casual spot that became so popular it was cloned in Altamonte Springs (on Maitland Ave., tel. 339-0790). That Seven Stars Around the Moon dish ($20.75 for two), by the way, is for two of the starving, or one desert-island escapee. Other tasty selections include lots of seafood and a sizzling wor ba with seafood and Chinese vegetables served over crisp rice. You won't break the bankroll either: Prices are in the $5 to $10 range. Open from 11am to 10:30pm daily and from noon on Saturday and Sunday.

John Rutherford, one of Orlando's best-known promoters, would *never* be caught far from a good restaurant. I so rely on his proven good taste for tastes that I bring you today one of his most heartfelt recommendations: **Forbidden City,** 948 N. Mills Ave. (tel. 894-5005). John, who's in the running for underground gourmet of the year (at least), loves this spot which began life as a gas station! Despite the City's humble past, its present is going very well, thanks to a talented chef who specializes in what some dare to call "nouvelle chinoise" cuisine. Such scrumptious options as sesame shrimp and orange beef are beautifully presented and perfectly cooked, and a particular favorite here is a taco-like creation incorporating Boston lettuce, chicken, and pine nuts. MSG is forbidden at this city which certainly provided the fodder for one of my most memorable evenings. Entrées are in the $8 to $10 range at this sweetly pretty restaurant which is open from 11:30am to 2:30pm weekdays and 5 to 10pm daily except Sunday.

Those who know a *wor* from a *wok*—and perhaps especially those who don't—are candidates for **Ming Gardens Chinese Cuisine,** 5432 International Dr. (tel. 352-8044), or **Ming Court Restaurant,** 9188 International Dr. (tel. 351-9988). Ming Gardens has a seafood bar with lobster, crab shrimp, and scallops, Chinese vegetables, and the like, plus a wide variety of Chinese cooking from Szechuan to Hunan, Cantonese, Mandarin, and Shanghai. Rosewood furnishings and Oriental lanterns make the Gardens a cozy dining spot while a limpid reflecting pool is the focal point at Ming Court where objets d'art are designed to re-create the refinements of the original Ming Court of long ago. Entrées are served family-style so everyone can get in on the taste testing of selection from the grill or the wok. There's a dim sum appetizer bar, exotic drinks, entertainment and dancing in the lounge, and, last, perhaps least, shark's-fin soup. Prices are in the $12 to $18 range, and court is in session from 5pm to midnight daily. Ming Garden is open 11am to 3pm and 5 to 11pm daily.

## FRENCH

Tiffany glass is worth a small fortune these days in even the smallest quantities, so as you dine at **La Belle Verrière,** 142 S. Park Ave., Winter Park (tel. 645-3377 or 642-0277), you can contemplate the size of the fortune displayed around you. The glowing stained-glass creations you see here are the works of Tiffany, that master craftsman, and they glow in all the colors of the rainbow. You'll glow, too after lunch or dinner in this dramatic setting sparked by masses of plants and fresh flowers, brick and wood trim, and glimmering candles. On the menu, you'll find such delicacies as panaché Parisien, grouper Caprice, tournedos Opus, goat cheese, orange tart, and gratin of raspberries. The bottom line on your bill will be in the $14- to $19-per-person bracket for dinner entrées, which are served from 6 to 10pm daily, lunch from 11:30am to 2:30pm. Closed Sunday.

**Le Cordon Bleu,** 537 W. Fairbanks Ave., Winter Park (tel. 647-7575), is a subtly elegant restaurant, and from its kitchens pour some of the area's best-loved culinary triumphs: things like chateaubriand, rack of lamb, mushrooms stuffed with crab and topped with mornay sauce, escargots, crisp breads, and sinful pastries baked right here. Many an award has been bestowed on this restaurant, and every one is well deserved. For a memorable dinner you'll pay $16 to $30. Le Cordon Bleu is open Monday through Friday for lunch from 11:30am to 2:30pm and for dinner from 5:30 to 11pm.

A Winter Park friend of mine swears she owes her Ms. America proportions to a diet she pursues at **Maison des Crêpes,** 348 N. Park Ave. (tel. 647-4469). Here's how it works, she says: She downs a couple of these paper-thin delicacies stuffed with creamy rich, incredibly delicious fillings, tosses off a crisp cold salad of spinach, mushrooms, and avocado, and perhaps a chilled glass of white wine . . . then doesn't eat for three days. Knowing what it's done for her, I'd certainly like to give this Winter Park Diet a shot. Maison des Crêpes is open 11:30am to 3pm for lunch and 5:30 to 10:30pm for dinner daily except Sunday and on Monday evening. Prices are in the $10 to $25 range or less for dinner.

Last and far from least we come to **Maison et Jardin,** 430 S. Wymore Rd., Altamonte Springs (tel. 862-4410). Take Hwy. I-4 to the Altamonte Springs exit, head west and turn left at the first road on the left, and be prepared to be swept off your feet by the dramatic beauty of this high-on-a-hill restaurant. Huge trees spread their massive branches over the grounds, fountains burble, a stream meanders through the woods. From the moment you roll up the shady drive, you are transported from the mundane to the marvelous. The "maison" is an elegant old home transformed into a warren of beautiful dining rooms. My favorite's the patio room, where a bay window offers a view of perfectly manicured lawns bordered by tiny clumps of flaming flowers. Every room has its own delights, be it an ornate chandelier, a painting, or an elegant set of furniture. There's even an Austrian shade in the powder room! From the kitchen come such treats as escargots, mushrooms thermidor, and zucchini and hearts of palm salad.

Recent renovations—$100,000 worth—have made this lovely restaurant even lovelier with more Venetian crystal chandeliers, Rosenthal china, and hand-blown crystal. Winner of numerous awards, Maison et Jardin, which is lovingly called the Mason Jar by un-Frenchified Orlandoites, charges prices that will bring dinner to about $40 each but it really is worth it in elegance and excellence. Hours are 6 to 10:30pm daily and from 11am to 2:30pm weekdays for lunch. Jackets are required and making reservations is very, very wise. Closed Sunday in summer.

## GREEK

You do recall that the world's original epicurean was the Greek Epicurus, so it's fitting that Jimmy Hansis should have named his

**Epicurean Restaurant,** 7900 E. Colonial Dr., Orlando (tel. 277-2881), after his famous countryman. If you fancy grape leaves, creamy moussaka, the feta-strewn Greek salads with tangy olives, not to mention sarmades, pastitsio, lamb, and kalamarakia, drop in here. Finish it all with thick Greek coffee and that irresistible wafer-thin pastry stuffed with walnuts, drenched in honey, and called baklava. Heaven knows what a Greek—or any—chef can do with shark and alligator tail, but those are two of the latest items to join the list here. Epicurean is open from 5 to 11:30pm, an hour later on weekends, every day except Sunday. Entrées are in the $10 to $18 range.

## ITALIAN

My favorite Italian restaurants are La Scala, Gus's Villa Rosa, and Anthony's.

Let's start with **La Scala,** Lorraine Drive at Douglas Road, Altamonte Springs (tel. 862-3257), where former opera singer Joseph del Vento brought both his vocal and his culinary talents some years ago. He named his new stage after an old one, and here he will show you why the Renaissance man was a product of Italy. Not only can Del Vento sing, he can cook up veal sautéed with peas, prosciutto, and artichokes; red snapper with parsley, garlic, white wine, oregano, and lemon; fresh pastas; steaks; seafood; and veal. Prices are in the $14 to $28 range, and La Scala is open from 5:30 to 10pm daily, except Sunday.

Next comes **Gus's Villa Rosa,** 5923 Old Winter Garden Rd., in the Orlando suburb of Orlo Vista (take Hwy. I-4 to Rte. 435 and drive north; tel. 299-1950). Orlo Vista is not exactly a household word, but here in Central Florida, Gus's place is well known in many a household. It's a simple but great spot for pastas, veal, seafood, and steaks, all created under the watchful eye of Gus Stamatin, who has rung up a long list of culinary credentials. Your bill will only be in the $10 to $17 range, however. Here's a special tip: Try the shrimp Onassis with feta cheese. Villa Rosa is open 4:30 to 11pm for dinner.

"Eating at **Anthony's,**" an Orlando friend reports, "is like having dinner in someone's home." What she says is quite true, with one exception: None of *my* friends can cook like this. Here you dine in a small restaurant, an intimate setting enhanced by handsome paintings and fresh flowers. From the kitchen pour tantalizing treats, all the usual Italian favorites, and wonderful pasta choices. Some Continental options are available, but this is a restaurant that specializes in good Italian food served in a charming atmosphere. You'll pay $12 to $16 for most menu selections; the hours here are 5:30 to 10pm for dinner Monday through Saturday, closed Sunday (tel. 628-1277). You'll find Anthony's at 407 S. Orlando Ave. in Winter Park.

## MEXICAN

You're already well south of most borders, but for a gastronomic trip even farther south, try **El Torito,** 275 W. State Rd. 436 in Village Shoppes, Altamonte Springs (tel. 869-5061). A sassy margarita or two, a quesadilla, a tostada, perhaps some camarones flores wrapped in bacon and served with grilled pineapple and Mexican corn and you'll be warbling *en español*. For all this fun you'll probably pay considerably less than the $10 top menu price. The hours are 11am to 11pm daily, later on weekends, and the lounge is open to 1am.

**Chi-Chi's,** 655 Maguire Blvd., Orlando (tel. 894-0655), is decorated in a contemporary style. A chain operation that's made a name for itself here and in many another locale, Chi Chi's delivers healthy margaritas, whopping tacos and tostadas, and wild creations of all kinds. Plenty of choices here, where you'll probably pay well under $10 for chow (I'm not counting your margaritas but you'd better), available from 11am to midnight weekdays, later on weekends.

**Jo Ann's Chili Bordello,** 1710 Edgewater Dr. (between Princeton and Ivanhoe streets; tel. 425-9865) is just too good a name to resist. If you love chili, you'll adore this crazy place where the wallpaper is red flock, the carpet is red plush, and all is offset by chandeliers and fancy drapes, à la bordello style—at least, I suppose it's bordello style. Waitresses dressed in French corsets and black high heels add their bit to X-rated chilis, each of which is named after a famous, er, lady. Chilis are also rated PG and R for those who like it hot but not quite so hot. Dinners are a little more elaborate and may feature, for example, smoked beef and pork or chili macs. For dessert? Cheesecake, of course, and Häägen-Dazs ice cream pie. Prices are in the $5 to $7 range for dinner, lots less for chili, and hours are 11am to 9pm daily. Never on Sunday.

**Chili's,** 7021 International Dr. (tel. 352-7618), serves South-of-the-Border chow in a casual atmosphere with prices easily in the under-$10 range.

**Las Palomas,** 3552 E. Colonial Dr. (tel. 894-2610), is a very handsome spot, all decked out in Spanish arches, hand-painted tiles, wrought iron balconies, and fountains. Chefs here come straight from Mexico City and turn out marvelously authentic Mexican treats. Las Palomas is open daily from 5 to 10pm and for lunch weekdays and Sunday brunch from 11:30am to 3pm. Prices fall easily in the $10 to $15 range with plenty on the menu for prices lower than that.

## SEAFOOD

Orlando's quite a distance from the sea but that doesn't stop restaurateurs here from ferreting out some good fish, treating them kindly, and serving them up to you in some interesting surroundings.

Wear your jeans and an expendable shirt, not to mention an expandable belt, when you try the **Chesapeake Crab House,** 9495 S. Rte. 17/92, Maitland (tel. 831-0442). A small spot much frequented by residents who delight in the informal atmosphere, the huge piles of crabs you hammer into shreds, and the big pitchers of beer. If you're looking for atmosphere, look elsewhere, but if you'd like to latch onto a hammer and pound away at some delectable blue crabs, head for the Chesapeake. Prices are in the $5 to $10 range (plus a $9 all-you-can-eat blue crab special). Doors open at 5:30pm Monday through Saturday; closed Sunday. Dinner is served until 10pm, later if there's a crowd.

For more of the same atmosphere with a little different seafood focus, try **Lee and Ric's Oyster Bar and Seafood House,** 5621 Old Winter Garden Rd., Orlando (tel. 293-3587). The center of attention here is oysters on the half shell, raw or steamed. Trenchermen can order oysters by the bucket and non-fans can choose rock shrimp by the dozen, smoked mullet (definitely an acquired taste), snapper, flounder, snow crab, or scallops, all washed down with pitchers of beer. Opening hour here is noon daily, closing 11pm. Your tab will be in the $10 to $15 range per person.

**Gary's Duck Inn,** 3974 S. Orange Blossom Trail (tel. 843-0270), has been around a long time and has racked up many awards for good seafood, simply prepared and presented in a casual atmosphere enjoyed by families, singles, couples—everyone. Gary's swears that if you stop here once you'll be back, and they must be right: They've passed their 40th anniversary. Fried butterflied shrimp's a favorite with many habitués of Gary's, but there are plenty of other choices, including brimming seafood platters, lobster, scallops—you name it. You'll pay entrée prices in the $10 to $17 range for dinner, which is available from 11:30am to 10pm daily, later on weekends. Saturdays the doors open at 5pm

**Red Lobster,** 4010 W. Vine St., Kissimmee (tel. 846-3513), probably won't be much of a surprise to you since this chain has spread far and wide. You'll find a casual comfortable atmosphere, plenty of what the name advertises, lots of other seafood choices, and even a few selections for those who can live forever without seafood. Prices are moderate at this family favorite—in the $10 to $15 range—and the Red Lobster's open daily from 11am to 10pm, later on weekends. There's now an oyster bar here, too, and a lounge open until midnight. There are seven other Red Lobsters in the area.

**Charlie's Lobster House,** 2415 Aloma Ave., Winter Park (tel. 677-7352), is a yuppie favorite and for good reasons: good food served in a casual but chic atmosphere at good prices in the $10 to $15 range for dinner. Hours are 11:30am to 10pm daily at this spot that used to be called Charlie's Blue Crab "but we didn't have much blue crab on the menu so now it's Charlie's Lobster House because we have lobster." Can't beat reasoning like that. People here at this casual spot are as pleasant and frank as that quote suggests. They're also successful: They've opened two more of these restaurants, **Charlie's Lobster House** in Mercado at 8445 International Dr. (tel. 352-6929) and **Riverview Charlie's** over on the east coast at 101 Flagler Ave. in New Smyrna Beach (tel. 904/428-1865).

If there's nothing more beautiful in your world than a fat lobster claw staring up at you, head for **Murphy's Lobster House,** 4736 W. Irlo Bronson Memorial Hwy., Kissimmee (tel. 396-7469 or in Orlando, 239-7171), where that crustacean occupies a prominent place on a menu that also features steaks and other varieties of seafood for prices in the $13 to $36 range, depending on how the commodities market is ranking lobster prices these days. A yuppie or aspiring-yuppie haven, this enclave also has a big dance emporium next door at Murphy's Vine Street Emporium. More on that under nightlife.

**Shells,** 852 Lee Rd., Winter Park (tel. 628-3968), is a restaurant chain that showed up in Florida recently and has met with considerable success. Small wonder, for the seafood here is good, simply prepared, and priced to please minimalist wallets. A very casual spot with picnic tables and minimalist decor, Shells has such bargains as a dozen oysters for under $2 and full dinners for prices in the $5 to $13 range. Hours here are 5 to 10pm weekdays, closing an hour later on weekends.

Crowds of the hungry have been beating a path to **L & N Seafood Grille,** 1375 Semoran Blvd., Casselberry (tel. 657-0201), for years now to tuck into the mesquite-grilled seafood prepared by skilled cookers here. If there's a fish that's not on the L & N menu, I can't imagine what it is. And best of all, the workers here *know* fish and can reel off the list of possibilities then answer your questions about the more unfamiliar options. Good service, homemade biscuits, and a "bottomless" bowl of salad (translation: All you can eat) are what keep them so busy here. You'll find complete dinner prices in the $9 to $25 range and hours are 11:30am to 10pm daily, closing an hour later on Friday and Saturday. Sunday brunch is served from 11am to 3pm. You'll find the restaurant 5.5 miles from I-4 and just north of Howell Ranch Road.

Their name may not be glamorous, but **Bucket's Bar and Grill,** 1825 N. Mills Ave., Orlando (tel. 894-5197), is a handsome spot that draws crowds in search of top quality food with an emphasis on seafood and, of course, buckets of oysters. Plunked down right on one of Orlando's lovely blue lakes, Bucket's offers lovely views through big windows yet retains a nice intimate atmosphere. It's right across the street from Loch Haven Park if you're stopping by one of the attractions there. You'll pay about $12 to $18 for dinner and the hours here are 11am to midnight weekdays, closing at 2am weekends.

**Shucker's Oyster Bar of Orlando,** 5620 S. Orange Blossom Trail (tel. 857-2754), is a lively place brimming with fresh seafood, buckets of oysters and plenty of beer, wine, and margaritas for accompaniments. There are always all-you-can-eat specials here at Shucker's, where you can begin your oyster aphrodisiacs early: Hours are 10:30am to 2am daily.

## STEAKS

Probably the best-known and certainly one of the longest-lived steak houses in the area is **Freddie's Steak & Seafood House,** 7355 Hwy. 17/92 on Rte. 17/92 in Fern Park (tel. 339-3265), where a kind of good-ol'-boy masculinity has determined the decor and the menu. Not much fancy French stuff here, just big thick steaks, a brimming relish tray, crocks of Cheddar cheese, several hearty breads, delicately pink prime rib, some seafood selections, ham glazed in rum, bananas, and coconut. You'll struggle out of here as content as the thousands who have preceded you. Bills will run in the $15 to $20 range, and Freddie's is open from 5:30pm to 2am, later on weekends. Entertainment in the lounge evenings.

I love restaurants that offer a challenge, and 2.5 pounds of T-bone is *definitely* a challenge. Where? **La Cantina,** 4721 E. Colonial Dr. (tel. 894-4491). This gargantuan eating has been going on here for nigh onto 40 years, in an attractive dining room that features a fireplace, fountain, and sunken conversation pit. Beef is aged and cut right here, and when the butchers are not slashing away, they're stirring the sauce for delicious manicotti, ravioli, and veal. Prices are in the $10 to $20 range, and the restaurant's open from 5pm to 11pm (later on weekends). Closed Sunday and Monday.

**Charley's Steak House,** 6107 S. Orange Blossom Trail (tel. 851-7130), prides itself on the care and feeding of the multitudes who never met a steak they didn't love. Aged beef is cooked over a natural wood-burning fire using a method the restaurant says was inspired by Seminole cookery. Seafood fans will find Australian lobster tails—big ones—on the menu, plus a fresh-catch item daily, and langostinos. Charley's also is one of the few places in town you can find pork chops. A big salad bar is included with dinner entrées, which range in price from $10 to $20. Charley's is open seven days for dinner from 4:30 to 10:30pm (half hour later on Friday and Saturday).

**Barney's Steaks and Seafood,** 1615 E. Colonial Dr., Orlando (tel. 896-6865), gets rave reviews for its top-notch steaks and prime rib and seafood creations, and more top marks for a gigantic salad bar with more than 30 offerings to satisfy the rabbit in you. Many, many Orlandoites swear by Barney's, which has been serving top-quality beef long enough to win a dedicated following. Try it, and you'll join the throngs. Open 11:30am to 4:30am daily. Prices are in the $11.50 to $22 range.

Crocodile Dundee's homeland gets a little attention here in Orlando at the **Outback,** an elegant woodsy, plantsy spot "down under" the Buena Vista Palace Hotel, Lake Buena Vista, in the Walt Disney World Village Hotel Plaza (tel. 827-2727). Thick steaks and giant lobsters are the fare here and can be so large they're downright unfair fare. Occasionally, a British favorite, like Yorkshire pudding, steak-and-kidney pie, or bubble-and-squeak turns up on the menu. Still, for my money, it would be sacrilege not to take advantage of the steak-sizzling efforts here. Outback prices are in the $16 to $25 range for dinner entrées, and hours are 6 to 11pm daily. English ales? You betcha. Something like 72 different kinds of bubblies on the list here.

## LIGHT MEALS

Who cares what they serve at a restaurant called **LePeep.** That's one you have to try just because. So what do they serve? Well, LeBreakfast, LeLunch, and LeBrunch, of course. Silly question. You'll find lots of interesting egg and skillet dishes on the menu here, plus pancakes, salads, soups and what they like to call "knife and fork sandwiches" for prices in the $3 to $5 range for most selections. Hours are 6:30am to 2:30pm weekdays, opening at 7am and closing at 7:30pm Saturday and Sunday. LePeep chirps at 250 S. Orange Ave. in the Sun Bank Building (tel. 849-0428) and at 4666 Kirkman Rd. (tel. 291-4580).

Crispy pecan waffles, yummy ice cream, towering sandwiches —do I have your attention? I thought so. Now that you're listening, take this culinary advice: try **Elliott's**, 327 Park Ave. S., Winter Park (tel. 629-0222), serves such delicacies by the carload every day of the week. There's no dearth of attendees here, you can bet, for two good reasons. One is those sin-laden desserts supplemented by deli sandwiches and crispy, crunchy salads; creamy cheesecakes; and strudels to die for. The other is the decor: brick walkways, an absolute jungle of growing things, paddle fans that cool inside, and a cozy little patio that lures al fresco diners outside. Prices are wonderful, too; most are in the $5 range. Elliott's is open from 8am to midnight Monday through Thursday, to 1am on Friday and Saturday, and from 10am to midnight on Sunday.

## INDIAN

Once you tune into the exotic tastes of India, you'll be a devotee forever, guaranteed. Get a start on those tastes at **Punjab Indian Restaurant,** 7451 International Dr., Orlando (tel. 352-7887). From the clay ovens called tandoors pour marinated meats and unleavened bread, curries, and herbed treats not to be missed. Entrée prices are in the $6 to $12 range at Punjab, which is open 11:30am to 11pm daily.

At **Darbar,** 7600 Dr. Phillips Blvd., #28 in Orlando's The Marketplace shopping center (tel. 345-8128), Moghul mystics are conjured up with early-17th-century decor and the fabulous flavors of India. Darbar is open from 6 to 10:30pm daily, closing an hour earlier on Sunday. Prices are in the $8 to $15 range.

## BUDGET AND FAMILY SPOTS

Many are the fans of **Mack Meiner's Country Store,** 921 N. Mills Ave., Orlando (tel. 896-5902), where you down chili, soups, barbecued specialties, and heavenly hash pie in an atmosphere that's just what the restaurant's name implies. Add oilcloth and kitchen chairs, old movie posters and ads, a player piano and sheet music, and you've got a spot to tie on the feedbag while keeping the young ones amused. Prices are in the $7 to $12 range, and Mack's is open from 10am to 10pm daily.

A longtime favorite in many areas of Florida is **Morrison's Cafeteria** at 7440 International Dr. (tel. 351-0051). Morrison's serves food much loved by many and plenty of it in very reasonable price brackets: $5 to $7 for dinner or less, depending on the state of your gluttony. It's open 7:30 to 10am and 11am to 9pm. There are three other Morrison's—in Winter Park, Altamonte Springs, and on Colonial Drive.

Pianist George Shearing loves the matzoh ball soup, and jazz star Maynard Ferguson has stopped by to sample the goodies at **Ronnie's,** 2702 E. Colonial Dr., in the Colonial Plaza Shopping Center, Orlando (tel. 894-2943). At Sunday breakfast you need a shoehorn to wedge yourself into the crowd here. No wonder, with prices in the $5 to $10 range for nearly anything in this famous place, less for many selections. Bowls of kosher dills and sauerkraut, cheesecake fluffy as cotton, rated the city's best by critics, guilt-spawning pastries. Hours are 7am to 11pm weekdays, two hours later on weekends.

**TGI Friday's,** at 227 Rte. 436 W., Altamonte Springs (tel. 869-8085), is a place where the waiters are liable to break into song. Bells ring, things whirr and buzz, and everyone has a great, if a little crazy, time here. There are several TGI Friday's in Florida, and all of them offer a multipage menu of soups and salads, desserts and appetizers, sandwiches and full-course meals. Things can get pretty weird here, but the food attracts the young, with-it set, who munch happily on potato skins and the like as waiters cavort among the moose heads and old buckets. Prices are in a reasonable under-$10 bracket, and hours are 11:30am to 2am daily. An outstanding Sunday brunch is on from 11 to 3pm.

If you're staying on International Drive, you'll find **Darryl's 1883 Restaurant and Tavern,** 8282 International Dr. (tel. 351-1883), a pleasant place to while away a couple of hours. All weathered wood, etched glass, and the like, the restaurant has something for absolutely every taste bud ranging from pasta to salads to Mexican food, burgers, steaks, sandwiches, seafood, ribs—you name it, they've got it somewhere. Prices are quite reasonable, falling easily in the $5 to $7 bracket for many menu selections, $8 to $13 for full dinners. Hours are 11am to 2am daily.

Here's a place you'll find most anywhere you turn in Central Florida: **Holiday House.** There are 14 of these attractive and inexpensive restaurants around, including one at 1522 Orange Ave. (tel. 425-1521), and another at 2037 Lee Rd., Orlando (tel. 293-4930), more in Winter Park, Mount Dora, and Deland. You eat well here, if simply, and are served likewise. Best news, however, is the price of $6.69 for a dinner buffet, $5.39 for lunch. They're open from 11am to 3pm and from 4 to 8:30pm daily.

Many near-Disney motels also operate restaurants where the atmosphere is family-casual and the prices are, in a word, wonderful.

One of these is **Davis Brothers Motor Lodge,** 6603 International Dr. (tel. 351-2900), which has a long and luscious smörga[dt]sbord, all you can eat, for $4.95 at breakfast, $4.95 for lunch, and $6.95 for dinner, children 2 to 8 half price. It's open from 7 to 10:30am, 11:30am to 2pm, and 5 to 8:30pm daily.

**Village Inn,** 345 W. Fairbanks, Winter Park (tel. 645-5767), offers good food at reasonable prices in a quiet, attractive atmosphere. You'll pay about $5 to $10 for a long list of choices that range from steaks to fantail shrimp—and those prices include beverage and dessert. Hours are 7am to 11pm Sunday through Thursday, around the clock Friday and Saturday.

Some gourmets, or is that gourmands, of my acquaintance will drive to the ends of the earth for a product born and bred in the Midwest and called Chili Mac. Producer of this delicacy is none other than a chain operation called **Steak and Shake,** which much to the regret of a few, at least, operates in Florida only from Central Florida north. So if you're planning to head south after Disney, get your fill of Chili Mac here at 2820 E. Colonial Dr. (tel. 896-0827), where burger prices are under $3. There are other representatives of these midwestern gourmet delights scattered about town, too, and they're open 24 hours.

Cuban restaurants have proliferated all over Florida, thanks to the hard work and culinary talents of the many Cubans who have settled here in the past three decades. Many of those have finally made it up to Central Florida, where they discovered that even among meat-and-potato folks there's a taste for cheap and quite wonderfully exotic *Cubano* cuisine. You can always feast for $10 to $15 for dinner at a Cuban restaurant, and often for about half that.

Tops among the choices in these parts is **Numero Uno,** 2499 S. Orange Ave., Orlando (tel. 841-3840) where the menu tops out with bountiful order-in-advance paella for two for $30 but most selections are $6 to $15. Hours are 11am to 9:30pm daily except Wednesday.

Every bit as good is **El Bohio Café,** 5756 Dahlia Dr., Orlando (tel. 282-1723), a favorite of many localites who flock in here for boliche, ropa viejo, and the like for prices in the $5 to $15 range. Hours are 11am to 9pm daily except Monday.

Two others with the same price range and similar offerings: **Medina's Café,** 2405 E. Washington St., Orlando (tel. 894-2206), open 11am to 10pm daily except Sunday; and **La Lechonera Restaurant,** 2420 Curry Ford Rd., Orlando (tel. 894-6711), open 11am to 9pm daily.

**Olive Garden,** 7653 International Dr. (tel. 351-1082), has become a favorite throughout Florida in recent years. You will find one of these modestly priced Italian restaurants here in Orlando on International Drive, where its handsome architectural accoutrements help it stand out from the crowd of eateries around it. You'll find a variety of pasta and Italian specialties on the menu here, at prices that fall easily in the $6 to $13 range. That includes lots of tossed salad, a vegetable, and quite good garlic bread sticks. Open from 7:30am to 10:30pm daily, the Olive Garden doesn't take reservations and is popular enough to draw a crowd on many evenings.

## A SPECIAL PLACE

A restaurant called **Al E. Gator's** obviously doesn't fit into just any category, so I'm putting it in this special one, by itself. It is Sea World's best sit-down restaurant, where you can try—are you ready?—a piece of alligator tail. Don't fret. Alligators have been so carefully protected in Florida, they're no longer an endangered species, so Sea World can sell the meat and never fear the forest ranger. That, of course, is not all they offer at Al E. Gator's, far from it. There are sandwiches and full meals, salads and desserts, plenty of choices from conch chowder to crab quiche, and other exotic specialties like mango muffins and Caribbean foods including Jamaica jerk pork and a Bermuda Triangle salad. Open daily during park hours, Al E. Gator's is at Sea World, 7001 Sea World Blvd. (tel. 351-3600). Prices range from $10 to $15 for full meals.

# V

# AFTER DARK IN DISNEY WORLD AND ORLANDO

Mature and adult as you think you are, there will come a moment when you seriously consider pushing some little kid out of the way so you can get a better view of Mickey and Minnie as they go cavorting by in the Main Street Electrical Parade. While children love Disney World, adults who have learned all too much about the differences between reality and fantasy tend to worship this place.

Sooner or later, however, the general wear and tear of the crowds, the lines, the hot dogs and popcorn—the sheer thrilling exhaustion of it all—grinds away some of the magic for grownups. (Everyone knows those youngsters would go on riding the rides for a week, nonstop, if it weren't for the fun-squelching presence of parents.)

When the consensus finally reaches a no-more-that's-final stage, that is a sign it's time to ease off a bit, to slow down and consider taking a breather. Working on the assumption that parents are people, too, it would be wise to seek relief in the form of some evening entertainment that excludes ducks who quack jokes.

Because Central Florida is an area geared to families, you'll find plenty of wholesome entertainment that's as intriguing for adults as it is interesting to children. Fortunately, that means you can take the children with you, if you like, to many of the top fun spots and, in fact, to all activities inside Disney World, where *wholesome* is practically emblazoned on the Disney family crest.

Orlando's not much on razzle-dazzle nightclubs though, so if that's your style, you'll have to travel a little farther south to Miami and environs or wait for a trip to Las Vegas. There is this good news, however: What entertainment you do find here is not expensive, so a night on the town won't cost you two days on the job.

One more thing: Except for the main events, which I'll outline, nightlife in the Orlando area changes frequently, so don't hold me to every word. Hotels and clubs that do offer diverting evening entertainment will always have something going, but you'd do well to give them a call to find out what exactly is happening this week or this season.

Here then is a look at the amusing and amazing ways you can

spend an evening in Central Florida. Once again, I've divided all the action up into two parts. That way, if you're staying in or near Disney World and don't feel like straying far from home, you'll be able to see at a glance what's happening in WDW. On the other hand, if you feel like exploring a little, you can turn to the Orlando section of this chapter and — go.

# IN DISNEY WORLD

Perhaps the most wonderful thing about fantasies is that you can have them any time, any place, at any hour of the night or day. That's probably part of the reason Disney World keeps its fantasies going from early morning until well into the dark hours. You'll find everything here, from stirring tributes to a nation the British once considered a fantasy to laughing, lollygagging parades of the cartoonist's fantastic characters.

You'll find hula hands telling stories of distant Polynesian lands, ingenuous young faces forming human Christmas trees, Broadway's hottest performers belting it out, jazz artists playing it cool, campfire singers, sparkling parades, and an explosion of fireworks that dazzles your senses as it shatters the silence and sends pinpoints of fiery light into ebony skies.

It's all waiting for you in this, the most magic of Magic Kingdoms, so without further ado, let's take a look at all the things there are to do after the sun goes down here in the world Walt Disney created.

Tops among the entertaining possibilities for both youngsters and adults is the Magic Kingdom's **Main Street Electrical Parade,** which takes place at 9 and 11pm daily in busy seasons, including Easter, summer vacations, and Christmas. Quite a dramatic event it is, too. An announcer solemnly says the parade's about to start, the twinkling lights of Main Street suddenly go black, and at the top of the street . . . there they are! Mickey, Minnie, Pluto, Dumbo, Snow White, and Pinocchio happily waving from their perches aboard dozens of floats, trimmed wheel to whistle in a glittering rainbow of tiny lights. Slowly the parade, augmented by bands and at Christmas by hundreds of choral singers, winds its glowing way down the darkened street, back-dropped by the towers and turrets of Cinderella Castle soaring into dark skies. Everything sparkles, including an occasional teardrop, as the fantasyland's procession moves slowly down the packed street.

Women's liberation has at last arrived in Mousedom! Mickey's cohort Minnie now sometimes struts her stuff as star of the daily character parade down Main Street, U.S.A. Of course, Mickey is still there cavorting his way down the macadam. She's now also starring in a show at Tomorrowland's Fantasy Faire pavilion, where you can see her kicking up her heels several times a day, accompanied by a supporting cast of Disney characters. Folks at City Hall can tell you when you'll be able to see this famous mousette.

Where should you go to see the parade? Well, this is one jam-packed event, so chances are you won't have much choice. The best spot, however, is in the center of the platform at Walt Disney World's Railroad Depot, where you get a fabulous view of the floats as they twist around the Town Square. If you don't manage a good spot there, settle happily for a place along the curb of Main Street, where hundreds of others will be settling as well.

Try to stake out a spot for yourself an hour or so ahead of time, but if you can't keep the squirmers in your crowd busy that long, just join all the others. It doesn't matter all that much since the floats tower over the crowds, and it's the general impression of light and music and laughter that's the magic of it all anyway.

Naturally, the 9pm parade is the busiest, since most of the small fry need to be tucked away before the 11pm extravaganza. If you're looking for the least crowded conditions, opt for the later parade. It's every bit as glittering.

There's one more possible viewing spot: a stool at Pecos Bill's restaurant in Frontierland. It's right on the parade route, which incidentally begins at Main Street, then goes around the east half of the Hub, across Liberty Square Bridge, and through Frontierland.

More electrical magic? Step right up to the beach and see the **Electrical Water Pageant,** featuring 1,000 feet of illuminated creatures floating merrily across the lake on which the Polynesian Village, Fort Wilderness, the Contemporary, and River Country are located. This watery wonder winds its way around the lake, appearing at the Polynesian about 9pm, at River Country and Fort Wilderness at 9:45, at the Contemporary about 10pm, and in the park itself about 10:20pm, on nights the park is open late. Check at Guest Services of City Hall to see if the show's going on while you're there and when and where you can go to get a look.

If you've read the section about hotels in Disney World, you've already discovered two other major evening events here, the luau at **Polynesian Village** and the every-evening entertainment at the **Contemporary Hotel's Top of the World Show.**

That luau is a touch of exotica that provides a different kind of fantasy altogether, the fantasy of sandy islands, waving palms, seductive music of the South Seas, graceful dancers, and brave warriors. Presented every night at 6:45 and 9:30pm, the luau features a rib-sticking dinner of Polynesian treats. Here's your chance to try some poi and wash away the taste with pineapple, to watch beautiful dancers tell island stories with graceful hands and assorted other parts, and to listen to the hypnotic thudding of the war drums. Cost of the show is $29 for adults, $23 for children 12 to 20, and $15 for children 3 to 11.

Meanwhile, over at the Top of the World in the Contemporary Hotel, there's a razzle-dazzle "Broadway at the Top" show in full swing. Featuring Broadway tunes, the Top of the World packs them in for its dinner and entertainment, which goes on stage at 7:45 and 11pm nightly (dinner seating at 6 and 9:15pm). Entertainment and hours may change, so call to find out what's going on this week. Charge for the show is $42.50 for adults, $19.90 for children 3 to 11.

You and/or the youngsters can dine at the **Trophy Room** in Disney Inn. You'll munch on prime rib, chicken, or fish. Dinner is $13 to $35 and reservations are required. Make them at 824-8000.

An evening aboard the **_Empress Lilly_** is among the more memorable events you can pencil in on your visit to Disney World. Dine in one of the handsome restaurants aboard this fairy-tale craft, then stop in for some rip-roarin' fun at the Baton Rouge Lounge, where you may be treated to some lively banjo-strumming entertainment, a guitarist, a group of entertainers—who knows what? Always funny and always fun, this is an amusing way to while away some evening hours. Things keep going until 1am here, and you can order specialty drinks by the pitcher. There's no cover charge or minimum either.

Those who prefer to keep their entertainment on an informal jeans-and-plaid-shirt level will love the **Hoop-Dee-Doo Musical Revue** at Fort Wilderness campgrounds. An every-evening event that goes on stage at 5, 7:30, and 10pm, this is one of the park's most popular shows and is often booked far in advance. Call 824-8000 for reservations and don't waste any time doing it. It's so popular partly because children love it, partly because adults love it, and partly because it's so good. First they feed you to a fare-thee-well with ribs and chicken, corn on the cob, strawberry shortcake, and the like, and then they get you laughing so hard you don't know whether you're choking from laughter or all that food. Vivacity they've got, these performers, and enthusiasm they've got—and get—from an appreciative audience that joins right in for these whoop-and-holler evenings. Join them. Show and dinner price is $30 for adults, $24 for youngsters 13 to 18, and $16 for children 3 to 12.

One other good time in Fort Wilderness is a good old-fashioned campfire evening. Called the **Marshmallow Marsh Excursion**, this novel evening of summer-only activity begins with a canoe excursion through the waterways, moves along to a campfire sing-along, and winds up with a marshmallow roast at a lakeside vantage point from which participants ogle the 9:45pm Electrical Water Pageant. Cost is $6 for adults, $5 for children 3 to 12, and reservations are necessary for these shows which take place only in June, July, and August. Call 824-2788, or go to the ticket booth at Pioneer Hall.

There's also a nightly **Campfire Program** at Fort Wilderness's Meadow Trading Post, complete with sing-along, Disney movies and cartoons, and Chip 'n' Dale often on hand to keep'em giggling. It's free.

Movies? Of course. For evenings when the feet simply will not go a foot farther, head over to the Contemporary Resort, where WDW guests can watch Disney features in the theater near the Fiesta Fun Center. Hours are usually 6pm to 2am, but you might check at the hotel to be sure and to find out what's playing.

Although there's a no-liquor policy in the Magic Kingdom itself, there are a number of cocktail lounges in Disney-MGM Studios, EPCOT, the four Disney resorts areas, and in the Walt Disney World Shopping Village in Lake Buena Vista. Here's a look at some of the lounges where you might find a respite from the activities around you.

You'll find that Polynesian theme right in your glass at Polynesian Village Hotel. There's a long list of exotic tropical drinks, ranging from basic piña coladas and Mai-Tais to creations with names like Blue Lagoon—it really is blue—Seven Seas, and Chi Chis. All these and more are stirred up at **Tambu Lounge** beside the Papeete Bay Verandah, where there's also nightly entertainment, and the **Barefoot Bar** out by the swimming pool.

In the Contemporary Resort, the fourth-floor **Outer Rim Lounge** is a tranquil spot to contemplate days past and future from seats overlooking the lake. Appetizers are served here until 11:30pm each night. There's a pleasant lounge adjoining the hotel's Top of the World room. From a seat there you can hear the lively entertainment that goes on there although you won't be able to see the show from the lounge. Finally, the resort's Sand Bar down by the marina features a piña colada with a twist—ice cream.

Special concoctions are a feature at the Disney Inn's lounge, where you can gaze out over the greens while you sample a Double Eagle (tequila sour floating on Kahlúa) or an Unplayable Lies (champagne and Southern Comfort nestled around a whole frozen apricot).

In Lake Buena Vista at Walt Disney World Village Hotel Plaza, all five hotels have cool hideaways, some with entertainment, some just for sitting.

At Grosvenor Resort **Moriarty's** has a pubby atmosphere, darts, and chess.

Hotel Royal Plaza's **La Cantina** sparks cocktail hour with oyster, shrimp, and crab raw-bar specialties, and the **Giraffe** disco maintains a frenetic pace to the wee hours. That disco, by the way, is the only one in WDW, thus making it a popular spot for Disney employees. It features a purple, yellow, and deep-green color scheme that's a dazzler, plus substantial happy-hour hors d'oeuvres that make the Giraffe a popular spot for early evening snacking, too.

Viscount's **Top of the Tower** offers a Magic Kingdom view that is nothing short of spectacular, and there's dancing and entertainment to boot.

**Howard Johnson Resort Hotel** has a cozy lounge, too.

Finally, there are a couple of lively locales in Walt Disney World Shopping Village. **Cap'n Jack's Oyster Bar** produces a happy combination of potables and seafood treats, and the **Village Lounge** features excellent jazz entertainment in comfortable surroundings.

The *Empress Lilly* has two lounges in addition to the lively Baton Rouge Lounge mentioned earlier: the **Promenade Lounge** and the **Starboard Lounge.**

Disney World's answer to Orlando's famed Rosie O'Grady's Church Street Station is **Pleasure Island,** a new Disney-thing-to-do that is also the park's first real attempt at an evening entertainment area and the first time it's delved into the world of alcoholic beverages.

Here, too, Disney has dreamed up a legend around which it has built a theme. Pleasure Island, you see, is an abandoned waterfront district and in it are six nightclubs, a half dozen restaurants and snack facilities, and a dozen shops, interspersed with street entertainment.

According to this "legend," Merriweather Adam Pleasure began calling this six-acre island home a hundred years ago when leisure yachting was capturing the imagination of the monied. Then, lo and behold, Merriweather, by now a millionaire, headed off to circumnavigate the globe but was soon numbered among the lost-at-sea. His private island, Pleasure Island, of course, fell into disrepair, abetted by the sloth of Merriweather's lazy kin.

The island became a lost island of abandoned lofts, warehouses, and factories with, nevertheless, something for everyone.

For openers you can combine dancing and dining here at the **Zephyr Rockin' RollerDrome.** All this rocking and rolling takes place in what, according to legend, was once a wind tunnel where Merriweather developed a weird flying vessel. Here you dance in the middle of the room outside, and ogle a band and disc jockey as they hang suspended from the ceiling in a moving space vehicle.

**Mannequins** is a cavernous warehouse in which merry ole Merriweather stored his canvases. High tech turns on here in a world of stage rigging, lights, and catwalks trimming a turntable dance floor. Animated and live mannequins don different costumes each night, machines make bubbles—and snow!

There's nothing more important to a teen than being seen, so for them: **Videopolis East,** a place rife with nonalcoholic beverages, music videos, a stainless steel dance floor, banks of video monitors, flash, and glitter.

Guests at this club must be *under* 18; if you're older than that, you must be accompanied by someone under 18, so there. A dance-till-you-drop spot, Videopolis has interactive video screens—if you get the right answer to the video Q & A, you get to control the lights and sounds for a few minutes. Wild, child.

Ooooooooo, who is that wisp? Perhaps it is Merriweather himself, dropping his ghostly form in for an evening of merriment at **Adventurers Club.** Right at home here among the handsome paneled recesses and glowing mahogany bookcases, Merriweather and his ghostly friends are joined by club members intent on swapping sea sagas in storytelling sessions. "Explore the unknown, discover the impossible" is the advice posted at the entrance and this spot certainly seems a likely place to do just that.

Get your yuks in the **Comedy Warehouse,** where comedians get you giggling in another unusual environment, Merriweather's former power plant. Improvisational comedy troupes host a bill of stand-up comics and vaudevillian performances.

What would life be like without a neon armadillo? You won't find out at the **Neon Armadillo Music Saloon,** where country-and-western, jazz, and cabaret performances take place in a lounge decked out in Southwest memorabilia—including a spur chandelier!

As for food:

**Portobello Yacht Club** features pizzas created in a wood-burning oven and outstanding pasta creations served in Merriweather Pleasure's former home, an elegant pastel architectural wonder with Bermuda overtones.

Spicy barbecued treats fit fittingly in at the legendary **Fireworks Factory,** where gunpowder-blackened floors attest to Merriweather's somewaht dubious pyrotechnic skills. Here long-necked beers are served from big tin buckets.

Grazing, the new gourmet rage, is the order of the day, however, with fun-food grazing stands set up to tempt with fancy ice creams, frozen yogurt, candies, and coffees at all the dance clubs, too.

You'll find all these treasures in Lake Buena Vista Village, right near the *Empress Lilly* riverboat, which remains at its dock. To keep the island theme going, footbridges connect Pleasure Island with the rest of the world. There is no admission charge to the island.

# ORLANDO NIGHTLIFE

To start at the top of Orlando's evening entertainment offerings is without question to start at **Rosie O'Grady's** (Church Street Station; tel. 422-2434), the Disney World of Orlando's nightlife. Rosie's is—here comes that word again—wholesome, and, above all, Rosie's is *fun.*

From the first moment you hear the wheezing wail of the huge calliope that occupies center stage outside Rosie's, you'll know you've landed somewhere special. Rosie's and all the wacky fun that now surrounds it got started a few years back, after Orlando lured Disney World here, thereby giving the city a hearty shove into Tomorrowland.

That successfully accomplished, Orlando began to seek its roots. It wasn't long before developers discovered Church Street, where a decrepit but historic hotel and railroad depot somehow remained standing after years of neglect. Here began a concerted effort to bring the past back to life. That aging railroad station, topped by a shining silver cupola, became the center of redevelopment, and Rosie O'Grady's moved in to become the center of the center.

Today you'll find here a rip-roarin' Gay 90s (or is that Roaring 20s?) atmosphere in the restaurants, the saloons, and even a whirling dervish of a disco. Step in the door and you're surrounded by an array of plants, antiques and brass, stained glass and skylights, and a rabbit warren of fascinating places to prowl. Peek around a corner and you come face to face with an ornate confessional from a French monastery (it's in the pub). Turn a bend and stumble on train benches from an old railroad station, cast-iron tables from an English pub, huge brass chandeliers salvaged from a Boston bank, teller's cages (vintage 1870) from a Pittsburgh bank.

When you've absorbed all that, move on to Rosie's four fun centers. First, there's Rosie O'Grady's Good-Time Emporium, complete with a red-hot mama in a slinky dress, a crooning minstrel singer who dances his way around the room—across the tops of the benches you're sitting on—and kicky cancan girls clacking across the bar. Then there's Apple Annie's Courtyard, where you can dine on fat sandwiches, salads, and plum daiquiris to the sounds of bluegrass music. Next there's Lili Marlene's Aviator's Pub and Restaurant (see Chapter IV on dining in Orlando) for dinner in smashing surroundings.

Finally, you can hit the heights—literally—with a hot-air balloon trip under the auspices of Phineas Phogg's Balloon Works (about $148 per person) and a stop at ole Phineas's other hangout, a trendy disco complete with a balloon-basket balcony from which you can watch dancers cavort amid flashing strobes and puffs of fog.

Open from 11am to 2am daily, Rosie's is the top star in the Orlando firmament, a not-to-be-missed winner for fun and frolic. The evening cover charge is $14.95 adults, $9.95 children 4 to 13, and drinks are in the $3 range. You can take the huge glasses your drinks come in with you as a souvenir.

Across the street from Rosie's is the Cheyenne Saloon & Opera House, which features a whoop-de-doo country and western evening complete with twanging guitars, soulful singers, and stomping cloggers.

Children are welcome at Rosie's, and they won't feel a bit out of place, since many parents bring their youngsters here for a big night on the town. Skip the disco with the young ones, however.

**Sea World** lets very little seaweed grow under its feet in competition with Disney World for the tourist dollar. That's part of the reason you'll find, here, at the second most popular attraction in the Orlando area, a nightly Polynesian luau with everything from poi to pulsating Polynesian music and those talented dancers with 78-r.p.m. hips. This show is very popular, so take the time to make reservations at 351-3600 (ext. 442) for the 7:15pm event (seating begins at 6:45pm). Charge for dinner and show is $24.95 for adults, $17.95 for children 8 to 12, $9.95 for children 3 to 7.

Britain's lusty King Henry VIII and his bevy of beauteous brides are the focus of Orlando's nighttime fantasy spot, an evening of fun, feast, and general frolic known hereabouts as **King Henry's Feast.** Enter the fortified royal court and find yourself dropping back a few centuries to days of yore when that overstuffed monarch presided over many a zany evening.

Here in Orlando the fun begins with a sip of mead, that fermented honey-based drink that kept heads rolling back in Henry's day. From there, it's on to a five-course banquet accompanied by limitless quantities of beer, wine, and soft drinks. Lift a flagon with Henry as you work your way through a feast that begins with soup and proceeds through freshly baked brown bread, salad, a palate cleanser of rainbow sherbet, chicken and ribs with sauces, vegetables, potatoes, and a finale of chocolate mousse.

As you dine, court jesters clown around, a magician shows you some fancy digital work, singers warble up a madrigal storm, and dancers in traditional court dress of the period perform for sovereign and royal hangers-on. Reigning over it all is portly but happy Henry, king of all he surveys.

All this takes place in what surely is one of Orlando's stranger sights: a moated fortification that rises up in the midst of sleek hotels like a medieval hallucination. Created by a British company of considerable imagination, King Henry's Feast is a $3.5 million creation of English stone, brick, timber, and fancy roofing tiles, topped by a 60-foot tower.

You can dine here with royalty at $25.95 for adults, and $17.95 for children 3 to 11. Show and dinner start at 6 or 8:30pm. You will find Henry devouring everything in sight at his palace at 8984 International Dr. (tel. 351-5151 or toll free 800/776-3501).

The same British company went on up the street a piece, changed their accents from British clip to Creole drawl, and created another entertaining evening called **Mardi Gras** (tel. 351-5151 or toll free 800/770-3551). Designed to cash in on the nation's fascination with all things *Louisienne,* this new nightspot is tucked away in a shopping complex called Mercado Festival Center at 8445 International Drive.

Fun begins at 6 or 8:30pm each night, when you're presented with a frosty mint julep. From there, the evening moves on to thick gumbo, a pasta salad, and a choice of mustard-sauced "blackened" chicken created by a special quick grilling process using very high temperatures that seal in flavors, or the spicy flavors of Cajun-barbecued fish. Skillets of spicy red beans and jambalaya appear, accompanied by cornbread muffins and long-grain rice cooked with a Cajun smoked-pork sausage called andouille. All that's topped off by a praline parfait.

A jazz orchestra entertains during dinner, then the house lights dim and you're off on a fantasy trip to carnivals around the world— an evening in Paris, Carnival in the Caribbean, a night at the circus, complete with magicians, cancan girls, and glittery costumes. Admission is $25.95 for adults, and $17.95 for children 3 to 11. Dinner and show are at 6 or 8:30pm daily with seating beginning earlier and the show's about two hours.

Not content with Shakespeare and New Orleans as fanciful evening entertainments, that same group, Orlando Entertains, went on the warpath with a gaggle of cowboys and Indians who whoop it up every night at **Fort Liberty,** 5260 Irlo Bronson Memorial Hwy., Kissimmee (tel. 351-5151; or toll free 800/641-5151; in Florida 800/521-5152). Get out those pointy-toed boots and that 10-gallon hat and hie on over to the fort for a rollicking evening of food and fun. Sprawling across 11 acres, this huge fort offers more than a good horse and a plate o' beans: here they toss in barbecued pork and southern fried chicken, unlimited wine and beer. As with this organization's other two shows, you can get in on the act yourself if you like—there's lots of audience participation. Or you can just sit back and watch the antics of a Buffalo Bill traveling medicine show. Price of this Western chuckle is $25.95 adults, $17.95 children 3 to 11.

As long as you're in the spirit of the thing, how about an evening among jousting knights and fair damsels? This one's called **Medieval Times,** a family entertainment that comes complete with dinner and show. Here medieval days come to life as armored knights on horseback race off to defend their honor—or someone else's. Lots of swordplay accompanied by plenty of chicken, ribs, pastry, and light potables. You're welcomed into the castle at 6 or 8pm and the show begins at 7 or 9pm daily at Medieval Times, 4510 Irlo Bronson Memorial Hwy. (US 192), Kissimmee (tel. 396-1518). Prices are $26 adult and $18 children 3 to 12.

Want to change that shoot-em-up scenery a bit? Then pack up your tents and head over to **Arabian Nights,** 6225 W. Irlo Bronson Memorial Hwy., Kissimmee (tel. 351-5822; or toll free 800/553-6116; in Florida 800/443-0492). On these grounds live more than 60 horses, ranging from those high-stepping airs-above-the-ground Lippizan stallions to purebred, worth-a-fortune Arabian stallions, fancy-stepping Percherons and Andalusians, speedy quarter horses, big-footed Clydesdales—even a 30-inch-high miniature pony named Mike, who will certainly steal your heart. A princess and her genie, seated on a magic carpet, reign over this horsey event, which features riding of all kinds from dressage to speed-for-speed's sake. As one employee put it: "This is really the horses' show; people are riding them but it's the horses that are important." Now that's a true horse lover's view of it—maybe it will be yours, too. Fee for a visit is $25.95 adults, $16.95 children 3 through 11 and that includes a dinner of French onion soup, a whole chicken, ribs, the works including beer, wine, or soft drinks, plus the show, of course. Show time is 7:30pm most of the time but may vary by as much as an hour in some seasons; sometimes there are two nightly shows.

If you simply cannot make it to Oktoberfest this year, settle for a yodel and an oom-pah-pah at **Bavarian Bierhaus,** 7340 Republic Dr., Orlando (tel. 351-0191). Fat pretzels, rollicking good humor, strudel, wienerschnitzel, spaetzle, dumplings, and barrels and more barrels of German—and homemade—good spirits, literally and figuratively. There's no cover charge here at this Bavarian hideaway tucked in behind Wet 'N Wild. Dinners are in the $7 to $12 range, and the Biergarten's open every night but Monday from 5pm until the last reveler pours out the door.

Whooooeee-eeee, what have we here? First you spot strings of lights. Then you realize they really *are* strings, the strings of a massive guitar that also happens to be the region's wildest new night restaurant, **Hard Rock Café.**

Part of a phenominally successful chain of restaurants, this Hard Rock Café is Florida's first. It's also the first to be built from the ground up by the company which usually incorporates its rocking spots into existing buildings. It's also the world's largest Hard Rock Café, nearly four times as large as the original London restaurant.

Designed in the shape of a huge electric guitar, this three-story showplace may be entered from Kirkman Road where you walk right down the 300-foot neck of the guitar, past silver tuning keys and under a translucent roof laced with fiber-optic guitar "strings." From Universal Studios you enter a record-shaped patio.

Once inside the three-story showplace, you can belly up to the guitar-shaped red cherrywood bar, gaze at two-story stained-glass tributes to Elvis, Chuck Berry, and Jerry Lee Lewis.

Here you'll find a huge collection of rock-and-roll memorabilia including an Elton John costume and an Elvis suit of lights, a jeweled outfit he wore in Las Vegas.

In the two shops here, walls are trimmed with bricks taken from the Beatles' first stage at the Tavern Club in Liverpool.

Outside two 1959 Cadillacs appear to have crashed into the building. Over the door is mounted yet another Cadillac.

Hard Rock Café focuses on burgers, chicken, salads, and desserts in the $6 to $13 range and plenty of the music that keeps packing 'em in here. Hard Rock Café, which has counterparts in London, Stockholm, Tokyo, New York, Dallas, Boston, and Washington, D.C., is open daily from 11am to 2am. Drinks are $2 to $4 and there is no cover charge. You'll find the cafe at 5800 Kirkman Rd. (tel. 363-ROLL).

As you might have noticed, theater plays a big part in everything that goes on here in Orlando, including nightlife. **Mark Two Dinner Theater,** 3376 Edgewater Dr., Orlando (tel. 843-6275), features a buffet dinner at 6:30pm and a Broadway musical at 8pm, Tuesday through Sunday, for $24 to $28. Dark Mondays, matinees at 1:15pm Wednesday and Saturday. Reservations are required.

Many, make that most, hotels in the Orlando area feature regular entertainment, ranging from country and western music (especially popular in this section of Florida) to easy listening and dancing music to a little comedic touch here and there.

Included among the most popular evening stopping spots are the **Days Inn Central** (4919 W. Colonial Dr.; tel. 299-8180), which at last check was featuring top 40 music; the **Hilton Inn Gateway** (7470 W. Hwy. 192; tel. 827-6257), where you can dine on homemade cornbread, barbecued ribs, and corn on the cob at a western cookout that's served with country music every Wednesday night from 8 to 10pm; two other **Hilton Inns** (at 7400 International Dr., tel. 351-4600, and at 3200 W. Colonial Dr. at John Young Pkwy., tel. 295-5270), both of which feature music for listening and dancing; **Limey Jim's** at the Orlando Hyatt (Hwy. I-4 and U.S. 192; tel. 239-4100); and the **Piccadilly Pub** in the Gold Key Inn (7100 S. Orange Blossom Trail; tel. 855-0050).

More? Of course. The **Langford Hotel** (at Interlachen and 300 East New England Ave. in Winter Park; tel. 644-3400) is among the top hotel entertainment spots in the area and features music for dancing, as well as showy entertainment and dazzling revues. Open Thanksgiving to Easter.

Also in Winter Park Le Cordon Bleu Restaurant's bar, **Harper's** (tel. 647-7575), is popular with students at nearby Rollins College and has entertainment every night except Sunday and Monday.

Young-but-getting-older white-collar types can be found in droves at **Bennigan's** (6324 International Dr., Orlando; tel. 351-4435) where happy hours are well-attended events.

**Shooter's** draws throngs of lookers and lookees to its sleek chic at 4315 N. Orange Blossom Trail (tel. 298-2855). Opened in 1990, this Orlando addition to an hysterically popular chain of watering holes is a likely candidate when you're in need of a view-ful sipping spot—it's on the shores of shimmering Lake Fairview—and can probably fulfill one or two other needs as well. It's open daily from 11:30 to 2am.

On a somewhat more esoteric level, the **Florida Symphony Orchestra** (tel. 896-0331) performs from September through May and the **Orlando Opera Company** (tel. 896-7575) warbles from about November to late March for ticket prices in the $16 to $45 range.

A Bach Festival of Winter Park (tel. 646-2110) takes place in the last week of February.

Orlando's **Southern Ballet Company** (tel. 628-0133) performs several times a year including presentations of the *Nutcracker* at Christmastime. Another dance group, **Dance Unlimited** (tel. 671-2155), has an annual February concert and a spring art festival at Leu Gardens, while the Dance Company of the **Academy of Dance and Theatrical Arts** (tel. 645-3847) has both a senior and children's company performing in spring and in June.

These dance, opera and symphonic events normally take place at the Bob Carr Performing Arts Center, a 2,500-seat auditorium at 401 Livingston St. (tel. 843-8111). Zev Bufman, Florida's premier play producer, brings his Broadway road shows here to the Carr also.

Lots of famous entertainers—folks like Engelbert Humperdinck, Jerry Vale, Patti Page, the Mantovani Orchestra, Roger Whittaker—turn up at the **Tupperware Convention Center,** P.O. Box 2353, Orlando 32802 (tel. 847-1800 in Kissimmee; 826-4475 in Orlando), which has a big auditorium for concerts. You'll find the center three miles north of Kissimmee on Fla. 17-92/US 441. Ticket prices vary.

Add to that **Annie Russell Theatre,** Box 2735 at Rollins College, a fascinating theater in the grand-Baroque style. A regular series of five productions here runs from October through May with children's theater in summer. Learn what is when by calling them at 646-2145. Rollins College is on Holt Avenue, just off Park Avenue in Winter Park and the theater is on the campus next door to Knowles Memorial Chapel. Tickets are in the $20 to $45 range.

**Central Florida Civic Theater,** 1010 Princeton St., Orlando (tel. 896-7365) has been lighting up the night with amateur and semiprofessional actors for nearly 60 years now. A community theater, the group now takes to the boards at Loch Haven Park, 1010 Princeton St., where the theater has been located for 10 of those 58 years. Curtain time for each of the theater's six plays from September to June is 8pm Wednesday through Saturday, with a 2pm matinee on Sunday. Season ticket prices are $60, about $25 less for students under 21. Individual tickets are $9 to $11.

To find out everything that is happening in the arts in Central Florida, pick up a copy of *Center State,* a monthly magazine with a centerfold calendar of events. Tickets can be booked at Select-A-Seat (tel. 628-5747). Another number for entertainment information is 644-1006. Check also the entertainment section of the *Orlando Sentinel* or several tourist-helper publications including *Orlando Magazine, Florida Tourist News,* and *See Orlando.*

Not far from Disney World, **Hollywood Lites,** once called The

Worst Bar (at Court of Flags Hotel, tel. 351-3340) has turned out to be one of the best in town. It's jam-packed almost all the time and features Hollywood memorabilia, drinks in the $2 to $4 range, and plenty of outrageous party happenings. Top-40 entertainment is the style produced here by live bands that begin about 9pm Tuesday through Saturday and keep things lively until 2am.

**Café on the Park** in the Harley Hotel, 151 E. Washington St. (tel. 841-3200) is a somewhat more sedate atmosphere—and a beautiful one—for dancing. It's open Monday through Saturday from 8pm to about midnight.

**Freddie's,** the popular steak house in Fern Park (Hwy 17/92, tel. 339-3265), has a vocalist entertaining every night but Sunday in the Lamplighter Lounge.

The elegant **Maison et Jardin** (430 S. Wymore Rd., Altamonte Springs; tel. 862-4410) has a warbling guitarist who entertains at dinner hours here and will serenade you with your favorite love song. You'll be enchanted.

**Townsend's Fish House and Tavern,** 35 W. Michigan St., Orlando (tel. 422-5560), has lots of yuppie-ville woodsy-plantsy atmosphere, marble bars and plenty of brass and copper trim. There's live entertainment here Wednesday through Saturday, a wine bar, and lots of burgers, fried vegetables and, of course, fish. There's no cover charge and hours are 11:30am to 2pm weekdays, and 5:30 to 10:30pm daily, with much later hours in the tavern. Early bird dinners are served from 5:30 to 6:30pm.

If you have a pressing desire to meet some of the Kids of the Kingdom on their off-duty hours, begin your search at the **Giraffe Lounge** at the Hotel Royal Plaza in Lake Buena Vista (tel. 828-2828) where they congregate. Top-40 music is on tap daily except Sunday here.

**J.J. Whispers,** 904 Lee Rd. (tel. 629-4779), has become quite a hot spot—perhaps the region's hottest—in recent years. Several nightclubs under one roof, this rocking spot is unmarked but you'll find it—just look for a million or so cars! The disco is called Shouts and is open Wednesday through Saturday. Whispers Show Room features a band for dancing Tuesday through Saturday and several smaller rooms are for those who want to hear themselves along with the music. Hours are 7pm to 2am and cover charge is $3 to $5.

**Sullivan's Trailway Lounge** is one of the few stayers on the Orlando nightlife scene. It's been around since the early 1970s. Often jammed, Sullivan's features such performers as Mel Tillis and Moe Bandy, but most of the time it's top touring and local country and western bands onstage at 1108 S. Orange Blossom Trail (tel. 843-2934). There's a $3 cover charge.

There's always a laugh to be had at the **Laughing Kookaburra,** in the Buena Vista Palace, 1900 Buena Vista Dr., Lake Buena Vista (tel. 827-2727). Billed as a "good time bar," it's also home to 99 bottles of beer on the wall—literally. They serve 99 varieties of domestic and imported suds. Contemporary show bands play for dancing and listening, and there are nightly specials and happy hours complete with hot and cold hors d'oeuvres. Open daily 4pm to 3am.

Upstairs, the **Top of the Palace Lounge** is much quieter as befits a spot with one of the region's most spectacular views of sunsets over Walt Disney World. You can sample a variety of different wines by the glass here.

**Murphy's Vine Street Emporium,** 4736 W. Irlo Bronson Memorial Hwy., Kissimmee (tel. 396-7469 or 239-7171), is where yuppies go for fun and games. For openers, there's dining in the Lobster House, where steak, seafood, and what the name would suggest are available at prices in the $13 to $25 range. There's also the Liberty Lounge, and, in a barrel of a building seating nearly 600 people, Murphy's Vine Street Emporium, a dance center with lots of flash and sizzle plus live entertainment weekdays and Sunday, a disc jockey and big-screen television entertainment on Sunday. Cover charge in the emporium is $2 weekdays, $3 Friday and Saturday.

A Florida land salesman once went to court to defend his sale of land to a buyer who claimed the land was worthless. That hapless buyer told the judge he'd bought the land because the developer told him he could grow nuts, coconuts, on it. Aha, the quick-witted land seller retorted, "I never said you could grow nuts on it. I said you could *go* nuts on it." You can decide which is of those things is happening at **Coconuts,** 745 Orienta Plaza, 745 Orienta Ave., at the intersection of Maitland Avenue and Fla. Rte. 436, Altamonte Springs (tel. 767-7557). This lively spot gets livelier about 9:30pm daily when the band goes into high gear and stays that way well into the wee hours. There's no cover charge.

**Bailey's Crocodile Club,** in the back room of Bailey's Restaurant at 118 W. Fairbanks Ave., Winter Park (tel. 647-8501) rocks your socks off from 9pm to 2am Thursday through Sunday. There's a $2 cover charge for gentlemen, free for ladies, and drinks are in the $3 to $5 range.

**READER'S RECOMMENDATION:** "Rock-and-roll is here to stay at Little Darlin's Rock N Roll Palace in Kissimmee, 5770 Irlo Bronson Memorial Hwy. (tel. 396-6499), in the Old Town complex near Xanadu and Medieval Times. Open every day 8:30pm to 1:30am, Little Darlin's charges $8.50 entrance fee for nightly shows featuring the greatest '50s stars—the Diamonds of 'Little Darlin' fame, Joey Dee and the Starlighters of the 'Peppermint Twist' and The Shirelles of 'Soldier Boy' renown, for instance. Wear your poodle skirts, saddle shoes, and letter sweaters . . . hula hoops and juke boxes are available. A fun place if you dig nostalgia" (Judie Carbaugh, Sykesville, Md.).

# VI

# SPORTS IN DISNEY WORLD AND ORLANDO

You don't think for a minute, do you, that those same Disney creators who invented a lovable mouse would stop at that?

Certainly not. Once they'd figured out how to entertain you in their fanciful world, they set out to dream up ways to keep golfers, tennis players, swimmers, joggers, and even professional shoppers happily occupied. Now there are so many sports available, in so many locations around this vast acreage that you need a scoreboard to keep track.

## SPORTS IN DISNEY WORLD

Since there's everything here to play on and with, from golf courses to outrigger canoes, let's start with that most popular of sports, golf, and then see if we can't find a sport for everyone.

### GOLF

Those links take up plenty of space in Walt Disney World's huge complex. For openers there are three golf courses here, the **Magnolia,** the **Palm,** and the course at **Lake Buena Vista Club.** All three started life as desert sands but have been miraculously converted into tree-lined, water-dotted, hilly areas, interesting enough to challenge golfers on the PGA Tour route, which visits here each year. If you're a golfing fan, you'll find them challenging but not terrifying. All are par-72 courses in the 7,000-yard range. Carts are required on the courses, the fee for which is included in the $55 greens fee for guests of Walt Disney World Resorts. If you really want to save money, plan your outing for the hours after 3pm, when twilight rates go into effect for all golfers, resort guests or not.

If you're staying at a Disney World resort, you can confirm starting times as soon as you have a confirmed reservation. If you're not, you can make reservations up to seven days in advance from January through April, when the courses see the most play. Guests at hotels in the Walt Disney World Village Hotel Plaza, by the way, are included. Starter's telephone number is 824-2270.

If you've got a young golf fanatic in your crowd, Disney can provide. Called the **Wee Links,** this youngsters' golf course features six holes with a total of 1,150 yards. It comes complete with all the nail-chewing difficulties of any golf course—traps, water hazards—but they're just a little easier to escape. Greens are artificial turf. Financed by the PGA Tour in the hopes of encouraging more young golfers, the Wee Links charges a $11 fee for youngsters under 18, and that includes clubs, a lesson on basic golf rules and etiquette, and 12 holes—that's two rounds—of golf. All the traveling done on the course is done on foot, so there are no cart charges. Adults needn't feel left out here: They can play, too, for $14 (tel. 824-2270).

If you'd like to get in some lessons while you're here, sign up for the **Walt Disney World Golf Studio.** You'll be part of a small class in which instructors highlight your skills and help you add to them. After class you get a look at the lessons on videotape and are treated to a critique of your style, which is recorded on an audiotape you can take home. Disney's Golf Studio operates at 9 and 11:30am and at 2:30pm Monday through Friday, at 9 and 11:30am on Saturday, and lasts for about two hours. Fee is $50; $25 more if you want to play nine holes after the lesson to practice what you've learned.

Private lessons are also available for $40 a half hour. Book private lessons at 824-2250 for the Disney Inn golf resort courses—the Magnolia and the Palm—or 828-3741 for instructions at Lake Buena Vista Club.

Rental equipment costs $20 for clubs, $4 a bucket of balls, and $6 for shoes. Get them all at the Pro Shop.

If you've always dreamed of playing in a **tournament,** you may even be able to satisfy that dream à la Disney. Local tournament play is organized by a Tournament Coordinator (824-2275), who may be able to include you in one of the local play-offs. If you're *really* into this thing and have the bucks to back it, you can play the annual Walt Disney World Classic/Oldsmobile each fall. To play with three pros during the tourney you must join the Classic Club for a $5,000 one-year membership fee, which includes six nights' hotel fees, greens fees for a year, and admission to the Magic Kingdom for a week. Details on the club are available at 824-2255.

## TENNIS

Those who want their contact with a small white ball to include strings and a net can chase that elusive orb at several interesting locations around Walt Disney World. You'll find three courts at the **Lake Buena Vista Club,** two at the **Disney Inn,** and six at the **Contemporary Resort Hotel.** At the latter you'll also find a speedy ball machine that will keep you running, plus a backboard. All are open from 9am to 8pm daily and are lighted hard courts. Fees are $10 an hour for singles, or doubles for WDW hotel guests. Those ball machines and the practice alleys that go with them are $10 for 30 minutes, $4 per hour racquet rental, but you can use the backboards free unless the courts are very busy, and then you'll pay regular court fees. Reserve court time at the Contemporary at 824-3578 (ext. 3578), at the Disney Inn at 824-2288, and at the Lake Buena Vista Club at 828-3741.

If you'd like to improve your tennis, there are lessons available for both adults and youngsters 4 to 16. Video cameras help the pros show you how to expand your talents. Details on the instructional programs are available at 824-3578.

If you want to rent a racquet, you'll pay $4 an hour, and you can buy a can of three tennis balls with the mouse's visage emblazoned on them for $4.98.

## BOATING

So many watery activities are there at Walt Disney World, your only problem may be drying out wrinkled fingertips. There are all kinds of boats, from speedy little craft to outrigger canoes, plenty of places to swim, and some favorite fishing holes.

If you like to stay atop the water while exploring, roam the byways of lovely, 450-acre Bay Lake and the adjoining 200 acres at the Seven Seas Lagoon. Marinas at Contemporary Resort, Fort Wilderness, and Polynesian Village will rent you small sailboats called Sunfish ($10 an hour), one- to six-passenger Capris ($15 an hour).

If you prefer power, you can start small and slow with motor-powered pontoon boats topped by canopies. Rental rates are $35 an hour, $50 for boat with driver.

If you're not in a hurry, you can provide your own power on pedal boats that rent for $10 an hour.

When speed's the thing, zip off across the waters on small boats called Water Sprites that fly like the wind and rent for $10 a half hour (children must be over 12 to rent or drive the boats, although younger sailors may ride in them accompanied by an adult). For even closer contact with the water, attach yourself to the back of a ski boat and water-ski for $65 an hour, including equipment, boat, and captain.

You'll find sailboats and speedboats, pontoon boats and pedal boats at Contemporary Resort, Polynesian Village, Fort Wilderness, and the marinas in Walt Disney World Village, where you can explore three more small connected lakes named Club Lake, Lake Buena Vista, and Buena Vista Lagoon. Canopy boats are available at all these locations, canoes at Fort Wilderness Bike Bar, and water-ski boats at Fort Wilderness and Contemporary Resort.

You'll need a Disney resort identification card or a driver's license to rent the craft. Can you sail a privately owned craft in Disney World? No.

## SWIMMING

One hardly expects to find a sandy white beach here in the land-locked center of Florida, but as usual Disney creates—with five miles of soft white sand. You can't miss that silica, in fact. On a monorail journey you'll spot the sands at Polynesian Village and behind the Contemporary, stretching around to Fort Wilderness.

As for swimming pools, there are nine of them on the grounds, one or sometimes two at every hotel and villa area. Although there's no charge for using them, they are not open to day visitors, only to guests of the WDW resorts. More pools for hotel guests are at the Walt Disney World Village Hotel Plaza hotels (Grosvenor, Royal Plaza, Buena Vista Palace, Pickett Suites, Viscount, Hilton, and Howard Johnson). Most interesting of the swimming holes is the pool at Polynesian Village, a fanciful creation with a waterfall and slide set among huge artificial rocks.

Pools and beaches are only for the use of guests staying at the Disney-owned hotels or campgrounds, so if you're intent on watery fun, head for River Country, or, better yet, Typhoon Lagoon, where Disney has created another Magic Kingdom using water as the main ingredient. Read more about those wonderlands in Chapter VIII.

## FISHING

Fishing is another guests-only sport at Walt Disney World and can be done in two ways: on your own in canals near the villa areas or at Fort Wilderness on a special Disney-organized expedition. Those two-hour expeditions leave every two hours from 8am to 6pm daily from the Fort Wilderness campgrounds and are $110 for two hours, including equipment, boat for up to five anglers, guide, and snacks. If you're staying in a Disney accommodation with a kitchen, you can keep your catch—usually bass—and cook it, but if you don't have a kitchen, just sigh a contented, triumphant sigh and toss it back into the deep. You don't need a fishing license. Reserve at 824-2760.

## HORSEBACK RIDING

Trail ponies carry you off into the lovely wooded countryside here on daily treks that take off at 9 and 10:30am, noon, 1 and 2pm. Quiet hour-long rides with a guide are $12 a person, and both day visitors and resort guests are welcome, although the kiddies must be at least 9 years old. Reservations can be made at 824-8000.

## JOGGING AND WALKING

Perhaps the best way of all to see the wondrous world Disney has created is on foot, walking or running. If you're a runner, all the hotels in WDW and in the Hotel Plaza carry jogging maps that show you how to plan the run (or walk). It's wise to do these activities early in the morning or after dusk, since other times of day can feature more Florida sun than you can handle. Fort Wilderness has an official jogging trail, 2.3 miles of it, complete with exercise stations. Otherwise you're pretty much on your own, so it might be wise to take a look at your prospective jogging or walking area by car or bus before you set off (or at least be very sure of your directions). If you miss a turn, a leisurely two-miler can become a sweating six-mile morning. Following *that* with a visit to the Magic Kingdom or EPCOT, and your feet are liable to make their displeasure known.

Walkers should head to the River Country area, where you can stroll down a nature trail, or over to Marshmallow Marsh at Fort

Wilderness, where a mile-long path takes you along the lake and through the woods.

## BICYCLING

You can rent a bike at the Fort Wilderness Bike Barn or at the Pool Pavilion in the Vacation Villas ($3 an hour, $7 a day, and $4 per hour and $9 a day for bicycles built for two), then pedal along miles of bike paths in Walt Disney World Village and at Fort Wilderness. Call 824-2742.

## WORKING OUT

Contemporary Resort has a health club complete with most of the usual exercise equipment and a sauna. The fee is $5 per person all day. Hours are 7am to 8pm and are coed. Closed Sundays. Massage appointments can be made at 824-1000.

## VOLLEYBALL, BASEBALL, HORSESHOES

Facilities for these sports, plus tetherball, are available at Fort Wilderness, but only to guests of Walt Disney World resorts. You need your own equipment for softball and baseball.

## WATERSKIING

**Ski Holidays** likes to call itself the largest water-ski instructional group in the world, and who can prove otherwise? Superlatives notwithstanding, the ski center is near all Lake Buena Vista area hotels and many other hotels in the area, too. Skiing takes place at Lake Bryan, a clear 350-acre spring-fed lake just minutes from the Disney hotel complex. Services range from special instructional programs for first-time skiers to hourly charters for intermediate to advanced skiers.

Rates are quite reasonable too: regardless of the number of skiers, $75 an hour, $40 a half hour. Those prices also include instructions and equipment.

They'll even teach you barefoot waterskiing here for $30 for 30 minutes and take the kids on ski rides for $5. Jet-skis and waverunners here, too. Hours are 11am to 5pm.

You can write to the company for a brochure at Box 22007, Lake Buena Vista, FL 32830. To get to the skiing area take I-4 to the Lake Buena Vista exit, turn south on Rte. 535 toward Kissimmee (away from Disney World) and about 200 yards east you will see a sign directing you to the school and the lake (tel. 407/239-4444).

# IN ORLANDO

Although Disney World has some of the best Orlando sporting life on its grounds, you'll find plenty of places to play in the rest of

Orlando as well. You have quite a range of choices, too, from wild rides on airboats that skim across the water to hot-air balloon rides high into the air.

Let's start with the nation's most favored sports, golf and tennis, and work up to the more unusual activities available.

## GOLF

Golfers staying within range of Disney World can head for Kissimmee's **Buenaventura Lakes Country Club** (301 Buenaventura Blvd.; tel. 348-2395), two par-30, nine-hole courses with greens fees and cart charges of $6 for nine and $10 for 18 holes.

Another nearby course is **Poinciana Golf and Racquet Resort,** on U.S. 17/92 west of Kissimmee (tel. 933-5300), where you can play 18 holes, a total of 6,697 yards of par-72 golf for $10 plus tax including cart.

Closer to downtown Orlando is **Fairways Golf Club** (14205 E. Colonial Dr.; tel. 282-7535), an 18-hole, par-70 course of 5,317 yards, which charges $15.90 plus $16.96 for an electric cart.

## TENNIS

Tennis players should head for the **Orlando Vacation Resort** (west of Hwy. I-4 on U.S. 27; tel. 904/394-6171), where you'll find 17 asphalt tennis courts (no fee), or **Vistana Resort** (east of Hwy. I-4 on Rte. 535, the Lake Buena Vista exit; tel. 239-3100), where guests play free on 14 clay courts, and there's a free tennis clinic daily except Sunday, private lessons, group lessons, and tennis clinics. Court hours: 8am to 11pm.

**Orlando Tennis Center** in Exposition Park (W. Livingston St. and Parimore St. in downtown Orlando, tel. 849-2161) has 15 lighted courts, open from 8am to 10pm daily (earlier closings on weekends) and charges $2.62 per person on hard surface, $4.74 on clay.

Free asphalt courts are available at **Oak Street Park** (Palm and Oak Sts., Orlando; tel. 847-2388). More free courts are located in parks in Orlando and Kissimmee. To find out just where they are, call the Orlando Recreation Department at 849-2288 and its counterpart in Kissimmee at 847-2388.

There are more free courts at **H.L. Godwin Park,** Fourth and Wyoming Sts., St. Cloud (tel. 892-7356), and **Orange Lake Country Club,** 8505 W. Irlo Bronson Memorial Hwy., Kissimmee (tel. 239-2295), which charges a small fee if you need to rent tennis rackets.

## BOATING

Kissimmee was carved out of flat sands and cypress swamps, some of which have been kept intact with huge cypress trees dripping eerie Spanish moss into the black water. It's quite a sight, and you can see it in some interesting ways—aboard a canoe, an electric boat, or an airboat. Rent any of those from **U-Drive Airboat Rentals,** 4266 W. Irlo Bronson Memorial Hwy., Kissimmee, six miles east of Disney World (tel. 847-3672). Hourly fees are $16 for airboats, $13 for electric boats, and $4.50 for canoes.

For first-class travel, rent a houseboat with galley, bath, and air conditioning, and tour the crystal springs of St. John's River. Boats are provided by **Go Vacations,** 2280 Pontoon Rd., Deland (tel. 904/736-9422). The company is located at a marina on Pontoon Road, and the rates are $595 to $895 for four days, $1,195 to $1,595 a week.

## PARIMUTUEL SPORTS

Watch those canine racers streak after the electronic bunny at **Seminole Greyhound Park,** Rte. 17/92 in Casselberry (tel. 699-4510), and at **Sanford-Orlando Kennel Club,** Dog Track Rd. (tel. 831-1600). Seminole is open May to September; Sanford, November to May, with racing nightly (except Sunday) from 7:30pm, matinees on Monday, Wednesday, and Saturday at 1pm. Admission is $1.

**Orlando-Seminole Jai-Alai Fronton** in Fern Park (211 S. Hwy. 17/92; tel. 339-6221) gives you a look at that unusual and thrilling sport nightly (except Sunday) in annually changing seasons, usually from May to September. Admission begins at $1 and games start at 7pm daily, with noon matinees on Monday, Friday, and Saturday.

From October to May, harness racers trot off daily except Sunday at **Ben White Harness Raceway** (1905 Lee Rd.; tel. 293-8721).

## BASEBALL

In March and April the **Minnesota Twins** play at Tinker Field, the Orlando Stadium, at 287 Tampa Ave. South (tel. 872-7593). Tickets are $3 to $7.

If you'd like to see whether you might just qualify for a team yourself, go hit a few at the **baseball batting range** (on U.S. 441, two miles east of Kissimmee; tel. 847-6502). There are three pitching machines plus a golf driving range and miniature golf course.

Over in Haines City, where Circus World once resided, you'll find the winter home of the **Kansas City Royals.** You can see them or their up-and-coming players practicing when you visit this attraction.

Newest residents of Kissimmee are the **Houston Astros** baseball team which now turns up here for spring training. A new 6,000-seat stadium adjacent to the Kissimmee/St. Cloud Convention and Visitors Bureau on U.S. 192 and 44 at 1925 E. Irlo Bronson Memorial Hwy is their playground. Contact 407/933-2520 for more information. Tickets are $3 to $7.

## SWIMMING

There are lakes and swimming pools scattered about. The Orlando Recreation Department (tel. 849-2288), the Orange County Parks Department (tel. 420-3640), or the Kissimmee Parks and Recreation Department (tel. 847-2388) can tell you where the best swimming's located.

There's much water fun to be had at a local attraction called **Wet 'N Wild** (6200 International Dr.; tel. 351-3200). You can ride bumper boats and speedboats, or paddle around a surf pool in which constant four-foot waves are created by a machine. Slide down white-water slideways or careen down a Kamikaze slide that sends you into a pool from a platform six stories high! There are squirting games and other fun for kids, a Corkscrew Flume that spirals you through a figure-eight and a tunnel, even a Bonzai Boggan water roller coaster that races at 30 m.p.h. then plunges you into a pool. You can picnic along the lake, snack at snack bars, and just generally spend an uncomplicated day in watery surroundings. Admission is $17.95 for adults, $15.95 for children 3 to 12, free to toddlers, and the attraction's open from 10am to 6pm daily. There's usually a bargain-rate discount (about half-price) after 3pm, too.

There are other smaller but similar versions of that $H_2O$ attraction. One of those is **Water Mania,** 6073 W. Irlo Bronson Memorial Hwy., Kissimmee (tel. 396-2626), where you can surf and swim and splash and go 'round and 'round on a maze of water slides. Admission is $14.95 adults, $11.95 children 3 to 12, and the mania continues from 10am to 7pm daily, closing two hours earlier in summer.

## FISHING

With lakes everywhere you look, there's certainly no dearth of fishing holes. **Bass** is the big catch in these parts, and a favorite spot to fish for them is Lake Tohopekaliga (much easier to get around than to pronounce). Kissimmee River's another spot that's good for fishing, and the Kissimmee–St. Cloud Convention and Visitors Bureau (Box 2007, Kissimmee, FL 32742; tel. 847-5000), can send you information on fishing, boat rentals, camping, and the like in the area.

If **deep-sea fishing** is more to your taste, you'll naturally have to head to the sea in the Cocoa Beach/Port Canaveral area where the Cocoa Beach Chamber of Commerce (400 Fortenberry Rd., Merritt Island; tel. 459-2200), headed by one very friendly Floridian, Larry Malta, can supply you with directions to marinas. Deep-sea fishing on charter boats is likely to run about $150 to $200 a day, higher in busy seasons.

If you're looking for an **inexpensive fishing trip,** try the *Miss Cape Canaveral,* an 80-foot party boat that sails at 8am daily returns at 5pm from Port Canaveral, about an hour's drive due east of Orlando. Price is $35 for adults, $25 for youngsters 12 to 15, $20 for children under 12, plus $5 for rod and reel. The boat's docket is at Commercial Road behind Fisher Seafood (tel. 783-5274).

**Pier fishing** is available at Canaveral Fishing Pier, just north of Cocoa Beach.

## HORSEBACK RIDING

This is horse country, so it's not difficult to find equine entertainment. **Devonwood Farm,** 2518 Rouse Rd., Orlando, about a half mile east of Alfaya Trail & Hwy. 50 (tel. 273-0822), for instance, offers horseback riding for $10 an hour for guided trail rides, lessons and riding trips by reservation only. They're open Friday, Saturday and Sunday 9:30am to 3:30pm by appointment. Another trotting spot: **Poinciana Horse World,** 3705 Poinciana Blvd., Kissimmee, FL 32758 (tel. 847-4343), where you can visit a real ranch and go on a $14-an-hour trail rides through some interesting countryside. Billed as a one-stop dude ranch, this working ranch has 600 acres on which you and your equine friend can roam. If you don't know which side of the horse is the up side, they offer riding lessons here. There's also a tack store, petting zoo, fishing pond, hayrides, ponies, and picnic areas. Whinnying is welcome here daily from 9am to 6pm, but call first for trail ride times.

## ICE SKATING

Never let it be said that we did not provide you with every option. If you can't bear to be without a little of the cold stuff, try the **Orlando Ice Skating Palace** (3123 W. Colonial Dr., in the Parkwood Shopping Plaza; tel. 299-5440). It calls itself an Olympic-size arena and is open Saturday through Thursday, charging $4.95 for adults, ($5.95 weekends), $4.45 for children under 12 ($5.45 weekends). Skate rentals (in case you forgot to pack those for a Florida vacation) are $1.50. There are hockey and figure skating clinics here, too.

## BALLOON TRIPS

**Phineas Phogg's,** part of the amazing Rosie O'Grady's complex (tel. 422-2434), takes you up, up, and away early in the morning at 6am when the winds are breezes gentle enough to waft you across the countryside on an hour-long journey which includes a champagne breakfast. The fee is $148 per person for an experience you'll never forget.

Ballooning is big news up this way where everyone is in search of a way to combine hobby and vocation. Among the companies offering hot-air balloon rides are **Above It All Ballooning,** 633 Dartmouth St., Orlando (tel. 422-0088), **Rise & Float Balloon Tours,** 5931 American Way, Suite 107, Orlando (tel. 352-8191), **Orange Blossom Balloons** in Old Town Shopping Center at 5770 Irlo Bronson Memorial Hwy., Kissimmee (tel. 239-7677), and **Balloons by Terry,** 3459 Edgewater Dr., Orlando (tel. 422-3529). Figure to pay $250 a couple or $125 to $150 single at these up-up spots.

## WATERSKIING

**Dee's Ski Center,** Rte. 1, Box 595, north of Lake Juliana in the town of Auburndale (tel. 813/984-1160), sports a lakefront clubhouse, five regulation slalom courses, and two fiberglass jumps. About a 30-minute drive from Disney World, the ski center is open year round and offers camping, cottages, a pro shop, and a fishing pier as well. To get there, take Exit 21 (S.R. 559) from Hwy. I-4, go one mile south toward Auburndale, and turn right on Lundy Road. A half hour of skiing is $20 and jet-skis rental is $20.

**Ski Holidays** likes to call itself the largest water-ski instructional group in the world. It offers a free shuttle service from all Lake Buena Vista area hotels and from many other hotels in the area, too. Skiing takes place at Lake Bryan, a clear 350-acre, spring-fed lake just minutes from the Disney hotel complex. Services range from special instructional programs for first-time skiers to hourly charters for intermediate to advanced skiers.

Rates are quite reasonable too: regardless of the number of skiers, $75 an hour. These prices include instructions and equipment, too. Parasailing is $45 per flight.

You can write to the company for a brochure at Box 22007, Lake Buena Vista, FL 32830 (tel. 407/239-4444). To get to the skiing area take I-4 to the Lake Buena Vista exit, turn east on SR 535 toward Kissimmee (away from Disney World) and about 200 yards east you will see a sign directing you to the school and the lake.

Another ski spot: **Splash-n-Ski,** 10,000 Turkey Lake Rd., Orlando (tel. 352-1494), where you can zip across a 148-acre private lake with coaching by British water-skiers; instruction is available for adults or children. When you get good—and brave—enough you can try out the six-buoy slalom course and the ski jump. Open daily, this skiing center charges $30 to $40 for jet- and waterskiing.

## FAMILY FUN

If you'd like to get in a little mini-golf or a couple of rounds on bumper cars, bumper boats, Ferris wheel, waterslides, or go-carts, stop in at **Fun 'N Wheels Family Fun Park,** 6739 Sand Lake Rd., corner of International Drive and Sand Lake Road (tel. 351-5651). It's open 10am to midnight and a book of 20 tickets is $20; golf is three tickets per adults, two for children 3 to 11, a round. Rides are one to four tickets.

Those who harbor a secret desire to smash their way through traffic can crash and crumple it up in a harmless gridlock at **Jungle Falls Go-Karts & Amusements,** 5285 W. Irlo Bronson Memorial Hwy., Kissimmee (tel. 396-1996 or 239-7053 in Orlando). There are go-carts and bumper boats, batting cages and video games. Rides are $2 to $5; this diversion is open from 10am to midnight, opening and closing an hour earlier in quieter spring and fall seasons.

**Pirate's Island Adventure Golf,** 4330 W. Irlo Bronson Memorial Hwy., Kissimmee (tel. 396-4660), puts you into Blackbeard's cave, across a waterfall and into the dens of some fierce fellows who zealously guard this miniature golf course. Rates are $5 adults, $4 children under 12, and hours are 9am to 11pm daily.

More of the same at **River Adventure Golf,** 4535 W. Irlo Bronson Memorial Hwy., Kissimmee (tel. 396-4666), and **Action Kartways Family Fun Park,** 2120 E. Irlo Bronson Memorial Hwy. (tel. 846-8585).

## SOMETHING FOR ESCAPISTS

When Orlando catapulted into the forefront of Central Florida life, developers practically wiped out any traces of what Floridians like to call Old Florida, relentlessly replacing the natural with the modern (and commercial). Having said that, let me add that there are still some tranquilly lovely hideaways here, and one of them is the Wekiva Wilderness.

To start at the very beginning: you can pronounce it Wah-KEY-vah or Wok-EYE-va, whether you'll be right or not just depends on which part of this riverside wilderness you're visiting. I like Wok-EYE-va because it sounds pretty to me but you can take your choice, they're both right.

Whatever you call it, there are some beautiful spots here to slip into a reclusive mood and contemplate the beauties of the Florida-that-used-to-be. One of them is **Katie's Landing,** 190 Katie's Cove, Sanford, FL 32771 (tel. 628-1482). Right on the river, this spot offers canoe rentals for $3 an hour, $12 a day, and guided canoe trips for $12 adults, $6 children 3 to 12. Katie's is open daily from 7am to 6pm. You'll find the landing by taking I-4 east to Exit 51 (the Sanford-Mount Dora exit), exiting onto Fla. 46, and going about five miles west.

At **Wekiva Falls Resort** you can rent canoes for $7 a day or take a boat cruise along the river, swim, camp, or picnic. Admission is $2 for adults, $1.50 for children 2 through 11, and the park is open from 8am to 7pm daily (tel. 830-9828). To get there take I-4 east to Exit 51 (Sanford-Mount Dora), turn left, go five miles, cross the bridge over the river, and stay in the left hand lane to turn left onto Wekiva River Road, where you'll find the entrance to the resort.

**Wekiva Springs State Park,** 1800 Wekiva Circle, Apopka, FL 32703 (tel. 889-3140), is yet another place to rent canoes, go camping, swimming, and picnicking on the lovely Wekiva river. Take I-4 east to the Longwood Exit (Fla. 434), turn left, follow Fla. 434 to Wekiva Springs Road, and turn right on Wekiva Springs Road, where you'll find the park about four miles down the road. Park admission is $2 for the driver, $1 for each additional passenger older than six. Canoe rentals there are $12 a day.

Florida has so many gently flowing rivers meandering quietly across the flatlands and rolling hills that escapists here soon discovered the pursuit of tubing. To do it, you rent a huge truck inner tube and then launch it and yourself into the river, where you do nothing more strenuous than let the current take you away from it all. At Rock Springs/Kelly Park, you can rent a tube for a dollar or so and have a go at this lazy tourist's sport. Rock Springs/Kelly Park is free and is open daily from 9am to 5pm (tel. 889-4179). To get there takes a little pathfinding ability; you'd best call in advance for directions.

# VII

# SHOPPING IN CENTRAL FLORIDA

If you like souvenirs, you will *adore* Orlando and environs, where there are more—and more bizarre—interpretations of that word than you could conjure up in your wildest dreams—or nightmares!

Where else in the world could you find a high-powered executive discussing millions of dollars on a telephone receiver lifted from the firm grip of a white-gloved Mickey Mouse telephone? For that matter, how many places do you find people strolling the streets wearing black plastic mouse ears?

It's contagious, this junk-abilia fever that hits Orlando visitors, so don't think for a minute that you're immune. Rare is the soul who can head home without a picture of the mouse—or Shamu the Killer Whale, or one of their fanciful buddies—triumphantly emblazoned somewhere on something or somebody.

So if you're a collector of almost anything, you can be sure you'll find something here in Orlando to collect. If you're not a collector, you probably will be by the time you leave, since there are few places to escape the barrage of sales pitches.

Despite appearances, however, real people do live in Orlando, and some of them have taste good enough to produce some interesting treasures you may enjoy after mouse mania has subsided.

Because there are so many hundreds of places to buy typical souvenirs, including every hotel gift shop and hundreds of shops in Disney World, Sea World, and Universal Studios, I'm going to trust you have enough ferreting ability to find those yourself.

What you'll find in this chapter instead are tips on some spots to seek out for bargains on souvenirs that do not scream "souvenir"!

Orlando's accent on families, supplemented by its comparatively youthful population, has led to the rise of many cut-rate and discount shops that offer interesting bargains on name-brand items. What's more, some area shops are in locations so intriguing, they're as interesting to visit as they are to explore for your special kind of treasure. Finally, best of all, there are some fascinating boutiques, particularly in the nearby suburb of Winter Park, that feature exotic creations difficult to match anywhere.

Let's take a look then at some of the top spots for a shopping break from the fun and frolic of Orlando's attractions.

Right on **Disney World grounds** in Lake Buena Vista is one of

Orlando's favorite shopping spots, **Walt Disney World Shopping Village.** Throngs of locals sweep in here on weekends to raid this interesting conglomeration of 27 boutiques, featuring everything from delicate handcrafted Christmas ornaments to gourmet kitchen necessities.

There's a candle shop; a shop featuring the finest—and most expensive—in crystal, china, and silver; a card and gift shop; and a shop that can engrave your photograph on a platter. Spain contributes its wood, metal, and porcelain products to a shop called Toledo Arts, and there's an around-the-world boutique with treasures from everywhere.

Toys of all kinds turn up at Pooh's Place and Toys Fantastique; there's a photo studio where you can have your picture taken in turn-of-the-century clothes; and there are stores featuring children's clothes, men's clothes, and women's tropical outfits. You can buy fancy bathroom accessories, perfumes, gourmet goodies including freshly roasted coffee beans and straight-out-of-the-oven pastries, exclusive and expensive chocolates, sundries and cards, liqueurs and liquors, wines and things to serve them all in, shoes, batiks, brass goodies, and ships in bottles.

All those treasures are interspersed with some intriguing restaurants (see Chapter IV on dining) and spiced with some attractive architecture. At night, tiny white Italian lights twinkle in the trees, turning this shopper's haven into the kind of fairyland even Tinker Bell would approve. One final don't-miss here: In Toys Fantastique is a dollhouse so elaborate and so fabulously appointed you'll gasp at the crystal and etched glass, miniature treasures of such beauty they're not for sale, although you can acquire reproductions with determination and money.

In Disney World's Magic Kingdom, MGM Studios, and EPCOT, you'll find dozens, nay hundreds, of shops, which I've outlined in Chapters VIII and IX.

**Downtown Orlando** is just beginning to come into its own as a shopping area. The prettiest parts of it to date are Church Street Station on Church Street, the **Orange Quarter & Shops,** Orange Avenue and Washington Street, and the **French Market** on North Orange Avenue. There are just nine shops and two restaurants in the Orange Quarter, but the setting's a delight of cedar and brick elegance, much of it preserved from days long gone. At the French Market, an enticing European flavor prevails.

**Church Street Station,** long the city's number one entertainment arena (see more on that under nightlife in Chapter V), recently added to its allure with several blocks of shops. One can spend some entertaining hours there roaming cobblestoned streets, poking around the Sharper Image's collection of high-tech oddities, checking a Coca-Cola collector's haven, hoisting a few at the local pub, and even rocking the night away at a lively disco/restaurant.

Over in **Winter Park,** Central Florida's Little Europe, you'll find silk scarves spilling over a counter, pearls and diamonds dramatically displayed in glittering windows, small treasures and large ones, all while wandering in Zurich or on Paris's Rive Gauche. All this elegance is centered on Park Avenue, one of the state's poshest shopping streets, ranking right up there with Palm Beach's famed Worth Avenue.

There's a tiny jewelry shop here with a royal-blue enameled bracelet I covet, another pretty little shop selling scented and intricately designed candles that look almost lovely enough to eat, and some boutiques that do indeed sell things to eat, items so appetizingly displayed you're likely to make one of the village's elegant restaurants your next stop.

If you like **shopping malls,** you will be thrilled with Altamonte Mall (on S.R. 436 between Hwy. I-4 and U.S. 17/92, Altamonte Springs exit from Hwy. I-4), which sports no less than 150 stores to help separate you and your greenbacks. Quite an attractive setting in which to spend, too.

**Colonial Plaza Mall** (E. Colonial Dr. at Bumby St.) has more than 100 stores to wander among, and **Fashion Square Mall** (E. Colonial Dr. at Maguire St.) has 92 shops in all price brackets.

A comparative newcomer among local malls is **Florida Mall,** 1500 Sand Lake Rd. (tel. 851-6255). Anchored by one of the loveliest hotels in Central Florida, the art-deco–style Holiday Inn Crowne Plaza, this mall is an airy, open place that rarely seems crowded and never seems frenetic. There are more than 150 shops here, dominated by Sears, Penney's, Maison Blanche, and Belk-Lindsey.

To combine fun and games with shopping and dining, stop by **Mercado Mediterranean Village,** 8445 International Dr. (tel. 345-9337). Something's always going on here, be it juggling, magic tricks, singing, dancing, or a combination of the above. There are also several quite creditable restaurants here, so you won't starve while you're waiting for someone to try something on for the umpteenth time.

If you feel like a little drive, head over to the village of Brooksville, where **Rogers' Christmas House Village** (103 Saxon Ave., Brooksville; tel. 904/796-2415) keeps Christmas going all year long. Billboards all around Central Florida lure you here— where it's always December 25 except on December 25, when they celebrate what they sell all year long. Open 9:30am to 5pm daily, this extensive shop shimmers with Christmas lights, multitudes of animated displays, and ornaments so entrancing not even Scrooge could resist them. You'll find the shop at the intersection of U.S. 98, Rte. 50, and U.S. 41, about 10 miles west of Hwy. I-75.

Multitudes of bargain seekers have moved Orlando's entrepreneurs to provide **factory outlet shops.** So popular has this form of shopping become in Central Florida, that there's now even an entire shopping center composed solely of shops billing themselves as factory outlets.

One of the best-known and best-advertised of the factory outlet stores is **Dansk** (7000 International Dr.; tel. 351-2425), importers and creators of sleek Danish contemporary pottery, gorgeous teak trays, and other teakwood ware, stainless steel, and glassware.

Supplement that with a trip to the **China & Glass Factory Out-**

**let** (62 W. Colonial Dr. or 6811 Visitors Circle, across from Wet 'N Wild on International Dr.), where companies represented include Wedgwood, Royal Doulton, and J.G. Durand.

**Pfaltzgraff,** 5490 International Dr. (tel. 345-9313), is a factory outlet store specializing in sleek contemporary china and appliances.

**Villeroy & Boch,** purveyors of sleek and chic contemporary china now found in many of the nation's finest restaurants, has a factory outlet here at 5451 International Dr. (tel. 352-7633).

Those who love the Bass Company's now-famous shoes can find that comfortable footwear at bargain prices at the **Bass Shoes** factory outlet, 5401 Oak Ridge Rd. at International Drive (tel. 351-2588).

Kingpin of the discount delights is the **Belz Factory Outlet Mall** (5401 W. Oak Ridge Rd., tel. 326-9600 or 351-3487; at the end of International Drive at the Oak Ridge Road intersection, follow the signs on International Drive after exiting I-4 at the Sand Lake Road exit and head east). Here you'll find 90 cut-rate shops open 10am to 9pm Monday through Saturday, and 10am to 6pm Sunday. These shops are positively jammed with most any treasure you can dream up—housewares, perfumes, gifts, entertainment items, shoes, clothes—you name it, they're all here at prices they say are 25% to 75% lower than retail tags.

Among the shops represented there is **Polly Flinders** (tel. 351-1404) which carries those much-loved hand-smocked dresses that look so cute on little girls, and **Danskin Factory Outlet** (tel. 351-2364) which offers tights, skirts, tops, and all the rest of those elasticized products essential to the survival of female athletes and fashion plates.

Finally, let's not forget the one thing that distinguishes Florida tourists at airports all over the nation: bags of **grapefruit and oranges.** You can stock up on these mandatory purchases at hundreds of small shops scattered around Orlando. There are several citrus sellers on International Drive, including **Citrus Circus** (across from Wet 'N Wild at 6813 Visitors Circle).

A biggy in the business is **Orange Ring** (Drawer 2107, on U.S. 27 north at Haines City, tel. 813/422-1938). Here you can even pick your own oranges on 10,000 acres of groveland and tour a packing and juice plant as well. While you're at it, indulge in a free glass of OJ, and try a piece of citrus candy or some orange jelly.

**Florida Citrus Tower** (Hwy. 27, 25 miles west of Orlando and a mile north of the intersection of S.R. 50 and U.S. 27 in Clermont; tel. 904/394-8585) does indeed tower over the miles of groves surrounding it. You can go up to the top of the tower for a fabulous view of silver-blue lakes and emerald-green groves, or visit a citrus packing plant, a citrus-marmalade factory, a citrus candy factory, a restaurant, an ice-cream parlor, and a glassblower's workshop at this citrus store-cum-attraction. (Tower rides are $1.75 for adults, $1 for students 10 to 15, others free.)

You say you'd rather make a deal than buy by the price tag? Then head right out to **Flea World,** Hwy. 17/92 (tel. 645-1792), a 33-acre flea market/mall in Sanford. Opened in 1982, this combination of junk and *junque* recently spent $2 million on an expansion program designed to create still more space for Turkish bedspreads, $3 haircuts, macramé plant hangers, antique furniture, old clothes, new clothes, and general treasure.

You'll find both indoor and outdoor marketing here at this very large bargain-up-a-storm playground, which features covered and paved walkways, especially pleasant for elderly and handicapped treasure hunters. You'll find restaurants here in air-conditioned buildings. You'll even find a chimney sweep! It's open Friday, Saturday, and Sunday from 8am to 5pm and admission and parking are free. Entertainment too. To get there from the Kissimmee/Disney area, take I-4 to the Sanford exit (about a 40-minute drive, 20 minutes from the downtown Orlando area), turn right to U.S. 17/92 and south to Flea World. Or take U.S. 17/92 directly from downtown Kissimmee north to the market. Tell them to send a search party if you're not back in 12 hours.

**Altamonte Park Plaza,** 995 Fla. 434 N. (tel. 862-2929), has a number of specialty shops, some discount, some not, all of them occupying an attractive indoor marketplace with a bit of a European air about it. Hours are 10am to 9pm daily, closing at 6pm Saturday and Sunday and opening at noon Sunday. To get there take the Longwood Exit from I-4.

Add to that another shopping center, **The Marketplace,** 7600 Dr. Phillips Blvd. (just north of Sand Lake Road and west of I-4, take Exit 29 from I-4, turn right at stoplight) where some creative souls have opened a pretty little woodsy shopping center with Victorian overtones. Makes an interesting, casual place to stroll as well as to shop. You'll find a pub and restaurant here, children's and women's fashion shops, an antiques store and assorted other boutiques. It's open daily from 10am to 9pm (tel. 351-7000).

Finally, we come back to the beginning, in a manner of speaking. It's called **Old Town,** and it's a delightful re-creation of an old-timey shopping street, right down to a surrey with the fringe on top. You'll find it at 5770 Irlo Bronson Memorial Hwy., Kissimmee (tel. 396-6233 or toll free 800/843-4202, in Florida 800/331-5093). Here you can ride on an antique wooden-horse carousel and hark back to simpler days, when catching the brass ring was one of life's major events. When you get off the merry-go-round, you can walk the brick road past more than 70 boutiques, dine in a couple of casual restaurants, down a 5-cent Coca-Cola or sample 52 flavors of popcorn! Dedicated shoppers will find everything here from Mexican paper flowers to Irish linens, pottery, fancy kites, and colorful tropical duds.

Those to whom shop is a four-letter word can partake of other diversions: a wood-carving museum and a tethered hot-air balloon ride, for openers.

Can't get enough? Okay, one more for the mall crawlers. **Maingate Outlet Mall,** 7521 W. Irlo Bronson Memorial Hwy., Kissimmee (tel. 396-4310 or in Orlando, 239-6574), stores are open from 10am to 9pm Monday through Saturday, noon to 6pm Sunday. Some label-lovers' favorites here are London Fog for everything from bumbershoots to shoes, Barbizon Lingerie for sweet nothings, Van Heusen for shirts, and Polly Flinders for hand-smocked children's dresses. A free mall trolley stops at hotels on the western corridor of U.S. 192 (that's everything west of I-4), and they're so obliging that they'll put your name in lights (on their marquee) and give you a photo memento of that big event.

This is the end of this list, believe it or not. Don't forget to take a look at downtown Kissimmee, where you can shop at some sweet little places tucked away near a serene spot called **Lake Toho-pekaliga.** Call it Lake Toho; everyone else does.

# VIII

# EXPLORING THE MAGIC KINGDOM

**A**t last you're here, in a place so captivating more than 15 million people visit it every year, a place sprinkled with stardust and glittering with the prestidigitation of imagination.

It's a special place, the Magic Kingdom, a place where reality remains at the ticket booth and fantasy goes exploring, where the mantle of maturity lifts, to be replaced by that star-struck child who lives deep inside all of us.

Jaded as you may be, cynical as you are about this magic, you too will feel the effect of this place the moment you step onto the macadam of Main Street. It doesn't matter that a child is crying, that you're a little lost, that bells are clanging on the horse trolley, and hooves are rattling on the cobblestones. In one heart-stopping moment distractions disappear. In that moment of awe, days of innocence, sun-filled moments long forgotten, people and places that can never return are recaptured, remembered, relived.

Into the sky above you, Cinderella Castle soars, and on the street before you, a grinning mouse looms into view. All around the homes, hearths, and hopes of another era transport you from a spinning 20th century to the era of your imagination, into a time when anything can happen, if you let it.

Let it.

## ORIENTATION

Enchanting as are these opening moments—and quite a few of the intermediate ones—in the Magic Kingdom, reality does have a way of intruding. There are things with which you must cope, chief among them the exigencies of entry, arrival, and survival. To help you do that, let's take a look at some of the things you'll need to know before you go and when you get there.

### WHEN TO GO

Disney World is a *very* popular place. That translates into crowds, all the time, all year long, at all hours of the day and night.

Lest you panic at the thought, however, let it be known that the Magic Kingdom is a huge place that can absorb thousands and leave you feeling there's hardly anyone around. Also, there are ways to avoid the most crowded times and days. One of the easiest is by getting to the park quite early, say 7 or 8am, during the busy holiday and summer seasons. At less crowded times of year (hold on, I'm coming to that), a 9 or 10am arrival will help you avoid traffic and lines.

What are the **hours** of the park? Well, they vary by season, but in the fall and winter—that is September, October, most of November, and early part of December, and January—hours generally are 9am to 8pm. At Thanksgiving, Christmas, New Year's Eve, and Easter, holiday hours are extended to 11pm or midnight. During the week of Washington's Birthday—that's February, in case you forgot—and college spring-break weeks toward the end of March, the park may open earlier and usually remains open to 10pm. Park operators sometimes decide to change the hours so it's a good idea to call **Disney information,** 824-4321 or 824-2222, to find out what's happening today.

Most people expect to find the **biggest crowds** at Disney World in the summer, when children are out of school and everyone's vacationing. Actually, however, the really monstrous crowds come at Christmas, when this fairyland becomes even more magical than usual. From Christmas through New Year's Day, 60,000 to 80,000 people *a day* troop through the turnstiles here.

Next most popular visiting days are in late November around Thanksgiving, two weeks at Easter, during college spring breaks in late March or early April, Washington's Birthday week in mid-February, and finally those summer holidays June through August. At any of those times, you can expect to find 40,000 to 65,000 people sharing the magic.

If you're intent on avoiding crowds, the slowest days at the park occur from the beginning of January to mid-February, March, September, October, and most of November, when the crowds ring in at a low of 15,000 a day to a high of about 40,000.

As panicking as those figures are, it may ease your mind to know that this is a very big place. When you and all those other people are moving about on 100 acres of ground, even a crowd of 40,000 is not an uncomfortable mass and often doesn't even mean interminably long lines. When, however, the numbers get into the 60,000 to 80,000 range, you can be sure you will wait in line for everything from a hot dog to a hot-dogging ride on the Space Needle (which I'm convinced would have a long line even in the middle of a hurricane).

Whether you can bear up under the crowd strains or not is a decision only you can make. Some people think it's well worth it— and Christmas at Disney World does indeed have many memorable moments—while others won't come within miles of the park at those super-busy times.

If you'd like to narrow your choices even more scientifically: In summer the busiest day at the park is Tuesday, followed by Monday, Wednesday, Thursday, and Saturday, pretty much in that order. In fall Saturday is the busiest day. Just about all year round you'll find the smallest crowds on Friday and Sunday. Reader Sara Drower of Wilmette, Ill., points out that during school vacations when the park stays open till midnight, the lines seem to diminish after dinner and "from 10pm to midnight you can see more than you could all day."

**Shopper Alert:** If you're planning on buying up your usual storm in this park's hundreds of shops, make your momentous decisions and whip out the cash or credit card *before* 2:30pm. Wait any later than that and you'll join what seems like every one of the other 50,000 mouse-ear fans in line after line at shop after shop. Shop early and check your loot. Clerks will be happy to describe the simple checking procedures.

## WHAT TO WEAR

Let's start with the hour or so preceding your departure for the Magic Kingdom, when you're deciding what to wear. What to wear may not sound important—this is just a day in a park, for goodness sake—but, believe me, four or five hours of sunshine and miles of steps later, what you have on, or off, will become all-consumingly important.

Wear comfortable clothes and layer them on, so you can add or subtract without multiplying stares. In Florida's sunshine you may think that a minimum of clothing is best, but keep in mind that desert dwellers do not by chance wear long, enveloping gowns and head-covering turbans. Clothes keep *out* heat too and ward off sunburn, a condition that can inflict itself on you with great rapidity in Florida—even on cloudy days.

I'm not quite sure how to put this next suggestion tactfully, but those with less hair atop their domes will appreciate—make that, need—a hat. Even the hair-endowed are likely to appreciate a hat's shade on hot days.

Disney officials say shoes and shirts must be worn at all times in the Magic Kingdom, but I'm afraid that rule, especially as it applies to shirts, is broken as often as it's kept. You must have both aboard transportation vehicles, however. They'll insist.

Shoes? Definitely, and comfortable ones, shoes you've come to know and love and absolutely no new ones, whose idiosyncrasies have not yet made themselves known. You will walk . . . and walk . . . and walk . . . and just when you think you don't have to walk another step, you discover you have to walk another step. There's a strong possibility that no matter what you do, your feet will be aching at the end of the day, but you can reduce the groans by getting as comfortable as possible before you take the first step.

One more accoutrement: sunglasses. Glare is everywhere.

## GETTING THERE

Now let's get on the road and get on over there, which you do by taking Highway I-4 (west in the direction of Tampa) or U.S. 192 east or west, depending on where you're staying. Huge signs on both roads make the Magic Kingdom so easy to find, even the White Rabbit could get there on time.

As you follow the entrance road leading to the Magic Kingdom, you can tune into a radio station, 640 on the AM dial of your car radio, for some basic information on entry to Disney World grounds. On very crowded days, signs also indicate how long you may be stuck in traffic approaching the Toll Plaza. Beyond that Toll Plaza, where you pay a $3 parking fee (waived if you're a guest of a WDW resort), are two miles of attractively landscaped roads to the parking area.

On the way you'll pass the **Disney Car Care Center** (tel. 824-4813), where you can buy gas and have minor repairs done from 7am to 9pm. AAA cards are accepted for towing needs. Employees there will drop you wherever you need to go in Disney World and pick you up later, so you don't lose the day baby-sitting your car. In and around the parking areas, there are tow trucks with emergency equipment available for minor troubles, like dead batteries or empty gas tanks.

Once you reach the parking area, you'll find a multitude of Kids of the Kingdom on hand to wave you into a parking spot. Be sure to note the name of the parking lot you're in—they're named for the Seven Dwarfs and other assorted Disney characters—and the number of your parking line. On busy days there can be 80,000 people in the park—that's a lot of light-blue station wagons. (If you don't trust your memory, there's a place to write parking information on the back of your parking stub. Keep the stub if you leave the park with plans to return that day—it's good all day long.) Handicapped visitors can park in a special lot adjacent to the Transportation and Ticket Center. Ask at the Toll Plaza for directions to the special lot.

Now, collect all the things you've brought (cameras, jackets, sunglasses, this guidebook, of course), step out of the car, look around, and you will shortly see a jeep-drawn tram snaking its way around the parking lot. Board the tram, and in a few minutes it will deposit you at the Transportation and Ticket Center, where you buy tickets for entrance to the park. Those who arrive *very* early may be lucky enough to find a space in Bashful, Sneezy, Donald, or Daisy parking lots, which are within walking distance of the Ticket Center.

Back to business. If you arrive at Walt Disney World by bus, you'll alight at the bus stop near the Transportation and Ticket Center. That's where you will reboard the bus at the end of the day, too. You'll also find lockers here, if you'd like to stash some of your belongings and pick them up before you leave.

## BUYING A TICKET

So here you are at the row of ticket booths where you'll have to make another decision: How many days can you spend exploring the Magic Kingdom, roaming Disney-MGM Studios, and taking a look at the wonders of the world in Disney's brand-new Experimental Prototype Community of Tomorrow, otherwise known as EPCOT?

Since that may take some consultation, I've allotted a special section a little further along in this chapter to a discussion of ways to see Disney World. Recommendations on how many days it takes to see it all, or the part of it in which you're most interested, come from the best brains at Disney and from my own assessment, acquired after walking many a mile around the Magic Kingdom, the new MGM Studios, and EPCOT Center. Take a look at that section on making the most of your (one, two, or three) days in the Magic Kingdom. Then, make some decisions, and then turn back here for a look at the prices.

A few years ago Disney World simplified life for us all by abandoning its former ticketing system which involved separate tickets for "A," "B," "C," and "D" attractions. In its place the park now sells one-, four-, and five-day tickets called "Passports," which can be used at any attraction in the park and allow you aboard all the park transportation from the monorail to the horseless carriage.

When EPCOT Center was completed in October 1982, and Disney-MGM in 1989, those massive sections of the park were included in multiday Passports, so you can travel around at will skimming back and forth, if you like, between the Magic Kingdom, Disney-MGM, and EPCOT Center.

Here are the prices of those Passports, but first a word of warning: *I am not guaranteeing these prices!* In 1987–88, Walt Disney World raised its prices *seven* times, and the hikes were substantial. There's no reason to think the park's ever-upward syndrome is over. Don't be put off by that, but *do* be prepared to pay a few dollars more than the prices I've quoted here.

A one-day ticket admitting you to the Magic Kingdom, Disney-MGM, or EPCOT Center, but not all three, is $30.65 for adults (10 years and up), and $24.30 for youngsters 3 through 9. Children under 3 are free at both attractions.

There are no two- or three-day tickets available.

A four-day Passport, including admission to all three parks, is $100.30 for adults, $79.15 for children.

Finally, a five-day Passport is $118.25 for adults, $95 for children.

There is some good news, however, amid these escalating prices: In 1990 Walt Disney World introduced an experimental pricing structure aimed at broadening the inclusivity of the four- and five-day Passports. Heretofore these passports permitted entry only into Walt Disney World and EPCOT. During the experiment, however, four- or five-day Passports will also allow entry to Typhoon Lagoon, Pleasure Island, Discovery Isle, and River Country. These latter attractions can be visited for one week beginning with the day of your first use of your passport. After those seven days, only the theme park admission days remaining on your passport can be used.

Tickets must be paid for in cash or by travelers' checks, American Express or MasterCard credit cards. Personal checks are accepted with proper identification, and WDW resort guests may charge tickets to their rooms with proper identification.

You can order tickets by mail by writing to Ticket Mail Order, Walt Disney World, Box 10030, Lake Buena Vista, FL 32830, but do allow at least 15 working days for the processing of your request and include $2 for handling costs.

If you leave the Magic Kingdom and want to return the same day, have your hand stamped at the exit.

If you're staying at one of the Walt Disney World resorts or in one of the hotels at the WDW Village Hotel Plaza, you can buy tickets right at your hotel. Village guests can get them at the Reception Center. WDW hotel guests save a few dollars on each, four- or five-day Passport.

## GETTING TO THE MAGIC KINGDOM

Once you've bought your tickets, you still have another journey ahead, and an exciting one it is, too.

To get to the door of the Magic Kingdom, you must find your way around or across the Seven Seas Lagoon (really a big lake). There are two ways to do that: Whoosh over on a monorail or chug over on a ferryboat. Either one can be boarded at the Transportation and Ticket Center, and both let you off right on the threshold of the Magic Kingdom.

On the five-minute monorail journey to or from the park, you'll ride alongside that sparkling lagoon, pass right through the lobby of the Contemporary Hotel and beside Polynesian Village, so you can get a look at both resorts. Peer below you as the monorail streaks along the water, and you'll spot bushes and trees shaped by talented gardeners into fascinating animal topiaries. My favorite's the Nessie sea monster, whose curving backbone rises up from, and disappears back into, the ground. Try *that* with your yew tree!

On the ferryboat, you ride merrily across the water and get a fascinating look at the Magic Kingdom as it rises up before you like a mirage. It's about a five-minute trip, not much longer than the monorail, but you do have to walk a little farther to the ferry dock. On crowded days, however, you can sometimes find a spot on the ferry faster than you can wait out the line to the monorail. Handicapped guests can use either form of transportation, although holding a wheelchair in line at the ramp to the monorail could be a bit tedious when the line's long, as it often is.

## SPECIAL NEEDS—CHILDREN, HANDICAPPED, FIRST AID, AND MORE

Having faced all those decisions and gotten yourself to the entrance of the Magic Kingdom, now what? Well, if you have **toddlers or small children** with you, you can be sure an exciting day with Mickey and Minnie will tire them out. To save your shoulder, your energy, and perhaps your temper, rent a stroller at the Stroller Shop for $4 a day. The shop's located at the far right of the Magic Kingdom entrance.

If that tiny one is a baby with a **baby's needs,** you can satisfy those at the Baby Center, a Gerber-sponsored endeavor. It's not far from the entrance of the Magic Kingdom, just off Main Street, U.S.A., next door to the Crystal Palace Restaurant. Here you'll find disposable diapers and a place to make the change, baby bottles and a place to warm them, pacifiers, baby food, and formula.

If you think you or one of your party might have trouble maintaining the pace, you can **rent a wheelchair** for $5 a day plus a $1 refundable deposit. You'll find the chairs at the Stroller Shop, too. If you have your own wheelchair, that's fine too, of course.

Just a note here about wheelchair travel: You can go just about anywhere in the Magic Kingdom in one, but wheelchair guests can't get off or on the monorail at the Contemporary Hotel. All the attractions except Space Mountain, Peter Pan's Flight, Swiss Family Treehouse, the Skyway, and the WEDway PeopleMover are accessible to guests who can be lifted from wheelchairs.

Attractions that can accommodate guests right in their wheelchairs are Main Street Cinema in Main Street, U.S.A.; Tropical Serenade in Adventureland; Hall of Presidents, Liberty Square Riverboats, and Diamond Horseshoe revue in Frontierland; and Mission to Mars, Circle-vision 360 "American Journeys," and Carousel of Progress in Tomorrowland. Many rest rooms in the Magic Kingdom also are equipped for people in wheelchairs.

Disney World visitors who are **blind** or have difficulty seeing should stop by City Hall on Main Street, U.S.A., and pick up a free tape cassette and a portable tape recorder (with a $10 refundable deposit) which will help them find their way around the Magic Kingdom via sound and smell descriptions. There are braille keys on the tape players.

For the **deaf,** the park provides a free written booklet on the attractions and for the hearing-impaired there's a translator unit that amplifies sound. Charge for the unit is $3 plus a refundable $10 deposit.

One would hope the need for **first aid** won't arise, but if you need a Band-Aid or an aspirin or even something more complicated, head for the first-aid station beside the Crystal Palace, just off Main Street, U.S.A., or a similar facility at the Transportation and Ticket Center. There's a registered nurse there to help you. If you need certain kinds of pills or medical supplies, however, be sure to take them with you. There's no pharmacy at the park.

It's possible that soon after you arrive, you will find that some of the things you thought you would need have become needless burdens. Naturally this book will not fall into that category. For those things that do, however, go over to the **lockers** located directly under the Main Street Station (and at the Transportation and Ticket Center as well), and for 25¢ or 50¢ you can keep your extra baggage secure while you traipse around the park. If you have something so large it won't fit the lockers, they'll take care of it for you at City Hall or Guest Relations at the Ticket and Transportation Center.

One thing you can't take into the Magic Kingdom is **pets,** be they parrots, poodles, ocelots, or a lovable turtle. Despite Disney's love for mice, dogs, elephants, ducks, and the like, you must park *your* Pluto here at the kennels, just next door to the Ticket and Transportation Center.

Your pet will be cuddled, loved, kept fed, watered, and pam-

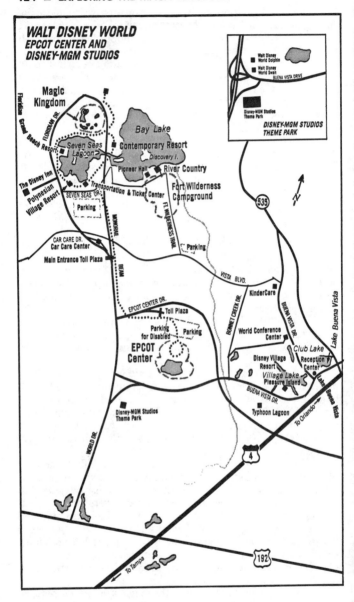

pered in air-conditioned quarters. If you have exotic pets, you must bring their cages or containers with you, and pets must have a certificate of vaccination just in case they bite someone.

If you're just at Disney World for the day, you can't leave Fido in the kennel overnight, but if you're staying in the WDW resorts or in a WDW Village Hotel Plaza you can. Kennels close an hour after the Magic Kingdom and EPCOT and the daily rate is $6. Rates for WDW resort guests or those staying in Lake Buena Vista Hotel Plaza hotels are $6 a day for dogs or cats, no charge for birds.

Some of us could lose things in an empty room. If you recognize yourself in that description (as I regrettably do), relax, Disney has the problem handled. Lose it, then rush over to the **Lost and Found,** where you can retrieve everything from your sunglasses to your sister. You can also report the loss at City Hall in Main Street, U.S.A., or at Guest Relations at the Ticket and Transportation Center.

As for **lost children,** you may find them here at Lost and Found or over at the Magic Kingdom Baby Center (by the Crystal Palace Restaurant), where hostesses will calm you down and find the missing little one.

If the **missing person** is an adult who's strayed or failed to show up at noon, as you'd agreed, etc., etc., then head for City Hall, where Kingdom Kids keep a message book. It might be a good idea to tell your whole group about this handy service, so you'll all know where to look if you get separated.

You can find **telephones** directly beneath the Main Street Train Station and at the Transportation and Ticket Center. Calls from within the Magic Kingdom are 25¢.

---

## Key to the Numbered References on the Magic Kingdom Map:

**(Main Street, U.S.A.)** 1. The Walt Disney Story; 2. Main Street Cinema; 3. Magic Kingdom Baby Care Center; 4. First Aid Center; 5. City Hall **(Tomorrowland);** 6. Swan Boats; 7. Circle Vision 360 "American Journeys"; 8. Dreamflight; 9. Mission to Mars; 10. StarJets; 11. WEDway PeopleMover; 12. Tomorrowland Theatre; 13. Carousel of Progress; 14. Skyway; 15. Space Mountain; 16. Grand Prix Raceway **(Fantasyland)** 17. The Mad Tea Party; 18. Mr. Toad's Wild Ride; 19. Snow White's Scary Adventures; 20. Dumbo, the Flying Elephant; 21. Cinderella's Golden Carousel; 22. Cinderella Castle; 23. 20,000 Leagues Under the Sea; 24. It's a Small World; 25. Peter Pan's Flight; 26. Skyway **(Frontierland & Liberty Square);** 27. Haunted Mansion; 28. Mike Fink Keelboats; 29. Liberty Square Riverboats; 30. Tom Sawyer Island; 31. Hall of Presidents; 32. Diamond Horseshoe Revue; 33. Frontierland Shootin' Gallery; 34. Country Bear Jamboree; 35. Frontierland Railway Station; 36. Big Thunder Mountain Railroad **(Adventureland)** 37. Pirates of the Caribbean; 38. Jungle Cruise; 39. Swiss Family Treehouse; 40. Tropical Serenade.

---

Then we come to the matter of **money.** Did I not tell you Disney thinks of everything? They thought, of course, of money and provided for it in the form of the Sun Bank, located just inside the Magic Kingdom on Main Street. It is open daily from 9am to 4pm

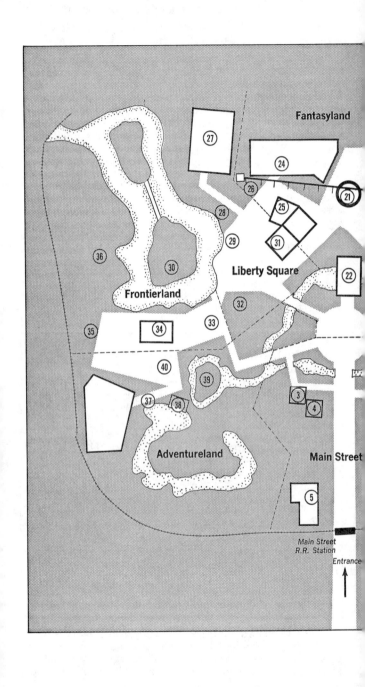

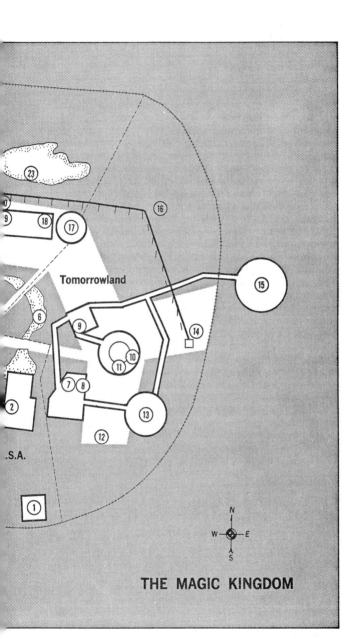

23

0
9
18
17

Tomorrowland

16

6
9
15
14
11 10
7 8
2
13
12
.S.A.

1

N
W E
S

THE MAGIC KINGDOM

and can help you with all the details of travelers' checks—selling, cashing, and refunding lost checks. Bankers here can also can issue cashier's checks and money orders, exchange foreign currency, provide emergency check-cashing for those with American Express or bank-issued credit cards, and cash personal checks, if you have a driver's license and major credit card. There are other Sun Banks in Disney World at Lake Buena Vista and in EPCOT.

Foreign currency can also be exchanged at City Hall, at the Guest Relations window at the Transportation and Ticket Center, and at the ticket booth in the Train Station on Main Street.

More on money. You can receive money by wire through Western Union offices at the Contemporary Hotel, in Kissimmee (tel. 847-4838) and on International Drive (tel. 352-5640).

You can pay for purchases in Magic Kingdom shops with cash, travelers' checks, or American Express, VISA, or MasterCard and for meals in the Magic Kingdom's sit-down restaurants with cash, travelers' checks, or credit cards, but in the fast-food dining areas, cash is the word.

Everything you ever wanted to know about the day's **entertainment** is available at the City Hall Information Center, where you can pick up maps and information on just about every facet of the Disney operation, including transportation facilities and times.

If you forgot or didn't bring a camera and have an urge to remedy that situation, head for **camera rental** in the Kodak Camera Center on Main Street, U.S.A. They'll rent you a Kodak camera free. All you do is leave a $50 deposit (cash or credit card).

You'll find **film on sale** here in the Camera Center and at Tropic Toppers in Adventureland; Frontier Trading Post in Frontierland; Heritage House in Liberty Square; and Kodak Kiosk or the Royal Candy Shoppe in Fantasyland. All hotels carry camera supplies, too.

**Postcards and stamps** can be bought at the Emporium and Penny Arcade on Main Street and mailed in antique-looking olive mailboxes. They'll be postmarked Lake Buena Vista, however.

If you buy **plants** in one of the shops and don't want to carry them around, park them in the kennels at the Ticket and Transportation Center.

**Alcoholic beverages** are not permitted in the Magic Kingdom but are available at all the hotels and in EPCOT. You must be 19 in Florida to buy alcoholic beverages. Younger travelers are permitted into hotel lounges but can't sit or stand at the bar.

If you run out of **cigarettes,** you can buy them at the Main Street Book Store on Main Street, Elephant Tales in Adventureland, the Trading Post in Frontierland, the Royal Candy Shoppe in Fantasyland, Heritage House in Liberty Square, and Mickey's Mart in Tomorrowland. There are vending machines at Columbia Harbour House in Liberty Square, King Stefan's in Cinderella Castle, Pinocchio Village Haus in Fantasyland, Tomorrowland Terrace, and the Mile Long Bar in Frontierland. Hotels have them, too, of course.

Finally, if you somehow forgot to buy those **mouse ears** for Aunt Tillie, don't despair. Once you're back home, just call (tel. 407/824-4718) or write Walt Disney World, Box 10,000, Lake Buena Vista, FL 32830, Attn. Mail Order Dept., and they'll send you what you want by mail.

# GETTING AROUND IN THE MAGIC KINGDOM

There's no doubt about it. The fanciful mind of that creative cartoonist has given new meaning to transportation. Here in the Magic Kingdom you can get around in fascinating ways that range from an antique horse-drawn trolley to a flying futuristic monorail.

Not only are those clanging, tooting conveyances fun to look at and to ride, but they save your feet from the tortures of pounding pavement. At the end of a long day in the Magic Kingdom, you'll look upon *any* step-saver with gratitude. What's more, all the transportation in the Magic Kingdom and in all of Disney World is free.

Let's start our explorations of Magic Kingdom transport with the most exciting way of all to go: **the monorail.** This sleek bullet-shaped train, with "fronts" on both ends, runs in a circle around the Seven Seas Lagoon, stopping at the Transportation and Ticket Center, Contemporary Resort Hotel, Polynesian Village, and the Magic Kingdom. You can also board a monorail at the Magic Kingdom's Ticket and Transportation center and zip over to EPCOT. To ride in the very first car, just ask the driver.

Inside the park, an old-time steam train makes a wide circuit around the perimeter of the park with a stop at Frontierland.

If you're a railroad buff—as was Walt Disney—and even if you're not, you'll enjoy a look at and a ride on these **railroad cars** that have an intriguing history stretching back to the turn of the century when they were constructed. Disney creators found them in Mexico, where they had been converted from coal- to oil-burning trains. Overhauled then and frequently now, as is everything in Disney World, the colorful trains operate on clean diesel fuel, and have lots of shining new parts to supplement the original equipment. Several different kinds of engines, named after Disney and his family and friends, pull the cars.

It's a lovely, breezy ride on a warm day and gives you a good introductory look at all the lands plus a glimpse of some of the animated creatures operated by the complex computer system WDW calls AudioAnimatronics.

I've already mentioned the ferryboat alternative to the monorail, but a little repetition never hurts, so: You can catch a **ferryboat** to or from the Transportation and Ticket Center to the Magic Kingdom. Although it takes just about the same time to traverse the water as the monorail takes to make its circuit, the ferryboat seems longer to most people, so lines for the boat are often shorter at the busy opening and closing hours of the park. What's more, it's a cool, relaxing ride across the lagoon and offers you an unusual view of this wonderland.

A quick and relaxing way to get from Peter Pan's Flight in Fantasyland to the center of Tomorrowland is the **Skyway to Tomorrowland.** A cable-car-in-the-sky ride, the Skyway gives you an eagle's-eye view over the Magic Kingdom before landing you in Tomorrowland. You can also take the ride from Tomorrowland and back to Fantasyland, but you'll first have to get off and get in another line to go back again. In short, the Skyway's a one-way trip in either direction.

In Main Street, U.S.A., there are several ways to travel. My favorite's the **horse-drawn trolley** that rattles its way down the middle of Main Street pulled by the rippling muscles of European plow horses. Those equine heavyweights haul visitors down Main Street to the Town Square and back up Main Street to Cinderella Castle all day long and live in a fancy barn at Fort Wilderness on their days off. You can see them there and watch them being shod if you're staying at Fort Wilderness.

You can almost feel the shock—not to mention the disdain— people felt at the turn of the century when you first spot a **horseless carriage** clipping merrily along Main Street. What a sight those first automobiles must have been to people who had never seen a motorized vehicle! In fact, those antique cars remain a strange sight today, but that doesn't make them any less fun to ride. What's more, you'll never have to get out and crank, since the cars sport modern engines and chug around the Main Street area with considerably more confidence than those early models.

**Double-decker buses** ply that busy Main Street thoroughfare too, joined by a merrily clanging, bright-red fire engine that's the stuff of many a youngster's dreams. You can ride both of them, but if you miss an actual ride on the fire engine, you can go look at it over at the Firehouse, a sight in its own right. It's next door to City Hall.

---

# LAND-HOPPING

---

It's time to start trekking, so let's take a look at the "lands" of Disney World. Attractions, restaurants, shops, and service centers are described as you explore each land, and you can see where the attractions are located by matching the number in the description with the numbers that appear on the map.

## GETTING ORIENTED

When you enter the Magic Kingdom you will pass underneath the railroad station and find yourself in Town Square. Stretching out in front of you is Main Street, U.S.A. Way at the end of that picturesque turn-of-the-century street looms the grandeur of Cinderella Castle, turrets glistening in the sunshine.

Just in front of the castle is an area known as the Hub, although its official designation is Central Plaza. Like Town Square, the Hub forms a circle. Think of it as the center of a wheel whose spokes run off left and right to the other lands in the Magic Kingdom. As you face the castle, the streets to Tomorrowland and Fantasyland are on your right; the avenues which will take you to Liberty Square, Frontierland, and Adventureland are on your left.

Since there are waterways circling the Hub, there's also a bridge to each of the lands. Again, as you face the castle the first bridge on your right goes to Tomorrowland. Moving counterclockwise, the second one to your right goes to Fantasyland, the next one which you'll find on your left goes to Liberty Square and Frontierland, and the final one on your left goes to Adventureland.

That may seem a little complicated, and an abundance of waterways, trees, flowers, curves, bridges, and dazzling distractions does complicate things a bit, but don't worry. Just keep an eye on the Magic Kingdom map, and if you still begin to feel a little lost, ask directions of any employee—you'll see hundreds of them cleaning, selling, and helping all over the grounds—and you'll soon be back on track again.

## A LOOK AT THE LANDS

Okay, oriented and anticipatory, off we go for a gleeful romp among fat bears and leering pirates, mysterious haunted houses and runaway railroad cars. . . .

### Main Street, U.S.A.

It's the queen of Main Street, U.S.A., the first thing you'll see and the last thing you'll remember. It's none other than Cinderella Castle, and it towers over the far end of Main Street in glittering magnificence. Somehow it fits there, despite the juxtaposition of medieval upon the turn-of-the-century prettiness of Main Street.

Here in the shadow of Cinderella, bells clang, horseshoes clatter, painted gingerbread facades sparkle, and there you are, suddenly cast out of the racing bustle of the 20th-century, back into a time when life moved more slowly. Glittering gaslights trim the curb, flags flutter atop window's walks, bay windows jut out over a sidewalk, wrought iron intricate as a spider's web rims a roofline, and an attic glass is carefully trimmed in ornate woodwork white as snow.

It is doubtful any Main Street in the U.S.A. was ever so picture-pretty. You'll want to explore every one of the emporiums here, and there are plenty, for each of them has something fascinating to show you.

To help you tour the Magic Kingdom's attractions, shops, and restaurants, I've numbered the attractions beginning at Main Street, U.S.A., and worked around counterclockwise to Tomorrowland, Fantasyland, Frontierland, and Liberty Square, ending in Adventureland.

To make a systematic tour of Main Street, you can start by turning to your right in the Town Square and heading over to a wide verandahed porch where a film, *The Walt Disney Story* **(1),** will give you a look at the life of the Mouse's "daddy."

Right next door is the **Town Square Café,** a Victorian delight gleaming with brass trim and woodwork. Breakfast is popular here, since you can sit outside in the relative cool of early morning and watch the square come to life. Simple home cooking, baked chicken, crisp salads, hefty sandwiches, chocolate cake, and the like also keep the Town Square Café crowded at lunch and dinner. Table service is available here, by the way.

An important upon-arrival stop is **Hospitality House,** tucked in between the "Walt Disney Story" and the Town Square Café. Here you can make reservations for "The Diamond Horseshoe Jamboree," a very popular live floor show about which you can read more in the section on Frontierland and Liberty Square. Suffice to say here that reservations are taken at Hospitality House on a first-come, first-served basis each morning for shows occurring that day only. So if you want to go, get your name in here first thing; the show is very popular.

One of my passions is hats, so I never miss a visit to the next shop along the way, **The Chapeau.** Here you'll find some frothy confections of lace, ribbons, and feathers incongruously paired with the monogrammed Mouseketeer ears you'll see everywhere. A great place to stock up on costume-party accessories or to pick up a little something for those people whose favorite cliché is "Now let me put on my other hat for a moment. . . ."

Next door, just at the corner, is that helpful place I mentioned earlier, the **Kodak Camera Center,** where you can borrow a camera by leaving a refundable $50 deposit. Video cameras are also available for $40 per day plus a $400 deposit via cash or a major credit card. Lots of other camera products there, too, including film, flashcubes, and various camera paraphernalia. You can also have an instantly developed shot taken of you and the gang in Victorian costume making a whistle-stop visit to the park aboard the back of a caboose.

Armed with film, photograph someone crunching happily away at the treats offered next door at the **Main Street Confectionery** where homemade peanut brittle's a lure.

You certainly need not fear starvation along Main Street. All along this make-believe boulevard you'll find ice cream, hot dogs, cookies, beverages, popcorn, and my all-time favorite, chocolate-covered frozen bananas, hawked by pushcart purveyors.

As you continue along the right-hand side of the street, you see the **Main Street Cinema (2).** Chortle over some of the classic films of a bygone era with stars like Charlie Chaplin and Fatty Arbuckle. Don't miss the early Mickey Mouse cartoon, *Steamboat Willie,* the first cartoon with sound and with the famous mouse and his mate.

More Disney World souvenirs—it's amazing how many things people can theme dream—at the **Disney & Co.,** shop next door. It may be hard to drag the kids out of this one.

Even harder to drag the distaffers out of the next shop along this side street: **Uptown Jewelers** carries a captivating line of antique-looking jewelry and some Disney character charms that may be among the more long-lasting souvenirs of your visit here.

Everything's old-fashioned everywhere you look on Main Street, but the **Main Street Market House** gets my vote for best "old" interpretation. Here a potbellied stove of the general-store variety is the center of things, surrounded by oak cases full of goodies that aren't old-timey but seem that way—Smucker's jams and jellies, Cracker Jacks, and other old favorites.

Shadow boxes, those black profiles created with an artist's eye and a sure hand on the scissors, are made as you watch at **The Shadow Box**—and there are always plenty of watchers. Plenty of buyers, too, since the paper portraits are just a few dollars, complete with frames.

Every time I see a glassblower at work I wonder what would happen if he *took* a deep breath instead of exhaling one. Somehow those artisans always manage to keep their mind on their work, which is just as well since they're working on molten glass so hot one misstep would required lots of burn remedy. Watch them twist their fiery product into fascinating forms at **Crystal Arts,** where you can also see a glass engraver at work.

Back on the main part of Main Street, cool off from watching that fiery glass at the **Main Street Bake Shop,** a charming little tearoom, where you can pick up some delicious coffeecake and Danish pastry. Then go next door to combine it with an ice cream creation at the **Plaza Ice Cream Parlor.**

If it's meal or snack time, you're right in place for a stop at the **Plaza Restaurant.** You can sit down, soak up the art nouveau decor, and let a waitress bring you a sundae dripping with sweet things or a substantial lunch or dinner that might include a hearty casserole or a pasta selection, a fat sandwich, or an overstuffed salad. For something lighter, there's a wildly colored pavilion next door that raisin-lovers should adore: Everything you order comes with a little side treat of raisins.

Or cross the street and have a jumbo hot dog and a soft drink in the pleasant, airy, red-and-white decor of the **Refreshment Corner,** a spot that will be appreciated by anyone who's hooked on old Coca-Cola memorabilia. Lots of it here.

If you continue on down the side street, you'll come to another popular Main Street, U.S.A., stopping spot, **Crystal Palace Restaurant.** This glass-domed barn of a restaurant is a cafeteria with some lovely views out over a courtyard or across the flower-bedecked sidewalks. Breakfast is a popular meal here, since there's a wide selection of goodies, usually plenty of room, and not much waiting time at early hours.

Here, too, is the **Magic Kingdom Baby Care Center (3)** and the **First Aid Center (4)** See the beginning of this chapter for a description of the services available at both centers.

You can now work your way down the opposite side of the street (that is, the left side as you face the castle, the west side of the street for those with a good sense of direction), aiming back toward Town Square.

Books are to some an irresistible lure. They're also the mainstay of the next shop along the avenue, **The Main Street Book Store.** This shop also sells some unusual greeting cards, stationery, and writing accessories.

Think you can't buy anything for a penny anymore? You can at Disney World where the **Penny Arcade** is the perfect place to lighten the load of coppers in your pocket. Use them to watch the first "movies," which were flipping cards that moved fast enough to fool your eye into thinking the characters were moving. Some slapsticky humor, and some fun things like a kiss-power tester, will keep you laughing.

If you know someone who's a practical joker—or are one yourself—you won't want to miss the next shop, the **House of Magic.** Well stocked with the gag items so loved by the world's lampshade wearers, this emporium also answers the dreams of would-be Merlins with things that pop up, disappear, reappear, and turn up in someone's ear.

If there's someone you'd like to clothe in Mouse-y fashion, stop by **Disney Clothiers,** just around the corner from the House of Magic. Every character in Mousedom is emblazoned on clothing for all ages.

Don't get your hair cut before you leave home. Wait until you get to the Magic Kingdom, and get those locks shorn in the style provided by **Harmony Barber Shop** (tel. 824-6550 for appointments). Likely as not you'll be serenaded during your shearing by —what else?—a barbershop quartet. If there's a moustache in the crowd, buy him his very own moustache cup.

Entries and exits wind all around these stores, so you'll easily find one of the largest stores in the Magic Kingdom, **The Emporium.** Its towering facade makes it a good landmark on Main Street, U.S.A., and inside you'll find zillions of souvenirs from T-shirts to towels to those ubiquitous ears.

When you walk out the door of The Emporium, you'll see **City Hall (5),** number-one information center in the Magic Kingdom and the place to go when you need help with just about anything. **Sun Bank** is right next door to provide you with financial services (see beginning of this chapter where those services are outlined).

Now you're back where you started at the Town Square and the **Railroad Station.** Here are two more possible stops, a snack bar called the **Station Break** and a **Newsstand** that's really a souvenir shop, no news.

From here in Town Square you can grab a ride on the railroad, if you're planning to make Frontierland, Mickey's Birthdayland, or Liberty Square your next stop. Or jump on the horse-drawn trolley, an antique jitney or horseless carriage, fire engine, or the Omnibus double-decker. Pick one and hitch a ride up to the Hub in front of Cinderella's Castle, where you can decide which of the lands to visit next.

## Tomorrowland

Ah, future shock. Here at Walt Disney World you can see what that means by walking a few steps from the old-time atmosphere on

Main Street, U.S.A., across a bridge, and there it is—the crystal ball of tomorrow gleams before you, inviting you to take a peek, if you dare.

Here you can play on an intriguing new transportation system, go on a mission to Mars, and soar through the black hole of infinite space on an innovative roller coaster.

What are we waiting for? Let's leave yesterday behind and race off into tomorrow. Once again, the attractions are keyed by numbers to the Magic Kingdom map.

As you cross the bridge to Tomorrowland (it's the first street on your right just as you end your walk up Main Street toward the castle and reach the beginning of the Hub area), you'll see a lovely blue canal. Floating serenely on it are enchanting craft called **Swan Boats (6).** Float down the waterways of the Magic Kingdom on one of these graceful creatures, a popular summer cooling-off spot.

Once across the waterway you'll find on your right one of the all-time favorite exhibits in the park, **Circle-Vision 360 "American Journeys" (7).** The wonders of the world roll out before you, behind you, and all around you as you watch a film that encircles the entire room. What a strange feeling it is to stand there in the center of the room and watch waters stretching out in front of you and see those same waters rolling away behind you. Reams of equipment are used to show this most unusual 20-minute film which many Disney-goers consider a must every time they visit the park.

Next door is Delta Airlines' exhibit. **"Dreamflight" (8)** is a ride-and-film combo that takes you on a historic journey in the world of aviation, the Caribbean, then ends up with some swooping special effects on a "hypersonic" flight. Exciting.

On your left as you enter Tomorrowland is **Mission to Mars (9),** where for a moment you become an astronaut heading off into space after a briefing by Mission Control. McDonnell-Douglas created this attraction, which includes some bizarre sounds, seats that shudder as you take off into space, and satellite photos of Mars' surface. Young explorers with good imaginations may like this one better than adults who have become inured to it all after watching many a rocket launching on television.

Next door is a spacey gift shop junior astronauts will find irresistible. Called **The Space Port,** it's filled with wire sculptures, "rain" lamps, and lots of chromy futuristic items.

Once you manage to drag yourself away from the glittering wonders of The Space Port and get back on the sidewalk, look up in the air and you'll see two other Tomorrowland attractions, **StarJets (10)** and the **WEDway PeopleMover (11).** On a StarJet you pilot your own spacecraft, a bullet-shaped car that moves in a circle as you "pilot" it up and down a few degrees—breezy and fun if you're a ride enthusiast.

As for the PeopleMover, it's a series of small trains moving on a track, a story or so above the grounds of Tomorrowland. Relaxing if you're footsore by now, the PeopleMover is an innovative concept in transport, in that it is powered by a motor that has no moving parts, uses little power, and discharges no polluting chemicals. You travel about a mile on the trains enjoying views of the monorails zooming by, some racing cars zipping along below, and at one point you even get a preview look at that scary Space Mountain roller coaster. Good place to decide whether Space Mountain is going to be part of your future.

Right here, too, by the PeopleMover and the StarJets is a snack bar called **The Space Bar,** offering a variety of sandwiches and snacks, soft drinks, and desserts.

Since this area forms a rough circle, let's move to the right (as you face StarJets and Space Mountain, that futuristic volcano-shaped building that towers over Tomorrowland). Back of the beaten path tucked away in foliage around the corner from Eastern's "Wings" exhibit is the **Tomorrowland Theatre (12),** where Kids of the Kingdom and Disney characters present a romp through fantasyland.

Next door you'll see a saucer-shaped building that houses the **Carousel of Progress (13),** a General Electric show which was first presented at the New York World's Fair. This 20-minute production features those life-sized, animated, computer-controlled figures Disney does so well. At this exhibit the AudioAnimatronic characters are a family group that tells you about the ways in which electricity has changed the history of this nation.

Moving along to your right you'll find the **Skyway Station Shop** filled with more mouse ears, T-shirts, and typically Disney souvenirs.

Beside the shop is the **Skyway (14),** a very popular attraction I mentioned earlier as a clever way to save your feet the journey from Tomorrowland to Fantasyland. Skyway's a cable car suspended high over the lands, and you move at a slow pace from Tomorrowland to Fantasyland, getting a marvelous view of the goings-on below. Lines here, they tell me, are often considerably shorter than Skyway lines at Fantasyland, so it might be a good idea to see all of Tomorrowland first, then take the five-minute Skyway ride to Fantasyland.

Here we are at last, the one Disney attraction every thrillseeker is determined to ride: **Space Mountain (15).** Enter here, and an eerie outer-space feeling descends upon you as you spot Disney employees in a control room from which a strange blue glow emanates.

Trepidation mounts as you hear the shrieks of riders, and culminates in some serious second thoughts when you see the bullet-shaped cars that are about to rocket you into this black-hole journey. It's comforting to have company on this ride since you sit directly in front of your companion, more or less on his/her lap.

Both of you are buckled in together and off you go into the wild black yonder, accompanied by wonderfully spooky sound-and-light effects. Meteors hurl themselves at you, stars shoot through the darkness, white lights zap. Slowly, slowly, you roll off into the blackness, then your speed increases, and suddenly you're whizzing through the inky darkness, your rocket tearing off at what seems to be 90-degree angles, flying up and down inclines.

Scary it is, but not as terrifying as some of the more diabolical roller coaster rides in amusement parks these days. Disney's Space Mountain thrills lie in spooky sounds and lights and the disorienting psychological effects of rapid, unexpected movement in darkness. It's also a short ride, just a little over two minutes, at speeds of about 30 miles an hour.

You're advised to pass this one up if you are subject to motion sickness, have a weak back or heart condition, poor health, physical limitations, or are pregnant. It's also a good idea to leave glasses, packages, and the like with a companion, since they can fly out of the car when you will be in no condition to attempt a retrieval. Lines here are enormously long almost all the time.

This is a ride much loved by youngsters, who take it over and over despite the wait, often an hour or more. You'll have to decide whether a two-minute ride is worth an hour-long wait. Thousands think it is.

Walk straight ahead as you leave the Space Mountain, and near the StarJets ride you will see a good snacking spot, **The Lunching Pad,** my candidate for Disney World's best pun. Here you can stoke up on some nutritious goodies like yogurt, trail mix, juices, sandwiches, salads, and natural foods, including carob-flavored treats.

To your right as you face The Lunching Pad is **Mickey's Mart,** filled with more Disney-theme treasures.

Next door to that a little farther along is **Tomorrowland Terrace,** a fast-food dining spot featuring performances by Michael Icebert, who makes strange sounds on electronic musical instruments. You can chow on some ordinary fare with extraordinary names like Moon Burgers and Galactic Pizza, a creation on sourdough bread.

Across the sidewalk is the **Grand Prix Raceway (16).** Racing-car buffs can get behind the wheel here and zoom in cars that run on a single metal track and seem to be racing even if they're really only going about seven miles an hour. Kids (you must be taller than 4'4" to ride) love it, but they aren't the only ones. The trick to steering, an aficionado tells me, is to turn the wheel all the way over in one direction or the other.

## Mickey's Birthdayland

Would that we could all age as gracefully as Walt Disney's famous rodent who doesn't look a day older than he did in his first film. Now cheerfully facing the seven-decade mark, the Mouse appears to have no need for a face-lift and is, in fact, quite cheerily celebrating his birthday every day of the year at Mickey's Birthdayland.

Designed as a 60th-birthday celebration spot for Central Florida's famous mouse, Mickey's Birthdayland proved so popular it became a permanent part of the park.

Shhh, don't anybody tell. Minnie and the gang are planning a surprise birthday party for Mickey and you're invited. First you find your way to the kitchen through Mickey's tiny house. Then you join the crowd in Minnie's kitchen where a rather disastrous baking day is under way.

Then it's on to the party where Pluto, Goofy, Chip 'n' Dale, and all the gang sing and dance a birthday greeting to their favorite friend. When the party's over, you can wander around this miniaturized "village," a particularly appealing spot for very young children who can also get a close look at some barnyard babies at Grandma Duck's Farm, home to chicks, piglets, and miniature horses.

## Fantasyland

Cloud pictures in the sky, rabbits with monocles, dwarfs and witches, glass slippers, and little boys with wings. That's the stuff of fantasies, those glorious moments when imagination is unfettered by reality and dreams are released to fly free.

Here colors glow, architectural ornaments glitter, and even the flowers seem to grow with a little more vigor. You would expect children to love Fantasyland's rainbows of colors and never-ending surprises—and they do—but I often think those who love it most are adults, who know too well the fragility of fantasies.

You can get here several ways. By coming straight up Main Street and around the Hub, you enter in the most glamorous way of all, right through the middle of Cinderella Castle; from any of the lands, just follow the streets around in the direction of Fantasyland (any Kingdom Kid, and plenty of signs, can tell you which direction to go); and finally, the way we'll go, right around the bend from Tomorrowland.

Since we're trying to do this systematically, let's start where we left off in Tomorrowland and just keep on going into the land of fantasies. Right in front of the Grand Prix Raceway, you'll see the first Fantasyland attraction you can visit, and it's a crazy one—**The Mad Tea Party (17).** You do remember that wacky soul in *Alice in Wonderland* who invited Alice over for some un-birthday party tea, don't you? Well, join the Mad Hatter here and go round and round in a king-sized teacup that spins crazily about a huge teapot.

Stagger out of your cups and just ahead you should see another wacky ride, **Mr. Toad's Wild Ride (18),** based on a Disney film about a toad who trades his manse for a car. This one reminds me a little of an electronic game. You ride in a car past all kinds of thrills—a chicken coop filled with protesting cacklers, a haystack, down a railroad track, and through the dark where you're threatened by all sorts of falling, banging things.

*Note to parents:* Mr. Toad's adventures and Snow White's scary trip into the forest (see below) are wild, giggly trips for adults, but very young children often find them more frightening than fun. Park officials advise you to consider the courage of toddlers before you subject them to the special effects of these rides.

If you need a little something to calm your nerves, stop in right next door to Mr. Toad's hangout at **Nemo's Niche,** a cuddly toy shop; **The Round Table** for a soft-ice-cream cone to soothe you at the adjoining **Gurgi's Munchies & Crunchies** for chicken nuggets; or at **Enchanted Grove** for swirly ice cream, slushies, and other assorted treats.

Think some gum drops or a peppermint stick will provide enough soothing? Get one next door to Gurgi's at **The Royal Candy Shoppe,** which also dispenses Disney memorabilia.

Between the candy shop and another souvenir store, **The**

**AristoCats,** is an adventure that takes you to the fairest of them all, Snow White. Go deep into the dark, forbidding forest of **Snow White's Scary Adventures (19)** to meet that wicked witch and shed a tear for gullible Ms. White. Just keep an eye out for the evil sourceress—she's got some surprises in store for you!

Around the bend from Snow White's Adventures, on the other side of The AristoCats giftshop, is **Mickey's Christmas Carol.** It's Christmas every day here in this wonderland of glitter and sugarplums.

Across the sidewalk from Snow White's place is darling Dumbo, the elephant world's answer to the Flying Nun. At **Dumbo, the Flying Elephant (20),** you'll see him whirling young riders up, down, and around in a simple ride that will thrill the little ones but is pretty tame for adult riders.

As you wander on in the shadow of Cinderella Castle, you will pass—or if you're like me, you will *not* pass, you will get on—**Cinderella's Golden Carousel (21).** What can you say about a merry-go-round? It's wonderful and, yes, I have a favorite steed, but I'm not telling which one. You'll take it, and it's mine. Besides, there are 89 others on this remodeled early-1900s carousel that once resided in a Detroit park, all of them glamorous equines that will carry you off in style. No expense was spared on this glittering creation which is something to see, whether or not you ride.

While you're right here, take some time to wander through the crowning glory of Disney World, none other than **Cinderella Castle (22).** This is Disney magic at its best, a fairyland structure crowned with needle-pointed spires and trimmed with turrets, chimneys, and lacy woodwork. Taller than Sleeping Beauty's manse in California's Disneyland, it seems to float among the clouds, its towering loveliness reflected in the waters that surround it.

Modeled after the architecture of medieval France and the incredible Bavarian palace of Mad King Ludwig (who may have been crazy but had the eye of a Michelangelo), the castle hides an interesting secret. Beneath it are the labyrinthian corridors used by Disney characters to traverse the park so they can turn up wherever they wish, like magic. Down here beneath the ground are stored the thousands of glittering costumes worn by Disney performers, who move through the corridors on electric carts. That's how Mickey and Minnie are able to be on Main Street one moment and turn up two "lands" away just a short time later.

You can't explore the whole castle, which also contains broadcasting facilities and an apartment meant for, but never used by, the Disney family, but you can walk straight through it and across the moat.

On your way through, marvel at the enormous mosaic murals composed of thousands of tiny slivers of glass in all colors of the rainbow, plus real gold and silver. It relates to the woes of lovely Cinderella and those nasty step-relations of hers. It's not hard to imagine her living happily ever after, here in this glittering monument to fairy tales.

Here in the castle is one of the Magic Kingdom's best and most elaborate restaurants, **King Stefan's Banquet Hall.** To dine here is to be served by lasses clad in ornate medieval gowns, in a setting of heavy wood beams and high ceilings, to drop back into another century, a time of royalty and riches, of knights in shining armor. King Stefan, by the way, was Sleeping Beauty's papa. Lunch and dinner are served here, and the preparations are more elaborate than you'll find elsewhere in the Magic Kingdom. You must make reservations at the door, and you'd better do that as soon as you arrive at the park, as seats go quickly.

Here, too, is an interesting gift shop, **The King's Gallery,** where you'll see fascinating chess sets and some lovely, if pricey, items ranging from music boxes to enamelware, lidded German beer steins, pewter and woodwork, and a special metal work done with silver and gold etched onto steel and called Damascene work after the Damascus creators of this skill.

Back in Fantasyland and behind the castle, you'll see a body of water dotted with boulders whose rough fingers reach out of the water to impede the progress of a submarine. A submarine? Yes, indeed, it's Fantasyland's **20,000 Leagues Under the Sea (23),** in which you board a submarine piloted by that awesome Captain Nemo of *20,000 Leagues Under the Sea* fame. These submarines carry you through millions of gallons of water in which dwell all kinds of imaginary sea creatures that loom up out of the blue. You even pass a polar ice cap before returning once again to terra firma.

Along the edge of Captain Nemo's playground is another snacking spot, the **Tournament Tent,** named for the tentlike enclosure from which are dispensed fruit drinks, ice cream, and submarine sandwiches.

Beyond that you'll see another tentlike structure, **Fantasy Faire,** where Mickey himself appears, accompanied by other characters who sing and dance for you several times a day. You can find out what hours they'll be performing at City Hall or on signs posted outside Fantasy Faire. Performances are great for photographs.

"Magic Journeys," a weird 3-D film that was once the hit of EPCOT Center, has reappeared here in Fantasyland. Don those funny 3-D glasses and fly over field and stream, meet a wicked witch who zaps you right in the eye with her jar of lightning, and a kite that persists in sitting right on your eyebrow. It's amazing and amusing and you'll love it—just watch out for those bats!

Here, too, you can get a look at an hilarious vintage Donald Duck short subject shown for the first time in three-dimensions.

As you might have noticed by now, there is absolutely no chance of starvation in Disney World. One more spot dedicated to staving off hunger pangs is **Pinocchio Village Haus** just across from the carousel. There's a European flavor about this warren of rooms where cuckoo clocks tweet away the hours. More of the usual child-pleasing fare here: fried chicken, hamburgers, hot dogs, and soft drinks. You can have breakfast here, too, if you decide to start your day in Fantasyland and nearby is the Pretzel Wagon.

Hard by Pinocchio's hangout is another all-time park favorite, **It's a Small World (24).** Some parkgoers tell me they stop here every time they visit Disney World. They just can't get enough of the hundreds of tiny dolls dressed up in folkwear of every nationality and singing their little hearts out. As you ride through this one, you're serenaded by the dolls, moving hands, feet, eyes, and assorted other parts. There are Hawaiian hula dancers, toy London Beefeater Guards, wooden-shoed Dutch dancers, Greek terpsichoreans, herds of singing animals, plus dozens more. Definitely one of Disney's cutest AudioAnimatronic displays. You'll love it. Everybody does.

Directly across the walkway from Small World is a big enclave which houses a number of shops and restaurants plus another favorite Disney attraction, Peter Pan's Flight.

Straight across from where you're standing when you exit Small World is another camera shop, **Kodak Kiosk,** which will develop film in two hours and is convenient if you've run out of film; a juice bar, **Troubador Tavern;** a **Disneyland Shop** with old and new Mouse memorabilia; and another hat shop, this one sponsored by that **Mad Hatter.**

Here, too, you'll find **Peter Pan's Flight (25),** on which you'll fly over the rooftops of London, Big Ben, Thames, and all, just the way Peter and Tinkerbell did. Watch out for that vicious Captain Hook, and cheer on the crocodile who's got a taste for captain-meat.

You can see more of these characters at **Tinkerbell's Toy Shop,** where pirate ships and their crews are the theme. Buy an Alice in Wonderland or Snow White costume here; who cares if Halloween is a year away?

Finally, on the very edge of Fantasyland near It's a Small World is the other end of that **Skyway (26)** I mentioned earlier. Board here and ride through the sky on a cable-car trip to Tomorrowland.

## Frontierland and Liberty Square

Americana in all its glory comes to life in these lands as Disney World, in its inimitable style, honors the American battle for liberty and the frontier spirit of those who fought and died in the struggle to expand the nation's boundaries.

Here America's legends, real and fictional, become the themes of rollicking entertainment, cozy cafés, and shops packed with the regalia of those bygone days.

It's sometimes corny and sometimes commercial, but beneath the surface runs a recollection that the nation we all share today is the gift of those who shed their blood on icy battlefields or fought their way through the wilderness to hack out a tiny piece of tomorrow for us all.

Just as Fantasyland merges imperceptibly into these two lands, Frontierland and Liberty Square flow together around a tranquil waterway that provides a setting for the re-creation of legends and legendary times in American history.

At the center of it all is a massive tree of such impressive girth and stature no one could bear to destroy it, so the giant live oak was dubbed the Liberty Tree and moved to its present location between The Hall of Presidents and Liberty Tree Tavern, where it has become the focus of these two lands. In its ancient branches are 13 tiny lanterns honoring the 13 original colonies that ignited the lamp of freedom in this nation.

You can enter these two lands from several directions, including the roads leading off to your left as you walk down Main Street toward the castle. Let's work on the assumption, however, that you're moving right around the park, counterclockwise, so you'll be near the Main Street exit when you've seen everything.

Okay, on we go then making our way from Fantasyland through Frontierland and Liberty Square.

As you leave Fantasyland past the Skyway ride, keep to your left and you'll pass right through to these two Disney lands. Happy will be the cooks who spot **Yankee Trader Gourmet Culinary Aids,** a shop packed with all the kitchen accoutrements you can think up, and perhaps a few you've never envisioned. Big wooden spoons, gadgets that cut french fries and flute radishes, mashers and mills, specialty foods, and lots and lots of cookbooks. No pioneer chef ever had it so good.

From there keep to your right and . . . shiver . . . it's the **Haunted Mansion (27),** rising in spooky splendor at a curve of the waterway. All the elements of horror are here—tombstones, cobwebs, see-through ghosts, and creaky noises—but you'll find it more fun than faint-producing.

As you enter a hall lined with portraits, you'll hear us dedicated cowards shrieking as the walls rise (or does the floor drop?). Once past that little thriller, you get a look at a most civilized, if somewhat ghostly, banquet where the transparent departed nod and chatter happily beneath spider webs and layers of dust.

Bats swoop, creatures appear and disappear, and you'll love every ghastly minute of it. Be sure to read the tombstones outside, too! This one's a top park attraction and definitely a don't-miss. (An interesting side note here: Workers have to struggle to keep this place *dirty* by importing dust and spreading it around.)

Back outside (sigh of relief) in the security of daylight, wander back the way you came and focus on water. That shouldn't be difficult, since you'll see quite a lot of it streaming by. To get out there on it, choose one of three ways: keelboat, double-decker riverboat, or a Tom Sawyer-inspired raft.

That brings us to three adventures located right here. **Mike Fink Keelboats (28)** was named for a riverboat captain of the early 1800s. One of the keelboats is named *Gullywhumper,* and the dock where the boats are moored is flanked by **Ichabod's Landing,** where you can buy some of the magic they make at the Haunted House.

The **Liberty Square Riverboats (29),** moored nearby, sail up and down the waterway here, so to avoid a repetitive trip, pick one or the other. Along the way on either boat you'll see Disney-created animals and pioneer adventures in action, not to mention more of the beautifully manicured grounds that you've been seeing all over the park. These paddlewheelers are real riverboat replicas run by a steam-driven paddlewheel. Hidden underneath the water, however, is a rail that keeps the boat on course.

If that youthful adventurer, Tom Sawyer, captured your childhood imagination, here's your chance to follow in his wake, so to speak, aboard a **Tom Sawyer Island (30)** raft journey that takes you across the river to Tom Sawyer's own island, where there are caves to explore, a rope bridge to traverse, and a shudder-causing water crossing made of barrels—a barrel of laughs for thrillseekers.

This island is a wilderness of deep tropical jungle growth that creates a restful serenity. There's plenty for kids to explore, ranging from **Fort Sam Clemens** guarded, in a manner of speaking (you'll see what I mean), by more AudioAnimatronically controlled characters and fitted up with toy guns the kids can blast away on to their heart's content. There's a dark tunnel to call echoes in, and for parents who want a moment's quiet, there's a pretty resting place called **Aunt Polly's Landing,** where you can munch on some basic sandwich and soft-drink selections.

Back at the riverboat dock and across the street from it you'll find a cluster of shops and eateries surrounding another premier attraction at Disney World, **The Hall of Presidents (31).** A favorite of history buffs, this production features life-size and lifelike figures of every president of the U.S., including the current one, answering a roll call while his predecessors listen, make notes, squirm about a bit, and even whisper to each other in the background.

Each president is dressed in the clothes of his time. All the outfits were carefully researched, as is everything about this show, from the furnishings to the minutest details of hair, eyes, cuff links, and tie pins. Preceded by a film outlining the importance of the Constitution to America, the Hall of Presidents' roll call provides a stirring show and one so realistic you will hardly believe your eyes.

On a side street here you'll find a cluster of shops and fast-food shops including **Heritage House,** where historical memorabilia—authentic-looking copies of historic documents on parchment paper—make attractive souvenirs, and Early American–replica housewares are sold; the **Silhouette Cart** purveyors of your favorite silhouette—you!; the **Umbrella Cart** custom-made personalized bumbershoots; and the **Courtyard,** sellers of topiaries and garden delights; **Old World Antiques,** which is jammed with antique furniture and bric-a-brac, the real thing plus reproductions; **Silversmith,** where you'll wonder how they keep all those polished silver spoons, pitchers, bowls, and candlesticks shining; **Sleepy Hollow Refreshments,** where you can find munchies and try a special Legendary Punch; **Columbia Harbor House** for batter-fried shrimp and sandwiches; and finally **The Fife and Drum,** an ice-cream shop (or shoppe).

That brings us to **Liberty Tree Tavern,** which is just a little too special to lump in with all the snack shops and quick stopping spots in the Magic Kingdom.

Here pillars soar at the wide entrance, and inside early Americana comes to life. You'll spot a spinning wheel waiting for its mistress to continue her work, a writing desk worthy of Ben Franklin, a tiny cradle, pewter, copper, and a fireplace. You'll feel as if you stepped right back into time in this wallpapered and draperied dining room where waitresses stride from the kitchens carrying heaped-up platters of food every bit as typically early American as the atmosphere: apple brown betty, pumpkin pie, pot roast, beef stew, and a very special walnut bread that's not to be missed. You can have lunch or dinner here, but do anticipate a crowd, since this lovely dining room ranks right up there with King Stefan's Banquet Hall in popularity.

As you stroll along the street on which dwells Liberty Tree Tavern, you'll be moving right into Frontierland, where there's more fun in store.

Just beyond Liberty Tree Tavern is one of the park's best-loved show spots, the **Diamond Horseshoe Revue (32).** Here leggy, beruffled damsels kick up their heels and some corny comics deliver punch lines that wouldn't play even in a rural area but are so silly you laugh anyway. All together, it makes a lively vaudeville show reminiscent of a frontier saloon performance that wouldn't raise even a schoolmarm's eyebrow.

There are several shows each day, and you need reservations, which you can make by presenting yourself at the door of the attraction in the morning of the day you want to attend. Reserved seats are on a first-come, first-served basis. First arrivals usually show up minutes after the park opens, so get there early. If you don't make it, drop by 45 minutes or so before a show and hope for a cancellation.

Next door to the revue is another chapeaux château, **Tricornered Hat Shoppe.** This one's big on frontier headwear—raccoon caps, cowboy gear, and the like. Once you've invested in the perfect ten-gallon topper, stride next door, pick up a gun, and mow 'em down at the **Frontierland Shootin' Gallery (33),** where you can fire away at toy buffalo, rabbits, and other frontier dinner fare. A dozen shots are 50¢ at the Shootin' Gallery, one of only a few attractions in the Magic Kingdom that charge a fee.

To complete the outfit you started at the Tricornered Hat Shoppe, stop at the **Frontier Trading Post** and stock up on all the things an urban frontiersperson needs—sunbonnets, belt buckles, moccasins, a six-shooter, even a Native American drum you can use to pound out a come-home-to-supper message for the kids.

One Disney visitor I know so enjoys the next attraction you'll encounter in the Magic Kingdom that he's seen it no less than 12 (!) times and says he can't wait to get back again to make it 13. He is not alone in his feelings about the **Country Bear Jamboree (34),** a rocking-and-roaring good time presented by some of the fattest, funniest roly-polys your imagination could conjure.

Performed in Grizzly Hall, this grin-and-bear-it, western hoedown is entirely peopled by bears (AudioAnimatronic all) who have exchanged hibernation for jubilation. Hear Five Bear Rugs, a country and western group, lay it on thick; watch Teddi Bearra flirt and flutter her boa; and Big Al, well, you have to meet Big Al to understand why he's become a park folk hero.

As the bear buffs exit the Country Bear Jamboree, many of them head right next door to the **Mile Long Bar,** which isn't quite a mile long but looks it, thanks to tricky mirrors and a gleaming brass rail. Mooseheads and the like offer some glassy-eyed stares as you munch away on snacks.

Next door, the **Pecos Bill Café** sports a rustic interpretation of Old West atmosphere with stick-and-twig ceiling and indoor and outdoor dining areas that serve hamburgers and hot dogs.

At the end of this boulevard is the **Frontierland Railway Sta-**

tion (35) mentioned earlier under ways to get around the Magic Kingdom. You can board the steam train here and travel back to Main Street, U.S.A., scenically circling the park, or, of course, get off the train here after boarding on Main Street.

There's still one more choo-choo you won't want to miss: **Big Thunder Mountain Railroad (36).** Board this train and whiz off over hill and dale, past a towering red stone outcropping, a flooded mining town, waterfalls, cackling chickens, hee-hawing donkeys, and authentic mining equipment. Just watch out for the sharp curves and at that last bend—prepare to get a little damp!

Other dining options here include the **Frontierland Wagon** which serves churros, a crispy Mexican pastry topped with sugar; **Westward Ho,** with snacks and beverages; and the **Nacho Wagon,** dishing up nacho chips topped with cheese.

Those who harbor a nearly unbearable love for those cunning country bears can stock up on memories of them at **Bearly Country** where the bruins show up in stuffed toys, country crafts, and clothing. At **Big Al's** you can get yourself outfitted in a Davy Crockett coonskin cap; at **Frontierland Wood Carving** artistic wood creations are the featured find; and at **Brier Patch** you can buy a pretty basket to cart this stuff around.

## Adventureland

Even the meekest among us harbor secret dreams in which we challenge a whitewater rapid or stride across an African veldt roamed by lumbering elephants and racing gazelles.

No matter that we trudge off instead to offices where the biggest adventure is a jaunt to the watercooler and the only roars are disapproval. No matter that we use the down payment on a Tahiti-bound sailing yacht to reseed the front lawn and relegate our fantasies to vicarious video excitement.

No matter, for in our secret dreams we're off sailing the seven seas, brandishing a sword, swigging rum from a gold chalice, and daring our enemies to fire at will. We hear the low growls of a jaguar prowling the primeval forest, swing across a stream on a sinewy jungle vine, and revel in the splashing joy of a cascading waterfall.

To begin your adventure in this part of the Magic Kingdom, stand facing the railroad station and follow the walkway around to your left. Curve around and you will soon see a collection of shops and snacking facilities called Caribbean Plaza.

Here the center of attraction is an adventure called Pirates of the Caribbean, which has spawned a treasure trove of shops offering everything from a skeleton-head flag to a ship in a glass bottle. Stop at the **House of Treasure** to outfit yourself in a pirate's hat, to grab up a shining musket replica, and to find a buried-treasure map.

At **Plaza del Sol Caribe** buy one of the huge straw sombreros you'll see all over the park, and at **Laffitte's Portrait Deck** have a photograph taken of yourself in full regalia surrounded by your booty.

Across the way, at the **Golden Galleon,** you can invest in a brass cannon or a spyglass—what respectable pirate would be without one? Or ferret out **La Princess de Cristal** and get your piratical monicker emblazoned on a goblet or on a ship in a bottle. If you're hungry, stop at nearby **El Pirata y el Périco** for a hot pretzel.

Then, in full gear, stride into **Pirates of the Caribbean (37)**, one of the best and liveliest of the Magic Kingdom's Audio-Animatronic tales. Here you sail on a pirate boat through the darkness as buccaneers lay waste to an unsuspecting village. Fearsome drunken pirates loll around, a dog barks, chickens cackle, and as you roll by, one of those brigands sits dangerously close above you, so close you can see the hair on his legs! It's great fun and an amazing display of imagination at work. Definitely a don't-miss at Disney.

Calm yourself (a little) after that adventure with a ride on the **Jungle Cruise (38)**, you'll feel like Hepburn and Bogart sailing off on *The African Queen.* You chug right among trumpeting elephants at bath time (and swear you're going to sail right into one) while jungle animals roar and chatter from the shoreline. Watch out for the headhunters, and don't get wet in the waterfall that is another remarkable part of this Disney jungle. In winter, when Orlando temperatures drop to chilly levels, a massive heating system keeps things steamy here. If all that water makes you thirsty, there's an **Oasis** next door.

Remember that Swiss family that ended up shipwrecked and marooned on an island, then learned to like it so well they stayed? You can get a pretty good idea why they found their retreat so tranquil by taking your own fantasy journey to their house, the **Swiss Family Treehouse (39)**. Climb up into the house (no, you don't *really* climb a tree) and peek inside to see the amazing results that can occur when people combine necessity with ingenuity. Wait until you see how they get running water.

Across the way is a warbling wonderland formally called **Tropical Serenade (40)**, but everyone knows it as Enchanted Tiki Birds. Hundreds of birds and other creatures inhabit this enchanted land, another of those incredible credibles only Disney can create.

Around the bend, the Florida Citrus Growers present the state's number-one product—orange and grapefruit juice—at the **Sunshine Tree Terrace.** Just about everything, including the ice cream, has that refreshing orange flavor in it, so this makes a good spot to stop before you tackle the enclave of tropical shops nearby.

Move from the juices and orange-flavored pastries to **Traders of Timbuktu,** where you can don a shark's-tooth pendant or buy a handsome wood carving in an appealing African atmosphere.

The products of China, Hong Kong, and other Asian points dazzle you with brilliant color at **Zanzibar Shell Company,** and I managed to find a safari hat I'd long sought at **Elephant Tales.** Need that staple of the tropics, a swimsuit? They've got one or two hundred at **Tiki Tropic Shop,** and to go with it, pick up a couple of dozen strands of shell necklace at **Colonel Hathi's Safari Club.**

If you're exhausted after all that browsing and buying, collapse at **Adventureland Veranda,** where you can dine in a Sidney Greenstreet paddle fan atmosphere on crispy salads and sandwiches with tropical fruit touches or full meals featuring the flavors of Polynesia and Asia. Next door at the **Aloha Isle,** you can nibble a Dole pineapple spear or sip a cool piña colada punch (without the punch, as are all liquid refreshments in this alcohol-spurning kingdom).

So there you have it, umpteen shops and cafés, pockets of hilarity and high spirits in the Magic Kingdom. When it's all over, you'll find yourself humming the tiki birds' songs and breaking out in an occasional chim-chim-cheree right along with the hundreds of others who come here in search of a few hours of Disney's magic, only to find it living forever in their hearts.

# EXPLORING RIVER COUNTRY, DISCOVERY ISLAND, AND TYPHOON LAGOON

It should come as no surprise that here in this kingdom where magic reigns, the wonder of water has not been forgotten. No matter where you go in Disney World, you're not far from its soothing serenity. There is, however, one special place, **River Country,** where you can give yourself over to its restorative powers, revel in the rapturous moments it has to offer. Tarzan enthusiasts can swing out over pools on ropes, and Tom Sawyer fans can experience a feeling of abandon at the ol' swimming hole.

Here creativity has carved from scrubby wilderness a giant water wonderland, piled with boulders, and lined with powdersoft sand. Watery delights challenge you to rocket down a giant slide, splash topsy-turvy and inner-tube–clad down a surface slick with ripples, to plunge through air to water.

Accomplished swimmer or aquatic amateur, there's something for everyone here at River Country, so let's take a look at some of the fun in store for you at this Disney World attraction.

Located on **Bay Lake,** which is also home to Fort Wilderness and Discovery Island and laps at the back door of the Contemporary Resort Hotel, River Country is divided into several sections, so everyone from toddlers to teenagers and parents can play here. For openers, there's a huge swimming pool, the largest in the country.

Better than that is **Bay Cove,** which most people call the ol' swimming hole, and is in fact part of Bay Lake. There's a special version of that swimming hole for youngsters, complete with beach, and around it all are beautifully landscaped grounds with picnic tables, a fountain, and a jungle nature trail.

In the huge swimming pool you can dive from some of those clever Disney-made rocks, or get yourself into the water by cannonballing down one of the two waterslides that streak high above the water. Don't look down, it won't help. So twisty is the slide you can't see the bottom anyway.

In Bay Cove board a rubber inner tube at **White Water Rapids** and challenge those swirling drops to do their darnedest. Here you board at **Raft Rider Ridge,** set off aboard your spinning wheel, and loop-do-loop down chutes and through whirlpools that spin and splash you downward as you bump and bound off other tumblers flying around the bends.

Or trudge to the top of **Whoop 'n' Holler Hollow** and leap into one of the two flumes where rushing waters send you spiraling down, faster than a speeding bullet (well, it seems that fast anyway) into the pool below. Sit up to create your own version of low gear or lie down to go into overdrive. To create a watery Indianapolis 500 run, arch your back so the least amount of body is in contact with slide and . . . whoooosh!

On hot summer days, Disney World-wise River Country visitors buy their tickets at the Transportation and Ticket Center *before* visiting the Magic Kingdom. They do that because they know so many people want to play here that River Country is often filled to capacity (and the ticket window closed) by noon or earlier. If you've already bought a ticket, however, you can go in anytime during the day. So if you're planning a visit to this wonderland of water fun, buy your ticket early and come back later for an afternoon swim. At any time of year, crowds begin to dwindle about 4 or 5pm, so if you're anti-crowd you may find these early evening hours appealing. There's usually also a $1 summer discount on admissions after 6pm, and the attraction remains open until 10pm most of the year. In summer this is the place to beat the heat. It's closed December to mid-February.

Some other things you'll need to know about River Country: Since some of the River Country adventures require swimming ability, children under 10 must be accompanied by an adult; you can bring your own towels or rent small ones for 25¢; men's and women's dressing rooms and coin lockers are available; you can bring your own picnic lunch and consume it on the beach or at well-shaded picnic tables; there are two snack stands, **Pop's Place** for burgers, dogs, beer, hot pretzels, and soda, and **The Waterin' Hole** with similar selections but fewer of them.

Admission to River Country is $11.75 for adults, $9.25 for children 3 to 9. Prices are a little cheaper for guests of Disney World resorts and Lake Buena Vista Hotel Plaza hotels.

Hours are 10am to 5pm, to 9pm in summer months, and you can get there by bus (look for those with a blue flag on the side) from the Transportation and Ticket Center, by boats which leave regularly from the dock near the gates of the Magic Kingdom, or by car (follow the signs as you enter the park). You do not need any identification for the blue-flagged bus, but you do need a ticket or hotel identification for the boat ride.

There's still one more adventure in store for you here in this part of the Magic Kingdom. It's called **Discovery Island.**

If you remember some of those enchanting Disney cartoon movies that brought favorite fairy tales to the celluloid screen, you'll recall that most of the human creatures often walked and talked with the animals. Birds helped Cinderella trim her ballgown with flowers, chipmunks stitched for her, rabbits scampered around Snow White and all the animals of the forest proved friends in time of need.

To visit Discovery Island is to live, like Cinderella or Snow White and their princes, in harmony with the animals, in a rainbow-hued garden where it's always springtime.

Meandering here across nearly 12 acres of island surrounded by the sparkling waters of Bay Lake, you'll find yourself in another world, the sounds of the World you left behind shut out, the chatter of birds and the scent of flowers your companions.

To create this zoological and biological wonderland, Disney creators built up the land, dug out waterways, piled up rocks, and sunk roots. Exotic plants from equally exotic climes were introduced to this wonderland; birds and animals from nations all over the world were transplanted to new homes here, endangered species pampered into procreation.

Nature owns this island, from the barnacles on the wrecked ship that lies mouldering on the beach and enhances the *Treasure Island* theme of this secluded spot, to tall trees where rare bald eagles nest.

You can amble through the paths and boardwalks here in less than an hour but you'll want to take longer. You'll find yourself stopping in **Flamingo Lagoon** to watch the pencil-legged creatures with salmon-pink feathers gangle their way across the water. You'll pause to watch a sassy peacock strut before a potential mate, showing off his royal blue feathers.

When something moves just over there, you'll stop to look again as you discover a tortoise eyeing you as curiously as you're eyeing it.

And you'll certainly spend some time at **Parrot Perch,** where brainy birds stand on their head for you, roll over, wave, cock an intelligent eye, and struggle to get your attention as demandingly as a small child.

No one could pass the trumpeter swans at **Trumpeter Springs** without stopping for a look at these ballerina-graceful creatures, and you'll want to linger in the great stands of whispering bamboo that create a shady glen known as **Bamboo Hollow.**

You'll pause many times as you roam this huge aviary, claimed to be the largest in the world and home to hundreds of vividly hued birds, ranging from albino peacocks to flaming-pink ibis and cocoa-brown pelicans, all of them squawking, warbling, and singing as sweetly as the tiki birds you met in the Magic Kingdom.

It's quite a sight, especially magnificent in spring when fancies turn to you-know-what and courting dances as elaborate as minutes turn this wilderness into a wonderland of nature.

Admission to Discovery Island, which is open all year long from 10am to 5pm, is $7.50 for adults, $5.50 for children 3 to 9.

You can save money by combining a visit to Discovery Island and River Country and buying one ticket to both spots for $15 for adults, $11 for children 3 to 9. If you're staying in a WDW resort hotel, you pay a little less.

Also if you're staying in a Disney resort, you can sail across to the island on water craft that leave from Polynesian Village, the Contemporary, and Fort Wilderness.

In 1989 Disney imagineers introduced a new watery diversion

here: **Typhoon Lagoon.** To create this wet fantasy, WDW quadrupled the size of River Country, dreamed up an earthquake, created an imaginary typhoon and tidal wave, and, *voilà*, out came Typhoon Lagoon.

Here you enter through a rain forest to find yourself in a rustic, ramshackle town dotted with storm detritus, like a shipwrecked fishing boat dangling at tether atop a mountain. White water cascades down Typhoon Mountain and dumps you into a lagoon where you splash and splutter in a rain forest among bat caves, spinning rocks, dinosaur bones, and other intriguing flotsam.

All this legend was dreamed up to add a little fantasy to your basic water flume park, which here includes a surfing lagoon large enough to surf in, activity pools for all ages and swimming abilities, geysers, fountains, bubble jets, slides, and a Tarzan swing across water obstacles and into a waterfall.

You can ride a lazy river on rafts and inner tubes, sailing into a hidden grotto that's a front-and-center seat for the rest of the action in this fun-and-frolic spot.

If the name Shark Reef doesn't scare you off, you can snorkel among brightly colored tropical fish or don a wet suit and try some more serious diving. Rental underwater cameras are available to record this adventure and there are changing areas, lockers and shower facilities, plus a couple of casual restaurants, Typhoon Tillie's and Leaning Palms, and a picnic area.

In 1990 WDW was experimenting with a new admission system in which Typhoon Lagoon was included in the price of four- and five-day tickets. If that experiment is rejected, however, the normal admission price to the attraction is $18.25 for adults, $14.50 for children 3 to 9.

# BACKSTAGE AT DISNEY WORLD

As you watch singing dolls and tiki birds, ride on electronically controlled cars, watch Mickey Mouse pop up here, then turn up there minutes later, somewhere in the back of your mind little questions begin to appear.

How do they do it? How do all these people dressed in all these elaborate costumes manage to get themselves around their Kingdom? Who makes all those costumes? What's out there in Disney World's thousands of acres of nature preserve?

You'll discover you're perishing to watch an artist draw some of the cartoon characters you know and love and get a look at the electronic wilderness that controls what goes on here.

There is a way you can do that but, alas, adult people, you must be a student in fifth through tenth grade.

If you're lucky enough to fall into that category you can join WDW's **Wonders of Walt Disney World** program, which takes youngsters on a six-hour tour focusing on one of three subjects: creative arts, ecology, or entertainment. Each participant can take only one of the programs, however, and there's a $70 fee, which includes books the kids are asked to read before they attend and some materials they can use to follow up on what they've learned when the six-hour course is completed. What's more, many schools give credit for the course, which was created by Florida educators, and/or excuse absences from regular classes if youngsters plan to attend. For parents that means you can plan a Disney trip during the school year without guilt. It's nice that crowds are smaller then, too, so the trip will be more fun in many ways.

Once youngsters sign up for one of the four programs, which I'll describe in a moment, they get a Kodak camera to use during their visit, and some film, all included in the $70 fee.

If you've got a budding Picasso in your family, send that one off to the **Disney Creative Arts** program. It features a visit with a Disney artist who shows kids how to draw some of the Disney cartoon characters, then offers them helpful hints as they follow those instructions on their own. Later, the course instructor visits the Magic Kingdom with the youngsters and shows them the behind-the-scenes design elements that keep old things looking old and explains some *trompe-l'oeil* effects that make things seem to be what they aren't.

**Exploring Nature** and the necessity of preserving nature's wonders is the focus of another course, which features a film describing Florida's ecological composition. After the film, youngsters roam with the instructor through Discovery Island and WDW's 7,500-acre nature preserve, where orchids grow high in the trees, alligators slumber in the marshes, and huge trees drip Spanish moss. Binoculars are added to the cameras for this jaunt, and kids get a nature notebook in which they can write down what they see for show-and-tell time back home. Instructors outline for youngsters the relationship between human, plant, and animal and explain the symbiotic relationship that keeps this World—and all the world—intact.

Finally, up-and-coming Julie Andrewses or John Travoltas will love **The Walt Disney World of Entertainment program.** Youngsters actually get to meet a Disney character and learn how to do what that character does. They go backstage and down into the "secret" tunnel labyrinth to learn what happens there to make the magic out front, and they get to talk with some of the performers in top Disney shows.

To find out more about the educational programs or reserve a place in one, contact Walt Disney World, Box 10,000, Lake Buena Vista, FL 32830 (tel. 828-1500).

# MAKING THE MOST OF ONE, TWO, OR THREE DAYS IN THE MAGIC KINGDOM

As you've no doubt gathered, there's so much to do here in Walt Disney World, you could spend ages peering and poking around the place and still not see it all.

There are, however, highlights, special shows that everyone agrees are wonderful, so I'm going to outline those and give you a few ideas I think might help make the most of your moments here.

Lucky are those who have a week or so to spend in Orlando, since they can spend some time at Disney World, then head off to see some of the other wonderful attractions in the center of Florida (more on those in Chapter XIII).

If you can only fit in a **one-day visit** to the Magic Kingdom, get there early—by that I mean actually be on Main Street, U.S.A. at 8:30 to 9am. Have breakfast and start moving. Despite the comparative brevity of each of the attractions here, lines do form early. Those lines can add up to an hour (or more at very popular stops) to each attraction's actual running time. Only real racers can see more than eight or nine attractions a day, so figure on those numbers as a maximum. If you're not given to a rapid pace, don't expect to cram even that many into your day.

No matter where you go in the world or how much you see, when you get home someone will tell you what you missed. It's the same at Disney World, of course, but most people do agree that the very **best attractions** in the park are: Space Mountain in Tomorrowland; Peter Pan's Flight and It's a Small World in Fantasyland; the Haunted Mansion and Hall of Presidents in Liberty Square; the Country Bear Jamboree and Big Thunder Mountain Railroad in Frontierland; and Pirates of the Caribbean and the Jungle Cruise in Adventureland.

For a one-day visit I'd opt to try and see as many of those as possible (timid types should skip Space Mountain, as should anyone if the line is very long, as it often is). I'd do that by working my way around systematically, counterclockwise from Main Street to Tomorrowland, Fantasyland, Liberty Square and Frontierland, and finally to Adventureland. You could, of course, go clockwise covering the same territory or, if you have very small children, plan to spend most of your time in their special land, Fantasyland.

For those with limited time, there's a special program few people know about that can get you around quickly and save much wear and tear on both your nerves and tootsies. That timesaver is called a **guided tour** and includes a guide who takes you around the park for 3½ hours. The price of the tour: $5.50 for adults, $3.75 for children. Guides know a great deal about the park and its operation, so you can learn more than you would on your own. They also know where the lines are the shortest, valuable knowledge in this busy kingdom. You can sign up for one of these morning tours at the Ticket and Transportation Center in EPCOT or the Magic Kingdom, and ask questions about it at Guest Relations or Guest Service (tel. 824-4321 or 824-2222).

If you have allotted **two days or more** for your Magic Kingdom visit (and if you possibly can, do, you'll use every minute), get there early both days and work your way through the lands, beginning perhaps at Tomorrowland and working your way around through Fantasyland the first day. Then start where you left off (or at Adventureland) the second day and continue on around and back to Main Street, U.S.A., adding other attractions that have caught your imagination.

If the park's open until 10pm or later, line up on Main Street about 8pm for the 9pm **Main Street Electrical Parade.** Active kids can amuse themselves in the Main Street attractions (Penny Arcade and Main Street Cinema), while someone with patience holds down the curbside space. Usually you can wedge in some time before and after the parade for an attraction stop or two. If you've already seen the parade, visit popular attractions, while it's tooting along. Lines are short then, since most people are out on Main Street ooohing and aahhing.

If you have time, try to work in a **special dinner** at one of the park's two top restaurants, King Stefan's Banquet Hall (you must make reservations at the restaurant—it's in Cinderella Castle—first thing in the morning of the day you're hoping to dine) or the Liberty Tree Tavern (same requirements: Make reservations at the restaurant, in Liberty Square, early in the morning of the day you're dining). Both offer delightful time-warp trips and some pretty good food to boot. If you can't get to either for dinner, try to work in a lunch stop. Lunch is less crowded, too. Frontierland's Diamond Horseshoe Revue also is a good spot for lunch, since you can watch the show while having a light lunch. Same reservation requirements as in the restaurants.

If you have **four days** allotted for Walt Disney World fun, plan on spending at least one afternoon relaxing on the sands of River Country or Typhoon Lagoon or uncovering the wonders of Discovery Island. You'll love both spots, and by this time you are likely to need the rest.

Naturally, if you have even longer, say **five days** just for the Magic Kingdom, you can go at a much more leisurely pace, perhaps visiting some of the fabulous breakfast, brunch, and lunch buffets in the Polynesian Village or Contemporary Resort and taking in a character breakfast or an evening show at either spot or at Fort Wilderness. Shopping's great at Lake Buena Vista Village, too.

If you can, try to spend **one evening** aboard the glittering *Empress Lilly,* dining at one of the three wonderful rooms there or just tuning in on the banjo music and fun that always seems to be going on in the Baton Rouge Lounge. Whatever you do, don't miss taking an evening jaunt over to the Village for a look at the *Empress* in its starlit evening glitter.

# SPECIAL EVENTS IN THE MAGIC KINGDOM

You think you've heard it all? Not by a long shot. Disney World pours its heart into entertaining you. All year long there are special events, some of them seasonal, some year-round activities, all designed to delight, amaze, enthrall, and keep you coming back for more.

Let's take a look now at some of the things you'll see going on around the Kingdom and some of the things you may want to know before you even set a date for your visit to the mouse's house.

## DAILY DOINGS

Every day you can tune in on some musical events in the Magic Kingdom. One of the first you're likely to see is the **Dapper Dans,** a harmonious quartet of barbershoppers who roam the byways of Main Street, U.S.A., and are at their most picturesque outside the barbershop where you'll often find them. It's located on the first side street on your left as you face the castle. These Dapper Dans are as typically Twenties as they can get, with red-and-white-striped vests, straw hats, and old favorite songs.

Each day at 5:10pm, the American flag that flies over Main Street comes down, accompanied by a small band and color guard which perform a ceremony known as **flag retreat.** It's a short but stirring performance, accompanied by the release of a flock of white pigeons symbolizing doves of peace.

**Steel drums,** those island-music mainstays, can be heard on-stage near Adventureland's Pirates of the Caribbean attractions. Those lilting calypso sounds fit this jungle atmosphere to a T.

Mickey Mouse and some of his cohorts plus the **Kids of the Kingdom** sing and dance up a photogenic storm of American patriotic tunes daily in the forecourt area of the castle. Good place for pictures and an entertaining show that includes medleys of popular favorites.

I've already mentioned that popular **Diamond Horseshoe Saloon** production, which despite the "saloon" in its name is more than suitable for even the youngest visitor. Perhaps this is a good time to repeat that no alcoholic beverages are sold in the Magic Kingdom. You must have reservations for these shows, which occur several times a day, so it's imperative to sign up early at the saloon.

Mickey Mouse, Goofy, and a host of Disney's favorites sing and dance several times a day at the **Fantasy Faire** stage just across the way from Cinderella's Golden Carousel.

You say you haven't heard a washboard lately? Well, don't be deprived of that experience. **Banjo Kings** have one, and they play it and other instruments on Main Street daily.

Naturally, you'll want to get a good look at those **cartoon characters**—Mickey and Minnie Mouse, Donald Duck, and the lot—so if you don't just run into them by chance, look for them at

City Hall, where they spend most of the day on one side or the other of the castle. They make an appearance at the castle forecourt at 12:30 and 5:15pm daily and on the Fantasyland side at other times.

Who's going to be **where and when** is posted each day at City Hall. If you have a special interest in the cartoon characters or one of the musical groups, go to City Hall when you enter the park, and find out when and where your favorites will be appearing.

Minnie Mouse reigns supreme in Tomorrowland where she performs daily in her own revue, "Totally Minnie," on the Tomorrowland stage. Performance times are posted at City Hall and at the stage.

For the little ones—and even perhaps for the not-so-little ones—a memorable Disney highlight is **Minnie's Menehune Breakfast with the Disney Characters.** You can see Minnie, Goofy, Donald, or one of the gang as you down some basic breakfast goodies at Minnie's bash in the Polynesian Village Hotel. Breakfast is 7:30 to 11am daily for $9.95 adults and $5.95 children. And you can reserve a seat by calling Central Reservations at 824-8000. At 9 and 10:30am, those same characters show up for **Breakfast à la Disney** on the *Empress Lilly* riverboat. **Breakfast at the Terrace Café** at the Contemporary Resort is a daily buffet feast (8 to 11am), with Disney characters. Price of the riverboat breakfasts is $9.75 for adults $6.50 for children ($8.95 for adults and $5.95 for children at Polynesian Village or Terrace Café.)

## NIGHT AND SEASONAL FUN

In summer the **All American College Marching Band** struts its stuff on the Fantasyland Fantasy Faire stage. You can find out when they'll be giving their daily performances there by calling Disney information, 824-4321 or 824-2222.

Mickey's Magic Kingdom really turns on at night—literally. Thousands upon thousands of white lights trim Main Street, U.S.A., to form a backdrop for the showiest Disney event of them all, the **Main Street Electrical Parade.** You can read all about that in Chapter V on nightlife in the Magic Kingdom, but let me remind you here that the hours are 9 and 11pm each night that the park is open until midnight. That occurs, by the way, at holidays like Thanksgiving, Christmas, Washington's Birthday in February, at Easter, and during summer vacation periods from about June to Labor Day. You'll find some tips on good spots to view the parade back there in Chapter V.

When the park is open until midnight in summer and on holidays, you can also count on a fireworks display known as **Fantasy in the Sky.** Fireworks boom for about five minutes in a kaleidoscope of bursting color that will knock your socks off (figuratively, don't panic). One of the most spectacular sights you can see here in the park, in fact, is the ebony sky above the turrets of Cinderella's Castle ablaze with rainbow-hued stars.

Another year-round evening event is the **Electrical Water Pageant,** which takes place every night on the waters of Bay Lake and features a 1,000-foot-long parade of floating creatures, all illuminated with tiny lights. Normal hours for the pageant are from about

9 to 10pm. Parade route begins at the Polynesian Village, moves past Fort Wilderness and then to the Contemporary Resort. When the park is open late, the floating pageant goes past River Country just before it gets to Fort Wilderness and then goes on to complete its showy journey at the Magic Kingdom about 10:30pm.

**More nightly activities** are outlined in Chapter V, including information on all kinds of evening fun, from a marshmallow roast to a sophisticated Broadway revue.

## HOLIDAY ACTIVITIES

Christmas is the beginning, or the end, of the Disney celebrations, depending on how you look at it, and it is a spectacular season to visit the Kingdom. Just be prepared to join thousands upon thousands of others who want to see this Christmas wonderland, too.

Each **Christmas celebration** is a little different, so you never tire of a return trip, but each includes the present of a huge trimmed tree ablaze with lights and ornaments, special presentations, and carolers who add the soft glow of candlelight and their lovely voices to the Main Street Electrical Parade. There's just enough cool in the air to give you the feeling of a very pleasant Christmas season but usually not so much cold you're shivering. Santa Claus—or Mickey in a Santa suit—is likely to be on hand somewhere, and top-name performers add their famous visages to shows that are nothing short of spectacular.

Naturally Mickey, Minnie, and friends celebrate **New Year's Eve** right along with the rest of us, so there are special festivities in the park that night, too, including a double set of fireworks. Plenty to see and do makes this an interesting place to spend the last hours of the year. Crowds are enormous, however, so be prepared for a Times-Square-South crush.

At **Easter,** Disney's decked out in its Sunday best, complete with those elaborate hats people have come to associate with this holiday, plus antique cars, and special celebrations. Mickey Mouse has a pretty impressive set of ears, but even they pale beside the magnificent appendages sported by the king of this day's activities, none other than the Easter Bunny, of course.

Since much of the Magic Kingdom focuses on the glories of this nation, **Independence Day** is a king-size holiday here. Throngs turn out on July 4 to spend this special day in the park and to ogle a double display of fireworks over Cinderella Castle and the Seven Seas Lagoon.

# IX

# EPCOT: A VISIT TO TODAY'S WORLD—AND TOMORROW'S

So quickly does the future seem to be coming at us these days, that we barely master one method of coping before the revised version appears. Even the simplest details of life change with lightning speed. We no sooner conquer one change than it's followed by another. Zap! We're back at step one, learning how all over again.

Just when you've conquered the intricacies of your bank's checking account system, you get a pleasant little note explaining, in steps 1 through 41, how to deal with a wondrous *new* system.

You succeed in setting your digital alarm clock only to be faced with a maze of bleeping video games and home computer budgeting. No more watching the needle climb on your speedometer . . . now you keep your eye on a dashboard of digitals. And restaurant bills? An incomprehensible computerized crazy quilt of PBCD, BR, SBT, SC, and BAL tossed in among myriads of numbers.

Things now pop up suddenly in places they've never popped up before, open and close automatically, appear and disappear at some unseen command. And to many, many people you're not a face anymore, you're not even a name, just a string of numbers and letters!

It's head-spinning, this awesomely rapid technological change, and sometimes it's even a little terrifying. Still, as unsettling as it may be, there's a thrill about it all, a feeling that you're part of something exciting, a small cog in a huge wheel turning a powerhouse of change that will alter the course of history for generations to come.

Long before the rest of us realized we were living in Flash Gordon's era, Disney imaginations had rocketed into tomorrow and tuned into the technology necessary to turn imagination into image.

You can see those first futuristic efforts in Tomorrowland, in Disney's solar-powered office building, in the park's computer-operated central energy system. Impressive as were those first forays into the future, they weren't nearly enough for Walt Disney and his dreamers.

For the cartoonist had a vision of tomorrow that focused on

man's ability to control his environment, to make technology a slave, not a master, and to use it to predict, manipulate, and control the future.

You can get a glimpse into the future at the newest and most ambitious Disney project: a daring enclave dubbed Experimental Prototype Community of Tomorrow and for obvious reasons nicknamed EPCOT Center. This "serious" amusement has a simple message, one that Disney held firmly in his heart and first spread around the world with the help of a little mouse.

It's a message of universality, of the oneness of this world we inhabit. At EPCOT Center the message is also one of caution, a warning that the world of tomorrow demands a commitment today to tolerance and understanding, a commitment, in fact, to community. EPCOT Center is Disney's way of alerting the world that one, without all, is impossible.

---

# ORIENTATION

Just as you discovered the immensity of the Magic Kingdom, so will you meet a similar, mind-boggling enormity at the Experimental Prototype Community of Tomorrow.

From the moment you step into the shadow of the huge geosphere that looms over the grounds here, you will know how that mouse must feel in the immensity of humankind's world. Towering architecture soars into the skies. Massive buildings stand on acre after endless acre of land. Intertwined throughout it all is a network of flower-lined walkways leading you mile after mile through the two new "worlds" Disneyites have created here.

As in the Magic Kingdom, you will soon discover there are things you need to know to survive in this civilized wilderness of worlds.

Let's begin then by taking a look at some of the basic survival tactics you will need in EPCOT Center, and some of the things you'll need to know to get the most from this trip to the world of tomorrow.

## WHEN TO GO

Because the Magic Kingdom and EPCOT Center share this World, they also share the crowds that visit here. Disney prognosticators figure those crowds will soon hike the park's 14 million annual visitors to a record 20 million people a year.

It's quite likely many of those will come here especially to see this new World. All of which means if you expect crowds, you won't be disappointed. Just a month or so after EPCOT Center opened, the early-morning line outside Spaceship Earth was one hour long!

It's safe to assume that EPCOT Center matches the Magic Kingdom's busy-day syndrome, with the turnstiles turning fastest during holiday periods—especially Christmas—and in the summer months. For a complete rundown on the crowds and when they're greatest, see the orientation section of Chapter VIII and expect history to repeat itself at EPCOT Center.

Here at EPCOT Center, too, crowds increase at attractions as the days go on, receding a bit at mealtimes when they increase greatly in all restaurants and quickie food stops.

If you can motivate yourself to get to EPCOT Center early in the morning—you'll find plenty of company already there at 8:30am when the doors open—you stand the best chance of getting restaurant reservations and working your way through the most popular attractions before the real throngs arrive.

Besides, it's pleasant to plunk yourself down at an outdoor table in, say, the Stargate Café and munch away on a simple breakfast ordered, entered, totaled, and sent to the kitchen by computer. What a way to get the day's first glimpse into the future!

**Shopper Alert:** If you're hoping that this EPCOT adventure will live on in memory via that simply gorgeous Eiffel Tower ashtray, then follow this advice: Make up your mind, difficult as that may be, and whip out the cash or credit card *before* 2:30pm. Wait any later than that and you're likely to join crowds that would make the Rose Bowl look intimate. Shop early and have your treasures sent over to Package Pick-Up. More on that later in this chapter, in the most logical of places: "Special Needs." Now who has more special needs than a dedicated shopper?

One other early-arrival tip: If you manage to get yourself moving early, don't wander into the first line you see, which will be the Spaceship Earth line. Everyone does exactly that, thus making the line at this first futuristic attraction longer in the morning than it is at just about any other time of the day.

Instead bear to your left and enter Earth Station, where you will find early-bird gourmets lining up to make reservations for dinner at World Showcase restaurants. More on that later, for now just get in line and get it over with.

## WHAT TO WEAR

If you didn't take my advice about shoes for the Magic Kingdom, please swallow your pride and take that advice here. That advice, in a few words, is *wear comfortable shoes.* No matter how unfashionable sensible walking shoes may look, your feet will love you for the gesture. Shoes are even more important here in EPCOT Center than they are in the Magic Kingdom. Distances are enormous, transportation is scanty and always jammed, lines are long, and there aren't that many chances, or places, to sit.

A corollary to that piece of advice is aimed at those who have the slightest, even the tiniest, concern over their ability to walk long distances. If for any reason you think you may tire—you're pregnant, have physical limitations as a result of age or infirmity, or have any kind of health problem affecting energy levels—don't be shy about **renting a wheelchair.** They cost only $4 a day plus a $1 refundable deposit. You can rent one at a wheelchair rental kiosk you'll find just to the left of the fountain as you enter EPCOT (that is, directly in front of the geosphere).

That's where you'll find **strollers** for the youngsters, too. Turn a deaf ear to little ones' protests that they are too old, and don't want to sit in a stroller. They may not want to be seen in one during the first few hours they're in this park, but it won't be long before the wailing protests become exhausted whimpers. If it helps you steel yourself to the protestations, just picture yourself walking a mile or so in the sun carrying a tuckered-out toddler on your shoulder. Strollers rent for $4 a day plus $1 deposit.

If you'd like to leave the little ones behind on an evening or weekend visit to EPCOT Center (or the Magic Kingdom), park them at the **Kinder-Care Children's Center** located in Lake Buena Vista (at the employees entrance to the park; tel. 827-5437 or 827-5444), where they'll be cuddled and fed for $5.50 an hour or $22 daily when space is available. This service is available to anyone from 6am to 10pm on weekdays, 6am to 9pm on Sunday, 7am to 6pm for infants.

If you're a Disney resort guest, the kids can stay and play at **Mouseketeers Clubhouses** (tel. 824-1000) in the Polynesian Village and the Contemporary Resort hotels for $4 an hour (50¢ an hour for additional children). Here they must be 3 to 9 years old and there's a four-hour maximum on child care. Reservations are required. In-room baby-sitting also is available at hotels for $7.50 an hour. Reserve 24 hours in advance.

## GETTING THERE

Since the Magic Kingdom and EPCOT Center are both part of Disney World, you'll use the same roads to get here. Sneak a peek back into Chapter VIII, where major highway routes to Disney World are outlined. Once you're on the road, you'll notice that signs directing you to Disney World or the Magic Kingdom now also include EPCOT Center, which is just three miles from the Magic Kingdom. From Highway I-4 there's a new interchange located halfway between the exits for Fla. Rte. 535 and U.S. 192.

If you're staying in one of the Lake Buena Vista hotels and driving to Disney World, just follow Hotel Plaza Boulevard to the Shopping Village entrance and turn left. Follow the road around and you'll find yourself right on the way to EPCOT Center's entrance.

Once you've found your way to the EPCOT Center parking lot, follow the same general rules you'll find in Chapter VIII, the most important of which is memorizing your parking lot location. Here the lots bear futuristic names, so you'll be leaving your old outdated combustion engine in a lot with a name like Communi-Cove.

Here, too, guest courtesy trams will pick you up near your car —just look around, you'll see the trams—and take you to EPCOT Center's Ticket and Transportation Center.

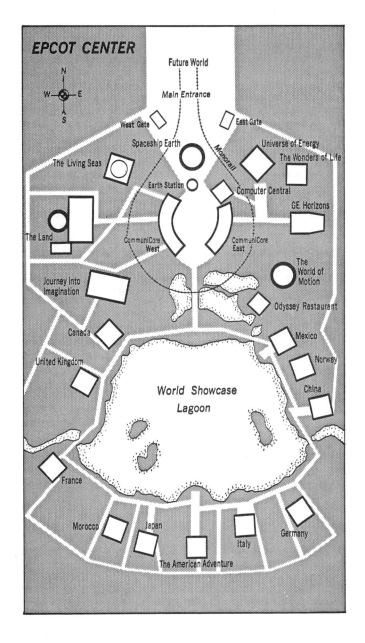

EPCOT CENTER

Future World

Main Entrance

West Gate

Spaceship Earth

East Gate

Universe of Energy

The Living Seas

The Wonders of Life

Earth Station

Computer Central

GE Horizons

The Land

CommuniCore West

CommuniCore East

The World of Motion

Journey into Imagination

Odyssey Restaurant

Canada

Mexico

United Kingdom

Norway

China

World Showcase Lagoon

France

Morocco

Japan

Italy

Germany

The American Adventure

Monorail

That same **Car Care Center** that will help you out with dead batteries and the like in the Magic Kingdom parking lot will come to your aid here too. So good are they, in fact, that a friend whose son lost his car keys somewhere in EPCOT Center called the Car

Care Center (tel. 824-4813) and not only had the door opened by a friendly Car Care person but was even presented with a duplicate ignition key so he could get home—and they didn't charge him a penny for that otherwise wallet-emptying service! Now those are knights in shining armor!

There's a special parking lot here for handicapped visitors. Ask one of the parking lot attendants, or look for a sign directing you to the lot, which is located a little closer to the entrance.

If you're taking a **bus** to EPCOT Center the bus driver will drop you off in the bus parking area and that's where you reboard the bus at the end of the day. Guests of hotels in Lake Buena Vista's Disney World Village Hotel Plaza can hop on a special EPCOT Center bus with a red-and-silver flag painted on the side. It's a short walk from the bus parking area to the Ticket and Transportation Center.

If you're in the Magic Kingdom and decide to whiz on over for a look at some future fantasies, just board an EPCOT-bound **monorail** which connects the Magic Kingdom, Contemporary Resort Hotel, and Polynesian Village with EPCOT Center. Go by monorail to EPCOT from those two Disney-owned hotels by taking the monorail to the Magic Kingdom's Ticket and Transportation Center, then hopping the EPCOT Center monorail from there.

Monorails to EPCOT Center leave only from the Ticket and Transportation Center at the Magic Kingdom, so you must make your way there first from hotels or from the Magic Kingdom. If you're staying in one of the other Disney-owned resort hotels—the villas or the Disney Inn—take an EPCOT Center bus to the Ticket and Transportation Center at the Magic Kingdom, then change to the TTC-EPCOT monorail. Same goes for Fort Wilderness guests.

That monorail, by the way, stops only at the entrance to EPCOT, not inside the EPCOT Center complex, although you'll see it inside EPCOT Center as it completes its circular journey on the way back to the Magic Kingdom. I mention that so you won't hope to hop the monorail when exhaustion strikes you somewhere in the middle of EPCOT Center.


## BUYING A TICKET

All the scoop on buying a ticket to the Magic Kingdom or EPCOT Center is outlined in Chapter VIII's Magic Kingdom rundown, but here are the prices again:

A one-day ticket admitting you to the Magic Kingdom, Disney-MGM Studios, or EPCOT, but not all three, is $32.75 for adults (13 years and up) and $26.40 for youngsters 3 through 9. Children under three are free.

A four-day Passport, again including admission to Disney-MGM, the Magic Kingdom and EPCOT Center—use of all transportation facilities in either—is $105.60 for adults, $84.45 for children.

Real devotees of Walt Disney World who have plenty of time to spend at Walt Disney World can buy a five-day Passport at $123.75 for adults, $100.30 for children. Those who simply cannot get enough can buy an annual pass for $190.80 for adults, $164.30 for children.

As with the Magic Kingdom, tickets may be paid for in cash or by travelers' checks, by American Express or MasterCard, or by okayed personal checks. Walt Disney World resort guests may charge tickets to their rooms with proper identification.

If you leave EPCOT Center and want to return the same day, have your hand stamped at the exit, even if you have a multiday passport.

## SPECIAL NEEDS—CHILDREN, PETS, HANDICAPPED, FIRST AID, AND MORE

I've already given you the word on renting strollers for children and wheelchairs for *anyone* who might entertain even the slightest doubt about walking capabilities. Both are available at the **Stroller and Wheelchair Rental** kiosk at the base of Spaceship Earth just to your left as you enter EPCOT Center.

A word for wheelchair guests: You can take the monorail to the Magic Kingdom and Polynesian Village and the Contemporary Resort, but you must go by bus to other destinations. To find out what bus goes where, stop by the Bus Information counters near the bus parking lots.

Rest rooms and telephones accommodating wheelchair guests are marked with the international wheelchair symbol.

Keep your receipt for the wheelchair or stroller—you can use it again at the Magic Kingdom and Disney-MGM Studios or here if you return later.

EPCOT rides that cannot accommodate wheelchairs include Spaceship Earth, Body Wars in the Wonders of Life, Horizons, Journey into Imagination, and the Maelstrom ride in the Norway pavilion. Wheelchair travelers can, of course, visit all the exhibits in those pavilions and those who can get out of a wheelchair and transfer to the ride car can go on the ride-through attractions.

If you have a small child with you, those demanding special needs can be met at **Baby Services,** near the Odyssey Restaurant. Here thoughtful Disneyites have provided facilities for changing diapers, warming bottles, and nursing, and there are even diapers, food, and formula for sale.

**Pets** must be parked at the EPCOT Center Kennel Club right at the Ticket and Transportation Center, where they'll be lots happier and cooler than they'd be parading around the park all day. The charge is $6 a day ($6 overnight, but overnight stays are only available at Magic Kingdom and Fort Wilderness, and only to WDW resort hotel guests).

If you get blisters from sun or pavement or suffer from any of the myriad of other little unexpected first-aid emergencies that can crop up, head for the **First Aid Station** adjacent to the Odyssey Restaurant, where a registered nurse is on duty to help you. If you take special medication, however, be sure to have it with you; there are no pharmacies in Disney World.

If you buy a few things the minute you enter EPCOT Center—not a bad idea, since most shoppers jam the shops on their way *out* of the park—you can stash them in **lockers** in the Entrance Plaza just to the right of the Spaceship Earth entrance. The charge is 25¢ for large-size lockers, 50¢ for even bigger storage space.

Those who lose things can find them at the **Lost and Found** at the Entrance Plaza, to the right of the turnstiles as you face the entrance to EPCOT Center. You can also call Lost and Found at 824-4245.

If it's a **lost child** you're seeking, take your hysteria to Baby Services adjacent to the Odyssey Restaurant. If the **missing person** is an adult, look at Earth Station in Spaceship Earth, where you can leave a message. Don't keep this message service to yourself. Tell your group, so you and the lost one can simplify regrouping.

There's another convenient EPCOT service that as yet is taken advantage of by only an in-the-know few. That service shares quarters with Lost and Found and is called **Package Pick-up.** It works like this:

First, you troop through the dozens of shops in World Showcase, spending and buying with the fervor of a sailor on a one-day pass. Do you have to carry all that loot around with you on the long return trip to the entrance? Certainly not. Wherever you buy, just tell the shop to send it over to Package Pick-up. The shop will give you a receipt and deliver your package to this handy pick-up spot at the entrance, thus saving you pounds of parcels. Deliveries are taken from shops to the pick-up center every hour, so there's virtually no chance you'll get to Package Pick-up before your package.

As for that little matter of **money,** see to that need at the Entrance Plaza, where credit-card cash advances, foreign currency exchange, and other credit-cardholder services are available. American Express cardholder services are also available at Travelport in CommuniCore East. For details on what requires cash and what can be paid by credit cards and which one, check the Orientation section of Chapter VIII. Same rules apply at EPCOT Center.

There are few things more frustrating than knowing what you want to say but being unable to say it in the prevailing language. If you think you or someone in your group might be faced with that difficulty, seek **foreign language assistance** at Guest Relations in Earth Station, adjacent to Spaceship Earth. Information in Spanish is also available on World Key Information Satellites, which are the television monitors set up throughout EPCOT Center to help you find your way around and discover parts of the place you might have missed. More on that later.

**Camera equipment** and even rental cameras are available in a Camera Center at the base of Spaceship Earth and at Journey Into Imagination, which is presented by Kodak.

To find out what **entertainment** is scheduled today at EPCOT Center, ask any of the hosts or hostesses in Earth Station at the Guest Relations desk. They know all about hours for parades, shows, live entertainment, and special events—and quite a lot more besides. Similar information is available on World Key Information Satellites, which I'll explain shortly.

For **general information** on anything at all, call World Center Information, 824-4500.

---

# A LITTLE GEOGRAPHY

---

Before you plan your EPCOT Center visit, you'll need to know a little about the geography of this huge "community" that's more than twice the size of the Magic Kingdom.

Here goes. EPCOT Center is divided into two separate sections: Future World and World Showcase.

As the name suggests, **Future World** offers a peek into the world of tomorrow as seen by some of the nation's largest corporations—Kodak, United Technology, Unisys, General Motors, Exxon, Kraft, American Express, and AT&T.

You certainly can't miss Future World, not only because it's the first thing you'll see as you enter EPCOT Center, but because its landmark is the landmark of all EPCOT—that giant geosphere lovingly known as the "golf ball." Flanking it on the left and right are two arcing buildings called CommuniCore East and CommuniCore West. Scattered about the perimeter are the various corporation exhibits, all of which are housed in huge buildings featuring soaring, innovative architecture.

CommuniCore's long arms enfold a central plaza, crowned by an enchanting fountain that's particularly beautiful at night, when colored lights play across its waters. At the edge of the lake, boats and buses gather in a wide area known as World Showcase Plaza. From here, you can see the whole World Showcase spread out around shimmering waters—terrific for photographers.

All of this occupies the north bank of a 40-acre lake. Rimming the lake is the section of EPCOT Center known as **World Showcase,** a complex of international enclaves, each featuring architectural landmarks of the nation represented. As you face the lake and move around it to your right counterclockwise (that is, west), you pass Canada, the United Kingdom, France, Morocco, Japan, U.S.A., Italy, Germany, China, Norway, and Mexico.

Overall, EPCOT Center is entered on the north side so all your normal direction-seeking is backwards. That means the geosphere and Future World are on the north side of the lake, World Showcase on the south side, CommuniCore East on your left as you face the lake and CommuniCore West on your right. A little confusing, but you'll figure it out with the help of plenty of signs you'll find everywhere.

If you walk all around that lake, you'll hike 1.2 miles, and the distance from exhibit to exhibit in Future World will keep you pacing about the same distance. Add to that the dozens of shops and restaurants you'll want to explore in both places, not to mention the lines you'll wait in, and you're likely to stride at least three to five miles before the day is over.

# GETTING AROUND

You can avoid some of that walking by learning a little about getting around in EPCOT Center, an activity which can be as much fun as finding your way around the Magic Kingdom—and even more necessary.

You can arrive by monorail, a pretty slick way to turn up anywhere. Once there, you can travel by **antique double-decker, open-sided omnibuses** that toot their way around the World Showcase, or by sleek **sailing craft** that chug across the waters of the lake in the center of this complex.

To get around here, keep in mind that EPCOT Center is divided into two sections, Future World, which offers you a glimpse into tomorrow and into yesterday, and World Showcase, which takes you on an international sojourn, complete with replicas of famous architectural landmarks of the nations represented.

All these wonders are spread over a land area that's more than *twice* as large as the Magic Kingdom. That means that what looks like lots of transportation really isn't much at all, so you'll have to count on walking many a mile in this part of the World.

It is, however, a lovely place to walk, trimmed with flowers in all the colors of the rainbow and filled with nooks and crannies where fountains soar, and dazzling views come suddenly into sight.

As interesting as it may be to walk the miles of land around the lake and through Future World, the transport provided is just as entertaining.

Those double-decker omnibuses, decked out in shining emerald green, fire-engine red, or buttercup yellow, travel clockwise around the lake. Official starting point is an open area called World Showcase Plaza, just at the end of the long walkway that leads from the geosphere to the lake. Buses stop at marked bus stops located just short of the China pavilion, in front of the German enclave, just beyond the U.S.A. pavilion, in front of France's contribution, and just between the United Kingdom and Canada.

One problem is that not every one of the buses stops at each of the stops, so it may not do you much good to go chasing after a bus. Easiest way to latch onto one is to hike to the nearest bus stop and wait until one comes along that's going somewhere near where you're going.

Once you're standing in World Showcase Plaza, ready to journey off for your tour of the World Showcase, you may be lured by the boats you see on the waters. Called *Friendship I, Friendship II,* etc., they also make specific stops before returning to the Plaza.

These *Friendship* launches travel to a dock just opposite the German pavilion and to Morocco.

# A VISIT TO A FUTURE WORLD

Now that you know what's where and how to get there, let's start right off for a peek at the weird and wonderful days of tomorrow.

First thing you'll see as you pass the ticket booths and step onto the Entrance Plaza is that EPCOT Center logo and landmark—the geosphere.

## SPACESHIP EARTH

Soaring 18 stories high, this massive conglomeration of triangles forms a shining silver globe that stands on giant concrete legs. Visible from miles away, the towering sphere casts its huge shadow over intricately landscaped grounds below and shelters AT&T's **Spaceship Earth** exhibit, as well as the information center known as **Earth Station.**

Board a Spaceship Earth car and journey off through history to explore humankind's age-old questions—Who are we? Where do we come from? Travel past life-like cavemen carefully recording their prehistoric hunts on cave walls as they did in the framed ancient caves of Altamira in Spain. Journey on along the Nile, where a Cleopatra, seated proudly on her royal throne, gazes deep into your eyes.

Sail with those skilled Phoenician sailors and see scribes working on the first alphabets. As you roll along in time, Greek tragedies take to the boards in the first theater productions. Imperial Rome is born and dies as you glide by, looking out over the smoking ruins of the glory that was Rome.

Islamic monks, working in tiny cubicles, painstakingly copy the learning left intact, saving it for that great rebirth, the Renaissance, and bequeathing it finally to that magical invention that changed the world: the printing press. You'll see Michelangelo lying on his scaffolding putting final brushstrokes on the ceiling of the Sistine Chapel; watch the newspaper, telegraph, telephone, radio, television, and computer spread their message fingers around the world.

Finally, your transport spins you into today and tomorrow, where all of us are linked as passengers on Spaceship Earth, rocketed by technology beyond this planet "into the age of choice, the age of opportunity. . . ."

Back down on Earth whether you like it or not, you exit directly into Earth Station, City Hall of the Future, where Guest Relations hosts and hostesses can help you with questions about EPCOT Center.

Here you can get your introduction to an amazing creation called **World Key Information Service,** which uses touch-sensitive television screens to give you all the latest information about EPCOT Center attractions, special events, and restaurants. Presented in English and Spanish, the information is retrieved automatically from video discs and computer data banks and carried on lightwave transmission facilities provided by Western Electric. There are 29 terminals throughout EPCOT Center where you can watch and actually talk to information attendants.

Here, too, representatives of the seven World Showcase restaurants requiring reservations can help you make **dinner reservations.**

A word about reservations seems apropos here. Be forewarned that France, Italy, and the United Kingdom have the most popular dining spots in EPCOT Center and reservations at those restaurants are often gone by 9am. (Les Chefs de France and Le Bistro de Paris, L'Originale Alfredo di Roma Ristorante, and Rose & Crown Pub and Dining Room, respectively). Reservations are such a popular business in fact, that it would be wise to walk right to Earth Station the minute you enter EPCOT, walk up to the bank of television-computers, and tell the face you see on the television screen there where you would like to dine for dinner or lunch. Don't worry that you won't be able to figure out how to work the computers; this reservation business is so active that everything's set up for you—all you have to do is talk.

If you're too late for a dinner reservation at the most popular spots, opt for lunch at one of them instead. Menus differ some, but quality is uniform at both meals and the atmosphere never changes. Besides, lunch is a way of sampling fare at less expensive prices.

Restaurants at which reservations are required are: Bistro de Paris and Les Chefs de France in France; Restaurant Marrakesh in Morocco; Biergarten in Germany; Mitsukoshi in Japan; the San Angel in Mexico; Nine Dragons in China; the Rose and Crown in U.K.; and L'Originale Alfredo di Roma Ristorante in Italy.

If you're unsuccessful in securing a reservation, don't despair. You'll never go hungry at EPCOT, which also has a number of nonreservation restaurants—Le Cellier in Canada, Au Petit Café in France, La Cantina in Mexico, Lotus Blossom Café in China, Liberty Inn at the American Adventure, and Tempura Kiku and Yakitori House in Japan.

If you can't get either lunch or dinner reservations and you're absolutely determined to try a certain restaurant, there's still one more chance. You can line up at the restaurant at about 11am or 6pm and hope for no-shows. Lots of people will join you in line and some are able to get in, despite their lack of reservations, although I wouldn't take bets on your chances. Still, it's worth a try.

## COMMUNICORE EAST

Let's move along now from the womb of that huge geosphere to **CommuniCore East,** to the left as you face the lake. In this arc-shaped wing you'll find the **Stargate Restaurant,** a popular breakfast and fast-food lunching spot where you can dine indoors or outside on a terrace overlooking the huge fountain that dominates the plaza between the East and West CommuniCore buildings.

Star of the show here is **Backstage Magic,** presented by Unisys and starring a computer-wise secretary and a little character called I/O. They hop around the computers explaining how MACS (Monitoring and Control System) keeps watch on EPCOT productions to make sure all is going according to plan and how ECS (Entertainment Control System) works the elaborate lighting on all the shows in the park at one time. It's an amusing production, particularly for those who have never seen a massive bank of computers in operation.

In CommuniCore East you'll also find American Express's look at future travel, **TravelPort,** where you step up to a television set, touch a circle in the center, and look over a vast range of vacation possibilities complete with films of skiing sojourns, beach journeys, and off-beat adventure trips of all kinds. If one of the possibilities thrills you, you can sign up right here with an American Express travel counselor whose computers have all the latest information on prices and places.

Unisys has gone all out here, with computerized oddities including an American-flag mobile whose stars and stripes are independently hung and move about forming different patterns. There's a raft of computer creations that will intrigue adults and youngsters alike. One is a revolving wood carving with tiny figures that makes a complete revolution about every three minutes. Under them you can see population figures change rapidly as new babies are born.

There's a robot that talks with youngsters and answers their questions and a huge crystal ball flowing with color and crisscrossed by airplanes.

Exxon has an **Energy Exchange** display that tells you about a lot of energy sources, ranging from solar photovoltaics—don't ask me—to nuclear fusion and home and car conversion projects. There's a display of coal mining methods buried in the mouth of a huge earth mover and an explanation of oil-retrieval methods. Star of the exhibits is a 30,000-pound piece of shale rock formed in the age of the dinosaurs and containing 500 gallons of oil, enough to keep a car running for a year. You can touch the massive rock and see the oil pockets buried deep within it.

At the **Centorium** gift shop futuristic metal sculptures are the most intriguing items, but there are plenty of the usual T-shirts and toys—and for when it's raining, raincoat-ponchos that are terrific for keeping out the damp without tying you up in plastic.

At an **Electronic Forum** you send 'em a message by recording your opinion on world events at a special **Future Choice Theater.** Soon you'll enjoy an electronic arcade, featuring games based on advanced technology—things like interactive video discs, 3-D graphics, lasers, and body-sensing devices.

## UNIVERSE OF ENERGY

As long as we're on the east side of Future World, let's roam over to the **Universe of Energy,** my candidate for EPCOT Center's most fascinating exhibit.

You enter a large room where you'll see row after row of long pews stretching out in front of you and on both sides. They look as immobile as Winchester Cathedral, but they're actually moving cars, part of a "traveling theater," as you will soon discover. Once seated, you are treated by Exxon, which produces this spectacular show, to an elaborately screened production tracing the cycles of life and death that have created oil deep beneath the earth's surface. On a 220-degree screen you'll see the struggle to build the Alaskan pipeline, the impressive technology involved in seeking and recovering oil and gas, then delivering it around the world by tanker.

As the seat you're sitting in turns and begins to move, traveling along a wire only one-eighth of an inch in diameter and powered by solar energy gathered by thousands of solar cells on the roof, you suddenly are thrust into the "dark and mysterious past," the terrifying dawn of history when huge dinosaurs roamed the earth. You see and smell dripping swampwaters as thunder and lightning roars around you and huge dinosaurs tower over you, one chewing rather placidly on a string of seaweed.

Slowly you travel deeper and deeper into the dark, dank swampland where giant tree ferns soar high above you and a monster-lizard shows its teeth. Overhead pterodactyls, ugly as buzzards, soar menacingly. From the land sulfurous smoke oozes and steams. As you move slowly through this nightmare land, a water-dwelling monster of prehistory suddenly thrusts a long neck and huge jaw up from the depths of a placid pool and roars in rage. Volcanoes erupt, spilling streams of flaming lava, as the earth hisses and bubbles in internal consternation.

It's terrifying and fascinating, a dramatic and devastatingly effective presentation of the dawn of humankind and of the world in which the black gold of today's primary energy source was born.

## WONDERS OF LIFE

Look out, stomach, here I come. It took a mere $100 million to produce this trip down the gullet and into the pancreas but then rides like that don't come cheap, as Metropolitan Life, the sponsors of this newest EPCOT pavilion, can testify.

Here you're greeted by a 72-foot-tall DNA molecule and move right along to discover that goofy Goofy going from couch potato to fitness fan.

Anacomical Players Theater features an improvisational theater group that gets the audience into the act as they deliver another health message.

A quite graphic film on childbirth, called "The Making of Me," includes actual footage of the birth of a child which you may or may not consider suitable for viewing by your child.

In this newest of the EPCOT adventures you can ride stationary computerized bicycles through filmed locales including Disneyland in California, have your golf, tennis, or baseball skills analyzed, play feelsies in the Sensory Funhouse or punch in some basic information on your life-style and discover just what a stress mess you are and what you can do about it.

All that takes place in the **Fitness Fairgrounds** where you can also see some exhibits describing the newest discoveries in science and medicine and sneak into **Desserts & Things** for a good-even-if-it-is-healthy oat bran waffle or frozen yogurt cone.

Die-hard shoppers can roam in **Well & Goods** where all the paraphernalia you need to pursue the fitness habit can be had.

Star of this show, however, is EPCOT's only thrill ride, **Body Wars,** a rip-roaring ride aboard a flight simulator exactly like those used in airline pilot training programs. A very rough ride, Body Wars is not for the faint of heart—literally or figuratively—or for the easily queasy, pregnant women, children under 3, or those with back problems.

On this wild ride you journey into the body, meeting up with some very scary body stuff along the way. I think I'd rather stay outside, thanks.

Finally, at **Cranium Command,** you try to do the impossible: figure out what goes on in the mind of a 12-year-old kid. A character called General Knowledge gives you a little help through this whimsical wonderland inhabited by a cute little adrenal gland, stomach, and, surprise, even a heart.

## HORIZONS

From oil reserves buried deep beneath the land, let's travel out to the Horizons for a peek into the future. Horizons, presented by General Electric in an unusual multilevel pavilion with strange jutting architectural angles, offers you a look at those now-humorous future-visions of the 1930s. You can see how right Jules Verne was in his predictions. From there you move on to Future Port where you drop in on families of the next century via three-dimensional scenes outlining life in apartments, on farms, out in space, and even under water. Take your pick!

In something called an Omnisphere you visit microworlds and macroworlds in crystal formations and DNA chains and become "part" of a fiery rocket blast-off projected on an eight-story-high screen!

In an undersea habitat, youngsters wearing gills go off on a school field-trip to a seaweed farm, and in a desert, robots harvest the crops—after all, *they* don't suffer from sunburn. When it's all over, you choose your ideal future and ride off into your special Horizon production.

## WORLD OF MOTION

If you're going to get anywhere, you first have to move. General Motors, perhaps needless to say, has been counting on that for some years now. In its EPCOT Center exhibit, dubbed World of Motion, GM has chosen to focus on the human desire to move by wheel. The giant automobile manufacturer has rounded up hundreds of Disney's finest AudioAnimatronic creations to bring you a rollicking roll back through the ages to humankind's first experimentation with a form that was to become vital to us all—the circle.

Presented in a circular building that bears an uncanny resemblance to a giant wheel, World of Motion keeps tongue firmly in cheek as it takes you on a ride—what else?—through 24 different scenes, beginning with an early wanderer who just might have discovered the wheel because his feet were sore! From foot power, you move on to animal power as an early mover-and-shaker shoves futilely at a recalcitrant zebra. Then you journey on to sail power.

Finally, the wheel really got things rolling, although it took a few unsuccessful attempts with wheels shaped like triangles and squares before round got around. After that, today was in sight in the form of the first car lot where determined dealers—"Hi, I'm Bob, the world's wildest trader"—could get you a terrific deal on a barely used . . . chariot (only a few hundred Roman miles on it, and owned by a little old charioteer)!

When people discovered it was such "fun to be free," the theme of this exhibit, they started moving in anything that would float (riverboats), roll (stagecoaches), chug (Old West "iron horses"), or fly (hot-air balloons). You'll see all those modes of transport up to and including an amusing big-wheeled bicyclist's hapless tumble into a hog pen and the first downtown traffic jam, which, come to think of it, hasn't changed all that much.

Through it all, chipmunks flip their tails, roosters flap their wattles, pigs squeal, a ukelele player's fingers move so realistically you'll swear he's real, and as for that cop hiding behind the billboard . . . well, hiss right along with the rest of us.

Antique cars, the real thing painstakingly restored, play a big part in the scenery of these mini-dramas, so you'll probably have to drag car buffs away from this amusing spectacle. Futurists will love it, too, since this historic journey ends with a 3-D-ish, you-are-there ride through a scenic wood, a thriller of a bobsled ride, and a wild night plane landing.

Just before you come back to earth, you get a glimpse into the future, a vision created by liquid neon and laser beds that form a vision of a futuristic cityscape.

It is, as they say, quite a trip.

When it's over, there are still more things to look at here as you discover, or rediscover, what makes that horseless carriage move and how much more smoothly it's likely to roll in the future.

At the **Aero Test Center,** for instance, you'll see an almost full-size replica of a wind tunnel GM used in Warren, Michigan, to test a car's wind resistance, a crucial factor in energy conservation. There's a **Bird and the Robot** demonstration of robot-compilation of car parts and a **Water Engine** film outlining a futuristic engine construction.

**Aero 2000,** GM's experimental four-seat subcompact car sports no steering wheel, only a central control bar, plus orthopedically shaped seats and a video view of the road ahead. Another car on display here, **Concept 2000,** is an 1,800-pound silver streak of aerodynamic knowledge. There's a futuristic truck model that's a Smokey-and-the-Bandit dream machine.

My own choice is a cuddly little creature called the **Lean Machine.** It's shaped just like a bullet, so you crawl in, pull the roof over your head, and lean—literally, the whole upper half of the three-wheeled vehicle actually tilts—into curves. They stole the leaning idea from horses that are able to negotiate those quarter-pole race-track curves by leaning into them. What's more, this little cutie gets *200* miles to a gallon!

Finally, there's a hands-on display of some of GM's newest and sexiest models, an irresistible lure for look-at-me-in-my-new-car photographers.

Not far from the World of Motion is the outsize **Odyssey Restaurant,** which also includes the Baby Center and First Aid Station. Stop here for lunch or dinner fare like Voyager Hotdogs and Explorer Beef Stew, and enjoy a watery view across the lake to World Showcase.

## COMMUNICORE WEST

Moving across to the other side of Future World (that's to the right, or west, side as you face the lake), you'll find CommuniCore West. Here AT&T has surpassed itself with one of the most creative displays you'll see anywhere in the world.

Granted this exhibit is not exciting in the sense of fire-breathing dinosaurs and steamy swamps, but AT&T's **Fountain of Information** is a masterpiece of creative thought.

Designed in the rounded curves of the art deco style, this "fountain" pours out never-ending streams of the informational material with which we are besieged every day. Down these "streams" flow stock certificates, newspaper clippings, paperback and record covers, video discs, and advertisements. Neon messages and moving letters join rivers of video monitors and strips of flashing movie film, telephones, video games, playing cards, sheet music, IRS forms, road signs, stoplights—all the endless flood of messages that demand our attention, streaming endlessly, endlessly on. It's a marvelously graphic look at what our brains absorb, discard, and file every day of our lives.

Sharing this enormous room with the Fountain of Information is a giant map, on which an attendant displays the vast AT&T network that's in operation even as you watch. On this display, called **The Intelligent Network,** you'll see the constant growth of telephone communication. When the brief lecture's over, you get a chance to try touch-sensitive devices that light up any state across the nation and tell you a little about entertaining events and sights there.

At **Face to Face** you get a look at a new kind of picture phone, called teleconferencing, that will enable you to attend a convention thousands of miles away without ever leaving your desk.

Send the kids off to **The Amazing Microchip,** a large model of an integrated circuit chip magnified 420 times. They can crawl and move around through this maze while adults learn how microchips are designed and manufactured by Bell Labs and AT&T.

See the best television picture of them all—yourself on the screen—and get a peek at new telephones that do everything but wash windows. Some help the deaf "hear" through encoded messages, others link to a computer to show you the number dialed, the time, day, and date, then store information in an electronic directory and date book. Pretty slick.

Spread across one wall are dozens of tiny animated figures that form a lighted, musical display outlining modern telecommunications in **The Age of Information.**

Best of all to many people, of course, are the **electronic games** here—all of them free. One, Lost for Words, turns your spoken word into electronic patterns so you can help a mouse find its way through a maze to the cheese. This machine speaks seven languages, including Russian, and provides the basic technology for use of voice commands to control machines, even to dial your phone, no hands.

Another fascinator is a "phraser," which challenges you to type any word into its system and it will pronounce the word back to you. If you can spell supercalifragilisticexpialidocious, this speech synthesizer, using stored rules of English pronunciation, will say it back to you. Fun.

Think you have a terrific memory? Pit it against AT&T's Bit by Bit game, which compares your superstar retention powers with AT&T's newest memory device, a 256,000-bit chip. This little devil will show you just how hard it is for human minds to remember a piddling 16 bits of information for even a few minutes.

If all that memory-straining has made you hungry, stop off in the Sunrise Terrace Restaurant where you can munch on fried chicken, corn muffins, and clam chowder while you store up energy to tackle the fascinating exhibits on this western side of EPCOT Center.

## THE LIVING SEAS

Here we are aboard the Hydrolator sinking down into the depths on our way to Seabase Alpha, where we'll be getting together with a couple of dolphins to discuss life down here in the "under" world.

Latest addition to EPCOT's Future World, the Living Seas exhibit circles around 6,000,000 gallons of sea water in a huge aquarium that is home to 6,000 undersea creatures.

Your adventure begins inside the Living Seas pavilion, where you board a 20-passenger Hydrolator for a 30-second ride to the ocean floor. As you ride, the sea rushes by you and electronic indicators show you how fast you're descending. Soon you're down at **Seabase Alpha,** an ocean research and communication station on the floor of the ocean where you board a Seacab to ride through an acrylic tunnel for an eye-to-fang look at sharks, rays, barracuda, and hundreds of less fearsome coral reef residents.

Next stop: **Seabase Concourse,** a preview of an ocean-research station of the future. Here you wander from place to place, spending as much time as you like examining this Jacques Cousteau wonderland. You'll get a look at: the **Scuba Tube,** an acrylic cylinder through which divers descend into this Disney sea; a 24-foot-high tubular aquarium that houses the **Pacific Coast Kelp Forest** where you'll learn some of fishdom's clever camouflages; newsreel reports on ocean discoveries; underwater gardens that may someday be harvested just like Kansas wheat fields; **Nature's Buried Treasure,** a display of the enormous wealth of minerals just lying there under the sea waiting to be retrieved; and dolphin and sea lion research centers where you can watch researchers trying to learn dolphin language—and to teach Flipper to speak Sea-nglish!

Seabase Concourse is divided into several modules—Ocean Ecosystems, Ocean Resources, Marine Mammals, Earth Systems, and Undersea Exploration. Games, hands-on exhibits, and animated displays make all this education not only palatable but a whale of a lot of fun as well. A star of the show is Jason, an AudioAnimatronics submersible robot who cavorts his way through a presentation on the pressure and temperature extremes that limit human exploration of the sea, but that don't bother him at all.

Sponsored by United Technologies Corp., the exhibit winds up with a slick film compiled by UTC photographers who traveled all over the globe to create this two-minute mind-boggler played on 35 different video screens. It makes a fitting accompaniment to your rise out of what WDW calls the "world's sixth-largest ocean" back up to the world of terra firma.

But wait, it's not over yet! One of the biggest stars in Living Seas these days is not the exhibit itself but **Coral Reef Restaurant** where you munch on seafood treats as you gaze through towering acrylic windows, watching some of that seafood still on the swim!

A 264-seat restaurant, Coral Reef features more than a dozen kinds of sea treats ranging from Dover sole to Maine lobsters, from scallops to shark, swordfish, and salmon trout (yes, there really is such a thing). Seafood selections naturally vary according to what found its way into the fisherman's net today, but choices may include such tempters as shark steak or filet of tuna with a walnut-orange butter; bay scallops flavored with basil; salmon trout swimming in lime butter; or swordfish steak in a Cajun rémoulade sauce. Prices are in the $15 to $25 range for entrées.

If all that sounds pretty good, it should. EPCOT Center's executive chef was twice named the state's Seafood Chef of the Year for blue-ribbon dishes he dreamed up, including one teaming citrus and red snapper.

## THE LAND

One of the most popular and certainly one of the most fascinating exhibits in EPCOT Center is just to the right of CommuniCore as you face the lake. The Land is every gardener's dream world, a place where things grow in sand or in nothing at all, where huge pink squash hang on vines, and a field of corn is likely to share the field with another vegetable as well.

Set in an architecturally impressive building topped by a glittering glass triangle, The Land focuses on humankind's relationship with the earth and the products we coax from it. In this six-acre pavilion Kraft offers you everything from a giant Farmer's Market of restaurants to a look at some of the innovative ways agricultural experts expect to use the land in future generations to provide more and better for all.

In the **Harvest Theater** you can watch an 18-minute motion picture, "Symbiosis," which outlines the interdependence between humans and their environment. "Symbiosis" highlights humans' amazing ability to control temperamental environments with creations like Peru's Machu Picchu, France's ancient aqueducts, and the rice terraces of the Philippines. You even get a look at some of the world's successes in reversing its own mistakes: cleaning of the Thames River in England and reclamation of Europe's Lake Constance.

A bilevel building, The Land features the intriguing **Land Grille,** a revolving dining room which offers you a glimpse of several sections of the pavilion as you dine on steak with green peppercorns; chicken marinated in lime juice; a Cheddar cheese, mushroom and nut-roll appetizer (dinner prices in the $12 to $20 range).

The Harvest Theater and Land Grille occupy a balcony overlooking the massive **Farmer's Market** below. In this Americana setting, you can dine under colorful umbrellas after collecting delectables from a wide choice of kiosks, including a bakery, an ice-cream shop, a beverage house, cheese shop (Kraft, naturally), potato store, barbecue, sandwich shop, and soup/salad store.

The **Kitchen Kabaret** is an amusing presentation that will get you cooking, so they say. Hostess Bonny Appetit is accompanied by the Kitchen Krackpots band (a mayonnaise jar playing canned food "drums," singing bananas and eggplants, a barbecue-sauce bottle strumming a whisk). A sexy Ms. Cheese, who's "a delightful array of curds," is joined by Ms. Ice Cream, the Cereal Sisters singing "Boogey Woogey Bakery Boy, the Toast (literally) of the Town," the comedy team of Hamm 'n Eggz, even a rocking broccoli stalk who's a member of the Colander Combo band and wears a conga outfit and sunglasses. It's funny, a little crazy, and a hilarious way to learn what you ought to be eating when you're chowing down on junk food.

The stellar production in The Land, however, is the **Listen to the Land Boat Ride.** After boarding a boat, you sail through some of the most innovative agricultural advances you'll ever see. First, you journey through three ecosystems—a rain forest, a desert, and the prairie. Then you move on to an experimental greenhouse where horticulturists, physicists, metallurgists, chemists, and agricultural experts are experimenting with plants and aquatic creatures in hopes of increasing the world's food production.

On a 40-acre site, you'll find plants growing under artificial gravity to simulate spacecraft growing conditions, and crops planted alternately in a process called "intercropping," which allows a plant like sugar cane to use nitrogen produced by peas or beans grown alongside it.

You'll see loofah gourds (those nubby creatures used as bath scrubbers) flourishing, pole beans climbing up cornstalks, tomatoes, lettuce, even strawberries growing on conveyer belts that move them to feeding areas where their roots are sprayed with nutrients. Plants grow in giant rotating drums; hormones are used to stimulate pineapples to flower in about one-third the time it normally takes; and lettuce thrives on space-saving plastic A-frames.

You'll see cucumbers that grow 12 inches a day, tomatoes whose huge roots dangle in the air, fed and watered through pipes. You'll learn how scientists can use pure seawater to irrigate plants. You'll discover a winged bean with pods that taste like spinach, flowers that substitute for mushrooms, and roots that can be eaten like potatoes!

Aquaculture is part of the activity going on here, too, so some of the chemicals that drip from roof-hung plants fall into ponds where they help fertilize water plants. Even fish get in on the act, as scientists study ways to increase shrimp and fish populations.

If you want to see even more than you'll see on this quickie trip, you can sign up at the end of the journey for a 45-minute **Tomorrow's Harvest Tour** that gives you an even closer look at the fascinating things going on here.

## JOURNEY INTO IMAGINATION

Sometimes imagination can be more fun than reality. No one knows that better than Kodak, which whisks you away into a strange "adult playground" where you can step on a color to create a sound, journey through a rainbow, feel strange feelies, and create a symphony or a computerized art masterpiece with a wave of your talented hand.

Journey Into Imagination rises over Future World in glassy magnificence, its glittering façade towering over a geometric crystal sculpture and a spray of fountains. An eye-catching triangular construction, the building housing this exhibit is a study in geometric forms and contemporary color play.

Inside, Kodak continues to challenge your imagination with an amazing array of hands-on displays you create yourself in a wonderland of electronic effects.

Your hosts are Dreamfinder, an elfin character who pilots a strange Dream-Catching machine, and his sidekick Figment, a purple dragon. Together, they roam a universe of the imagination collecting colors, sounds, and shapes, which they convert into new creations of all kinds. When you travel with them, nebulae explode, you hold lightning in a jar, and you play with a bubble machine and colorful rainbows.

You can try a few of Dreamfinder's tricks yourself upstairs in the **Image Works,** a creative playground of the future, where you'll be a child again but not in any childish way. Instead you'll make **Bubble Music** by projecting bubbles on a screen and accompanying them with some very odd electronic sounds.

At **Dreamfinder's School of Drama** you can get right up on stage yourself and follow instructions on video monitors. While you're acting, your talents are appearing on a screen behind you where you become part of the play, enlarged or miniaturized as the script demands.

Walk right over the rainbow in **Sensor Maze,** where you're assigned a color by a tunnel of neon rings. Listen to your voice activate a light show and visit **Stepping Tones,** where your footsteps set off a blaze of color, light, and sound effects.

At **Light Writer** create patterns with light, and at the **Magic Palette** pick a shape and color, then use a magical pen to create bizarre designs or to color in a sketch.

A **Kaleidoscope** creates changing patterns of color, and odd tables full of blunt-tipped gold dressmaker's pins offer you a weird tactile and visual sensation. Or try **Electronic Philharmonic**—just wave your hands in front of a caseful of musical instruments and out come whatever sounds you command.

Ride a glass elevator to the **Magic Eye Theater** to see a slide show that uses wonderful photographs to outline the history of photography. Move on then to the star show of this Kodak pavilion, the 3-D production that's won the hearts of the crowds.

White-gloved rocker Michael Jackson has now joined Dreamfinder, Figment, and the rest of the Disney family to take you on a Journey into Imagination. Here Michael becomes Captain EO, star of a new three-dimensional space-fantasy film directed by Francis Ford Coppola. Weird and wonderful, this 3-D whizzer also stars Anjelica Huston and Dick Shawn, along with a cast of impish new Disney characters who accompany the captain on a space adventure.

Outside the building, the show goes on with a maniacal fountain that acts like no self-respecting fountain you ever saw. This one persists in leaping right over your head, disappearing down a hole, and leaping right back out again to spring its way around and around you.

# A JOURNEY THROUGH
# A WORLD SHOWCASE

Awed with the future and all its possibilities, let's journey now into the present—and perhaps even a bit of the past—for a look at the world we know but never well enough. Let's visit Walt Disney World's World Showcase, an international exposition that will show you around much of the globe almost as fast as the Concorde supersonic jetliner could get you to Europe.

World Showcase is spread around the edges of a vast lagoon. America's pavilion sits smack in the center, flanked by a variety of other cultures ranging from Japanese to Italian, Mexican to Canadian.

Because the buses and boats which can save you some steps around this showcase move on a clockwise course, in this case from east to west, let's start at Mexico's eerily enchanting pavilion and work our way around the clock to the westernmost entry, Canada.

## MEXICO

As you enter World Showcase Plaza, which runs alongside the lake opposite the geosphere, look to your left and you'll see the golden stones of a great, stepped pyramid rising out of the flatlands like a south-of-the-border mirage. Street signs announce the presence of Avenida Esplendida as you stroll to a walk-up window for a taco or a burrito at **La Cantina de San Angel.**

Inside, you're greeted by a display of 2,500-year-old pre-Columbian art created by artisans who had deciphered the mysteries of astronomy and time measurement long before the U.S. was even a gleam in some revolutionary's eye.

Walk on, and suddenly you're no longer in America but in the middle of **Plaza de los Amigos** surrounded by typical adobe *casas* where flowers bloom, candles flicker, and romantic wrought-iron balconies are just waiting for a troop of mariachi singers to serenade an ebony-haired señorita. A shell fountain tucked away in a wall burbles merrily, and in the distance mysterious, deep-blue light illuminates a pyramid.

In the center of it all, a busy marketplace is jammed with sturdy baskets, colorful pottery, pastel paper piñatas, delicate lace dresses, and rainbow-hued paper flowers big as hats. At **Artesanias Mexicanas** pick up a soft woven serape, an onyx carving, a delicately crafted ceramic cathedral or tree of life, intricately carved wooden candlesticks, ornate birdcages, leather huarachis, guayaberas, and colorful Mexican glass.

You can dine in the eerie glow of that towering pyramid as jungle birds chatter around you, silenced occasionally by the distant snarl of the jaguar. In the **San Angel Inn Restaurante** you'll be greeted by a pretty señorita in a long white dress, and you're entertained by that mariachi band as you dine on mole poblano, carne asada, huevos rancheros, tacos, tamarind water, margaritas, tamales, chili rellenos, and the like, for prices in the $10 to $20 range for dinner, about half that for lunch.

Step into a flower-trimmed boat and whiz off on a cruise through Mexican history brought to life with AudioAnimatronics, beautiful three-dimensional settings, and film. Back you'll fade into ancient Mexico when the Mayan civilization flourished. A stone priest comes to life to greet you as you wander through time, accompanied by singers and dancers, even an occasional determined vendor or two, working hard to strike a bargain. Finally you sail into the excitement of Mexico in this century and then bid adios in a burst of fireworks.

## NORWAY

The latest country to join Disney's World Showcase of nations is Norway, the land of fjords and fairy-tale trolls. Here in Norway you can munch on Scandinavian open-faced sandwiches, then board a Viking ship and set sail from a scenic Norwegian village up a fjord, over a waterfall, and back in time. Settled cozily into your dragon-headed craft you float along a river through whitewater rapids and into a 10th-century Viking village, complete with full-size Viking ship about to set sail.

You journey on into a mythical Norwegian forest ruled by wicked trolls and playful water spirits who cast a spell on your boat causing it to—whoops!—plummet backwards down the river into the rapids of Jutenheimen mountain country.

You crash through a narrow gorge and narrowly miss disaster as you get caught in a spinning whirlpool, then swirl through a rock passageway in the North Sea. Whew!

Lightning crackles and waves roar as that fabled sea produces a raging storm that shakes the foundations of a towering oil production platform looming up before you. After a narrow miss, you float again into a serene fishing village, where you dock and begin your exploration.

Down a wooden gangplank that meanders between a rocky

ledge and a waterfall, and you're back in Norway, this time via a wide-screen film that transports you from cozy mountain hamlets to colorful seaside villages.

Outside awaits the Norwegian village, which features the ornate architecture of the Norwegian cities of Oslo, Alesund, Bergen, and Setesdal surrounding a cobblestone plaza.

If it's snack time, you can stoke up in a Norwegian bakery that produces this land's famous pastries. If it's let's-eat time, step into the castle, a replica of the 14th-century **Akershus** fortress that stands in Oslo's harbor, and roam through a vast array of smörgåsbord selections. You dine accompanied by the whoosh of a nearby waterfall.

To get a look at a "real" Viking ship, step out to the Showcase Lagoon, where a replica of the Viking ships used more than 1,000 years ago by 10th-century Norse explorers is moored. A 50-foot ship, the **Norseman** was a gift from a Norwegian maritime organization. Could this be the ship that Leif Ericsson sailed when he discovered America?

On sale in the castle and elsewhere are the best-loved Norwegian crafts ranging from colorful and intricate hand-knit sweaters and shawls to pewter and Norwegian tole painting on wood. Glass and metal creations in chic contemporary styling are tempters, too.

## CHINA

Now the music changes as you wander into the strange sounds of Asia through the huge **Gate of the Golden Sun** and stroll across a tiny stone bridge over a serene lotus-laden pool. Above you soars the curving roofline of the **Temple of Heaven,** its royal blue tiles glittering in the sun.

Wander among art treasures in the **House of the Whispering Willows,** then go into the ornate **Hall of Prayer for Good Harvest,** where you'll step back more than 1,200 years as eighth-century poet-storyteller Li Po, Shakespeare's Chinese equivalent, appears on a 360-degree screen to introduce you to the wonders of this rarely seen country.

Amusingly, Li Po was reputedly a notorious drunkard who boasted that he wrote best when sozzled; his picture was often displayed as a trademark over wine shops in China. Regardless, he tells a good story and his presentation at EPCOT's China pavilion is likely to be one of the highlights of your visit here.

You enter the Forbidden City, visit the Dalai Lama's priceless palace, sail along the Yangtze and Yellow rivers, roam the Great Wall of China, visit the Harbin Ice Festival in Manchuria, and see a performance of the Peking Opera and a demonstration of shadow boxing at Hangzhou's West Lake. This 20-minute classic took seven months to film and contains footage of parts of China never before filmed by Westerners.

As you leave, a diminutive hostess garbed in emerald-green silk trimmed in gold threads bids you goodbye with a tiny bow.

Newest addition to China is the elegant **Nine Dragons Restaurant,** where petite Asian lasses scurry about toting loaded trays of steaming taste treats. A favorite for lunch, Nine Dragons features tall windows overlooking the lagoon and World Showcase promenade. Massive intricately carved wood panels, hand-rubbed until they shine, are a study in Chinese talent for detail while handsome brocaded chair cushions and elaborate Oriental fixtures set the stage for an evening of delicate tastes—and taste.

Chinese chefs turn beef, chicken, and seafood into an amazing maze of delicacies typifying the cuisine of several Chinese provinces up to and exceeding Mandarin, Cantonese, Szechuan, and Shanghai. Have a go at hot-and-sour soup, beef steak with jade tree, stir-fried lobster tails, Peking duck, Chinese teas, and finish with an ice-cream egg roll or red-bean ice-cream. When you're in the mood for light and delicate, this is the place. Dinner entrées are in the $10 to $20 range, lunch selections about $5 less.

One more new touch here in China: the **Lotus Blossom Café,** which offers quick counter service featuring all the favorite Oriental fast-food items, from egg rolls to stir-fry selections. Try the beef and broccoli stir-fry. The atmosphere's nice here in this roofed but open-air dining spot that looks out over the tranquillity of an Oriental garden.

## GERMANY

In the land of oom-pah-pah and dirndls, sausage and singers, beer and bratwurst, you're greeted by the painted walls and timbered architecture of the Alpine region, medieval spires, and a picturesque *Platz* (town square) where scarlet geraniums spill from flowerboxes and the German zest for life spills over. There's even the inevitable town clock chiming away as a fountain bubbles over gray stones.

In a huge **Biergarten** you can guzzle mugs of suds or down a glass of tangy German wine presented in etched, green-stemmed glasses. Amid massive stone walls hung with tapestries, begin lunch or dinner with the traditional white radishes carved and twisted into a spiraling stream. In this village-rathskeller atmosphere handsome *Herren* in lederhosen and *Damen* in dirndls yodel their hearts out, toot away on long, long Alpine horns, and dance up a storm of clap-slapping traditional dances. Your hunger will be dissipated here by sauerbraten and sauerkraut, huge platters of sausage and pork chops, and German chocolate cake, for prices in the $10 to $16 range for dinner and show.

Crafts in Germany are handsome, so expect to be lured into enchanting shops like **Der Bücherwurm,** which sells attractive original oil paintings and etchings. **Volkskunst** is stocked with candles in intricate designs; foot-tall ceramic mugs; angels dressed in elaborate gold-trimmed brocades; and large wood carvings, including one $1,500-plus masterpiece featuring a lamplighter carved in a thick slab of wood, his copper lantern lighted. Look up at the ceiling here and you'll see an entire mini-oom-pah-pah band in full swing.

Young ones will love the offerings of **Der Teddybär,** and wine lovers will find treasures in the **Weinkeller.** Chocoholics should avoid the **Süssigkeiten,** where products of the cocoa bean are joined by delicate cookies and confections. To put your goodies in a worthy setting, stop by the **Glas and Porzellanhaus,** purveyors of Germany's famed porcelainware, which here includes a $12,000 Hummel figurine!

## ITALY

Just a few steps away from Germany rises a tall column crowned by the Lion of St. Mark, talisman of Venice's most famous piazza, St. Mark's Square. Here a gondola is moored at dockside and the Doge's Palace beckons you into an arcade filled with handcrafted leathers, delicate Venetian glass, and hefty clay pottery filled with plastic fruit and vegetables so realistic you'd be wise not to mix them with the real thing.

Star of Italy's pavilion is **L'Originale Alfredo di Roma Ristorante,** a place created by the *original* Alfredo, who's certainly been flattered by plagiarism over the years. Naturally those delicate pastas are the lure here, and you'll see them created right before your eyes in the shadow of dozens of photographs of Alfredo packing his famous pastas into the willing mouths of the famous. One of the three most popular restaurants in EPCOT Center, Alfredo's is booked for dinner very early but often has more lunch spaces than you'd expect.

It's no wonder it's so popular, since you dine in a beautiful rust-colored room with sunshine streaming through tall windows curtained with heavy drapes. Chandeliers glitter and murals of Roman scenes beguile you as white-coated waiters deliver antipasto misto, spaghetti carbonara, linguine al pesto, cannelloni filled with spinach, veal in a cream sauce, bocconcini featuring veal and mushrooms in wine sauce, zabaglione, zuppa inglese, and cassata di ricotta. Entrées are in the $15 to $20 range or less, and there's a children's menu, here as in other restaurants, for $3 to $5.

Out of the piazza at **Il Teatro di Bologna,** commedia dell'arte actors present amusing skits, and Carnival in Venice dancers perform in the shadow of the Triton fountain. When the show's over, stroll by the shops to see the glittering gold jewels, delicate Venetian glass, and fragile Capodimonte flowers. **Il Bel Cristallo,** for instance, features beautiful Italian pottery, wood carvings, intricate coral cameos, and a flashing glass paperweight that's a beauty. Don't miss the music boxes, particularly the miniature grand piano with an inlaid wood mandolin, music, and pipes entwined in flowers. It plays Offenbach's "Barcarolle," and it can be yours for $1,000.

Terra-cotta pottery is a specialty at **Arcata d'Artigiani,** while 14-carat gold's the lure at **La Gemma Elegante,** where Venetian beads are a temptation. Finally, there's **i santi,** where glove-soft Italian leathers are downright irresistible.

## THE AMERICAN ADVENTURE

Occupying stage center at EPCOT Center's World Showcase is America, complete with Liberty Inn, hot dogs, and a brick replica of Independence Hall.

On your way to the fascinating AudioAnimatronics history lesson, you pass under the flags of America's first two centuries and walk a long formal hall carpeted in scarlet and lighted by candle lamps in wall niches.

America's animated production takes place in an impressive theater lined with white columns and arches showcasing marble-like statues of various "spirits"—the spirit of freedom, adventure, tomorrow, self-reliance, pioneering, and knowledge—set against a backdrop of burgundy velvet.

The crystal chandeliers glitter then dim, as 35 full-size animated figures, the most life-like ever developed by Disney's imagineers, tell the story of America's early days and the nation's struggles for liberty and justice.

The hosts are Benjamin Franklin, who has the distinction of being the first AudioAnimatronic creation to walk up stairs, and Mark Twain, as irascible and witty as ever.

Pride, Twain tells us, is our national heritage, and even those Americans who have overcome it manage, nevertheless, to be proud of their humility! It goes on like that: a look at the nation's struggle over slavery features a stirring speech on the subject by Frederick Douglass; a call for an end to Native American suffering is delivered by Chief Joseph; and an impassioned plea for women's rights comes from Susan B. Anthony.

You'll see soldiers fighting and dying in the Revolutionary War and watch brave men, women, and children fight the wilderness to survive and to expand the nation westward. It's a moving presentation and one that may bring a tear to the eye of many a proud American.

If you're suffering an attack of the munchies before or after the 29-minute show, stop by the **Liberty Inn** next door for hot dogs, hamburgers, and other oh-so-American fare, served in a covered outdoor café or beneath umbrellas in a patio overlooking the lagoon and the huge American Gardens stage on which various international stars perform.

## JAPAN

High above you, a massive red torii gateway welcomes you to the Japan pavilion, where you'll spot the flash of a golden fin in a koi pond and hear the wind whistling through a stand of bamboo. That tranquillity for which the Japanese are so justly famous pervades this serene enclave where everything, from pebbles to trees, seems made to measure.

Its front entrance guarded by a five-roofed, blue-tiled Shinto temple trimmed on each corner with bells, the Japan pavilion features the **Katsura Imperial Villa**, "best viewed in the romantic light of an autumn moon," they tell you. Here a palatial villa has become an intimate restaurant serving yakitori, skewered meats, and colorful, simmered vegetables inside or outside under a parasol, on a tiny serene patio where musical entertainment is provided by a tinkling waterfall.

Japan's **Mitsukoshi department store** stocks fragile mobiles of inch-high, kimono-clad maidens, plus silks, fans, wall hangings, Japanese lanterns, elaborate enamelware, and rubber gourmet hors d'oeuvres so realistic even the high price tags on the shrimp or the lemon slice seem worth their weight in realism. The department store is housed in a grand Sishinden Hall, and at its back door loom the towers of a forbidding feudal castle with huge brass-trimmed double doors and a heavy wooden bridge spanning a moat.

A priceless suit of samurai armor is displayed here and proves most intriguing. It's made of small scales of lacquered iron laced together with silk cords. It weighs only 25 pounds yet was far more impervious to the forces of war than heavy European chain mail. An accompanying sword was made of steel so strong it could cut through a pile of copper coins without a nick!

You can see a movie outlining some of the wonder of this lovely country, then climb the steep staircase up to the collection of restaurants and a pleasant cocktail lounge, the **Matsunoma Lounge,** that boasts the best view of EPCOT Center. Here you'll find the **Teppanyaki Dining Rooms,** where master chefs prepare grilled steaks, lobster, huge shrimp, and chicken right before your eyes as you sip Japanese beer, sake, or plum wine (dinner and lunch prices $12 to $19). Or try the **Tempura Kiku's** sashimi, batter-fried delicacies, brought sizzling to your lacquered tray at the tempura bar ($12 to $17 for lunch and dinner).

## MOROCCO

Visions of veiled ladies and ghostly-spooky caftans disappearing around the corner. Clandestine whispers. Humphrey Bogart in *Casablanca.* It all comes to life at EPCOT's new Morocco pavilion which itself came to life in 1984 but seems, like Morocco, to have been here since the beginning of time. At the Morocco pavilion you're welcomed by a gaggle of clapping, singing, fez-topped musicians who pound on drums and strum away at stringed instruments in the shadow of a replica of the 12th-century Koutoubia Minaret.

Disney artists are a magical lot, and here they've managed to re-create the labyrinthian splendor of Morocco, with its strikingly beautiful palace courtyards so like Spain's famed Giralda. In the small museum here you can examine some of the amazingly intricate artwork of the Moroccans. You even get a special invitation to a re-creation of a Moroccan wedding at which the bride in elaborately embroidered wedding gown and slippers sits high on a pile of pillows.

Artisans were brought from Morocco to build this pavilion with its intricate tilework and carved timbers. So realistic is the mélange of streets, gates, and minarets they have created that one workman is said to have looked down the street and pointed out the house in which he was born!

Some of those artisans remained here and you can watch them weaving beautiful Moroccan carpets, pounding brass into trays and pitchers, tooling leather. That and many, many other kinds of treasures—sheepskins, gold-trimmed caftans, ceramics, woodwork, silver, leather hats, and baskets—are sold in this bazaar.

Morocco sports one of the newest restaurants in EPCOT, the **Marrakesh.** A study in candlelight, ornately carved plaster, tiles, carpets, costumed waiters, and a belly dancer, Marrakesh is one of the most seductive of EPCOT's restaurants. For $13 to $17 you feast on a dinner of such Moroccan specialties as couscous—a bowl of semolina topped with vegetables, beef, lamb, and chicken—or saffron-flavored harira soup. Revel in the flavors of apricots, cinnamon, almonds, honey, and prunes delicately blended with chicken, beef, or lamb and top it off with glasses of hot mint tea.

## FRANCE

In the shadow of the Eiffel Tower stands the line everyone wants to be part of: the line for reservations at France's **Les Chefs de France** restaurant, created and cuisined by three superstar chefs— Roger Vergé, Paul Bocuse, and Gaston Lenôtre. It is well worth the wait, every delectable morsel of it.

Definitely the star of this charming enclave, the restaurant features what may very well be the best food in Central Florida, not to mention the best vittles in Disney World. Dream along these lines: salade de homard (lobster), snapper topped with salmon mousse and baked in a puff pastry, braised beef with scalloped potatoes, filet de boeuf au poivre et aux raisins in Armagnac sauce. For starters: French onion soup, aspic de foie gras, pâté de veau en croûte, oysters topped with spinach and a champagne sauce.

In one pretty glass-enclosed dining room, there's a tranquil garden atmosphere, in another dining area attractive booths, masses of silk flowers, gleaming brass and crystal, even an outdoor patio. You can feast on complete appetizer-to-dessert (chocolate cake layered with chocolate mousse) dinners for $17 to $21 and less ambitious feasts in the $9 to $15 range. Lunches are likely to run up to the $9 to $14 range when you see the tempting array of crisp salads and gorgeous desserts available.

While it's more than a little difficult to pull yourself out of this entrancing restaurant, you may be lured by the delectable scents emanating from the **Boulangerie Pâtisserie.** Delectable pastries draw a crowd of the hungry, many of whom can't wait: They sit right outside in a tiny patio, **Au Petit Café,** and consume the goodies from within this typical French bakery.

There's one more chance to sample this delectable French cooking: **Le Bistro de Paris,** an upstairs dining room just behind Les Chefs de France and near the bakery. Here you dine on earthy, provincial French cooking, things like cassoulet and boeuf bourguignon. Quainter and quieter than the downstairs operation, this Bistro is for me the winner in this French war of the whisks. Prices are in the same range as downstairs, about $19 to $25 for a complete dinner; lunch $12 to $15.

If you figure you can create delectables just as irresistible right in your own kitchen, give your talents a little boost at **La Casserole,** which sells all the accoutrements of a gourmet kitchen, from escargot dishes to huge whisks and special spices. At **Barton & Guestier** pick up a bottle of *vin* to carry under your arm along with your loaf of crusty bread, a little cheese, and all you'll need for a lakeside picnic is a thou beside you singing in the wilderness.

Art buffs will want to peek into **Plume et Palette** and perfume fans will find **La Signature** offerings hard to resist. Love silk flowers and baskets to put them in? Stop at **Les Halles** and fulfill your fantasies with their floral creations.

France also wants to show you its wonders—and they are

many—so it's produced a beautiful film, "Impressions of France," that takes you across the green French countryside and shows you why Paris is called the City of Lights. You'll go on an airborne trip across this picturesque land via a spectacular 200-degree screen presentation that takes place inside the **Palais du Cinema,** a replica of a famous Paris theater.

## UNITED KINGDOM

From Gallic shrugs to veddy, veddy British accents is only a hop, skip, jump, and a bridge here in EPCOT Center's World Showcase. As the last strains of the "Marseillaise" fade in the background, you'll stride into the land of tea and ale, transparent china, and cuddly woolens.

It is, of course, the incomparable kingdom, interpreted here at EPCOT Center with gabled rooftops, cobblestone streets, timbered architecture, and a pub so British they'd have difficulty duplicating that much atmosphere in the Mother Country.

Third of the triumvirate of most-popular restaurants in the Showcase, the **Rose & Crown Pub & Dining Room** is, old chap, British beyond British. Rest your weary foot on a brass rail as you quaff a pint, warmed at a special beer-warmer to a very British 53 degrees, or cooled to a Floridian 45. Shafts of sunlight sneak through the etched glass and café curtains to bounce off polished woods, and there's a lovely view across the lake from the tiled dining room out back or the small patio area.

As for the fare . . . well, talk about typical: steak-and-kidney pie, fish and chips, Stilton cheese, Scotch eggs (hard-boiled eggs and sausage with a mustard sauce), and raspberry fool. Lunches for $8 or less, dinner a dollar or two more, and at dinner a chance for beefeaters to try some roast beef. Ales, stouts, and the like are $4 a pint—try an ebony Guinness Stout for something different.

Outside in the cobblestoned courtyard you'll find **The Tea Caddy** occupying a white cottage with a thatched roof and purveying Twining's fancy teas and yummy jams. Complete the tea part with some biscuits from **The Biscuit Barrel** and wander over to **The Queen's Table** to select some elegant Royal Doulton china on which to present this masterpiece high tea you're creating.

Plaid kilts and wool sweaters in soft heathery colors, not to mention your clan's traditional tartan, are spread wall to rafter in **Pringle of Scotland,** while at **His Lordship** you can treat his lordship to a fancy pipe, a ship in a glass bottle, or a most unusual chess set.

Don't miss **The Toy Soldier,** where the "King" is a chubby bear complete with crown and royal robes. The highlight of this enchanting shop is a glass-cased display of a royal dinner, featuring tiny minstrels on the balcony, jesters spinning hoops and tottering on a teeter-totter, a winking maid, knights with bejeweled shields, and waiters delivering heaping trays of fancy viands to some of the dourest royal visages this side of Alice in Wonderland. Perhaps Alka-Seltzer hadn't been invented yet.

## CANADA

The star of our northern neighbor's exhibit is a stunning 360-degree motion picture **"O Canada!"** Surrounded by film you'll travel through this largest country in the Western Hemisphere as freely as the 50,000 wild geese that take to the skies in a flurry of feathers. Ride in the Calgary Stampede, then fly downhill on skis, and climb Toronto's C.N. Tower for a goose-eye view of that sophisticated city.

Back down on terra firma, wander through this Canadian village, which includes everything from a Northwest Territories native village to a 19th-century French château. As you near the abandoned gold-mine tunnel, you may get splashed by drops from a waterfall that cascades over huge rocks nestled beneath tall pines.

Some of the World's Showcase's most interesting—at least to Floridians—treasures are to be found at **Northwest Mercantile,** where you can buy soft rabbit skins, raccoon caps, plaid wool jackets, leather mittens, sheepskins, and figures carved from coal. Fur-collar-trimmed jackets, moccasins, tribal dolls and totem poles, maple syrup, and wild rice—they're all here in a most unusual Showcase shop.

If you're hungry, drop in at the buffeteria-style **Le Cellier** restaurant, a study in stone and wine-cellary atmosphere gleaming with candles, copper and pewter accessories, brocaded chairs, and a vaulted ceiling. You'll find some unusual treats, each representing a province or major city: Manitoba beef short ribs, baked salmon, Toronto sausages, and Canadian bacon, sauerkraut baked in cider, and a special Québec tortière (pork pie), all in the $10 to $20 range.

# ENTERTAINMENT AT EPCOT CENTER

Just as there's never a dull moment in the Magic Kingdom, there's always something to watch at EPCOT Center.

If you arrive here early in the morning, you'll get a musical greeting from the **Future World Brass,** a 12-piece contemporary group that begins its day's work near Spaceship Earth and makes appearances in other parts of the park in the afternoons.

Most of EPCOT Center's entertainment focuses on World Showcase. American Gardens Theater, an outdoor stage in front of The American Adventure, hosts changing shows featuring **national dance and folk singers.** Shows include music and dance traditions of 40 different nations by performers in handmade costumes of their countries. What's more, each World Showcase pavilion features entertainment representative of its culture.

**Mexico** has a five-piece marimba band on stage at the pavilion's Plaza de los Amigos and a strolling nine-piece mariachi group playing in the courtyard, cantina, and dining areas.

**Chinese artisans** create woodcarvings, clay seals, stamps, woven baskets, and the inimitable Chinese calligraphy in the China pavilion. There are even some of those huge papier-mâché lions, peopled by dancers, slinking around the pavilion and colorful, swirling ribbon dancers.

In Germany you'll see a Bavarian **Oktoberfest** complete with dancers and a seven-piece baskapelle band, plus one-man oom-pah band, a yodeler, and alpenhorn player. Join in—they'll love it.

A **street actors group,** Teatro di Bologna, performs in the centuries-old commedia dell'arte improvisational style in the piazza at the Italy pavilion. Some of their improvisations are a scream. In Alfredo's restaurant **singing waiters** warble opera classics.

**Voices of Liberty** sing in the American pavilion, and their drummer-piper counterparts, the **Sons of Liberty** fife-and-drum corps, pound the pavement much the same as they must have done in the Revolutionary War.

A **traveling candyman,** who magically turns rice toffee into dragons and birds, wins top marks from the small fry—and me—at the Japanese pavilion.

In France's enclave a **strolling musical group** plays favorite Parisian songs.

In London, **Renaissance Players** deliver some hilarious street theater reproducing in memorable—and fractured—style the dramatic masterpieces of Shakespeare.

Scottish **bagpipes** turn up in Canada's pavilion.

Light shatters the night at EPCOT Center these days as the park presents its new "IllumiNations" show. A dazzling spectacle that sends millions of colored lights and laser beams dancing over the landmarks and lagoon of World Showcase, IllumiNations turns Germany's Bavarian castle into a gingerbread toy shop, sets dragons atop the roofs of the China pavilion, cracks piñatas over Mexico and turns the chimneys of France into Paree-by-night. It's all quite a show.

# X

# DISNEY-MGM STUDIOS: A STAR-SPANGLED MOUSE

Lives there a soul who hasn't dreamed of fame, of stardom and screaming fans, of autographs and adulation?

Nahhh, we're all hams at heart and here at Walt Disney World's newest attraction we all get a chance to be a star.

Step onto the macadam here and you're transported to Hollywood of yore when Lana Turner soared from sodas at Schwab's to stardom on the celluloid screen. When Fred and Ginger danced up a terpsichorean swirl and Rhett courted Scarlett.

Even the Hollywood of today gets into the act with Indiana Jones and the Muppets, Dick Tracey and Roger Rabbit.

Once again, those imaginations that have made Walt Disney World the most visited attraction in *this* galaxy guide you from the world of reality to the world of celluloid make-believe where you become star for a day . . . at least.

## ORIENTATION

Some stars are lucky enough to reach the top the easy way—you can bet there were no casting couch experiences in Mickey's rise to the top of the Crossroads of the World landmark where he lords it over the entrance to this new park-within-a-park.

As in the other parks there are some basic survival tips, so let's take a look at some of the things you'll need to know to get this third of the Disney triumvirate under control.

### WHEN TO GO

I really wish I could tell you when to go but this park which just opened in 1989 has been so busy since its opening that the parking lot is often full by noon or even earlier.

That is bound to slow down in days to come but because the

park is small—just 110 acres—and there are double-digit thousands of people at Disney World on any given day, this park is always likely to be a busy spot.

My best advice is: Arrive early, perhaps 30 to 60 minutes before the park officially opens at 9am. It would also be wise to check on the opening hours which occasionally change. Typically, the hours here are 9am to 9pm, later in summer and on holidays. A call to Disney information at 824-4321 or 824-2222 will put you in the pictures.

Naturally, the busiest times of year are the same here as they are in the Magic Kingdom and EPCOT, so please take a look at what I've said about that back in Chapter VIII—basically mid-February, mid-April, June to September, and mid-December.

Once in the park, you would do well to head straight for the Animation Building where one of the park's most popular shows occurs.

If you wait until later to hit this one, expect to spend 30 to 45 minutes in line. Animators who work here head for home between 5 and 6pm so don't leave this stop until last—without them it's just not the same.

## GETTING THERE

Major routes to Walt Disney World are outlined back in Chapter VIII so take a peek there and you'll soon see how to get to the main entrance which is just off I-4 at US 192.

You can also exit I-4 at an exit ramp north of US 192 and south of Fla. 535 (it's about halfway between the two) and follow the signs to Disney-MGM Studios.

If you're staying in hotels within the 43-square-mile tract of Disney property, you need not go out onto main highways. You can stay right in the park and travel to the attraction by following the signs or maps available at all the hotels.

Specifically, you'll follow Hotel Plaza Boulevard to the Walt Disney World Village where you turn left and follow the signs, heading for EPCOT and quite nearby, Disney-MGM Studios.

If you're staying in hotels on WDW property, buses are the easy way to go and will deliver you from the door of your hotel to the entrance of the park. Leave the driving to them.

All the same kinds of service—i.e. the **Car Care Center** (tel. 824-4813) which helps you out with dead batteries—are available at this park, too.

Parking here is $3, the same as at the other parks, and there are trams to take you from your car to the ticket booth. Once again, don't forget to look at the name and number of the row you're parked in—or you and your car may be estranged for many a long hour.

## WHAT TO WEAR

Same advice here as elsewhere: Comfortable shoes are the most important. Beyond that, clothes and hats to keep the sun from frying you and sunscreen for the same reason.

And once again, if you have any kind of disability—or just

think you might get tired—**rent a wheelchair.** They cost just $4 a day plus a $1 refundable deposit and are well worth it when you're on the verge of collapse after a long day. There's nothing wrong with me—physically, at least—but I've many times gazed with longing at those being pushed back to the entrance at closing time.

**Rental strollers** are an absolute requirement as anyone who has walked a mile or so toting an exhausted toddler can testify. They're the same price as wheelchairs and worth far more on the hot days that are common here in Orlando.

Please look back in Chapter IX's discussion on "What to Wear" for information on baby-sitting services in case you decide this Hollywood stargazing may not mean much to your youngsters.

## BUYING A TICKET

Nothing new here, all the same info you've already read in other chapters. In case you missed those discussions, here it is in a nutshell:

A one-day ticket permitting entrance to one, but only one, of the three parks (the Magic Kingdom, EPCOT Center, or this one, Disney-MGM Studios) is $30.65 adults, $24 for children 3 through 9. Children under 3 are free.

There are no two- or three-day admissions to any of the parks.

A four-day Passport that includes admission to any or all of the three parks and use of all the transportation facilities is $105.60 adults, $84.45 children.

Five-day Passports are $123.75 adults, $100.30 children, and annual passes are $190.80 adults, $164.30 children.

Tickets can be paid for in cash, by travelers' checks, by American Express, MasterCard, or VISA, or by personal check with proper identification. WDW resort guests may charge tickets to their rooms with identification.

If you leave Disney-MGM Studios and intend to return the same day, have your hand stamped at the exit, even if you have a multiday Passport.

## SPECIAL NEEDS—CHILDREN, PETS, HANDICAPPED, FIRST AID, AND MORE

Strollers and wheelchairs can be found at Oscar's Super Service Station inside the main entrance but supplies are limited. Your rental receipt may be used on the same day in the Magic Kingdom, EPCOT Center, or again at the studios.

**Baby's needs** can be met at the Guest Services building at the main entrance.

If you need **a camera,** you can rent one or buy one at The Darkroom which is just to the right as you enter the park. Kodak Disc Cameras, camcorders, and 35mm cameras are available for purchase or for rent (see details in Chapter VIII, under Main Street, U.S.A.) and two-hour film processing is available. Many other shops also have film.

Minor medical problems can be treated at the **First Aid Station** in the Guest Services building at the main entrance.

**Hearing-help devices** and tape cassettes and players for the **blind** and sight-impaired are available at Guest Services.

**Locker facilities** cost 50¢ and can be found next to Oscar's Super Service Station.

If you lose someone, seek them at Guest Services at the main entrance or call 560-4668. Other **lost articles** also can be found at Lost and Found there (tel. 824-4245).

**Money?** Get some at the automated bank teller next to the production Information Window at the main entrance. Credit cards and travelers' checks are accepted at full-service restaurants but it's cash only at food carts and counter-service dining spots.

To find out what **entertainment** is scheduled, ask the friendly faces at the Guest Services Building. A prominent celebrity appears each day at various locations; Guest Services can tell you who it is and where to stargaze.

Streetmosphere characters, including a Hollywood gossip columnist, a flimflam man and assorted other oddities, are out day and night and on the outdoor stage on Hollywood Boulevard, the Mouse and his cohorts perform. Once again, show hours are posted at Guest Services.

# LET'S GO STAR-TREKKING

Now you know what's where and how to get there so let's begin climbing Disney's fantasy stairway to the stars.

## HOLLYWOOD BOULEVARD

Welcome to the most famous boulevard in stardom!

Mickey himself, certainly the star of *this* World, makes it perfectly clear from the moment you near this new theme park that he's top banana here: The Mouse's unmistakable ears top a water tower known hereabouts as the **Earffel Tower.**

Inside the entrance gate, you'll spot the World's number-one star again, this time atop the **Crossroads of the World,** a Hollywood-now-Mouseland landmark.

Your first step into the park takes you right into the past: Just ahead is **Oscar's Super Service,** a days-of-yore gas station complete with antique gas pumps and shiny old cars. Secreted away inside are things to keep babies happy, lockers, stroller and wheelchair rentals.

Right next door **Oscar's Classic Car Souvenir Shop** lures those with drive-away dreams.

Whether your fantasy is a feather-trimmed gown à la Cyd Charisse or a camouflage shirt circa Rambo, you are likely to be able to fulfill it at **Sid Cahuenga's One-of-a-Kind** shop where clothing at least purporting to have been worn by stars awaits, along with reams of Hollywood collectibles from posters to pottery.

Now that you're dressed, get your physog in print at **Cover**

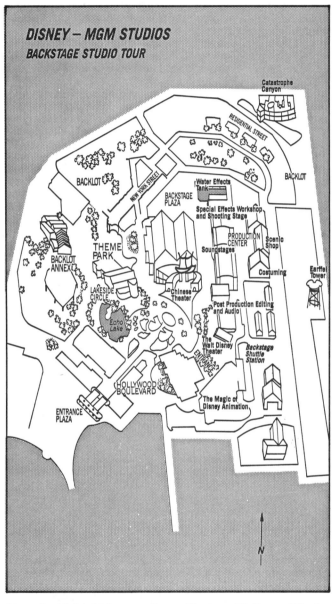

## DISNEY – MGM STUDIOS
### BACKSTAGE STUDIO TOUR

**Story.** In this intriguing spot, just a skip down Hollywood Boulevard, you can dress up in just about any gear you can dream up, then find your photo on the cover of your favorite magazine.

Photographers will help you look the part, then see to it that your perfect face graces a souvenir copy of any magazine you choose from *Barbie* to *Seventeen* to *Sports Illustrated.* Personally, I'm seeking a spot on the cover of . . . well, never mind.

Designed to plunge you into the Hollywood of the 1930s and 1940s, this park is awash in art-deco-streamlined-moderne-neon-chrome furbelows designed to time-warp you into the glories of Hollywood's heyday.

In a cluster of period boulevard buildings you'll find a camera supply store called **The Darkroom;** all the Mickey Mouse T-shirts you can bear at **Mickey's of Hollywood;** and, at the **Celebrity 5 & 100,** clothing, jewelry and even one of those black-and-white, Scene-One-Take-One things a director clacks.

Just around the corner from Mickey's of Hollywood is **Hollywood and Vine,** where the 20s come to life with costumed waitresses and chicly anachronistic art deco interiors.

As you amble back and forth on this wide boulevard, you'll meet folks Disney calls "streetmosphere" characters—budding starlets, a gossip columnist known as the "boulevard blabber," a flimflam man, hopeful starlets, and even street sweepers hoarding celebrity trash.

You can pick up some of your own, er, treasures at **Lakeside News,** a haven for comic book enthusiasts; **Sweet Success,** a candy shop; and **Keystone Clothiers,** purveyors of Disney-character clothing and Hollywoodized accessories.

Those who want themselves immortalized in film or disc can star in a home video at **Pacific Electric Pictures** or record a music video at **Sights & Sounds.**

Disney characters whoop up a storm of song and dance—you really *have* to see Goofy in white top hat and tails—at the open-air amphitheater in which they perform here.

It's just across from another Hollywood landmark, the **Hollywood Brown Derby** where you can dine on Cobb salad, steaks, seafood and pasta specialities.

If you arrive here early in the morning, head for this punning eatery: **Starring Rolls,** purveyors of freshly baked muffins, bread, cookies, and pastries.

At the head of the street is yet another famous landmark, Grauman's **Chinese Theater.** Inside is one of the park's favorite rides, **The Great Movie Ride.**

On this one you meet no less than 59 AudioAnimatronic characters ranging from Gene Kelly to Mary Poppins, from Tarzan to John Wayne, from James Cagney to a slimy monster of "Alien" fame. You get caught in a gangster shoot-out, help rescue a treasure Indiana-Jones style, kill off the Wicked Witch of the East, and trip along the Yellow Brick Road with Dorothy, Toto, and the troops to a triumphant entry into the Emerald City of Oz.

## BACKLOT ANNEX AND LAKESIDE CIRCLE

To keep all you hot stars thinking cool, WDW installed a lake called Echo in the middle of the park, then encircled it with diversions.

As you wind around the lake, turning left off Hollywood Boulevard, you can seek respite at **50's Prime Time Café** where fans of the 50s can tune in, quite literally, to their favorite sitcoms via television sets at every table. At the **Tune In Lounge** next door, you'll find living room decor designed to make couch potatoes feel right at home.

Don't get too comfortable—right next door you may get caught in the crossfire as guys and gals jump off buildings, escape from burning cars, and chase down runaway trucks. It's all part of the fun, if you can call it that, at the rip-roaring **Indiana Jones Epic Stunt Spectacular.** Real stunt artists show you some of the tricks of their trade—and scare you to death in the process.

Next door, the **Backlot Express** churns out burgers and hot dogs to get you fit enough to endure **Star Tours.**

George Lucas, of "Star Wars" fame, and the Disney imagineers teamed up here to create a galactic journey to the Moon of Endor planned by two most unusual travel agents, none other than R2-D2 and C-3PO.

Aboard a flight simulator that pulsates and gyrates, bumps and grinds with seat-beltable vigor, you rocket at Concorde-plus speed into the stratosphere where you get snared in a field of frozen ice fragments, stuck in a battle with a massive Imperial Star Destroyer, are forced to fight the dark forces with laser beams, and then barely miss a collision with the Death Star. Whew! Talk about a rough ride!

Right next door, **Endor Vendors,** home of extragalactic souvenirs, is stocked with memorabilia to help you keep alive the memory of that harrowing ordeal.

Completing the circuit are some get-in-there-and-try-it-yourself diversions.

At **SuperStar Television** you may be chosen to play a starring role in some of television's hit shows like "General Hospital," "Cheers," "The Tonight Show," "Gilligan's Island," "The Golden Girls," and "I Love Lucy." Live action on the part of superstars and would-be stars is merged by electronic wizardry so the audience watches one of its own "starring" in those series favorites.

At **The Monster Sound Show** you learn how eerie sounds get eerie as you help make creepy noises; and at a post-show playground called **SoundWorks,** you can team up with Roger Rabbit, make flying-saucer sounds, and enter a 3-D **Soundsations** world full of sounds both strange and strangely familiar.

Tucked in between the two attractions is **Golden Age Souvenirs,** stocked with goodies from the golden age of radio and television, not to mention, of course, Disney Channel logo products.

Those in search of a quiet moment lakeside can nibble at **Min and Bill's Dockside Diner** cozied away in a freighter or grab the cool at **Dinosaur Gertie's Ice Cream of Extinction.**

## BACKSTAGE STUDIO TOUR

Surely, there dwells in all of us a niggling little curiosity about what goes on behind the slick pictures presented on those celluloid screens.

Here at this working production center you can look in on everything from the wardrobe workers to the cartoonists as they put together the stuff of screen-star dreams.

A two-hour tour, the backlot visit requires a little stamina and a heartfelt desire to see what's going on backstage. You can, however, ease out after the first hour.

If starvation strikes at the entrance to the Backstage Tour, nip into the **Soundstage Restaurant,** a mini food court that occupies the set of the film comedy "Big Business." Here in the midst of a Hollywood "wrap" party is one of the park's few sipping spots, the Catwalk Bar suspended over the restaurant and offering beer, wine, cocktails, and specialty drinks.

On with the tour.

During the hour-long first half of this backstage visit, your tram car chugs past the glass-enclosed workshops of costume creators and scenery builders.

On you go, down a residential street that's home to some famous homes including the "Golden Girls" manse and, in one driveway, you meet none other than that snorting, snuffling sedan named Herbie.

Then it's on to a harrowing journey through Catastrophe Canyon, a perilous place fraught with roaring floodwaters and fiery explosions. A stunning special-effects production, the storm, fire, flood, and bucking tram car are well worth the wet you'll get if you sit on the left side of the tram.

Once safely past that peril, you'll see some memorabilia from M*A*S*H* strewn artfully around and get a look at a quite amazing fool-the-eye New York cityscape, complete with landmark skyscrapers created by forced perspective.

An hour later your tram drops you at Backstage Plaza where you can spend some time roaming among gag gifts and other oddities at **The Loony Bin,** dressing yourself up in the **Disney Studio Store** or sneaking a snack at the **Studio Catering Co.**

From there you're off again, this time on an hour-long walking tour that visits: a **water effects tank** where storms and other watery wonders are created; a **special-effects workshop,** home of optical illusions; **soundstages** where you may see a film in production; **postproduction and audio facilities;** and the **Walt Disney Theater** where you'll see sneak previews of upcoming Disney films.

At the beginning or the end of the Backstage Studio Tour awaits the Animation Production Center. Here you travel **Back to Never Land** for a look at artwork from the Disney Animation Collection and a giggly lesson in animation basics.

Every part of the animation studio is on display beginning with that very first step, story development. From there you move on for a visit to the studios in which artists create the animated drawings; pencil in details, backgrounds, and special effects; photocopy the cartoon; paint, ink, photograph, and edit it.

At the end of the tour, you see the results of all that work— some Disney cartoons that are now classics of the genre—and you can stop in the **Animation Gallery** where limited editio reproductions, books, figurines, and collectible cartoon stuff is sold.

# XI

# DISNEY AND THE BEANSTALK: GROWS, GROWS, AND GROWS

In recent years this park has burgeoned like the proverbial Topsy, adding more and more diversions to put fun and pun into your life.

A few of Disney's play places actually have been around for many years but the hoopla surrounding the Magic Kingdom and EPCOT have overshadowed them.

There seems no end in sight: Disney exec Michael Eisner recently promised yet a *fourth* park—although he wouldn't say what kind of park the imagineers are dreaming up next.

And who knows what might happen in years to come—with more than 25,000 acres and 43 square miles of land, there's plenty of room for most anything these fertile minds can dream up.

In the meantime, here's a look at some of the new and less-heralded parts of the park.

## TYPHOON LAGOON

Newest diversion of them all is this typhoon-created lagoon, a 56-acre water park with just one theme—water. Naturally, this new addition to the world of Disney has a "legend" and here it is:

Seems a typhoon hit a small resort village, then touched off an earthquake and a volcanic eruption. What with one thing and another, the village didn't fare too well.

Determined residents pasted and painted and did the best they could but nobody's perfect: Some of the structures still have trees growing out of the roof, others lean a bit to starboard and a couple are held up by ropes!

What nobody could do anything about was this shrimp boat, the *Miss Tilly,* which remains beached for all time atop magical Mount Mayday.

No matter, *you* don't have to live there. You're just here to roam the ruins, play a little, and keep an eye on *Miss Tilly* as it periodically spouts a 50-foot flume of water onto giggling watchers far down the "mountain."

As for that mountain, it's said to be the largest artificial watershed mountain and certainly it's the only mountain you'll see rising 85 feet from the flatlands of Central Florida.

You can easily spend a day here, splashing in the 2.5-acre Typhoon Lagoon that's larger than two football fields and has a wave-making machine that creates five-foot rollers that crash ashore every 90 seconds. You can body-surf on those whitecaps or rent a raft or board to ride the waves created when water collects in huge chambers above the lagoon, then drops through trap doors.

Those who just want to paddle about a bit can toddle off to smaller tidal pools, **Whitecap Cove** and **Blustery Bay** where quiet waters prevail.

Winding around and through the white sands and swaying palms is **Castaways Creek,** which begs you to rent an inner tube or raft and set off on the half-hour voyages down this lazy river. Just three feet deep, the waterway chugs along through a rain forest that sprays you with misty water, past shady grottoes and through the water works where pipes "broken" by the storm dump gallons of water on you.

You can race through a cave at 30 m.p.h. on two speed slides and twist and wiggle your way down two curving slides.

That viscious earthquake had its light side: It created two waterslides called **Humunga Kowabunga.** On these you take a 30-m.p.h. dive down a 50-foot drop that has its own grandstand for those who want to watch as the fearless try to keep the tops of their bikinis on as they roar down the waterways.

There's more of the same at **Jib Jammer, Rudder Buster,** and **Stern Burner,** three body slides that rocket you off at about 20 m.p.h. through rock formations, caves, and waterfalls.

I'm not at all sure why anyone would *want* to do this but then there are several things I don't understand. Anyway, those of a mind to swim with a shark can do so at **Shark Reef,** an artificial coral reef populated by a variety of denizens of the deep, up to and including some small nurse and bonnethead sharks, said to be quite uninterested in nibbling at people.

Jump on a fat, overgrown inner tube and into **Mayday Falls** where you ride a 460-foot slide that glides into a pool, then zooms you off again to the bottom.

At **Keelhall Falls,** you'll spiral around and around down a 400-foot slide at about 10 miles an hour and at **Gangplank Falls,** you can ride with a crowd on huge tubes that support three other water babies intent on riding the slides.

Youngsters can play and paddle at **Ketchakiddie Creek** which has plenty of supervision so you can leave the little ones there and go off on your own for a while.

All the usual accoutrements of a water park are here too, from restaurants to rest rooms and changing rooms, even a couple of shops stocked with lotions, bathing gear, towels, and beach paraphernalia. Admission to Typhoon Lagoon is $18.25 for adults, $14.50 for children 3 to 9. A two-day pass is $29 for adults, $23 for children, and annual passes are available for $75.

## RIVER COUNTRY

More of the waterborne wild life is available at **River Country,** which nestles into a corner of Bay Lake near Fort Wilderness Campground.

There's another small mountain here and lots of artificial attractions, but so skillfully done you can hardly tell the real from the not-so-real.

Here you can plop into the **Ol' Swimming Hole,** a huge swimming pool created by walling off a section of Bay Lake. Next door is a pint-size version of same for the youngsters.

A pair of waterslides offer a thrill a minute as you plunge to an invisible bottom and shoot through the air and into the blue.

In true ol'-swimmin'-hole style, you can swing out over the water on rope swings, a ship's boom, and assorted-other-methods flight machines.

Climb up Whoop 'n' Holler Hollow, jump on one of the two flumes and spiral down through the jungle greenery faster than a speeding bullet.

White Water Rapids takes you and your inner tube through chutes and cool pools on a swirling ride that gets you all tangled up with a giggling horde of other riders.

Food, changing rooms, lockers, and supplies are available at River Country, which is usually open all year but is best in spring, summer, and fall when temperatures are warm, warmer, and warmest.

Admission is $11.75 adults, $9.25 children 3 through 9. WDW resort guests get a $1 discount on those prices. A combination ticket with Discovery Island, which I'm coming to in a minute, is available for $15 adults, $11 children 3 through 9; same $1-off deal for WDW resort guests.

## DISCOVERY ISLAND

So populated with upturned wildlife is Discovery Island that I don't think anyone would be surprised to see Snow White strolling among the birds and bees of this little park-within-a-park.

An 11-acre wilderness, Discovery Island seems as wild and remote as WDW is a work of imagination. All that wilderness atmosphere is just as engineered as the rest of the park, however: Workers brought in sandy soil, added boulders and trees, created hills and lagoons, planted bamboo and palms, and created a jungley world out of nowhere.

Soon this Treasure Island look-alike sported an aviary filled with birds, a shipwreck on the beach, a bevy of screaming peacocks, and a crazy quilt of flowers, ferns, and jungle plants.

You can visit this diversion in about an hour but you can spend much longer here, particularly in spring when a young bird's fancy turns to thoughts of courting rituals.

Here a group of trained parrots, cockatoos, and macaws clown around on command at **Parrot Perch**—one even stands on its head.

At **Trumpeter Springs** trumpeter swans glide happily round and at **Crane's Roost** fancy cranes of several varieties prance and preen.

A vast grove of bamboo rustles and clicks at **Bamboo Hollow** and at **Avian Way** you'll visit a huge acre-wide, walk-through aviary that is home to some oddities including frothy white peacocks and scarlet ibises vivid as a sunset.

**Pelican Bay** is home to a cluster of brown pelicans too injured to survive in the wild and **Flamingo Lagoon** is the happy hunting ground for a breeding colony of those birds you see rendered in plastic on many a Florida lawn.

A huge 500-pound tortoise lumbers about with his friends on **Tortoise Beach** and at **Eagle's Watch,** a couple of bald eagles have set up housekeeping.

There's a snack bar and a beach here but nothing elaborate. Swimming's verboten but you can bring a picnic, if you like, and dine on the beach in view of that wrecked ship.

Admission is $7.50 adults, $4 children 3 through 9 and there are combination tickets available with River Country admissions (see above). You can get to Discovery Island on watercraft that leave from the Magic Kingdom, Fort Wilderness, and the Contemporary, Polynesian, and Grand Floridian resorts.

# XII

# A STAR IS BORN: ORLANDO'S UNIVERSAL APPEAL

**G**rrrrrrrrrrh. Aaaaaaaaaaaaahhhhh! No! No! Agggh!

What's going on here? Nothing, darlings, that's just the sound of Orlando on a roll.

That is, in fact, just the sound of Orlando, ripping into the last decade of the 20th century with all the vigor and enthusiasm that converted this once-hicktown from a cluster of unsophisticated rubes to a bevy of savvy fantasy-sellers.

It is, in fact, the sound of Universal Studios, a massive city-within-a-city, a wildly amusing theme park, and a deadly serious money-maker out to set the world on film.

Welcome to the melodrama of the decade: Can a mischievous Mouse live peacefully with an overstuffed Gorilla?

Such are the kinds of weighty questions they ponder here in Central Florida's never-neverland, which in 1990 welcomed a very big newcomer—none other than King Kong—and all his little playmates from E.T. to Ghostbusters and Woody Woodpecker.

All those characters and more are part of the region's quite spectacular new attraction—Universal Studios.

So Mickey meets the King and quite a Kongfrontation it is likely to be.

## GETTING THERE

Opened with full fanfare on June 7, 1990, this huge new attraction sprawls over 444 acres of Central Florida, 10 miles southwest of Orlando between the intersection of I-4 and the Florida Turnpike.

To reach the park take the I-4 exit from the turnpike. From I-4, take Exit 30-B to Kirkman Road (Fla. 435) and look for the studios a half mile north of I-4 on Kirkman.

Once you've found your way here and parked your car in the attraction's two vast parking lots, be sure to note the row and slot in which you're parked. You will need to find it someday and it might be nice not to be looking well into the night. Parking fee is $3. If you do lose your car, parking attendants can help you find it if you are able to tell them about what time you arrived at the park. They keep records that indicate which parking lot was in use at various times of the day. So do try to remember—at least—what time you get here.

## WHEN TO GO

Americans are inclined to travel in bunches, all arriving at the same time and, it sometimes seems, the same place. That means you will find the biggest crowds at the favorite go-to-Florida times of year: mid-February to early March, mid-April, June to September, and from mid-December to January.

Getting to the park early in the morning gives you the opportunity to hit the attraction's favorite rides—likely to be King Kong's Kongfrontation and the E.T. trip—before the throngs arrive.

Universal expects to be open from 9am to 9pm daily, later in summer, during special events, on holidays, and perhaps weekends.

## WHAT TO WEAR

In a few words, stay cool and comfortable. That means wear clothes but lightweight clothes. Wear shoes, comfortable shoes. Like its competitor, this is a very large park and you'll spend plenty of time walking and standing in lines, so dress and be shod accordingly.

## SPECIAL NEEDS—CHILDREN, PETS, HANDICAPPED, FIRST AID, AND MORE

You can **rent wheelchairs and strollers** here at the entrance gate for $4 a day. If you think you might have any need for either, don't hesitate.

USAir is the official airline of the park and Hertz is the official rental car rental agency.

**Baby services** are available at Guest Relations.

If you need minor medical services, you'll find **first-aid** help between the San Francisco and New York attractions.

**Pets** wouldn't like it here anyway so it doesn't really matter that the park prohibits them. They'll be perfectly comfortable and a great deal happier at the attraction's kennels where you'll pay $4 for their care and coddling. You'll find the kennels at the Toll Plaza as you drive into the park.

**Camera equipment** can be purchased or rented at Lights, Camera, Action just inside the gates to the park. They will loan you a 35mm camera free and rent you a camcorder for $45 a day. You must also leave a credit card imprint to ensure that you return the equipment.

For **general information** about the park call 407/363-8000.

## BUYING A TICKET

Ticket purchases are pretty straightforward business here. You can buy a one-day ticket for $30.74 adults, $24.38 children 3 through 10. Those odd numbers are the result of a 6% Florida sales tax added to the basic $29 and $23 admission prices. Children under 3 are free.

For a two-day adult ticket you pay $51.94. Children's two-day tickets are $41.34. An annual pass is $90 adults, $71.55 for children.

Southeast Bank operates a full-service bank at the Main Entrance Complex and the park will accept traveler's checks, American Express, MasterCard, and VISA credit cards.

Any questions about tickets or anything else in the park can be answered by the staff. You can write to them at 1000 Universal Studios Plaza, Orlando, FL 32819, or call 407/363-8220.

# STARS IN YOUR EYES

So let's go get star-struck at this striking cluster of Hollywood memorabilia.

A larger sister to the Los Angeles Universal Studios Tour that has captured the imagination and the wallets of travelers to California for nearly a quarter of a century, this Universal Studios Florida facility is bigger and showier than the LA attraction where growth was limited to preexisting studio conditions.

Universal moved in on Disney with aplomb for Universal is not new to this fantasy business. They have, after all, been creating celluloid dreamworlds for decades and running a live entertainment spectacle visited by 60 million of the awe-struck over the years.

Step right up to the gate of Universal Studios Florida and a whole new kind of fun begins. Here you'll quail at the sight of a roaring King Kong, fall in love with that AWOL astronaut E.T., and feel your knees buckle as the earth quakes.

Spread out over 444 acres, Universal's Central Florida studios cost more than $600 million and that's a lot of entertainment!

In business for 75 years, Universal Studios by now knows plenty about fantasy and how to make it happen. For openers they employed spook-movie creator Steven Spielberg as creative consultant.

To that they added attractions based on adorably ugly E.T., terrifying King Kong, box-office boffo "Back to the Future," toothy Jaws, squeaky Ghostbusters, and a terrifying earthquake.

Here you'll see a star—and be a star! You'll see how moviemakers do the impossible and even do it yourself. You'll go behind the scenes to see how years of cinema thrills and chills were created and relive some of the movie moments you've most loved.

A fabulous city, dotted with lagoons and beaches, this new universe is a massive study in fancy and fantasy.

A real working film studio, on duty 24 hours a day, Universal is making movies even as you play in this giant park. Who knows when your favorite star will stroll right up to you?

Set streets you'll stroll include: **New York/Metro**—featuring everything from Little Italy to Central Park and Coney Island; **San Francisco Bay**—starring Ghirardelli Square, Fisherman's Wharf, Embarcadero, even a BART subway station; **New England Vil-**

**lage** —complete with Amity Village, a New England Street, and Amity Harbor; **Hollywood**—starring Sunset Boulevard, Hollywood Boulevard, Beverly Hills, Rodeo Drive, and the Garden of Allah; **World Expo**—showing off a World's Fair site, Exposition Park, and Dr. Brown's Science Center; and **specialized sets** ranging from Angkor Wat to Psycho Hill and Bates Motel.

Adventures abound. Cartoonists Bill Hanna and Joe Barbera, who brought us **Yogi Bear, Huckleberry Hound and the Flintstones,** among others, now bring you a "slam-bang, high-speed chase that'll take you inside the cartoon, put you in the thick of the action and leave you stretched, squashed, smashed, bashed, crashed, crushed and open-mouthed with awe and amazement." When you've recovered, they'll teach you something about how animation gets animated and you'll get a chance to try it yourself.

Then it's on to a meeting with a major monk! He'll huff. He'll puff. He'll roar.

You'll scream a lot.

**King Kong,** they say, is 30 feet tall and 13,000 pounds of howling terror "ready to take things into his own hands. Crushing everything in his path. Swatting planes like flies. Rampaging! Daring you to face his colossal fury. And when you do, he'll blast you with his banana breath, then twist you, turn you and hurl your tram on the most terrifying trip you've ever taken!"

Shiver.

Rest up after that one with a trip to **E.T.**'s house. After all, he visited yours. Here you hop aboard your Star Bike and pedal across the moon . . . "through the purple perfume fog. To a planet where flowers shower you with songs. And Cloud Bearers, Water Sprites, Jumpums and tickly Moot Moots shower you with love." Only you and E.T. can save the planet and when you do he'll thank you for it with that sweet little glow of his heart light.

Awwwww.

Enough of that sweet stuff, let's have some 8.3 terror as the earth quakes beneath your feet at the park's shivery-scary **Earthquake.**

"It's a heart-pounding, palm-sweating, mind-boggling, trainwrecking 8.3 Earthquake that'll rip the ground out from under you," predicts Universal. "Bring the world down around you. And swallow you alive in the fire and flood of the most terrifying, natural disaster ever. So awesome you'll wish it was only a movie."

Eeeeeeek!

So you're starting to love this terror stuff? Then bring your teeny-weeny yellow polka-dot bikini but don't go near the water! Whoops, you did it. You're in there with . . . . . . . . aaaaaaaa!!!!!! No, no, it's . . . Jaws!

"The Great White is back and this time you're in the water with him! Right up to your neck in a part every actor would die for! Nothing can stop him! Nothing stands in the way of nature's most perfect predator as he relentlessly pursues his prey. And you'd better pray for a miracle," they warn.

Shriek!

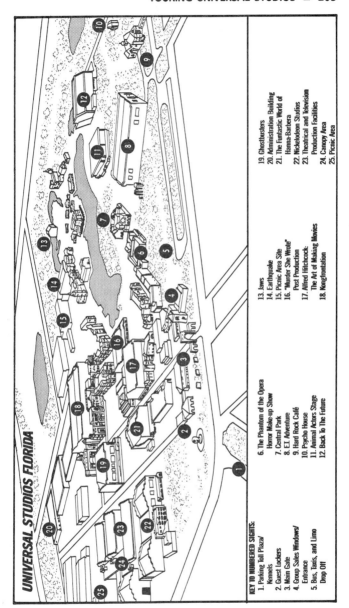

UNIVERSAL STUDIOS FLORIDA

**KEY TO NUMBERED SIGHTS:**
1. Parking Toll Plaza/
   Kennels
2. Guest Lockers
3. Main Gate
4. Group Sales Windows/
   Entrance
5. Bus, Taxis, and Limo
   Drop Off

6. The Phantom of the Opera
   Horror Make-up Show
7. Central Park
8. E.T. Adventure
9. Hard Rock Café
10. Psycho House
11. Animal Actors Stage
12. Back To The Future

13. Jaws
14. Earthquake
15. Picnic Area Site
16. "Murder She Wrote"
    Post Production
17. Alfred Hitchcock:
    The Art of Making Movies
18. Kongfrontation

19. Ghostbusters
20. Administration Building
21. The Fantastic World of
    Hanna-Barbera
22. Nickelodeon Studios
23. Theatrical and Television
    Production Facilities
24. Canopy Area
25. Picnic Area

Let's ease up a bit here and buckle up for a ride **Back to the Future** with Doc Brown.

"Climbing, diving, banking and blasting you back to the dinosaurs at the Dawn of Time. Rocketing you to Venice for a brush with

Da Vinci. Whooshing you right through Niagara Falls. Literally hanging you up on the brink of disaster and teetering on the edge, then taking you over, plunging you down, down, down in the steepest drop imaginable," they promise. "A sight, sound and total sensory combination of seven-story-high Omni-Max surround screens, space-age flight simulators, and live, cinemagic special effects. . ."

Wheee!

Is that . . . Is that . . . no, no, it's the Green Gobbler and the Terror Dogs.

Yes, it's Universal's "ghastly gathering of the ghoulish stars of one of the highest grossing films ever made! It's a brought-to-life attack by the dearly departed. An over, under, around, and see-through blitz of banshees, demons, spirits, and specters ready to slime at any time. But when the **Ghostbusters** fight back, look out! The Neutrana beams cross, the ectoplasmic energy explodes, the Staf Puft Marshmallow Man blows his top and everybody gets creamed!"

Ergggg!

Bzzzzzz . . . it's The Fly. And Frankenstein. And the Phantom of the Opera.

Naw, it's all makeup and you'll learn how it's done at the park's **Phantom of the Opera Horror Make-Up Show** under the tutelage of masters of makeup.

Uggggghly.

Whodunnit? You dunnit, working with Angela Lansbury at the **"Murder She Wrote" Post Production Theater.** Here you become executive producer and do all the work from picking the star to getting it in on budget and on time.

Hmmmm.

Well, that's just a sample—there's an **Animal Actors Stage** starring everyone from Lassie to a huge alligator, a **Screen Test Adventure Studio** where you'll be videotaped starring in a famous movie or one you plan yourself, **Nickelodeon,** the kid stuff that's been sweeping the nation.

Fun goes on and on and on here at this new attraction and at least some of the fun changes every day as this giant studio goes about its filming business, entertaining you at the same time.

There's no question about it—even Scrooge would love this place.

# XIII

# MORE THINGS TO SEE AND DO IN CENTRAL FLORIDA

Once upon a time—say all of six or seven years ago—Orlando's Chamber of Commerce suggested visitors plan a three- or four-day visit to see the area's attractions. Now, they say, you should plan three or four days for Disney World alone!

So fast have the whales and other assorted creatures followed the Mouse here in Central Florida, that there are now enough attractions to keep you busy for two weeks—moving fast.

There's simply no doubt about it anymore—Central Florida is the state's playground, a place filled with so many amusements you can go on day after sunny day touring and traipsing, ogling and ooohing, getting a look at everything from a re-creation of the dry Serengeti Plain complete with elephants to wet ocean depths complete with a performing killer whale.

It's fun, and it can provide a wonderful place to spend part, if not all, of a memorable Florida vacation. Let's take a look now at some of the other places to play, here in the land a Mouse built.

## ORIENTATION

Defining where exactly you'll find Central Florida is not as easy as it seems. Certainly Orlando forms the center of the center, but how far you can go in all the other directions and still remain central is a matter interpreted differently by every chamber of commerce within a 300-mile radius.

We'll have to be arbitrary about our definition, though, and say we're talking about an area that goes as far west as Tampa and St. Petersburg (which, come to think of it, is about as far west as you can go in Florida) and east to Cape Canaveral and Daytona Beach. For northern reaches let's count St. Augustine—it's such an intriguing place to visit—and Ocala. On the south, Sarasota's about as far as the attraction belt goes, although if soft, sunny beaches are your forte, you'll want to get down farther south where the sun *really* shines, and the ocean is the state's number one year-round attraction.

Okay, all defined and determined, off we go.

# OTHER ADVENTURES IN THE ORLANDO AREA

After you see the crazy ducks and looney tunes at Disney World, it's time to start exploring some of the other weird and wonderful attractions in and around this Central Florida city. Give yourself two days at least, three or four if you can manage it, just to visit some of the varied amusements you'll find hereabouts.

Here's a tip that may save you some money if you're thinking of getting a look at the largest of those adventurelands, SeaWorld and Cypress Gardens. You can buy a Platinum Pass, which is good for a year and allows you unlimited admission to both parks. At last check, the price of these year-long passes was $44.95 for adults, $34.95 for children. If you've already bought a ticket to one of these attractions, they'll sell you the Platinum Pass and subtract the amount of the ticket you've already bought.

## SEA WORLD

Right in there chasing Mickey's tail in popularity is Sea World (6227 Sea Harbor Dr. at the Highway I-4 Sea World exit; tel. 351-3600, toll free 800/327-2420, 800/432-1178 in Florida), largest marine-life theme park in the world. You can spend a whole day here without any difficulty, since they keep the entertainment going at a rapid pace practically from dawn to dusk.

Fifteen different shows are crowned by a performance of none other than **Shamu,** the gigantic 8,000-pound killer whale who's so sweet it's hard to believe he'd kill a shrimp. Shamu lets his trainer ride on his back, loves to kiss pretty girls and children, and seems to get the world's biggest kick out of performing a delicate ballet—no toe shoes.

Joining him are dolphins, otters, seals, sea lions, and water-skiers (the human kind) who cavort about to your amazement and amusement. And there's precocious Baby Shamu, the first killer whale born in captivity.

Sea World's $18 million Shamu Stadium, a marine mammal attraction, is home to a school of Shamu killer whale look-alikes. Eighteen of those big bruisers can be bred here and some of them perform in this huge stadium, which features 6,000,000 gallons of water and a performing pool three stories deep.

Shamu's relatives' home is the largest single-species research and display facility in the world. Just seeing these massive creatures is worth the visit, but seeing one of them merrily racing about with a proportionately teensy human being on its back is downright mind-boggling.

Newest residents on this very splashy block are some facy fellows all dressed up in tuxedos: They're fat and sassy penguins, happily waddling their way around 4,000 square feet of subantarctic environment, where you'll see Florida's only snowfall. At this new **Penguin Encounter** exhibit, you won't be at all sure whether you're watching them or they're watching you.

Nightlife has come to Sea World in the form of **Night Magic,** a series of nighttime shows that are as dramatic as they are amusing. You can attend Aloha, a Polynesian luau, or drop in on Shamu's Night Magic, starring Shamu and Baby Shamu. You can watch water-skiers racing around beneath a pyrotechnic display called Night Pirates, or see a special nighttime parody of the daytime sea lion and otter show. There's a magic show, some comedians, a Gator's Patio Party with live entertainment and an appearance by Al E. Gator, a chance to dance with Sea World characters, and a Boat Parade of Lights, all of it topped off by a fireworks ballet extravanganza. Tickets for the Night Magic concert series are $25.40 adults and $21.15 children.

Another show here is a hark back to days of bobby socks and rolled-up jeans. Called **Beach Blanket Ski Party,** the show is 45 minutes long and gives baby boomers a chance to reminisce on those melodious days of "A white sport coat, and a pink car-na-tion . . ."

There's yet another fun attraction here, **Cap'n Kid's Fun Ship,** a splashy playground built around a 60-foot pirate ship. Kids can play here on everything from ropes that reach out over the water and often drop them splashing and giggling into it, to splashy slides and tunnels.

A real spine-chiller at Sea World is the **Shark Exhibit,** a veritable *Jaws* come to life all around you. You enter a huge tank made of enormously thick, transparent acrylic and ride on a moving conveyor belt through a tunnel while those toothy denizens of the deep swim all around you.

At Sea World you can see what a coral reef looks like, watch Antarctic penguins play in the coolest home in Florida, examine the mysteries of a tidal pool, watch waltzing fountains, pet a manta ray, rise to the heights in a 400-foot skytower, and even buy an oyster—with a pearl inside, guaranteed.

You'll never starve here either. There are nine theme restaurants in the park, and they're all open when the park is, from 9am to 8pm, later in summer and on holidays. Most evenings there's a Polynesian luau, too, with swivel-hipped dancers, fire-bearing terpsichoreans, and a Polynesian buffet dinner (see Chapter V on nightlife). Sea World admission is $25.40 for adults, $21.05 for children 3 to 9, younger ones free. You can take a special 90-minute, behind-the-scenes tour for $5.95 adults, $4.95 children. Parking and kennels for Fido are free, too.

## WET 'N WILD

Orlando doesn't have a beach, so it dreamed up **Wet 'N Wild** (6200 International Dr.; tel. 351-3200), a water wonderland where you can splash and splutter to your heart's content. A surf pool produces constant four-foot waves, a whitewater slideway and a Kamikaze slide send you whizzing down into a pool from a platform six stories up in the air, and a Corkscrew Flume spirals you through a figure-eight and a tunnel before depositing you in the blue. A 25-acre water wonderland, Wet 'N Wild now has the Blue Niagara, a looping tube that sends riders screaming down more than 200 feet of blue inner space and The Bubble Up, a giant, colorful inflated bubble. Admission is $17.95 adults, $15.95 children 3 through 12. Wet 'N Wild is open from mid-February to November from 10am to 6pm, sometimes later in peak summer season.

## MYSTERY FUN HOUSE

Nothing's what it seems here, as magic takes over to trick you and treat you to a look at the world turned inside out. You can lose yourself in a mirror maze, try to fathom the topsy-turvy gravity room, play with lasers, walk a magic floor, and have a million laughs and an equal number of surprises. You'll find the Fun House at 5767 Major Blvd., just off Hwy. I-4 at Rte. 435 North in the Florida Center area (tel. 351-3356). Admission is $6.95 for adults or children 4 through 12. Open 10am to 11pm daily.

## MEDIEVAL TIMES

These days, Orlando's seemingly boundless fascination with fantasy seems to be taking medieval form. One of the newer attractions is called Medieval Times, 4510 Vine St., Kissimmee 32741 (tel. 305/396-1518). Here you can thrill to the sounds of yesteryear as knights on horseback race to defend someone's honor. Medieval tournaments, complete with jousting and good-guys/bad-guys swordplay, amuse you as you dine on chicken, ribs, pastry, and light potables. A rousing family entertainment, this dinner-and-show event begins at 6:45 or 8pm (castle opens at 6pm), lasts about two hours, and is $26 for adults, and $18 for children 3 to 12.

## XANADU

Excuse me, I must just ring Robutler for a towel so I can pop into my spa. If this is what life in the 21st century is going to be like, let us all hope we make it. At Xanadu, Box 2286, Kissimmee, U.S. 192 and Rte. 535 (tel. 305/396-1992), they are convinced they know just how we all will be living in days to come. You can see if it looks good to you by stopping in at this styrofoam mushroom of a house that sprouts in all fantasy just down the road from, of all things, Medieval Times. Talk about time warps.

At Xanadu, which certainly projects some other century in materials, design, and architecture, you'll find a really intriguing look into the future of home construction. Circular rooms flow into each other, there's an indoor pool, a waterfall-spa in the master bedroom, a solar sauna, a greenhouse, sunken conversation pit, electronic hearth, projection television, a "house brain," security center, computer-voice command center, a central vacuum system, elec-

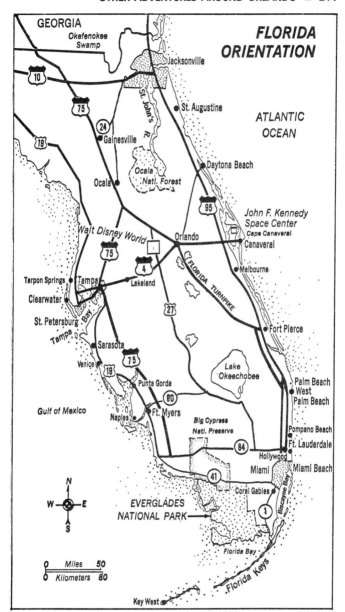

tronic exercise equipment, and best of all, a robot butler who never frosts you with a chilly "Really, Madam."

You cannot miss Xanadu—just look for the weirdest sight on U.S. 192 heading east from I-4. It's open daily from 10am to 10pm (be there 45 minutes before closing time to make the tour) and admission is $4.95; children under 10 are free.

## REPTILE WORLD

I'd rather write for a living than do what those people do at **Reptile World Serpentarium,** 5705 Irlo Bronson Memorial Hwy., at U.S. 192, St. Cloud (tel. 892-6905). They milk cobras and cozy up to all kinds of friendly vipers, 60 varieties of the crawly creatures, in fact, including everything from crocodiles to lizards. If you'd like to scare yourself silly, this is the place. It's open from Tuesday through Sunday from 9am to 5:30pm; closed September and some holidays. Admission is $3.75 for adults, $2.75 for children 6 to 17; under 6, $1.75.

## GATORLAND ZOO

I know one or two human morsels I'd like to throw to the alligators that slither around this attraction; perhaps you do, too. It's fun to think about, anyway, as you watch these oddities of nature attack a hunk of meat at feeding time. Besides, who doesn't want to get a close-up—without confrontation—of one of these marshland critters? You'll find the zoo at 14501 S. Orange Blossom Trail on Rtes. 17/92 and 441 just north of Kissimmee (tel. 855-5496). It may be worth the trip just for a picture of yourself fearlessly petting a boa constrictor. Hours here are 8am to 7:30pm daily, later in summer, and admission is $6.95 for adults, $4.95 for children 3 to 11. They've recently trained those toothy gators to leap into the air, a feat quite uncommon for these ground-loving creatures, and quite a sight indeed.

## ALLIGATORLAND SAFARI ZOO

If you just can't get enough of those slithery creatures, there's another chance to watch them slapping up a feeding frenzy at **Alligatorland Safari Zoo,** 4850 W. Irlo Bronson Memorial Hwy., Kissimmee (mailing address: P.O. Box 819; tel. 305/396-1012). Here you're greeted by some very large teeth, and some very big tails attached to some very small brains. Is this starting to sound like your office? A mile-long trail wends through the gators' favorite murky waters and takes you past some other indigenous Florida creatures including birds and monkeys. Admission is $5.95 for adults, $4.50 for children 4 to 11; this toothsome adventure is open from 8:30am to 8pm, sometimes closing an hour later.

## ELVIS PRESLEY MUSEUM

Somehow I just knew it would happen. Elvis Presley has joined the fantasy world of Orlando attractions. Step right up to the Elvis Presley Museum, 5921 American Way (across from Wet 'N Wild; tel. 345-9427). Here live Elvis's grand piano, Elvis's Mercedes 600 limo, Elvis's wardrobe, furniture, bed, jewels, paintings, Cobra race car, guitar, gun collection, and his very own karate ghi. Admission is $4 for adults, $3 for children 7 to 12. Hours are 9am to 10pm daily.

## CENTRAL FLORIDA ZOOLOGICAL PARK

This pleasant zoo, located at U.S. 17/92 at I-4, at Lake Monroe (tel. 843-2341), is home to more than 200 wild and exotic animals who occupy some very pretty acreage. Alligators, crocodiles, lions, and tigers stare back at you here, and the zoo also has pony rides, a children's zoo, animal-feeding demonstrations on weekends, and an elevated nature trail through a swamp. Hours are 9am to 5pm daily and admission is $5 for adults, $2 for children 3 to 12. Take Exit 52 from I-4 to find the zoo.

## ORLANDO SCIENCE CENTER

This scientist's dream attraction at Loch Haven Park, 810 Rollins St. at U.S. 17/92, Orlando (tel. 896-7151), amuses with an intriguing assortment of hands-on science exhibits and a planetarium. Hours at the center are 9am to 5pm weekdays, closing at 9pm Friday, and open noon to 9pm Saturday, noon to 5pm Sunday. Admission is $4 for adults, $3 for children 4 through 17. Sky shows are at 2:30pm weekdays, 2, 4, and 7:30pm Saturday, and at 2 and 4pm Sunday. On weekends, the center presents cosmic rock concerts, otherwise known as laser light shows, at 9, 10, 11pm and midnight. Admission is $4.

## MORSE MUSEUM OF ART

For my money the most gorgeous small attraction in all of Orlando, the Morse Museum of Art, 113 Wellbourne Ave., Winter Park (tel. 644-3686), is home to a fabulous collection of Louis Comfort Tiffany's pearls-without-price stained-glass windows, jewelry, lamps, and paintings. There's a long story behind this museum, which is owned by a Tiffany associate, who rescued much of this priceless collection when Tiffany's art nouveau mansion in Long Island, N.Y., burned. Other art nouveau works also may be on display there, including the work of Emile Galle, John LaFarge, Frank Lloyd Wright, Maxfield Parrish, George Innes (whose work can also be seen on Florida's west coast in the town of Tarpon Springs), and René Lalique. Morse Museum is my top don't-miss recommendation for any artist or art-lover, and is open Tuesday through Saturday 9:30am to 4pm, Sunday 1 to 4pm. Admission is $2.50 adults, $1 children older than 6.

## CENTRAL FLORIDA RAILROAD MUSEUM

Somewhere in most of us lies a desire to hear the wail of a train whistle and the thrum-thrum of wheels rolling over steel tracks. If you're one of those, stop by the railroad depot museum in the former Tavares & Golf Railroad Depot at 101 S. Boyd St., Winter Garden, just past the railroad track (tel. 656-5056 or 644-6777). Restored right down to the last detail, the depot is now home to 3,000 pieces of railroad history, from steam engines to whistles, switchlights, and antique memorabilia. It's open Sunday 2 to 5pm and is free.

## FIRE STATION NO. 3/LOCH HAVEN PARK

Orlando's oldest standing firehouse is the focal point of scenic downtown Loch Haven Park, 2416 N. Mills Ave. (tel. 896-4231). This red brick creation now houses fire-history treasures ranging from an 1885 hose cart to a 1908 horse-drawn steamer and a 1950 American La France. Admission to the firehouse at 812 E. Rollins St., Orlando (tel. 898-8320), is free and the station is open Tuesday through Friday from 10am to 4pm and weekends from 2 to 5pm. In this park, you'll also find the **Orange County Historical museum** detailing the history of the Orange County/Orlando area; the **Orlando Science Center** (see above); and the **Orlando Museum of Art,** which houses an impressive collection of pre-Columbian pottery and a rotating collection of 20th-century American and African art.

## LEU GARDENS

What time is it? About 50 chrysanthemums past a periwinkle. That's what time it will be for you at the flower clock in Leu Gardens, a 55-acre botanical garden at 1730 N. Forest Ave., Orlando (tel. 849-2620). Stroll here through forests of camellias, azaleas, roses, dogwood, orchids, and all kinds of colorful annuals, blooming their hearts out for you. You'll also find sculptures, fountains, oak archways, an avenue of camphor trees, and Leu House, a turn-of-the-century Florida farmhouse. Plunked down on the side of a lake and surrounded by these gorgeous gardens, Leu House is so scenic it's a favorite wedding spot. Admission to the house (tel. 849-2620) is $1, and it's open 9am to 5pm every day except Christmas.

## A CENTRAL FLORIDA COW TOWN

I always like to know a little about places I stay, and certainly the name Kissimmee gets you wondering! Here are some of the weird things I've discovered about this unusual hamlet in central Florida.

When you drive through the comparatively small downtown area of Kissimmee and feel there's something vaguely familiar about it, there is. Frank King, creator of the "Gasoline Alley" comic strip lived here for 25 years, marrying up Skeezix and Nina in an imposing—and very handsome—courthouse just like the Osceola County Courthouse you'll see here. That courthouse, built in 1889, is the oldest courthouse still in use in Florida.

Back in the 1880s a canny, and very rich, fellow named Hamilton Disston took advantage of a fiscal mess Florida had gotten itself into and did the state a favor—he bought no fewer than four million acres of land at 25 cents an acre, thus making himself a millionaire a few times over again. He called the trading post here Allendale but folks hereabout later renamed it Kissimmee, a Native American word for "heaven's place."

Attention, hardware store entrepreneurs, here's one for you. In downtown Kissimmee, on Broadway, you'll find Makinson's Hardware, which opened in 1884, making it the oldest hardware store in the state. Another historic site here is the 1925 Arcade Theatre on Broadway.

You'll find the name Narcoosee floating around and about in Kissimmee: That was a settlement here, used by some long-ago Brits who sent pensioners and second sons in search of an American fortune. There was a polo club, lawn bowling, tennis, and even an ostrich farm here!

Kissimmee still has its ranches and its cowboys, although you're not likely to see them these days unless you attend the weekly cattle auction. That takes place on Wednesdays, and is about as country as you can get now in this urbanized area. Read on a little farther for a description of the auction, which is listed under "Some Offbeat Attractions."

An early cattleman here, Milt Hinkle, is said to have been an acquaintance of Wyatt Earp, Annie Oakley, Pancho Villa, and Geronimo—quite a lively circle of friends! He is also said to have been the man who first brought the rodeo to Kissimmee, which now hosts a big semiannual bash—the Silver Spurs Rodeo, which takes place each February and July. A major competition in the national rodeo circuit, the Silver Spurs will give you a look at everything from ridin' and ropin' to a square dance on horseback!

All in all, Kissimmee is worth a few hours of your time. It's a pretty lakeside village that's quite off the beaten track. There are some quaint shops and some attractive restaurants at lakeside, too.

At last we come to what you *really* need to know, how to pronounce Kissimmee: Folks here like to say it's pronounced Kiss-SIM-ee during the day and KISS-i-me at night.


# WINTER PARK

Winter Park is a jewel of a town shaded by tall old trees and lined with some spectacularly beautiful homes. Everything about this tiny village is bandbox-perfect, from boutiques surrounding tiny courtyards, to some of the region's loveliest and best restaurants, to the vestpocket park that's the inviting heart of the two-street downtown. Don't miss a trip to this village; better yet, stay there (see chapters III and IV). In this lovely urban retreat is the **Morse Museum of Art,** where hundreds of Louis Tiffany works are housed, and here, too, is lovely **Rollins College,** a serene and scenic attraction in its own right. On the campus, **Cornell Fine Arts Center** (tel. 646-2526) is home to a fine collection of Old Master European paintings and 19th-century American paintings, along with an eclectic display of collections—including 1,200 watch keys. This is also where you'll find the Albin Polaske Foundation, the home, studio, and now museum of the sculptor and painter of reknown. A three-acre estate, it's open to the public free from October through June, from 10am to noon and 1 to 4pm, Wednesday through Saturday, and Sunday from 1 to 4pm. You'll find the house-museum and art collection at 633 Osceola Ave., Winter Park (tel. 647-6294).

## AUDUBON HOUSE

Bird-watchers and others interested in conservation can get a close look at some native birds of prey at the Audubon House and Center for Birds of Prey, a free attraction open from 10am to 4pm Tuesday through Saturday at 1101 Audubon Way, Maitland (tel. 647-2615).

## CARTOON MUSEUM

Up here, where almost nothing is as real as it seems, you knew this kind of attraction would have to show up someday. A small, gallery-style museum, the Cartoon Museum, 4300 S. Semoran Blvd., Suite 103, Orlando (tel. 273-0141), houses thousands of cartoons, comic books, radio and television premiums, and Big Little Books. Open from 11am to 6pm daily, closing at 4pm Sunday, this cartoon-buffs heaven is free but is not recommended for children younger than 11.

## CHRISTMAS

It is, of course, Christmas every day in the village of Christmas, Florida. Thousands of oddity collectors troop the 24 miles over here from Orlando every year to have their Christmas cards stamped in—you guessed it—Christmas, Fla. A replica of the 1837 Fort Christmas (tel. 568-4149) built during the Second Seminole Indian War from 1835 to 1842 is now dedicated to all races who fought and died here. In the fort are papers, treaties, and a gallery of Seminole Chiefs, where you can get a look at maps, weapons, and artifacts of the Seminoles and those who fought to remove them from this land. Fort Christmas, too, is a free attraction and is open from 10am to 5pm Tuesday through Saturday, opening at 1pm Sunday. You'll find Christmas on Fla. 429, 24 miles east of Orlando and two miles north of Fla. 50. Mailing address is P.O. Box 231, Christmas, FL 32709, and if you send them your stamped holiday cards, obliging post office workers will postmark them and send them on their way.

## GENIUS DRIVE

There is nothing lovelier than a peacock except, perhaps, 100 peacocks. You can listen in on their fearsome shrieks and get a look at some fabulous birds strutting their stuff. They fan their colorful tails along an oak-lined, winding road at a private estate in Winter Park. Peacocks wander about at will on the grounds, which are open free each Sunday from noon to 6pm. Folks at the Winter Park Chamber of Commerce, 150 N. New York Ave., P.O. Box 280, Winter Park, FL 32790 (tel. 644-8281) can tell you how to find this estate.

## SOME OFFBEAT ATTRACTIONS

If you're one of those city slickers who think steaks are created in the back room of a supermarket, it may be time for you to see the real thing on the hoof. Do that at Kissimmee's weekly **cattle auction,** where real honest-to-goodness cowboys cajole and caterwaul with future prime ribs. In the audience, cattle barons, looking more like punchers than princes, set the prices at this boots-and-jeans event that goes on every Wednesday at 1pm at the city's Livestock Market, just north of U.S. 17/92 and U.S. 441 at 150 E. Donegan Ave. (tel. 847-3521). When the bidding and the roping's over, you can lunch at the Auction House, while cow punchers shove those big bruisers around outside. There's no admission charge.

Now here's something you'll have to go far to top: a museum of food containers. By that I mean **Tupperware's International Headquarters,** where those famous plastic containers are lauded. You can learn how those plastic boxes and bowls are created and discover what you can create with them at this museum located on U.S. 441 and 17/92, just south of Orlando (tel. 847-3111). It's open from 9am to 4pm Monday through Friday, and it's free.

Citrus trees laden with fruit are among the most beautiful sights you'll see in Central Florida, and there's no better place to get a look at them than at the **Florida Citrus Tower** on North U.S. 27, Clermont (tel. 904/394-2145), the highest observation point in the state. Here you can gaze out across 2,000 square miles of emerald citrus trees laden with orange and gold fruit—quite a sight. Later, visit a glassblower's workshop, a citrus packing plant, and a citrus candy kitchen; send some oranges home to less fortunate frozen friends and buy some yourself (then see if you can resist eating all of them before you get home). Citrus Tower is open from 7:30am to 6pm daily and charges $1.75 for adults, $1 for students 10 to 15, others free, for the ride to the top.

Mormons own a huge 300,000-acre ranch in the center of Florida called **Deseret Ranch** (Star Route Box 1250, Melbourne, FL 32904). They're kind enough to invite tour groups in on Monday, Wednesday, and Friday to take a look at a working Central Florida ranch, but advance arrangements are required. It's free. Deseret is on Osceola County Road 419, just north of Rte. 192, about 25 miles east of St. Cloud (tel. 892-3672 or 892-2792).

It's uniforms, uniforms, everywhere and every one of them with razor-edge creases when the gobs graduate each Friday at 9:45am at the **Orlando Naval Training Center,** Bennett and Corrine drives, two blocks north of Rte. 50 (tel. 646-4501).

Watch oranges go in one side of a machine while gum drops and other delights roll out the other side at the **Citrus Candy Factory,** Box 800 (U.S. 27 in Dundee; tel. 813/439-1698). This factory, located between Cypress Gardens and Circus World, makes a toothsome visit and it's free. Open 8am to 6pm daily, later in summer. There's a marmalade and jelly tour each day and a tour through a fruit packing house—just ask.

Newest residents of Kissimmee are the **Houston Astros** baseball team, which began training here in the spring of 1985. A new 6,000-seat stadium adjacent to the Kissimmee/St. Cloud Convention and Visitors Bureau on U.S. 192 and 441 is their playground. Contact them at 305/847-5000.

**Big Tree Park,** south of Sanford off U.S. 17/92 on Gen. Hutchinson Hwy. near Longwood (take the Longwood exit from I-4), is home to the largest and oldest stand of bald cypress trees in the nation. So many of these fascinating maze-of-roots trees have been destroyed by the urbanization of Florida that there are few chances to get a close look at them, and very few chances to see a massive stand like this one. A very special resident here is "The Senator," a 3,500-year-old, pioneer landmark bald cypress, one of the oldest and largest trees in America. Its age has been authenticated by the American Forestry Association. Big Tree Park is open from 7am to sunset daily, from 9am on weekends, and it's free.

# OTHER ATTRACTIONS IN THE CENTRAL FLORIDA AREA

Moving a little farther afield to Tampa on the west, Cape Canaveral on the east, Ocala on the north, and Winter Haven on the south, you'll find still more places to play.

## CYPRESS GARDENS

Once dubbed "a photographer's paradise" by *Life* magazine, Cypress Gardens is one of Florida's most elegant attractions. No gardener should miss this beautiful acreage overflowing with exotic flowers and trees. Women dressed in antebellum hooped skirts pose in glamorous, green-lawned surroundings and are so perfectly turned out they look like human floral creations.

Once a huge cypress swamp, Cypress Gardens has retained much of that exotic marshy mystery but turned part of its acreage into gardens where the scent of rare roses joins the perfumes of jasmine, gardenias, orchids, hibiscus, and flowers in every color of the rainbow and quite a few hues even a rainbow would envy.

Visit **Animal Forest,** filled with 750 creatures, some of them tame animals who want nothing more from you than a pat; take photographs of the lacy domed gazebo that's been the setting for television films and weddings; and don't miss the frequent waterskiing shows. The stars of these performances are world famous for their performances and their precision on skis. There are trick skiers who ski barefoot, skiers who take their skis airborne aboard a kite, precision skiers who do carefully choreographed dances on skis while traveling 60 or 70 m.p.h. or more, and even a skiing dog! The grand finale of this magnificent—and very photogenic—show is a three-tiered pyramid of skiers balanced on each other's shoulders.

There's plenty to do and see, but perhaps the most satisfying of all is just a quiet walk or electric boat ride through these magnificent grounds, down deep jungle paths that wind through ginger plants and coffee trees, ancient cypresses centuries old standing in inky, haunting lagoons. There's a hushed air about this place that makes it a welcome relief from the noise and crowds that go with so many area attractions.

You'll never lack for something to eat here or something to do.

There are plenty of restaurants and dozens of boutiques full of treasures. You may have to drag devoted photographers out of here since there's something photogenic around every tree.

Cypress Gardens has recently added another photographer's delight, the Island in the Sky, a revolving platform that lifts riders slowly into the sky so they can photograph these lovely gardens from the air.

Few are those who come to Florida for ice but once you're here, why not? That's the way Cypress Gardens figured it when they introduced their newest show, "Southern Ice," an ice-skating extravaganza that turns the tropics into a snow scene with performances by 10 ice skating champs. Hoopskirted southern belles, the mascots of Cypress Gardens, turn up on the ice to cavort with skating alligators and an ice princess who appears beneath giant cypress trees laden with ice instead of the traditional Spanish moss. It's all done with special lighting and eight projectors. You'll find the 25-minute "Southern Ice" performances going on daily at the Ice Palace in the Southern Crossroads section of the park.

Railroad buffs will delight in **Cypress Junction,** an elaborate, multitrack model railway exhibit, and kiddies will love the small rides here.

It only seems fair that in this floral wonderland gardeners should have something special just for them. That something special is a November chrysanthemum festival, with thousands upon thousands of those blossoms blooming their rainbow-hued hearts out for all comers. If a riot of mums is not enough, there are 8,000 other varieties of plants here. The staff is quite knowledgeable about what is what and how its garden grows. Be sure to take a look at the 1,600-year-old cypress tree called The Chairman—it's a wonder!

In peak summer and winter seasons, the park also has after-dark shows, complete with fireworks lighting up the night skies.

You'll also see some fancy synchronized swimming and a group of talented, award-winning high divers at Aqua-cade, one of them a national champion diver who does two things even money couldn't get me to do: climb way, way up to a diving platform several stories high and then dive off it.

Open daily from 8am to sunset, Cypress Gardens (P.O. Box 1, Cypress Gardens, FL 33884) has shows all day long, and admission is $18.50 for adults, $12 for children 3 through 9. To get there head south from Orlando on U.S. 17 (or branch off Hwy. I-4 onto U.S. 27, picking up U.S. 17 in Haines City). Signs all over the Haines City area will help you find your way to the Gardens on Rte. 540, (tel. 813/324-2111 or toll free 800/237-4826 or 800/282-2123).

## RIVERSHIP ROMANCE

When the fantasylands overcome you, one way to escape to something different is to sail off on the *Rivership Romance,* which cruises the waterways of the historic St. Johns River on brunch, lunch, and dinner cruises. There's entertainment on board this triple-decked ship too, but just standing up on the observation deck and watching the world float by is entertainment enough. Lunch cruises depart daily at 11am, dinner trips at 7:30pm, Saturday brunch at 9:30am. Adult fare is $26.25 for lunch and $35 for dinner; children 3 to 12 pay half-fare. You'll find the boat at 433 N. Palmetto Ave. in Sanford (tel. 305/321-2627 or 321-5091, or toll free 800/423-7401).

A two-day cruise on the St. Johns, with a stop in historic Palatka and an overnight stay at the Holiday Inn there, is $201.40 including meals, the hotel, and the cruise. In April and November, the ship also occasionally sails on three-day river cruises.

## LAKE WALES

When you tire of other diversions, a lovely way to get a look at Florida as it was a century ago is to visit **Lake Kissimmee State Park's Cow Camp.** Here you walk along an eerily quiet trail beneath a shady canopy of ancient banyan trees to come suddenly upon a frontier cowboy camp, set up just as it would have been in 1876. A Florida "cracker" cowboy, his coffee tin bubbling on the open fire before him, sits in the shade of a palm-thatched lean-to spinning tales of the time in which he "lives." Later he'll show off his skills with the 14-foot-long rawhide rope used to drive the small, lean scrub cows to market. Those whips are, in fact, what gave the cowboys—and all Floridians—the nickname "Florida crackers."

An actual operating cow camp, the camp at Lake Kissimmee State Park raises cattle that are descended from the same scrubby Spanish cattle that once were a mainstay of the Florida economy. Smaller, and some say meaner, than the Texas longhorns which have evolved from the same Spanish Andalusian cattle, the cows are rounded up and branded each spring by the park rangers who will show you how it's done. To find the camp and the park, take Rte. 60 east from Lake Wales to Boy Scout Road and follow the signs or take Rte. S17B to the 5,030-acre park. Admission is $2 for car and driver, $1 for each passenger and the cowboy's living history presentation takes place from 9:30am to 4:30pm on Saturday, Sunday, and holidays. You can also camp, hike, picnic, and go boating in the park, which is open from 8am to sunset year round. For information or brochures, write to the park at 14248 Camp Mack Rd., Lake Wales, FL 33853, or call 813/696-1112.

There's a beautiful, albeit most unusual, place to stay and to dine here in Lake Wales. Called **Chalet Suzanne Country Inn and Restaurant,** on U.S. 27 and 17A, four miles north of Lake Wales (tel. 813/676-6011), this whimsical spot was created by a woman who needed to make enough money to support her children and began renting a few rooms.

Before long, her eclectic tastes and wonderful eye for the funky had turned her hideaway in the middle of an orange grove into this not-to-be-missed hostelry. Every room is different, and each is buried in a forest of antiques and oddments, up to and including a red British telephone booth. It's a wonderful sight on the shore of a tiny lake. It's been made even more wonderful by the woman's descendants, whose culinary talents have made the restaurant here one of the state's most-honored dining rooms. It's expensive—you'll pay $40 or more per person for dinner—but the food is memorable. So is the decor—no two dishes or chairs are alike, but all combine to create a charmingly harmonious whole. Room rates are $95 to $185, year round.

## BOK TOWER GARDENS

One of the most majestic sights in Florida is Bok Tower, which rises in ghostly magnificence high on a hill above the shores of glittering Lake Wales, just south of Orlando on U.S. 27 (tel. 813/676-1408). Few places are as tranquil as the 128-acre grounds around stately Bok Tower, where you'll be tempted to find a shady spot to just stare up at the magnificence of this Georgian Gothic Tower. It's set in the stillness of Mountain Lake Sanctuary atop Iron Mountain, once a sacred tribal site and the highest point in peninsular Florida. Donated to the nation by Dutch immigrant publisher Edward Bok, the 205-foot, pink-and-gray marble octagonal tower houses a 53-bell carillon whose gentle notes ring out each half hour, and there's a 45-minute recital presented at 3pm daily by resident carillonneur Milford Myhre. Admission to the sanctuary, open 8am to 5:30pm daily, is $3, children under 12 free.

## SPOOK HILL

While you're here in Lake Wales, it's fun to stop by Spook Hill, a wacky sight that's absolutely free. Spook Hill's just off U.S. 17 at North Avenue and 5th Street, and here's what you do when you get there: Just drive your car up to the designated spot, put it in neutral, remove your foot from the brake and watch the car move slowly backward . . . *uphill!* No one's telling why or how it works, but there are some local yarns about a Native American chief protecting his people, a pirate curse, and an alligator.

## BLACK HILLS PASSION PLAY

Another Lake Wales attraction, open from mid-February to mid-April, is this dramatic re-creation of the final days of Christ's life. Performances are each Tuesday, Thursday, and Saturday at 7:30pm, Sundays at 6pm, and on Good Friday evening. Tickets are $7 to $12. The natural outdoor amphitheater in which the play is performed is nestled in a citrus grove. It's a sight worth seeing, whether or not you make the play (tel. 813/676-1495). Write Box 71, Lake Wales, FL 33853.

## NASA KENNEDY SPACE CENTER'S SPACEPORT USA

It's an easy daytrip from Orlando (about a 90-minute drive) to Titusville and Cape Canaveral (quickest road is Rte. 528, the Beeline) and a pretty drive to this east coast area on the Indian River. From Orlando, follow the signs to Kennedy Space Center (not Cape Canaveral).

At the Kennedy Space Center's Spaceport USA, begin your visit with a stop at the **Visitor Information Center** (tel. 452-2121) on Merritt Island, between the mainland and the cape, about six miles east of Titusville. Huge rockets and spacecraft fill the yard here, and inside you can see a piece of moon rock and get a close-up look at Apollo capsules, rocket engines, and a lunar module.

In the Gallery of Space Flight a film traces the development of the space program. It's open daily (except December 25) from 8am to sunset and is free.

To get around this massive complex, line up for one of the two-hour, NASA-escorted, double-decker bus tours which leave every few minutes from the Visitor Center. The tour costs $4 for adults, $1.75 for children 3 to 12. You can take either the **Blue or the Red Tour.** The Red Tour includes the fascinating astronaut training building, where stimulators reproduce conditions of an actual space flight, and lights illuminate the craft as its components are explained by a narrator. The Blue Tour covers the Cape Air Force Station and Museum.

As you cruise around the enormous acreage, which happens also to be a wildlife refuge that harbors many an endangered species, you'll pass the 52-story **Vehicle Assembly Building** and the huge transporters that carry spacecraft to the launching pads. You'll get a look at a lunar launch pad and visit the mission control center from which the moon flights were organized and directed.

Astronauts in Earth orbit photographed much of a new film at the Space Center called *The Dream is Alive,* shown in Spaceport USA's IMAX Theater. A $3.6 million production, the film is narrated by Walter Cronkite and features footage shot during three missions in 1984. Price is $2.75 for adults and $1.75 for children 3 through 12.

Newest addition here is "Satellites and You," a new exhibit that teams Disney's animated Animatronics characters with weird visual and sound effects to turn you into an astronaut-for-a-day off on a walk into outer space.

As you probably know, shuttle flights were reduced after the January 1986 tragedy. Call NASA toll free at 800/432-2153 for information on the next launch. Make reservations for a pass by calling 407/452-2121 between 8am and 4pm, or write NASA Visitors Services Branch, PA-VIC, Kennedy Space Center Headquarters, Kennedy Space Center, FL 32899.

If you're thinking about staying over here—and it is a fair-to-middling drive back to Orlando—you'll find a couple of lovely large hotels like the **Cocoa Beach Hilton,** 1550 N. Atlantic Ave., Cocoa Beach, FL 32931 (tel. 407/799-0003 or toll free 800/445-8667), and dozens of small to medium-sized motels waiting to welcome you. Folks at the Cocoa Chamber of Commerce, 400 Fortenberry Rd., Merritt Island, FL 32922 (tel. 407/459-2200) have plenty of information on where to stay and what to see and do in their part of the state. There's more of that kind of information available at the Brevard County Visitor Information Center, which is conveniently located at Kennedy Space Center, FL 32899 (tel. 407/453-0823).

Restaurants in the region include a popular spot called the **Pier House** which is up on pilings stretching right out into the ocean with terrific views. You'll find it at Canaveral Pier, 401 Meade Ave., Cocoa Beach (tel. 783-7549). Other top restaurants in the area include **Bernard's Surf,** 2 S. Atlantic Ave. (tel. 783-2401) and

**Strawberry Mansion,** 1218 E. New Haven Ave., Melbourne (tel. 724-8627).

## BUSCH GARDENS

Over on the state's west coast in Tampa is one of Florida's top 10 attractions, Busch Gardens, an other-world place where Tarzan and Jane stroll blithely by and an elephant gives you a high-eyed stare.

Tops among the most popular attractions in the state, Busch Gardens earns its fame with a massive African jungle re-creation built by the famous brewery. To get here, take Highway I-75 to the Busch Boulevard exit, then just follow the signs to the park (tel. 813/977-6606 or 813/971-7978). Mailing address is Box 9158, Tampa, FL 33674.

It will take you every bit of a long day (about six or seven hours) to see all there is to see here, and you won't go astray if you allot a couple of days to add Busch's **Adventure Island** to your adventure list.

You can get around this vast complex on foot, on a monorail, or on a Skyride cable car that crosses the Dark Continent's Serengeti Plain for a giraffe's-eye view of things.

If you love trains, you can see everything from ground level aboard a little train that chugs around the park, passing by animals that roam free, separated only by moats or other natural barriers.

Out on the dusty Serengeti are 500 head of big game moving around a 60-acre veldt. Gazelles streak across the sands here, and elephants amble slowly about spouting water over their warm backs as water buffaloes and rhinos get their water the easy way—by sloshing in it.

Turn-of-the-century Africa, shades of that famous "Dr. Livingstone, I presume" era, is the theme here, and Busch creators do plenty with that theme. They've created a make-believe **Morocco,** where snake charmers hypnotize those slithery creatures and belly dancers hypnotize everyone; a **Congo,** where huge Bengal tigers prowl about their domain looking ever so much like sassy pussycats, until they leap into their river; a **Timbuktu,** where the Dolphins of the Deep perform; a **Nairobi,** where night creatures prowl Nocturnal Mountain; and a **Stanleyville,** where Tanzanian tribesmen practice their ancient woodcarving art.

Roam here among one of the largest collections of mammals, reptiles, and birds in North America—3,500 in all—then play on such amusements as the state's largest log flume ride. You can tour a tantalizing array of craft shops and when you tire, head straight for the **Hospitality House,** possibly the most popular stop in the park, where Busch gives you free samples of its famous product. Guzzle away at the edge of a pretty lagoon or under the trees of a bilevel patio where a piano player entertains.

While you're here, try not to lose your head on an *African Queen* boat ride up the river to the headhunters' village, or your tummy on the Python roller coaster which does a terrifying 360-degree loop.

Shows here include "Kaleidoscope," a splashy, Broadway-style musical revue with fancy lighting and flashy costumes; "Music Express," a musical history revue that takes you from big band sounds to top 40 hits; "Dolphins of the Deep," starring high-jumping dolphins and a sea lion; the "Busch Gardens Bird Show," with trained macaws and cockatoos, a Bavarian show, and a variety of animal acts.

Busch Gardens is open daily from 9:30am to dusk (about 6pm in winter, 8pm in summer), and one admission $23.95 per person (children under 2 are free) includes everything in the park except parking ($2 a car). One learned-the-hard-way piece of advice here: remember your parking lot number. This is a huge lot, and it's sickeningly easy to forget where you left Ole Hoss. Here, too, wear comfortable shoes and clothes—you'll do a lot of walking in the sunshine.

Next door to the gardens, you'll find **Adventure Island** (tel. 813/971-7978), a 13-acre water park complete with waterslides and endless surf, lots of kids games that are also fun for I'm-a-kid-again travelers. One-day admission is $14.95 per person, with children under 2 free. After 3pm prices drop to $11.65 per person. It gets a little chilly for this kind of fun in winter, so the park is open only from March to October. Hours are 10am to 5pm weekdays and 9am to 8pm Saturday and Sunday. Children under 8 must be accompanied by an adult.

## THE UNIVERSITY OF TAMPA/HENRY B. PLANT MUSEUM/TAMPA BAY HOTEL

This is not a honky-tonk sight, but instead a wonderful way to get a look at the posh early days of Florida, when people traveled in considerable style. Once one of the most elegant hotels in the state, this antique hostelry is now a National Historic Landmark university, but you're still welcome to tour it free each Tuesday and Thursday at 1:30pm. Its bright silver onion-domed minarets are a city landmark, and its long hallways, once traversed by rickshaws, no less, are worth a look.

When these elegant quarters were opened in 1891, the price tag on this hotel was a whopping $3 million—an enormous sum of money in those days! In the basement rathskeller here Teddy Roosevelt's Spanish-American War troops are said to have invented the drink that came to be known as Cuba Libre. There are priceless works of art here, too, collected by builder Henry Plant, whose treasures are in a free museum. You'll find the university by taking the Ashley Street exit from Highway I-275 and following Ashley toward downtown to U.S. 60 (West Kennedy Boulevard). Turn right across the bridge and you'll see the campus guardhouse on your left. It's free.

## ST. PETERSBURG'S MUNICIPAL PIER

You can see an intriguingly updated historic attraction by taking a trip over to St. Petersburg, where you'll find the **Municipal Pier.** It may not sound like an attraction, but it is. At the end of this long streak of concrete is a building you'll swear is upside down, but that's not all. This city landmark has been here in one form or another since 1889, when horse-drawn flatcars carried passengers from the boat docks, two miles away, to land. It's still a mile long and there's still a jitney to take you from one end to the other of this huge pier, which now features boutiques, craft vendors, a restaurant, lounge, observation deck, and a tiny strip of bathing beach.

## RINGLING MUSEUM/CA'D'ZAN/ASOLO THEATER

South of Tampa/St. Petersburg, you'll find the serene city of Sarasota, home to writers, artists, and other creative types now, but once home to a creator of a far different kind: circus king John Ringling. Ringling may be famous for his gaudy sequined performers and the Day-Glo colors of the Big Top, but in his own life he knew how to find lasting beauty of a far different nature.

He did that by collecting priceless works of art from all over the world and hanging them in a museum that is itself a work of art. **John and Mable Ringling Museum of Art** (5401 Bayshore Dr., Sarasota; tel. 813/355-5101) is a columned Italian Renaissance building of tranquil symmetry. It's a delight to the eye both outside, where a copy of Michelangelo's famous "David" casts a tranquil eye over the courtyard, and inside, where a top collection of baroque art masterpieces graces the walls. Admission is $6 for adults, $1.75 for children 6 to 12, which covers both house and museum, and the Circus Galleries. Hours are 10am to 6pm daily, closing at 10pm Thursday.

As if that weren't enough, Ringling went on to create **Ca' d'Zan,** a palatial bayside home where he lived with his wife, Mable, whose extravagant tastes are said to have been the inspiration for this palace. One of the 10 richest men in the nation before he died in 1936, Ringling gave the beautiful peach-colored art gallery and his rosy-cream stucco palazzo (the name means John's house in Venetian-Italian dialect), plus a 68-acre estate, his art collection, and entire fortune to the state of Florida, which gave it to everyone by opening it to the public.

More than half a million people come here every year to look at the 30-room mansion capped by a 60-foot tower and filled with carved and gilded furniture from the estates of the Astors and Goulds. Roam the 30 rooms here and you'll see priceless tapestries, a $50,000 Aeolian organ with 4,000 pipes, Venetian glass in every color of the rainbow, a bathtub hewn from a solid block of yellow Siena marble, and bathroom fixtures made of gold.

There's still more: the **Asolo Theater,** a jewelbox of a playhouse that looks like something in a dream. This froth of gold-and-cream baroque architecture was once part of the castle of deposed Cypriot Queen Catherine Coranor, who lived near Venice. Her tiny theater, filled with gold-leafed, festooned boxes, twinkling sconces, arcing tiers of white columns, and once visited by Robert Browning, was lost for some years after it was replaced in the palace by, predictably enough, a movie theater. An antique dealer found it, and it eventually ended up here, where it's one of the most glamorous lecture halls and the only baroque court playhouse in the nation, presenting lectures from December through August.

## SILVER SPRINGS

North of Orlando up toward Ocala racehorse country you'll find one of the state's many crystal-clear mineral springs and one of its most famous. **Silver Springs,** located five miles west of Ocala on Route 40 at 5656 SR 40 (tel. 904/236-2043), features a glass-bottomed boat that ferries you around as you look at the fish in their habitat and the lovely "mermaids" who go below to feed them by hand. More than two million visitors turn up here to gaze at these crystal waters every year, and you'll enjoy joining them for a look at both the springs and the exotic wildlife that roam alongside them. It's open daily from 9am to 5pm; admission is $15.95 for adults, $9.95 for children 3 to 11.

There's a water-theme park here too, **Wild Waters,** open from 10am to 5pm from late spring to September, $8.95 adults, $7.95 children.

---

# SIDE TRIPS FROM CENTRAL FLORIDA

---

Florida's a fascinating place wherever you go, but it can be especially so if you get off the main tourist treks and out into some of the places native or honorary-native Floridians go.

These range from a tiny village packed end to end with spiritualists and séance experts to a lovely country town where spirited horses are the most important residents. Let's take a look at some of the interesting side trips you can take in the Central Florida area.

## DAYTONA

Daytona's fame and fortune was born a couple of generations ago with the birth of the motorcar. Every famous automotive name from Olds to Ford came here in the early days to drive on the hard-packed sands of this oceanside city. You can still drive on the sands, although racing's out. After you've driven just inches from the briny deep, park the flivver and sit on that sand with the hundreds of other sand lovers who come here to do just that. Daytona's packed during its annual tribute to speed, known as Speed Weeks, in early February and July, so if you're planning to stay over, make sure you reserve hotel rooms far, far in advance for that busy time. **Marineland,** U.S. 1, Marineland (tel. 904/471-1111), is a popular attraction here and features performing dolphins of renown. Adults pay $12, children 3 to 11 $7. Open 9am to 5:30pm daily.

## CASSADEGA

This is the spiritualists' village, founded in 1874 by spiritualist George Colby, led here by an otherworldly guide. He founded a town and psychic center and donated 35 acres to the Spiritualistic church. Today, you'll see small signs outside many homes announcing the services within of a medium. These mediums claim not to permit charlatans among them, and all are registered by a national spiritualists' association.

## SEBRING

Sebring's another town made famous by speed—it's the home of the annual Sebring International Grand Prix of Endurance for sports cars in March—but it's also a pleasant citrus country village with sapphire-blue lakes and lovely old homes. A tranquil spot to visit.

## NEW SMYRNA BEACH

This once-sleepy seaside village is getting busier these days as the central Florida sprawl moves outward both east and west. A beautiful way to get a look at this village and its environs is to settle into the **Riverview Hotel,** an old cottage that once belonged to the man who ran the ferry that crossed the waterway to the mainland here. Really an inn, the **Riverview,** 103 Flagler Ave., New Smyrna Beach, FL 32069 (tel. 904/428-5858), was built by the same talented folks who restored and re-created the delightful Park Plaza Hotel in Winter Park.

The Riverview has an old-world feeling, with airy wicker furniture, four-poster beds, and paddle fans. Topped by a tin roof and trimmed out in yellow clapboard, urban sailors pull up to the dock and nip into the trilevel dining room to keep an eye on the water through big picture windows. Evenings, tiny white lights twinkle, and all is well with the world, wherever it is. Rates at the Riverview are $65 to $125 double, including Continental breakfast served in your room or on your balcony. Prices are higher for a honeymoon suite.

## GAINESVILLE/MARJORIE KINNAN RAWLINGS HISTORIC SITE

Gainesville's fame is its university, the University of Florida, which has a pretty campus that has bred many a governor and legislator. Just south of town lived Florida's Pulitzer Prizewinning author, Marjorie Kinnan Rawlings, who wrote *The Yearling, Cross Creek,* and *The Big Scrub,* based on her experiences in Florida. Her home, completely furnished just as she left it, is on Route 325, which you can reach from Route 20 East (tel. 466-3672). Its isolated location beside Lake Lochloosa gives you an idea how she got the setting for those touching Florida stories. At the **Yearling Cross Creek Restaurant** in Cross Creek (tel. 466-3033), you will be served dinners made with recipes suggested by the author in her *Cross Creek Cookbook.* Prices are in the $10 to $15 range and the restaurant's open daily.

## OCALA

Ocala's the home of many a Florida-bred champion thoroughbred, winners like Needles and Carry Back. About an hour's drive from Orlando, this small town has green lawns, and mile after mile of pristine white fences. These rolling hills, like Kentucky's famed bluegrass country, helped shape the sleek racers bred on 150 farms in the area.

If you speak horse, you'll fit right into this environment, where the impending birth of a white-blazed foal is likely to outrank a human baby's arrival. If equine talk isn't part of your vocabulary, stop by and learn something at places like **Castleton Farms** (Box 128, Trenton), about five miles west on Route 307, just off Route 26. Second-largest breeding farm in the world, Castleton raises trotters and pacers for harness racing. Give them a call (tel. 904/463-2686) before you drop in. Other farms are outlined on a map distributed by the Ocala Chamber of Commerce (110 E. Silver Springs Blvd.; tel. 904/629-8051). They can even tell you where to find greyhound breeding farms in the area.

## ST. AUGUSTINE

In few other cities in the nation can you travel from century to century as easily as you can in this community that was 55 years old when the Pilgrims landed on Plymouth Rock. In the quiet lanes of this seaside city, past and present merge into an amalgam of centuries.

There are, of course, the neon intrusions of the 20th century, but look beyond them and you will hear the echoes of a 16th-century cannon and the melodies of a ballroom where crystal sparkled in the glow of hundreds of candles as swashbuckling cavaliers and ebony-haired señoritas twirled across polished wood floors.

You'll find haunting echoes of the past in a tiny two-room soldier's cottage shaded by the huge branches of a live oak, and in the polished magnificence of a reconstructed home filled with shining silver and trimmed in jewel-colored velvets. You'll find them in the foot-thick walls of towering Castillo de San Marco and in the simplicity of the tiny red-cypress schoolhouse.

As the nation's oldest city, St. Augustine has many sights that will delight you, ranging from what some claim is the site of the object of early governor Ponce de León's search—the Fountain of Youth—to more certain historic sites like the huge Castillo that protected this city from a variety of invaders.

First visited in 1493 by Columbus and Ponce de León, the city was not settled until 20 years later, in 1513, when Ponce de León came searching for the fountain of youth reputed to be found here. He never found it—or perhaps he did, who knows?—but other Spaniards settled in and fought first the French and later the British for sovereignty.

Seminole uprisings were fought here, and the British and Spanish exchanged control over the city for several generations until finally ceding it to the U.S. In the late 1800s kingmaker and railroad builder Henry Flagler extended his railroad to the city, and life in St. Augustine began to focus on sun seekers who journeyed here by steamer and train. They spent the winter here in lavish style, dancing under the stars atop the old fort and parading in carriages down Avenida Menendez.

St. Augustine is about an hour's drive north of Daytona along sweeping strips of snow-white, hard-packed sand trimmed with sea oats. If you decide to stay overnight here, I'd recommend the **Kenwood Inn,** 38 Marine St., St. Augustine, FL 32804 (tel. 904/824-2116), an old hostelry built just after the Civil War and revamped in 1981 by talented restorers who have brought the magic back into these ancient boards. A perfect place to begin your return to another century, Kenwood Inn charges just $55 to $85, including Continental breakfast (year round).

Top sights here are the fortress, the Oldest House, all the restored homes and shops along St. George Street, called San Agustino Antigua. There is quite a lot more to see, too, and **Sightseeing Trains** (3 Cordova St.; tel. 829-6545) are a good way to see and understand much in a short time. For complete information on everything there is to do and see here, stop in at the **Visitor Information Center,** 10 Castillo Dr., right on the main road through town (tel. 829-5681).

# INDEX

## GENERAL INFORMATION

Accommodations:
  reservations, 26, 29–30
  *see also* Accommodations *index*
Air travel, 16
Alcoholic beverages, at Magic Kingdom, 126
Amusement parks, 109, 226
Animals: *see* Pets; Zoos
Aquarium, 208–9
Art museums:
  Central Florida, 225
  Orlando, 213, 215

Babysitters, 9
  EPCOT, 160
Baby services:
  Disney-MGM Studios, 191
  EPCOT, 163
  Magic Kingdom, 122
  Universal Studios, 202
Balloon trips, 108
Baseball, 106
Bicycling, Disney World, 104
Blind visitors, Magic Kingdom, 123
Boating:
  Disney World, 102
  Orlando, 105–6
Bus travel:
  from airport, 23
  to Orlando, 19
  within Orlando, 23

Camera needs:
  at Disney-MGM Studios, 191
  at EPCOT, 164
  at Magic Kingdom, 126

  at Universal Studios, 202
Camping, Disney World, 32–4
Cars and driving, 19–23
  Disney-MGM Studios, 190
  EPCOT, 161–2
  Magic Kingdom, 119–20
Cassadega, 226–7

Central Florida, 207–29
  art museums, 225
  Christmas (village), 216
  Kissimmee, 214–15
  map of, 211
  orientation, 207–8
  parks and gardens, 218–19
  tourist information, 9
  Winter Park, 215
  zoos, 218, 223–4
Christmas (village), 216
Cigarettes, at Magic Kingdom, 126
Citrus fruit, 13–14, 217
  shopping for, 114
Climate, 5–7, 9
  hurricanes, 6–7
  rain, 6–7
  tropical storms, 6–7
Clothing:
  for EPCOT, 159
  for Disney-MGM Studios, 190
  for Magic Kingdom, 119
  for Universal Studios, 202
Country club, Lake Buena Vista, 70
Credit cards:
  Disney-MGM Studios, 192
  EPCOT, 164
  Magic Kingdom, 126

Daytona, 226
Deaf visitors, to Magic Kingdom, 123
Discovery Island (Disney World), 148–9, 199–200
Disney-MGM Studios, 3–4, 189–96
  camera equipment, 191
  children's needs, 191
  clothing for, 190
  credit cards, 192
  entertainment information, 192

Disney-MGM Studios (cont'd)
  first aid, 191
  getting to, 190
  lockers, 192
  lost and found, 192
  map, 193
  orientation, 189–92
  shopping in, 192–6
  tickets for, 191
  when to go, 189–90
Disney World:
  accommodations at: see Accommodations index
  getting tickets for attractions, 120–2, 162–3, 191
  getting to, 15–20; by air, 16; by bus, 19; by car, 19; by ship, 20; by train, 16
  map, 125
  nightlife, 87–92
  restaurants at: see Restaurants index
  tourist information, 9
  see also Disney-MGM Studios; EPCOT; Magic Kingdom

Emergencies:
  pet, 9
  see also First aid
Entertainment: see Nightlife and entertainment
EPCOT, 157–88
  accommodations at: see Accommodations index
  camera equipment, 164
  children's needs, 163
  clothing for, 159–60
  entertainment, 187–8
  first aid, 163–4
  getting around, 166
  getting to, 160–2
  handicapped visitors, 163
  layout of, 165–6
  lost and found, 164
  lockers, 164
  maps, 125, 161
  missing children and persons, 164
  money, 164
  orientation, 158–65
  package pick-up, 164
  pets, 163
  shopping in, 169, 181–4
  tickets for, 162–3
  tourist information, 9

  wheelchair access, 159–60, 163
  when to go, 158–9
  World Key Information Service, 167–8

Film, 10
  at Magic Kingdom, 126
Films: see Movies
First aid:
  Disney-MGM Studios, 191
  EPCOT, 163–4
  Magic Kingdom, 123
Fishing:
  Disney World, 103
  Orlando, 107
Florida:
  tourist information, 8
  see also Central Florida
Food, 12–14
Foreign-language assistance:
  EPCOT, 164

Gainesville, 227
Gardens: see Parks and gardens
Golf:
  Disney World, 100–1
  Orlando, 105
Greyhound racing, 106
Groceries, 10

Handicapped visitors:
  Disney-MGM Studios, 191
  EPCOT, 163
  Magic Kingdom, 123
  Universal Studios, 202
Harness racing, 106
Health club, Disney World, 104
Historical museums, 213
Historic houses:
  Apopka, 73
  outside Central Florida, 227
Holidays:
  Magic Kingdom, 156
Horseback riding:
  Disney World, 103
  Orlando, 107–8
Hurricanes, 6–7

Ice skating, 108

Jai-alai, 106
Jogging, Disney World, 103

Kennedy Space Center, 221–3
Kissimmee, 214–15

Limousines from airport, 22
Lost children:
    EPCOT, 164
    Magic Kingdom, 124

Magic Kingdom, 117–56
    blind visitors, 123
    children's needs, 122–3
    clothing for, 119
    deaf visitors, 123
    entertainment    information,
        126
    first aid, 123
    getting around, 129–30 by
        double-decker bus, 130; by
        ferryboat, 129–30; by horse-
        drawn trolley, 130; by mon-
        orail, 129; by train, 129
    getting to, 119–20
    handicapped access, 123
    holiday activities, 156
    lockers, 123
    lost and found, 124
    map, 128–9
    missing children and persons,
        124
    nightlife, 155–6
    orientation, 117–29
    pets, 123
    shopping, 132–4
    special events, 154–5
    telephones, 124
    tickets for, 120–2
    top attractions, 152–3
    when to go, 117–19
Maps:
    Central Florida, 211
    Disney-MGM Studios, 193
    Disney World and EPCOT,
        125
    EPCOT, 161
    Magic Kingdom, 128–9
    Orlando, 57
    Orlando and environs, 21
Medical problems, 9
Missing persons:
    EPCOT, 164
    Magic Kingdom, 124
Money:
    Disney-MGM Studios, 192
    EPCOT, 164
    Magic Kingdom, 126

Movies, 132
Movie studios:
    Disney-MGM    Studios, 189–
        96
    Universal Studios, 201–6

New Smyrna Beach, 227
Newspapers, 10
Nightlife and entertainment:
    Disney World, 87–92; Adven-
        turers Club, 91; Barefoot
        Bar, 90; Campfire Program,
        89; Cap'n Jack's Oyster Bar,
        90; Comedy Warehouse, 91;
        Contemporary Hotel's Top
        of the World, 88; Electrical
        Water Pageant, 88; *Empress
        Lilly* cruise, 89; Giraffe Disco,
        90; Hoop-Dee-Doo Musical
        Revue, 89; La Cantina, 90;
        Main Street Electrical Parade,
        87; Mannequins, 91; Marsh-
        mallow Marsh Excursion, 89;
        Moriarty's, 90; Neon Arma-
        dillo    Music    Saloon,    91;
        Outer    Rim    Lounge,    90;
        Pleasure    Island,    90;    Star-
        board    Lounge,    90;    Tambu
        Lounge, 90; Top of the Tow-
        er, 90; Videopolis East, 91;
        Village Lounge, 90; Zeph-
        yr    Rockin'    RollerDrome,
        91
    EPCOT, 187–8
    Magic Kingdom, 155–6
    Orlando, 92–9; Academy of
        Dance and Theatrical, 97;
        Arabian Nights, 95; Bailey's
        Crocodile Club, 99; Bavari-
        an Bierhaus, 95; Bennigan's,
        96; Café on the Park, 98;
        Central Florida Civic Thea-
        ter, 97; Coconuts, 99; Dance
        Unlimited, 97; Days Inn
        Central, 96; Florida Sym-
        phony Orchestra, 97; Fort
        Liberty, 94; Freddie's, 98;
        Giraffe Lounge, 98; Hard
        Rock Café, 95; Hilton Inn
        Gateway, 96; Hilton Inns,
        96; Hollywood Lites, 97–8;
        J.J. Whispers, 98; Langford
        Hotel, 96; Laughing Kooka-
        burra, 98; Limey Jim's, 96;
        Maison et Jardin, 98; Mardi

Orlando (*cont'd*)
  Gras, 94; Mark Two Dinner Theater, 96; Medieval Times, 94–5; Murphy's Vine Street Emporium, 99; Orlando Opera Company, 97; Piccadilly Pub, 96; Rosie O'Grady's, 92; Sea World, 93; Shooter's, 96–7; Southern Ballet Company, 97; Sullivan's Trailway Lounge, 98; Top of the Palace Lounge, 99; Townsend's Fish House and Tavern, 98; Tupperware Convention Center, 97

Ocala, 227–8
Oranges: *see* Citrus fruit
Orlando, 1–5
  accommodations, 10–11; *see also* Accommodations *index for specific establishments*
  climate, 5–7
  getting around, 20–4
  getting to, 15–20
  maps, 57; and environs, 21
  nightlife, 92–9
  restaurants, 11–12; *see also* Restaurants *index for specific establishments*
  tourist information, 7–9

Parks and gardens:
  Central Florida, 218–19, 220
  Orlando and environs, 109–10, 214, 217–18
Pets:
  at EPCOT, 163
  at Magic Kingdom, 123
Photographic needs:
  at Disney-MGM Studios, 191
  at EPCOT, 164
  at Magic Kingdom, 126
  at Universal Studios, 202
Plants, at Magic Kingdom, 126
Postcards and stamps, at Magic Kingdom, 126

Rain, 6–7
Reservations:
  hotel, 29–30
  restaurant, 71–2; EPCOT, 168
Restaurants:
  Orlando, 11–12

  reservations for, 71–2; EPCOT, 168
  *see also* Restaurants *index*
River Country (Disney World), 146–7, 199

St. Augustine, 228–9
Science and technology museums, 213
Sebring, 227
Shopping, 111–16
  citrus fruit, 114
  Disney-MGM Studios, 192–4, 195, 196
  Disney World, 111–12
  EPCOT, 169, 181–4
  factory outlets, 113–14
  Magic Kingdom, 132–4, 140, 141, 144–6
  malls, 113, 115–16
  Orlando, 112
  souvenirs, 132–4, 136, 138, 140, 141, 144–6
  Winter Park, 112–13
Side trips from Central Florida, 226–9
  Cassadega, 226–7
  Daytona, 226
  Gainesville, 227
  New Smyrna Beach, 227
  Ocala, 227–8
  St. Augustine, 228–9
  Sebring, 227
Special events, Magic Kingdom, 154–5
Sports, 100–10
  Disney World, 100–4; bicycling, 104; boating, 102; fishing, 103; golf, 100–1; health club, 104; horseback riding, 103; jogging, 103–4; swimming, 102–3; tennis, 101–2; walking, 103–4; waterskiing, 104
  Orlando, 104–10; balloon trips, 108; baseball, 106; boating, 105–6; fishing, 107; golf, 105; greyhound racing, 106; harness racing, 106; horseback riding, 107–8; ice skating, 108; jai-alai, 106; swimming, 106–7; tennis, 105; waterskiing, 108–9
State parks, 109–10

Suntans and sunburns, 6
Swimming:
  Disney World, 102–3
  Orlando, 106–7

Taxis, 22
Telephones, 124
Tennis:
  Disney World, 101–2
  Orlando, 105
Tourist information:
  Central Florida, 9
  Disney World and EPCOT, 9
  Florida, 8
  St. Augustine, 229
Tour, Backstage Studio (Disney-MGM Studios), 195–6
Train travel, to Orlando, 16–19
Tropical storms, 6–7
Typhoon Lagoon (Disney World), 150, 197–8

Universal Studios, 201–6
  camera needs, 202
  children's needs, 202
  clothing for, 202
  getting to, 201–2
  handicapped visitors, 202
  pets, 202
  tickets for, 202–3
  when to go, 202

Walking, in Disney World, 103–4
Waterskiing:
  Disney World, 104
  Orlando, 108–9
Wekiva Springs State Park, 110
Western Union, 10
Wheelchair access, EPCOT, 159–60, 163
Winter Park, 215

Zoos, 212, 213
  Central Florida, 218, 223–4

# SIGHTS AND ATTRACTIONS

## Central Florida

**CENTRAL FLORIDA AREA**
Adventure Island, 224
Animal Forest, 218
Aquacade, 219
Asolo Theater, 225
Black Hills Passion Play, 221
Bok Tower Gardens, 221
Busch Gardens, 223
Ca' d'Zan, 225
Cypress Gardens, 218–19
Cypress Junction, 219
John and Mabel Ringling Museum of Art, 225
Lake Kissimmee State Park's Cow Camp, 220
Lake Wales, 220
NASA Kennedy Space Center's Spaceport USA, 221–3
Rivership Romance, 219–20
St. Petersburg's Municipal Pier, 224–5
Silver Springs, 226
Spook Hill, 221
The University of Tampa/Henry B. Plant Museum/Tampa Bay Hotel, 224
Wild Waters, 226

**ORLANDO AREA**
Alligatorland Safari Zoo, 212
Audubon House, 216

Big Tree Park, 217–18
Cartoon Museum, 216

Cattle Auction, 216–17
Central Florida Railroad Museum, 213
Central Florida Zoological Park, 213
Christmas, village of, 216
Citrus Candy Factory, 217
Desert Ranch, 217
Elvis Presley Museum, 212–13
Fire Station No. 3/Loch Haven Park, 214
Florida Citrus Tower, 217
Gatorland Zoo, 212
Genius Drive, 216
Kissimmee, 214–15
Leu Gardens, 214
Medieval Times, 210
Morse Museum of Art, 213
Mystery Fun House, 210
Orlando Naval Training Center, 217
Orlando Science Center, 213
Reptile World, 212
Tupperware's International Headquarters, 217
Wet 'N Wild, 209–210
Winter Park, 215
Xanadu, 210–12

## Disney-MGM Studios

Animation Gallery, 196
Backlot Annex and Lakeside Circle, 194–5
Backstage Studio Tour, 195–6
Back to Never Land, 196
Crossroads of the World, 192
Earfell Tower, 192

Hollywood Boulevard, 192–4
Indiana Jones Epic Stunt Spectacular, 195
The Monster Sound Show, 195
SuperStar Television, 195
Walt Disney Theater, 196

# E P C O T

Aero 2000, 172
Aero Test Center, 172
The Age of Information, 173
The Amazing Microchip, 173
Backstage Magic, 168–9
Bird and the Robot, 172
Body Wars, 171
Bubble Music, 177
CommuniCore East, 168–9
CommuniCore West, 173–4
Concept 2000, 172
Cranium Command, 171
Dreamfinder's School of Drama, 177
Electronic Forum, 169
Electronic Philharmonic, 177
Energy Exchange, 169
Face to Face, 173
Fitness Fairgrounds, 170
Fountain of Information, 173
Future Choice Theater, 169
Harvest Theater, 175
Horizons, 171
Image Works, 177
Intelligent Network, 173
Journey Into Imagination, 177–8
Kaleidoscope, 177
The Land, 175–7
Lean Machine, 172
Light Writer, 177
Listen to the Land Boat Ride, 176–7

The Living Seas, 174–5
Magic Eye Theater, 178
Magic Palette, 177
Nature's Buried Treasure, 174
Pacific Coast Kelp Forest, 174
Scuba Tube, 174
Seabase Alpha, 174
Seabase Concourse, 174–5
Sensor Maze, 177
Spaceship Earth, 167, 167–8
Stepping Tones, 177
Tomorrow's Harvest Tour, 177
TravelPort, 169
Universe of Energy, 169–70
Wonders of Life, 170–1
World of Motion, 171–4
World Showcase, 165, 178–87

**WORLD SHOWCASE**
America, 182–3
Canada, 187
China, 180–1
France, 185–6
Germany, 181–2
Italy, 182
Japan, 183–4
Mexico, 178–9
Morocco, 184–5
Norway, 179–80
United Kingdom, 186

# The Magic Kingdom

Adventureland, 145–7
Aunt Polly's Landing, 143
Bamboo Hollow, 149
Bay Cove, 147
Bay Lake, 147
Big Thunder Mountain Railroad, 145
Carousel of Progress, 136
Cinderella Castle, 139
Cinderella's Golden Carousel, 139
Circle-Vision 360 American

Journeys, 135
Coocoo Cabana Parrot Perch, 149
Country Bear Jamboree, 144
Diamond Horseshow revue, 144
Discovery Island, 148–9, 199–200
Disney Creative Arts, 151
Dreamflight, 135
Dumbo, The Flying Elephant, 139
Exploring Nature, 151

Family Treehouse, 146
Fantasy Faire, 140
Fantasyland, 138–41
Flamingo Lagoon, 149
Fort Sam Clemens, 143
Frontierland and Liberty Square, 141–5
Frontierland Railway Station, 144–5
Frontierland Shootin' Gallery, 144
Grand Prix Raceway, 137
Hall of Presidents, 143
Haunted Mansion, 412
Horse-drawn trolley, 130
Ichabod's Landing, 412
It's a Small World, 140–1
Jungle Cruise, 146
Liberty Square Riverboats, 412
Mad Tea Party, 138
Main Street, U.S.A., 131–4
Mickey's Birthdayland, 137–8
Mickey's Christmas Carol, 139
Mike Fink Keelboats, 412
Mission to Mars, 135
Parrot Perch, 149
Mr. Toad's Wild Ride, 138

PeopleMover, WEDway, 135–6
Peter Pan's Flight, 141
Pirates of the Caribbean, 146
Raft River Ridge, 147–8
River Country, 147–8, 199
Skyway, 136

Skyway to Tomorrowland, 130
Snow White's Scary Adventure, 139
Space Mountain, 136–7
The Space Port, 135
Starjets, 135
Swan Boats, 135
Tomorrowland, 134–7
Tom Sawyer's Island, 142–3
Tropical Serenade, 146
Trumpeter Springs, 149
20,000 Thousand Leagues Under the Sea, 140
Walt Disney World of Entertainment program, 151
White Water Rapids, 147–8
Whoop 'n' Holler Hollow, 148
Wonders of Walt Disney World, 150–1

# Universal Studios

Animal Actors Stage, 206
Back to the Future, 205–6
E.T.'s House, 204
Earthquake, 204
Ghostbusters, 206
Hollywood, 204
King Kong, 204
*Murder She Wrote* Post Production Theater, 206

New England Village, 203–4
New York/Metro, 203
Nickelodeon, 206
Phantom of the Opera Horror Make-up Show, 206
San Francisco Bay, 203
Screen Test Adventure Studio, 206
WorldExpo, 204

# ACCOMMODATIONS

## Disney World

**CAMPING**
Fort Wilderness, 32–4

**RESORT HOTELS**
Caribbean Beach Resort (*D*),
   29
Club Lake Villas (Club Suites)
   (*D*), 31
Contemporary Resort Hotel
   (*D*), 27–8
Disney Inn (*D*), 30
Fairway Villas (*D*), 31
Grand Floridian Beach (*D*),
   28–9
Polynesian Village (*D*), 26–7
Swan (*D*), 38–9

Treehouse Villas (*D*), 31–2
Vacation Villas (*D*), 30–1
Walt Disney World Dolphin (*D*),
   39–40

**WALT DISNEY WORLD HOTEL
PLAZA**
Buena Vista Palace (*FC*), 37–8
Grosvenor Resort (*FC*), 35–6
Hilton at Disney World Village
   (*FC*), 36–7
Hotel Royal Plaza (*FC*), 36
Howard Johnson (*FC*), 36
Pickett Suites Resort (*FC*), 38
Viscount Hotel (*FC*), 35

## Orlando & Environs

Best Western Orlando Inn, Or-
   lando (*B*), 55–6
Budget Host Inn Main Gate
   East, Kissimmee (*B*), 47
Buena Vista Motel, Kissimmee
   (*B*), 48
Casa Rosa Inn, Kissimmee (*B*),
   48
Central Motel, Kissimmee (*B*),
   48
Chalet Motel, Kissimmee (*B*), 49
Chalet Suzanne Country Inn
   and Restaurant, Lake Wales
   (*FC*), 220–1
Chateau Motel, Kissimmee (*B*),
   49
Colonial Motor Lodge, Kissim-
   mee (*B*), 46

Comfort Inn, Kissimmee (*B–M*),
   44
Court of Flags, Orlando (*FC*),
   52
Cypress Cove, near Kissimmee
   (*M*; nudist), 61
Davis Brothers Motor Lodge,
   Orlando (*B*), 53
Davis Park, Orlando (*B*), 55
Days Inn Lake Buena Vista, Lake
   Buena Vista (*M*), 42
Days Inn Universal Studios East,
   Orlando (*D*), 54
Days Suites, Kissimmee (*M*), 45
Econo Lodge Maingate East,
   Kissimmee (*B*), 46–7
Embassy Motel, Kissimmee (*B*),
   47

**KEY TO ABBREVIATIONS:** *B* = Budget; *B&B* = Bed-and-Breakfast; *CG* = Campgrounds;
*D* = Deluxe; *FC* = First Class; *M* = Moderate

Enterprise Motel, Kissimmee (B), 48

Fort Summit Camping Resort, Davenport, (camping), 63

Gateway Inn, Orlando (B), 53

Gold Key Inn, Orlando (M), 56

Grenlefe Resort and Conference Center, Grenlefe (D–FC), 60

Harley Hotel, Orlando (M), 55

Hawaiian Village Inn, Kissimmee (B), 48–9

Hilton Inn Florida Center, Orlando (D), 52

Holiday Inn-Kissimmee, Kissimmee (B), 47

Howard Johnson Midtown, Orlando (B), 55

Hyatt Orlando Hotel, Kissimmee (FC), 44

Hyatt Regency Grand Cypress Hotel, Orlando (D), 42–3

Key Motel, Kissimmee (B), 49

King's Motel, Kissimmee (B), 46

Lakeside Inn, Mount Dora (FC), 61–2

Lakeview, Kissimmee (B), 46

Langford Hotel, Winter Park (M), 58

Larson's Lodge, Kissimmee (B), 46

Las Palmas Inn, Orlando (M), 53

Maple Leaf Motel, Kissimmee (B), 49

Mission Inn, Honey-in-the-Hills (FC), 62

Orange Lake Country Club, Kissimmee (FC), 45

Orlando Marriott, Orlando (FC), 50

Orlando Motor Lodge, Orlando (B), 56

Orlando Vacation Resort, Clermont (M), 60

The Palm, Kissimmee, (B), 48

Park Inn International, Kissimmee (B), 47

Park Plaza Hotel, Winter Park (FC), 58

Peabody Hotel, Orlando (D), 50

Port O Call Campground, Kissimmee (CG), 63

Radisson Inn & Justus Aquatic Center, Orlando (FC), 50–1

Radisson Inn Maingate, Kissimmee (M), 45–6

Ramada Altamonte Springs, Altamonte Springs (M), 59

Ramada Inn West Gate, Clermont (M), 60

Residence Inn by Mariott, Altamonte Springs (FC), 59

Rodeway Inn Eastgate, Kissimmee (B), 46

1776 Resort Inn, Orlando (B), 53

Sheraton Lakeside Inn, Kissimmee (M), 44

Sheraton World, Orlando (FC), 52–3

Sonesta Village Hotel on Sand Lake, Orlando (FC), 51–2

Spacecoast Motel, Kissimmee (B), 48

Star Quality Resort, Orlando (M), 53

Stouffer Orlando, Orlando (D), 49–50

Sun Motel, Kissimmee (B), 48

Sunrise Motel, Kissimmee (B), 47

TraveLodge Gardens, Orlando (M), 56

TraveLodge Kissimmee Flags, Kissimmee (B), 47–8

Twin Towers Hotel, Orlando (D), 54

Unicorn Bed and Breakfast, Kissimmee (B&B), 54

Vistana Resort, Lake Buena Vista (D), 41–2

Yogi Bear's Jellystone Park Campground, Kissimmee (CG), 62

## Outside Central Florida

Kenwood Inn, St. Augustine (M), 229

Riverview, New Smyrna Beach (D), 227

# RESTAURANTS

## Disney World

Adventureland Veranda (Polynesian), 146–7

All American Sandwich Shop (*B*; deli), 69

Barefoot Snack Bar (*B*; hot dogs), 67

Baskerville's (*B*), 70

Breakfast à la Disney (*M*; family style/breakfast), 68

Brunch with the Disney Bunch (*M*; family style/brunch), 68

Campfire Snack Bar (*B*; hot dogs), 68

Cap'n Jack's Oyster Bar (*M*; seafood/oysters), 69

Chef Mickey's Village Restaurant (*M*–*E*; seafood), 69

Chez Donut (*B*; donuts), 70

Chip 'n' Dale's Country Morning Jamboree (*M*; family style/breakfast), 69

Contemporary Café (*M*; buffet), 67

Contemporary Café Character Breakfast (*B*; breakfast), 69

Contemporary Resort (*E*; American/continental), 67

Coral Isle Café (*M*; Polynesian/lunch/dinner), 67

Crystal Palace Restaurant (*B*; breakfast), 133

El Cid (*M*; seafood/Spanish), 70

The Empress Room (*E*; continental), 65

Fiesta Fun Center (*B*; snacks), 68

Fisherman's Deck (*E*; seafood), 66

Garden Gallery Restaurant (*B*; snacks), 68

Grill Room (*M*; family style), 67

Hotel Royal Plaza's Knight Table (*B*; pizza), 70

Howard Johnson's (*B*; American/family style), 70

King Stefan's Banquet Hall (*M*), 139–40

Liberty Tree Tavern (*M*; American), 143–4

Lite Bite (*B*; burgers), 70

The Lunching Pad (*B*; lunch), 137

Minnie Menehune Character Breakfast (*B*; family style/breakfast), 69

Outback (*M*; steaks), 82

Outer Rim (*B*; snacks), 67

Palm Grill (*M*; American), 71

Papeete Bay Veranda (*M*–*E*; Polynesian/brunch), 67

Pinocchio Village Haus (snacks/German), 140

Plaza Restaurant (*M*; American), 133

Polynesian Village's Polynesian Revue (*E*; Polynesian), 66

Pompano Grill (*M*; American), 70

Pop's Place (snacks), 148

Portobello Yacht Club (*M*; pizza), 91–2

Refreshment Center (*B*; hot dogs), 133

Sand Trap (*B*; snacks), 68

The Space Bar (*B*; snacks), 136

Steerman's Quarters (*E*; steaks/prime rib), 66

Sunshine Tree Terrace (snacks), 146

Tangaroa Terrace (*M*; Polynesian), 67

Tomorrowland Terrace (*B*; burgers/pizza), 137

**KEY TO ABBREVIATIONS:** *B* = Budget; *E* = Expensive; *M* = Moderate

Top of the World (*E*; family style), 67
Tournament Tent (snacks), 140
Town Square Café (*M*; Ameri can), 132
Trail's End Café (*B*; family style/buffet), 68
The Waterin' Hole (snacks), 148

## EPCOT

Akershus (*M*; Norwegian), 180
Au Petit Café (bakery), 185
Biergarten (*M–E*; German), 181
Boulangerie Patisserie (bakery), 185
Coral Reef Restaurant (*E*; seafood), 175
La Cantina de San Angel (*M–E*; Mexican), 178
Land Grille (*E*; American), 176
Le Bistro de Paris (*M–E*; French), 185
Le Cellier (*M*; buffet), 187
Les Chefs de France (*M–E*; French), 185
Liberty Inn (snacks), 183
L'Originale Alfredo di Roma Ristorante (*M*; Italian), 182
Lotus Blossom Café (*B*; Chinese), 181
Marrakesh (*M*; Moroccan), 184–5
Nine Dragons Restaurant (*B*; Chinese), 180–1
Rose & Crown Pub & Dining Room (*B–M*; English pub style), 186
San Angel Inn Restaurant (*B*; Mexican), 179
Tempura Kiku's (*M*; Japanese), 184
Teppanyaki Dining Rooms (*M*; Japanese), 184

## Orlando & Environs

Al E. Gator's, Sea World, (*M*; seafood), 85
Anthony's, Winter Park (*M*; Italian), 78
Barney's Steaks and Seafood, Orlando (*M*; steaks/seafood), 82
Bavarian Bierhaus, Orlando (*B*; German), 95
Benihana of Tokyo, Orlando (*M*; Japanese), 75
The Bubble Room, Maitland (*M*; American/continental), 74
Bucket's Bar and Grill, Orlando (*M*; seafood), 81
Café on the Park, Orlando (*M*; American/continental), 73
Chalet Suzanne Country Inn and Restaurant, Lake Wales (*E*; eclectic), 220–1
Charley's Steak House, Orlando (*M*; steaks), 82
Charlie's Lobster House, Mercado (*M*; seafood), 80
Charlie's Lobster House, New Smyrna Beach (*M*; seafood), 80
Charlie's Lobster House, Winter Park (*M*; seafood), 80
Chesapeake Crab House, Maitland (*B*; seafood), 79
Chi-Chi's, Orlando (*B*; Mexican), 79
Chili's, Orlando (*B*; Mexican), 79
Darbar, Orlando (*M*; Indian), 83
Darryl's 1883 Restaurant and Tavern, Orlando (*B*; mixed menu), 84
Davis Brothers Motor Lodge (*B*; American), 84
El Bohio Café, Orlando (*B*; Cuban), 85
Elliott's, Winter Park (*B*; light meals), 83
El Torito, Altamonte Springs (*B*; Mexican), 78
Epicurean Restaurant, Orlando (*M*; Greek), 78

Forbidden City, Orlando (*B*; Chinese), 76

Freddie's Steak & Seafood House, Fern Park (*M*; steaks), 81

Gary's Duck Inn, Orlando (*M*; seafood), 80

Grene Heron (*E*; American), 60

Gus's Villa Rose, Orlando (*M*; Italian), 78

Historic Townsend's Plantation, Apopka (*M*; American/continental), 74

Holiday House, Orlando (*B*; American), 84

Jin Ho, Winter Park, Altamonte Springs (*B*; Chinese), 75

JoAnn's Chili Bordello, Orlando (*B*; Mexican), 79

Jordan's Grove, Maitland (*M*; American/continental), 74

La Belle Verrière, Winter Park (*M*; French), 76

La Cantina, Orlando (*M*; steaks), 82

La Lechonera Restaurant, Orlando (*B*; Cuban), 85

La Scala, Altamonte Springs (*M*; Italian), 78

Las Palomas, Orlando (*B*; Mexican), 79

Le Cordon Bleu, Winter Park (*M*; French), 77

Lee and Ric's Oyster Bar and Seafood House, Orlando (*B–M*; seafood), 80

LePeep, Orlando (*B*; light meals), 82

Lili Marlene's Aviator's Pub and Restaurant, Orlando (*M*; American/continental), 74

Limey Jim's Restaurant, Orlando (*M–E*; American/continental), 73

L & N Seafood Grille, Casselberry (*B–M*; seafood), 81

Mack Meiner's Country Store, Orlando (*B*; family style), 83

Maison des Crêpes, Orlando (*M*; French), 77

Maison et Jardin, Altamonte Springs (*M*; French), 77

Medina's Café, Orlando (*B*; Cuban), 85

Ming Court Restaurant (*M*; Chinese), 76

Ming Gardens Chinese Cuisine, Orlando (*M*; Chinese), 76

Morrison's Cafeteria, Orlando (*B*; family style), 83

Murphy's Lobster House, Kissimmee (*M–E*; seafood), 80–1

Numero Uno, Orlando (*B*; Cuban), 85

Olive Garden, Orlando (*B*; Italian), 85

Park Avenue Grille, Winter Park (*M*; American/continental), 73

Park Plaza Gardens, Winter Park (*M*; American/continental), 72

Pebbles, Longwood (*M*; American/continental), 72

Piccadilly Restaurant, Orlando (*M*; American/continental), 73

Punjab Indian Restaurant, Orlando (*B*; Indian), 83

Ran-Getsu of Tokyo, Orlando (*M–E*; Japanese), 75

Red Lobster, Kissimmee (*M*; seafood), 80

Ronnie's, Orlando (*B*; family style), 83

Shells, Winter Park (*B*; seafood), 81

Shucker's Oyster Bar of Orlando, Orlando (*B*; seafood), 81

Steak and Shake, Orlando (*B*; burgers), 84

TGI Fridays, Altamonte Springs (*B*; family style), 84

Townsend's Fish House and Tavern, Orlando (*B*; American/continental), 74

Village Inn, Winter Park (American), 84

## Outside Central Florida

Yearling Cross Creek Restaurant, Cross Creek (*M*), 227

# NOW, SAVE MONEY ON ALL YOUR TRAVELS!
## Join Frommer's™ Dollarwise® Travel Club

Saving money while traveling is never a simple matter, which is why the **Dollarwise Travel Club** was formed 31 years ago. Developed in response to requests from Frommer's Travel Guide readers, the Club provides cost-cutting travel strategies, up-to-date travel information, and a sense of community for value-conscious travelers from all over the world.

In keeping with the money-saving concept, the annual membership fee is low—$18 for U.S. residents or $20 for residents of Canada, Mexico, and other countries—and is immediately exceeded by the value of your benefits, which include:

1. Any TWO books listed on the following pages.
2. Plus any ONE Frommer's City Guide.
3. A subscription to our quarterly newspaper, *The Dollarwise Traveler*.
4. A membership card that entitles you to purchase through the Club all Frommer's publications for 33% to 50% off their retail price.

The eight-page *Dollarwise Traveler* tells you about the latest developments in good-value travel worldwide and includes the following columns: **Hospitality Exchange** (for those offering and seeking hospitality in cities all over the world); **Share-a-Trip** (for those looking for travel companions to share costs); and **Readers Ask . . . Readers Reply** (for those with travel questions that other members can answer).

Aside from the Frommer's Guides and the Gault Millau Guides, you can also choose from our Special Editions. These include such titles as *California with Kids* (a compendium of the best of California's accommodations, restaurants, and sightseeing attractions appropriate for those traveling with toddlers through teens); *Candy Apple: New York with Kids* (a spirited guide to the Big Apple by a savvy New York grandmother that's perfect for both visitors and residents); *Caribbean Hideaways* (the 100 most romantic places to stay in the Islands, all rated on ambience, food, sports opportunities, and price); *Honeymoon Destinations* (a guide to planning and choosing just the right destination from hundreds of possibilities in the U.S., Mexico, and the Caribbean); *Marilyn Wood's Wonderful Weekends* (a selection of the best mini-vacations within a 200-mile radius of New York City, including descriptions of country inns and other accommodations, restaurants, picnic spots, sights, and activities); and *Paris Rendez-Vous* (a delightful guide to the best places to meet in Paris whether for power breakfasts or dancing till dawn).

To join this Club, simply send the appropriate membership fee with your name and address to: Frommer's Dollarwise Travel Club, 15 Columbus Circle, New York, NY 10023. Remember to specify which single city guide and which two other guides you wish to receive in your initial package of member's benefits. Or tear out the next page, check off your choices, and send the page to us with your membership fee.

**FROMMER BOOKS**
**PRENTICE HALL PRESS**
**15 COLUMBUS CIRCLE**
**NEW YORK, NY 10023**
**212/373-8125**

**Date_____**

Friends:

Please send me the books checked below.

## FROMMER'S™ GUIDES

(Guides to sightseeing and tourist accommodations and facilities from budget to deluxe, with emphasis on the medium-priced.)

| | | | |
|---|---|---|---|
| ☐ Alaska. . . . . . . . . . . . . . . .$14.95 | ☐ Germany . . . . . . . . . . . . . . . . . . . . . .$14.95 |
| ☐ Australia. . . . . . . . . . . . . .$14.95 | ☐ Italy . . . . . . . . . . . . . . . . . . . . . . .$14.95 |
| ☐ Austria & Hungary . . . . . . .$14.95 | ☐ Japan & Hong Kong. . . . . . . . . . . .$14.95 |
| ☐ Belgium, Holland & Lux-embourg . . . . . . . . . . . .$14.95 | ☐ Mid-Atlantic States. . . . . . . . . . . . .$14.95 |
| | ☐ New England . . . . . . . . . . . . . . . . . .$14.95 |
| ☐ Bermuda & The Bahamas . . .$14.95 | ☐ New York State. . . . . . . . . . . . . . . .$14.95 |
| ☐ Brazil . . . . . . . . . . . . . . . .$14.95 | ☐ Northwest. . . . . . . . . . . . . . . . . . . .$14.95 |
| ☐ Canada. . . . . . . . . . . . . . .$14.95 | ☐ Portugal, Madeira & the Azores. . . . .$14.95 |
| ☐ Caribbean . . . . . . . . . . . . .$14.95 | ☐ Skiing Europe . . . . . . . . . . . . . . . . .$14.95 |
| ☐ Cruises (incl. Alaska, Carib, Mex, Hawaii, Panama, Canada & US). .$14.95 | ☐ South Pacific . . . . . . . . . . . . . . . . . .$14.95 |
| | ☐ Southeast Asia . . . . . . . . . . . . . . . .$14.95 |
| ☐ California & Las Vegas. . . . . .$14.95 | ☐ Southern Atlantic States . . . . . . . . . .$14.95 |
| ☐ Egypt . . . . . . . . . . . . . . . .$14.95 | ☐ Southwest . . . . . . . . . . . . . . . . . . . .$14.95 |
| ☐ England & Scotland. . . . . . .$14.95 | ☐ Switzerland & Liechtenstein. . . . . . . .$14.95 |
| ☐ Florida . . . . . . . . . . . . . . .$14.95 | ☐ USA . . . . . . . . . . . . . . . . . . . . . . . .$15.95 |
| ☐ France. . . . . . . . . . . . . . . .$14.95 | |

## FROMMER'S $-A-DAY® GUIDES

(In-depth guides to sightseeing and low-cost tourist accommodations and facilities.)

| | |
|---|---|
| ☐ Europe on $40 a Day . . . . . .$15.95 | ☐ New York on $60 a Day . . . . . . . . . . .$13.95 |
| ☐ Australia on $40 a Day . . . . .$13.95 | ☐ New Zealand on $45 a Day. . . . . . . . .$13.95 |
| ☐ Eastern Europe on $25 a Day .$13.95 | ☐ Scandinavia on $60 a Day. . . . . . . . . .$13.95 |
| ☐ England on $50 a Day . . . . . .$13.95 | ☐ Scotland & Wales on $40 a Day. . . . . .$13.95 |
| ☐ Greece on $35 a Day . . . . . .$13.95 | ☐ South America on $35 a Day. . . . . . . .$13.95 |
| ☐ Hawaii on $60 a Day . . . . . .$13.95 | ☐ Spain & Morocco on $40 a Day . . . . . .$13.95 |
| ☐ India on $25 a Day . . . . . . .$12.95 | ☐ Turkey on $30 a Day . . . . . . . . . . . . .$13.95 |
| ☐ Ireland on $35 a Day . . . . . .$13.95 | ☐ Washington, D.C. & Historic Va. on |
| ☐ Israel on $40 a Day . . . . . . .$13.95 | $40 a Day . . . . . . . . . . . . . . . . .$13.95 |
| ☐ Mexico on $35 a Day. . . . . .$13.95 | |

## FROMMER'S TOURING GUIDES

(Color illustrated guides that include walking tours, cultural and historic sites, and other vital travel information.)

| | |
|---|---|
| ☐ Amsterdam . . . . . . . . . . . .$10.95 | ☐ New York. . . . . . . . . . . . . . . . . . . . .$10.95 |
| ☐ Australia. . . . . . . . . . . . . . .$9.95 | ☐ Paris . . . . . . . . . . . . . . . . . . . . . . . .$8.95 |
| ☐ Brazil . . . . . . . . . . . . . . . .$10.95 | ☐ Rome . . . . . . . . . . . . . . . . . . . . . . .$10.95 |
| ☐ Egypt . . . . . . . . . . . . . . . . .$8.95 | ☐ Scotland . . . . . . . . . . . . . . . . . . . . . .$9.95 |
| ☐ Florence . . . . . . . . . . . . . . .$8.95 | ☐ Thailand . . . . . . . . . . . . . . . . . . . . . .$9.95 |
| ☐ Hong Kong . . . . . . . . . . . .$10.95 | ☐ Turkey. . . . . . . . . . . . . . . . . . . . . . .$10.95 |
| ☐ London. . . . . . . . . . . . . . . .$8.95 | ☐ Venice. . . . . . . . . . . . . . . . . . . . . . . .$8.95 |

**TURN PAGE FOR ADDITONAL BOOKS AND ORDER FORM**

0690

# FROMMER'S CITY GUIDES

(Pocket-size guides to sightseeing and tourist accommodations and facilities in all price ranges.)

| | |
|---|---|
| ☐ Amsterdam/Holland . . . . . . . .\$8.95 | ☐ Montréal/Québec City . . . . . . . . . . . .\$8.95 |
| ☐ Athens . . . . . . . . . . . . . . . . .\$8.95 | ☐ New Orleans . . . . . . . . . . . . . . . . . . . .\$8.95 |
| ☐ Atlanta . . . . . . . . . . . . . . . .\$8.95 | ☐ New York. . . . . . . . . . . . . . . . . . . . . .\$8.95 |
| ☐ Atlantic City/Cape May . . . . .\$8.95 | ☐ Orlando. . . . . . . . . . . . . . . . . . . . . . . .\$8.95 |
| ☐ Barcelona . . . . . . . . . . . . . .\$7.95 | ☐ Paris . . . . . . . . . . . . . . . . . . . . . . . . . .\$8.95 |
| ☐ Belgium . . . . . . . . . . . . . . .\$7.95 | ☐ Philadelphia . . . . . . . . . . . . . . . . . . .\$8.95 |
| ☐ Boston . . . . . . . . . . . . . . . .\$8.95 | ☐ Rio . . . . . . . . . . . . . . . . . . . . . . . . . . .\$8.95 |
| ☐ Cancún/Cozumel/Yucatán . . .\$8.95 | ☐ Rome . . . . . . . . . . . . . . . . . . . . . . . . .\$8.95 |
| ☐ Chicago . . . . . . . . . . . . . . .\$8.95 | ☐ Salt Lake City . . . . . . . . . . . . . . . . . .\$8.95 |
| ☐ Denver/Boulder/Colorado | ☐ San Diego . . . . . . . . . . . . . . . . . . . .\$8.95 |
| Springs . . . . . . . . . . . . . . . .\$7.95 | ☐ San Francisco . . . . . . . . . . . . . . . . . .\$8.95 |
| ☐ Dublin/Ireland . . . . . . . . . . .\$8.95 | ☐ Santa Fe/Taos/Albuquerque . . . . . . . .\$8.95 |
| ☐ Hawaii . . . . . . . . . . . . . . . .\$8.95 | ☐ Seattle/Portland. . . . . . . . . . . . . . . .\$7.95 |
| ☐ Hong Kong . . . . . . . . . . . . .\$7.95 | ☐ Sydney . . . . . . . . . . . . . . . . . . . . . . .\$8.95 |
| ☐ Las Vegas . . . . . . . . . . . . . .\$8.95 | ☐ Tampa/St. Petersburg. . . . . . . . . . . .\$8.95 |
| ☐ Lisbon/Madrid/Costa del Sol. .\$8.95 | ☐ Tokyo . . . . . . . . . . . . . . . . . . . . . . . .\$7.95 |
| ☐ London. . . . . . . . . . . . . . . .\$8.95 | ☐ Toronto. . . . . . . . . . . . . . . . . . . . . . .\$8.95 |
| ☐ Los Angeles. . . . . . . . . . . . .\$8.95 | ☐ Vancouver/Victoria. . . . . . . . . . . . . .\$7.95 |
| ☐ Mexico City/Acapulco . . . . . .\$8.95 | ☐ Washington, D.C. . . . . . . . . . . . . . . .\$8.95 |
| ☐ Minneapolis/St. Paul. . . . . . .\$8.95 | |

## SPECIAL EDITIONS

| | |
|---|---|
| ☐ Beat the High Cost of Travel . . .\$6.95 | ☐ Motorist's Phrase Book (Fr/Ger/Sp). . . .\$4.95 |
| ☐ Bed & Breakfast—N. America \$11.95 | ☐ Paris Rendez-Vous. . . . . . . . . . . . . .\$10.95 |
| ☐ California with Kids . . . . . . .\$14.95 | ☐ Swap and Go (Home Exchanging) . . . . .\$10.95 |
| ☐ Caribbean Hideaways . . . . . .\$14.95 | ☐ The Candy Apple (NY with Kids) . . . . .\$12.95 |
| ☐ Manhattan's Outdoor | ☐ Travel Diary and Record Book . . . . . . . .\$5.95 |
| Sculpture. . . . . . . . . . . . . .\$15.95 | |

☐ Honeymoon Destinations (US, Mex & Carib) . . . . . . . . . . . . . . . . . . . . . . . . . . . .\$14.95

☐ Where to Stay USA (From \$3 to \$30 a night) . . . . . . . . . . . . . . . . . . . . . . . . . . . .\$10.95

☐ Marilyn Wood's Wonderful Weekends (CT, DE, MA, NH, NJ, NY, PA, RI, VT) . . . . . . .\$11.95

☐ The New World of Travel (Annual sourcebook by Arthur Frommer for savvy travelers) . .\$16.95

## GAULT MILLAU

(The only guides that distinguish the truly superlative from the merely overrated.)

| | |
|---|---|
| ☐ The Best of Chicago . . . . . . .\$15.95 | ☐ The Best of Los Angeles. . . . . . . . . . .\$16.95 |
| ☐ The Best of France. . . . . . . .\$16.95 | ☐ The Best of New England . . . . . . . . . .\$15.95 |
| ☐ The Best of Hong Kong . . . .\$16.95 | ☐ The Best of New York. . . . . . . . . . . . .\$16.95 |
| ☐ The Best of Italy . . . . . . . . .\$16.95 | ☐ The Best of Paris . . . . . . . . . . . . . . . .\$16.95 |
| ☐ The Best of London. . . . . . . .\$16.95 | ☐ The Best of San Francisco . . . . . . . . . .\$16.95 |
| | ☐ The Best of Washington, D.C. . . . . . . . . . . . .\$16.95 |

## ORDER NOW!

In U.S. include \$2 shipping UPS for 1st book; \$1 ea. add'l book. Outside U.S. \$3 and \$1, respectively.
Allow four to six weeks for delivery in U.S., longer outside U.S.
Enclosed is my check or money order for \$_____

NAME_____

ADDRESS_____

CITY_____ STATE_____ ZIP____

0690

# JESUS' TWENTY MEGATRUTHS